Political Parties in the Technological Age

Political Parties in the Technological Age

Stephen E. Frantzich
United States Naval Academy

Longman
New York & London

Political Parties in the Technological Age

Longman Inc., 95 Church Street, White Plains, N.Y. 10601

Associated companies:
Longman Group Ltd., London
Longman Cheshire Pty., Melbourne
Longman Paul Pty., Auckland
Copp Clark Pitman, Toronto
Pitman Publishing Inc., New York

Senior editor: David Estrin
Production editor: Halley Gatenby
Cover and text designs: Joseph DePinho
Cover illustration: Joseph DePinho
Text art: Bill Christ
Production supervisors: Pamela Teisler and Judith Stern

Library of Congress Cataloging-in-Publication Data

Frantzich, Stephen E.
    Political parties in the technological age.

    Bibliography: p.
    Includes index.
    1. Political parties—United States—History.
2. Political parties—United States—Technological
innovations.   I. Title.
JK2261.F83   1989   324.273'09   87-26157
ISBN 0-582-28605-0 (pbk.)

88 89 90 91 92 93 9 8 7 6 5 4 3 2 1

To my children—Mark, Matthew and Andrew—whose idea of a "party" is quite different from the subject of this book, but who will eventually reap the fruits of our efforts to invigorate or emaciate American political parties.

Contents

Acknowledgments

Over 100 party leaders and political observers in more than 25 states and on the national level offered their insights through interviews and provided background material. Their perspectives added life to the intellectual analysis of the parties. Donna Hurley and Gloria Perdew of the U.S. Naval Academy Library used their magic of data base retrieval to simplify the bibliographic searching. The U.S. Naval Academy funded a sabbatical and travel for me, resulting in some of the original research that eventually found its way into this book. Eric Goldstein, Rachel Bien, and Mike Vice served as research assistants through the Anne Arundel County Gifted and Talented Program. Numerous researchers will find their ideas begged, borrowed, or stolen (hopefully, with appropriate credit given). Irving Rockwood and Jarol Manheim initially talked me into the project, while David Estrin and the fine staff at Longman Inc. helped me carry it to fruition. Winifred K. Frantzich read the entire manuscript for grammatical errors and made the kind of suggestions only a mother could make. My wife, Jane, not only served as a talented editor and tough critic but maintained the household during research trips and when I was locked away in my writing loft. Any errors of commission and omission, of course, remain mine.

1

Mediating Groups in American Politics

As the sun rises across the country and most of the more than 250 million Americans prepare to start a new day, few have any realistic expectation that their individual efforts will directly affect the American political system. While supporting the concept of democracy and touting the role and power of the individual citizen, most also realize that, in fact, individuals usually have power only to the degree that they join with others to pursue common interests. Everyday conversation is sprinkled with simple, yet profound observations that "in unity there is strength" or "organization is power." In a large democracy, individual interests are mediated by a variety of collective groups that inform, organize and activate supporters. As mediators, groups such as political parties, unions, and clubs facilitate actions such as running an electoral campaign, organizing a strike, or planning a social event that would be beyond the capacity of an individual. In exchange for having someone else do it, the individual may pay a membership fee or help with some portion of the task, while giving up some control over the final outcome.

Mediating groups come in increasingly varied forms and sizes. Some are purely voluntary, depending on the free choice of individuals to support them, whereas other groups, such as unions and professional associations—where membership may be a legal or practical requirement to pursue an occupation— have a degree of guaranteed support. Some groups deal in the political process continuously. Political parties are continually assessing the last election or preparing for the next, whereas interest-group lobbyists plan each group action to support their political goals. Other groups dabble in politics selectively. The typical sports team, church, or social club, etc. is drawn into politics only when its special interests are threatened. Professional baseball, for example, was viewed as being about as far removed from politics as possible until

1

Congress began investigating policies concerning player trades and drug use. When its interests were at stake, representatives of America's pastime (baseball) got involved in America's spectator sport (politics) through lobbying. Despite the pervasiveness of politics, the majority of groups in American society generally have only a tangential relationship to the political process.

Although citizens of the United States can be divided into a wide variety of groupings based on attitudes (e.g., proabortion/antiabortion, liberal/conservative) or personal characteristics (e.g., black/white, northerner/southerner), the concept of a *group* implies some level of loyalty and organization. The loyalty of members could involve the entire spectrum from a feeling of kinship with other individuals with similar characteristics to supporting actively the group's organizational need for resources. To organize, groups need human resources (supporters, workers, leaders, and so on) and material resources (telephones, copy machines, computers, and so on) to communicate, to make decisions, and to carry out activities. Think of your own ethnic background. You may view yourself as Irish or, Asian or, German or, black, but this sense of loyalty or identity does not make you a member of an organized group with the capacity to take action. Until you join an organization such as an Asian-American club or the National Association for the Advancement of Colored People, you have not actively supported a group. The types and levels of requisite organizational resources depend on the complexity of organizational structure and the tasks attempted. The level of group organization can involve anything from simply choosing a set of officers and making a commitment to continuing activity to amassing a full-time staff and a complete set of operating procedures and marshaling the resources to carry out specific tasks.

The United States has always been known as a nation of joiners, far surpassing other nations in citizen involvement with groups outside the family circle (see Verba & Nie, 1972, p. 114). The average citizen is involved in a number of groups, and some citizens involve themselves in a multitude of organizations. Individuals link themselves to groups in a variety of ways. Many stay at arm's length, professing support for group goals but doing little or nothing to achieve those goals. A smaller number become members, formally expressing their support and, often, contributing resources necessary to maintain the organization. A much smaller number carry on the day-to-day activity of the group as voluntary leaders and, for some groups, as paid staff. The further one gets from participating in the day-to-day activities of a group, the less likely one is to see a direct translation from individual goals to group activity and effort. Within a group, then, activists serve as intermediaries, drawing on the support of less active supporters and formulating group activities and strategies. Robert Michels (1915/1949) described the process of a small set of activists having the motivation and skills to control groups as the "Iron Law of Oligarchy." The oligarchic leadership group, always fewer than the majority, may grasp and maintain its power through manipulation or may be willingly granted its leadership roles by a less-interested membership. We have all been in social or political groups in which decision-making positions were traded among the same small group of people. If deeply interested in the organization, we may fight to become part of the leadership group, but in most cases we willingly let others carry the burden if, generally, they seem to be working for our interests.

As a player in the larger political game, the group competes with other organized groups to help reach established goals and serves as an intermediary to translate interests into action. Groups vary in their motivation and capacity for representing faithfully the interests of their supporters. Some groups take pride in their internal democracy. They actively encourage the expression of supporter input, and they see their supporters as a legitimate force for directing and redirecting group goals, strategies, and activities. Smaller and more local organizations such as community property owners' associations, parent-teacher associations, and some political parties hold open meetings to solicit ideas and approve suggested policies. Some state and national organizations regularly poll their membership or hold conventions to establish organizational priorities and strategies. Other groups recognize the need for various types of supporters but work from the premise that supporters are not equal in their knowledge, interests, and activities. In these groups, upper-level activists *attempt* to chart a course for the organization that will maintain and, they hope, increase the approval of the less-active, passive supporters. They may also poll their membership or hold conventions, but the range of choices is determined by the leadership group, and soliciting membership is done more for public relations than for organizational guidance. The more homogeneous the interests of group members, the easier it is to get them involved in group decision making. But it also may be less necessary, since a consensus already exits.

Groups attempting to organize individuals with widely varying interests unintentionally encourage internal conflict by involving a wide range of supporters, however such openness may be needed to keep the group together. For example, members and leaders of a homogeneous group such as mink farmers are likely to have similar goals, and the leaders have freedom to act without constantly checking with the membership. A chamber of commerce, on the other hand, representing a wide range of businesses (large and small, importers and exporters, and so on) whose policy goals might vary, must carefully check with its membership before taking a policy position. As we shall see, groups vary in the degree of mediation practiced. *Mediation* may mean anything from organizing and carrying out on a larger scale well-defined goals and activities already established by supporters to stimulating undefined interests, offering solutions, and carrying out tasks beyond the interests and capabilities of the supporters.

Historically, political parties stood out as the preeminent set of mediating groups in the political process. Although I believe that political parties still play an important role, and one that may be increasing, the complex of organized citizen groups has increased in both number and activity. To maintain a viable position and compete for the resources necessary to maintain the organization, parties have been increasingly faced with the need to enlarge their effort and revise their activities.

THE POLITICAL AND GOVERNMENTAL SETTING

Whereas individuals form groups around their occupations, religious preferences, hobbies, and so forth, the focus of this book is on groups and, more particularly, on political parties that involve themselves in the political process. Although one can discuss various types of politics such as "office politics" or "campus politics," we limit ourselves here to the politics of the governmental process. Governments were established to carry out collective activities beyond the scope of individual or group efforts, from building roads and schools to providing national defense. To coordinate such tasks, gather resources, and settle conflicts, governments were provided the legal right to force compliance, using even extreme forms of sanctions if necessary. The preeminent position in society of government as the institution given the right to force compliance with an agreed-upon policy can be seen in the government's exclusive right to imprison, or even put to death, those unwilling to follow important policies.

The establishment of a government indicates little about how it will perform its tasks. No society exhibits total agreement about the goals and activities of government. *Politics* is the process by which collective goals are chosen, strategies for implementation decided upon, and the range of acceptable compliance techniques validated. As a conflict-resolution process, politics can take on many forms, from the elite rule of a small group to that of a pure democracy in which absolute equality of individual impact reigns. Between the two extremes lies the representative system in which we live.

Representative democracies vary in their degree of citizen impact, but all exhibit some common factors. Recognizing that in a large and complex society not all citizens can be, or wish to be, actively involved in politics, representative democracies exhibit a division of labor. A relatively small group of individuals is chosen by election to represent the rest of the citizens. To have meaningful elections, key problem areas for governmental concern must be identified, a variety of candidates must be presented for voter choice, the voters must be provided with adequate information to make a judgment, a significant proportion of the voters must become involved, and the candidate getting a majority of the vote is certified as the winner. None of these steps would happen on its own, and most of the requirements—from issue identification, candidate recruitment, and informing the electorate, to activating voters and ensuring fair elections—are better handled by groups external to the government. Giving the existing regime of officeholders exclusive control over the process of selecting their successors increases the potential for fraud and diminishes the possibility of changing leadership groups.

Representative government does not stop at the ballot box. After an election it is important to ensure that elected and appointed officials remain responsive to the citizenry and have the means for creating policy-making coalitions for carrying out citizen preferences. Responsiveness to citizen demands *between* elections is extremely important, particularly in a complex society in which elections are contested on the basis of generalities and policy decisions are established and implemented on the basis of specific criteria. For example, the passage of the 55-mile-per-hour speed limit during the energy crisis of 1974 to save gasoline precipitated more than a decade of citizen response. Some citizens argued for the basic premise, some asserted that the crisis was past, some thought that other goals (such as efficient use of time) were more important, and others claimed that variations in the enforcement administration brought the entire policy into question. By 1987 enough pressure had built to reverse the initial policy at least partially.

Mediating groups help carry out the tasks that make representative government possible. To understand the role that groups play, it helps to identify the various functions and who performs them. It would be convenient if groups specialized and no functions were shared, but that is decreasingly the case. Traditionally, interest groups played a more dominant role in merely identifying issues (*interest articulation*) before elections and communicated them to the elected officials after the election, but they played a much less significant role in the election itself. Political parties, on the other hand, dominated campaigns, having a virtual lock on recruiting candidates through the nominating process, dominating the information process (albeit sharing this function with the media), pervading the activation of voters, playing a major role in monitoring the honesty of elections, and bringing a fair amount of coherence to the behavior of elected officials and political appointees whose individual views varied significantly. Once in office, parties emphasized *interest aggregation*, bringing together relatively like-minded individuals and forging them into a political force by joining their resources and bringing about the compromises necessary for unified action. This compromise role begins in the election process through things such as "balancing tickets" to include various ethnic, geographic, or ideological groups and writing platforms to seek out areas of agreement. Once in office, the parties forge the compromises necessary to make policy through bargaining (see Pomper, 1980b, pp. 6–7). Although the lines have blurred, with parties attempting some increased interest articulation and, particularly, with other groups in society infringing on the electoral activities of the parties, much of the distinctiveness still has meaning.

DEFINING THE PARTIES AND APPROACHING THEIR STUDY

Defining Political Parties

Definitions of political parties are as numerous as the writers, theorists, and legislators who turn their attention to the parties. In the most basic perspective, *political party* is an organized group of relatively like-minded individuals joining together to control the personnel and policies of government through elections. This definition implies that parties are clearly *organizations* with a *purpose* and that they pursue their purpose primarily through the electoral process. Political parties vary in the way that individuals join, the methods by which they attempt to control political outcomes, and the relative focus they give to controlling personnel or policies.

Ways of Joining Parties

Although few parties discourage supporters, some make it more difficult to claim allegiance. *Ideological parties* require compliance with a preestablished set of principles as a prerequisite for support, whereas *electoral parties* are much more inclusive and constantly reassess the nature of support their principles attract. The dramatic contrast between the Soviet Communist party, which requires ideological purity, and the pragmatic American parties, which denigrate slavish commitment to ideology, indicates two extremes. When co-existing with electoral parties, ideological parties generally reflect a narrower set of interests and may not see winning elections as their primary or even a realistic method of changing governmental policy. Ideological parties are more common in the multiparty systems of Europe but exist in less vibrant forms in the United States. The various Socialist parties, the American Communist party, the Peace and Freedom party, the Libertarian party, and others woven through contemporary American history pride themselves on purity of belief more than electoral success. Electoral parties, on the other hand, present voters with a relatively comprehensive set of general policy positions and attempt to forge a majority knowing that few voters support every party position. The major American parties reflect the electoral approach and although not bereft of principles, make a conscientious effort to find principles that will sell.

The opportunity and method of revealing one's linkage with a party also varies. *Mass membership parties* seek out formal card-carrying members who express their commitment through supporting the party with their effort and resources. In exchange, members play a significant role in charting the course of the party. Frequent meetings involve the passing of resolutions and statements of principle that the elected officials are expected to carry out. In a number of European countries, for example, to be a Christian Democrat or a Socialist involves paying a membership fee and having the right to participate in the party meetings. Although usually less than 5 percent of the party voters are actual members, no one has an excuse for not getting involved if he or she really wants to. *Cadre parties*, on the other hand, assume a lower level of citizen interest and accept a party-policy process dominated by an almost permanent small group of highly involved activists. The interests of the larger bloc of potential party supporters are taken into account as the party leaders determine the most "saleable" policy positions, but the mass of supporters is only irregularly and reluctantly involved in party decisions. American parties fit more the mold of cadre parties. However, election laws requiring enrollment by party in order to vote in primary elections to nominate candidates, as well as attempts by the parties to broaden their participatory and financial base through the establishment of membership clubs, stand out as attempts to blur the distinction. In recent years, the more policy-oriented clubs (Young Republican League, College Democrats, and so on) have declined in strength, whereas the largely "paper" fund-raising membership organizations (Elephant Club, Donkey's Club, President's Club, and so on) have increased, with new members receiving fancy membership cards and other perquisites.

Party Goals

The question of whether parties attempt to win elections in order to frame policies or whether they frame policies in order to win elections is to some degree two sides of the same coin. The distinctions in comparing parties involve determining which side of the coin is emphasized more by a particular party. Pushed, one would have to conclude that the major American parties opt for controlling the personnel of government as opposed to policy goals.

The competing views of parties either as single-minded collections of individuals who recruit candidates and wage election campaigns in order to enact their favorite policies or, more cynically, as organizations that view winning elections as an end in and of itself both seem to miss the mark. As is often the case, reality is somewhere in between these extremes. In the desire to win elections parties must recruit candidates and formulate policies. These choices generally show a relatively consistent policy bias. The different success rates of party candidates are translated into increased probabilities that their particular policy bias will find its way into public policy.

Recognizing the predominance of the electoral goal helps distinguish political parties from other political groups in society and to highlight the uniqueness of American political parties from parties in many other countries. Although other organized interests in American politics have increasingly focused their efforts on elections and in some ways look like parties, these interest groups have little desire to control the personnel of government outside of its utility for affecting policy. The parties, on the other hand, have a continuing interest in getting their people in office and keeping them there above and beyond the policy implications. An interest group unsuccessful in backing the winning candidate regroups and attempts other methods of affecting policy. A party continually unsuccessful in reaching its election goals fears for its own demise as an organization.

The above comments on American political parties must be taken in the context of the Republican and Democratic parties at the various levels of government. Aside from the major parties, a whole range of minor parties exists or has existed in America. Those based on electoral goals that they did not reach faded from the scene. Other organizations going under the label of *party* but having little realistic aspiration for winning office look more like interest groups. They use the campaign to espouse their views but do not really expect their candidates to win. At best, some of their positions may be adopted by more viable major-party candidates.

Studying the Parties

Studying the political parties is like trying to herd snakes. Everything is slippery—from the definitions to the measurements of existence and strength. The search for truth is also clouded by the fact that analysts become "enamored with their subject matter and are tempted to imbue it with more significance than it deserves" (Epstein, 1980, p.7). Although I believe that, despite dramatic changes in the political environment and subsequent changes in the parties, the parties are still a significant force in American politics, I will attempt to give you enough information to make your own judgment.

Components of Parties

In reading the literature on political parties, one is drawn to the analogy of the blind men feeling different parts of the elephant and trying to describe it. The man holding the tail and confidently comparing the elephant to a rope, and his colleague grasping a leg and equally confidently asserting that an elephant is like a tree trunk were both captives of their particular perspectives.

From one perspective, a party is a set of symbols (Epstein, 1980) in the minds of voters. Voters develop gut feelings about which party is better in general and perceptions about which party is most likely to bring about policy goals such as peace or prosperity. Stereotypes of the Republicans as the party of big business and Democrats as the party of the little guy, for example, while simplistic, involve enough truth to guide and give confidence to many voters' electoral decisions. Focusing on the party as a symbol encourages analysis of the nature of the party image and a comparison of the types of voters holding various images, and it attempts to determine the link between party images and voter loyalty and behavior. In recent years such a perspective has led to extensive research on the impact of party identification on voting and other political behavior.

From another perspective, parties are seen as teams of candidates (Downs, 1957) and their supporters planning strategies for capturing office and outlining methods of making policy. Often borrowing economic models, such an approach is an attempt to evaluate various vote-maximizing strategies (Fishel, 1979, p. xiii).

One can also view parties as organizations (Cotter, Gibson, Bibby, & Huckshorn, 1984) attempting to marshal resources to maintain the organization. This approach requires analyzing the causes and consequences of organizational structure, and describing the nature and utility of organizational activities.

Although all of the above foci—symbolic, campaigning, and organizational—are covered in this book, the primary focus is on the party as an organization. The nature of the organization depends on the attitudes and support of the electorate (the party in the electorate). Campaign-strategy planning and the loyalty of officials elected under the party label (the party in office) are of vital interest to the party organization, but the party organization is what ties, or should tie, all components together.

THE CONTRIBUTIONS OF POLITICAL PARTIES

The path of history is strewn with the dinosaurlike relics of organizations that, failing to serve an adequate purpose, found it impossible to extract the resources necessary to maintain themselves. Unless political parties satisfy a recognizable and significant need of those who provide the human and material resources, they will vanish. A variety of people have a stake in maintaining the political parties. From the broadest perspective, parties contribute to the workings of the political system. More narrowly, they help political activists form coalitions and inform voters.

The concept of "function" defines the contribution an entity makes toward reaching some goal. In assessing the function of an organization, one might ask, "What would be missing if this organization no longer existed?" or "What things would remain undone or would have to be taken up by another organization?"

Any discussion of an organization's contribution must begin with an abstract evaluation of the potential contribution, fully recognizing that this potential may not be fully matched by reality.

Systemic Functions

Supporting Democracy
Political parties play a vital role in maintaining a democratic system of government, at least in the eyes of these observers:

> There is no America without democracy, no democracy without parties, no parties without compromises and moderation. (Rossiter, 1960, p. 1)

> The political parties created democracy and ... modern democracy is un-thinkable save in terms of the parties. (Schattschneider, 1942/1982, p. 1)

> Parties in general, and the two party system in particular, therefore, have come to be seen not only as the sail that keeps democracy in the United States moving, but also as the rudder that keeps it on a charted, predictable course. (Delli Carpini, 1985, p. 2)

Although seldom made explicit, a number of specific contributions by the parties to democracy stand out.

Managing and Contributing Conflict

Democracy requires giving individuals a responsible range of choices. Political parties have a continuing stake in interjecting enough conflict into the political system to guarantee choices. Parties, particularly at the national level, attempt to field candidates for every office as a symbol of their vitality, no matter how dim the chances for success. In some states (such as Texas and Louisiana) and localities, the parties have used a strategy of selectively contesting a limited number of races and focusing their efforts and resources.

In the realm of issue conflict, parties have provided some of the most fertile ground for defining impending policy problems and outlining creative approaches to their solution. This task has most often been taken by the party out of office in an attempt to differentiate itself from those in power and to seek a basis for challenging them at the polls. As a national conference on the future of the political parties concluded:

> At their best, American political parties are a great deal more than mechan-isms for filling offices. They can be—and frequently have been in the past—robust institutions which both facilitate social change and preserve public confidence. (American Assembly, 1982, p. 4)

As continuing organizations, they can be held responsible for past decisions and tend to avoid making unrealistic promises—no matter how electorally advantageous—that may come back to haunt them in the next election. Polit-ical parties, particularly in a two-party system, aggregate a wide variety of interests under one label. Parties must find a way to establish a set of policy positions that deal with a wide range of policy areas as well as different approaches to specific policy realms. The process of developing nonconflicting policy positions forces compromise among party activists, simplifying the choices given voters. Rather than being faced with the nuances of a wide panoply of options, the parties tend to agree on those positions shared by most voters and to focus their conflict on those relatively few issues that divide the electorate. In the 1984 presidential election, for example, both the Republican and Democratic candidates accepted as a given the need to reduce the deficit and guided the conflict to a discussion of whether this should be done by cutting domestic programs, cutting defense expenditures, or raising taxes.

Parties in multiparty systems, on the other hand, have more freedom to pursue single-issue areas (environmental parties, agricultural parties, religious parties, and so on) or to exclude advocates of different positions. In West Germany, for example, the Greens focus their concern on extreme environmental matters and appeal to a small segment of the voters for whom these items are the prime issues; the other parties, however, largely ignore the issues the Greens espouse. In a two-party system each party must be more responsive to the other party for fear that ignoring major policy areas or becoming too exclusionary will force large blocs of voters in the only direction they can go and still participate—into the hands of the one opposition party, strengthening its political hand.

Ameliorating the Separation of Powers

In their fear of concentrated power, the Founding Fathers created a system of separate institutions sharing powers. Although not mentioned in the Constitution and probably not anticipated by its authors, political parties became primary vehicles for making the new government structure work. By establishing general party principles in platforms and more indirectly through the policy preferences of nominated candidates, the parties set the scene for the possibility of coordinated action by the various branches and levels of government. Presidents seek out the support of their party members in Congress first, and those members feel a sense of shared policy goals and political destiny based on party. Similar linkages help coordinate other areas of potential organizational conflict.

As a *presidential system* in which the chief executive and the legislature are elected and often act independently, the U.S. system of government lacks the kind of party-based team approach of a *parliamentary system* such as that of Canada, Germany, or Great Britain. British Prime Minister Margaret Thatcher and her fellow parliamentary leaders must have viewed Ronald Reagan with bemusement in 1987 when his veto of the 55-mile-per-hour speed-limit revision was not only overridden by Congress but by a majority of his party and with the support of his party leader in the House of Representatives. In parliamentary government, the chief executive (the prime minister) is selected by the majority caucus in the parliament, which in turn creates a cabinet of party faithful from the parliament. In parliamentary systems, there is a sense of collective party responsibility, and a government loses power if a majority of the legislative party is dissatisfied. Although lacking some of the tools and traditions of parliamentary systems, American political parties do help make "compromise rather than veto the general form of [policy conflict] resolution" (Orren, 1982, p. 5). Ronald Reagan's inability to maintain party discipline concerning the 55-mile-per-hour speed limit was not uncommon, but it is not typical. Party members in the different branches of government are more likely to cooperate than disagree.

Despite their limitations, the parties are seen as positive forces for making the system workable:

These [American] parties are unique. They cannot be compared to parties of
other nations. They serve a *new* purpose in a new way. Unforeseen and
unwanted by the Fathers, they form the heart of the unwritten constitution
and help the written one to work. It is through the parties that the clashing
interests of a continent find grounds for compromise . . . . over such an area
[the United States], where there is no unity of race, no immemorial tradition,
no throne to revere, no ancient roots in the land, no single religion to color
all minds—where there is only language in common, and faith, and pride of
the rights of man—the American party system helps build freedom and
union. (Herbert Agar, *The Price of Union*, quoted in Broder, 1972, pp.
181–182)

Monitoring the "Rules of the Game"

As continuing participants in the electoral process, political parties have a
stake in the rules under which the game is played. Party leaders are quick to
point out procedural changes that will benefit the opposing party. With all
parties alert to procedural changes, there is less chance of new electoral rules
being totally unfair to one of the major parties. This does little to protect the
minor parties, though, which constantly face rules designed to maintain and
enhance the major parties.

Expanding the Electorate

Democracy implies a relatively broad base of citizen participation. Participation rates in all political systems are less than universal due to lack of citizen
interest, awareness, and ability to meet the legal requirements. Observing the
typical party headquarters during election time, one would be struck by the
efforts at registering new voters, encouraging interest in the campaign, and
getting voters to the polls. Political participation in the United States often
fails to match that in other developed nations because of the heterogeneity of
the American electorate and the strictness of legal requirements for registration
and voting, but without the impetus of the parties, the rates would be even
lower.

Party activists realize that elections are often won or lost before the first
campaign speech is given, since the size and composition of the electorate can
predetermine likely winners and losers. Political parties expend a great deal of
effort in making it possible for those most likely to support their party to vote.
Historically, the parties have been involved in expanding the electorate, under
the assumption that the party credited with allowing a new group to participate
would get a disproportionate percentage of its votes. Both parties, for example,
fought to get credit for reducing the voting age to 18. Once the legal boundaries of the electorate are determined, the parties play an important role in
getting people registered to vote and getting them to the polls.

In addition, the parties facilitate participation in other political activities
such as campaigning, fund raising, and issue development among the smaller
percentage of citizens with extraordinary interest. American parties generally

reflect a very inclusive process, encouraging and welcoming any and all to participate.

Recruiting and Training Candidates

Politics requires a constant influx of new individuals to fill elective and appointed offices. Political parties have a stake in making sure their people are prepared to compete for these offices in a viable manner.

> The activities of party organizations at all levels provide a means of attracting, nourishing, testing and assessing new public leadership from and for oncoming generations. (American Assembly, 1982, p. 4)

Political parties have begun to train candidates through formal campaign schools and informal experience. Parties are involved in the informal recruitment of elected officials through identifying potential candidates, urging them to run, and providing them with the resources to compete. In pursuing the goal of winning elections, parties are often active in expanding the types of people in political office. Parties function "as a back door antitrust mechanism, breaking up established power and allowing the entry of new groups into the political-economic system" (Edsall, 1984a, pp. 129–131). In recent years, both parties have recognized the political potential of seeking out blacks, women, Hispanics, and youth as candidates for political office. In many aspects of the formal nominating process, this political party backing in a primary election or through a convention process enhances a candidate's prospects.

Enhancing Campaigns and Informing Voters

To win elections candidates must find ways to identify, appeal to, and activate potential voters. Voters desire relevant information and a "truth-in-packaging" component guaranteeing that they are getting what they are voting for. Political parties have the potential for marrying these two sets of desires and in the meantime ingratiating themselves both to the candidates and the voters.

From the candidate's perspective, the existence of a pool of likely supporters who vote for party candidates and a cadre of volunteers and experts ready to work in the campaign are appealing. In exchange for party support in the election, the elected official will often repay with support for party-policy positions. The degree to which parties control access to electoral office through controlling nominations or elections largely determines the level of party loyalty evidenced.

The idealistic image of the aggressive and informed citizen eager to get involved in the political process is unrealistic. The low level of voter interest and knowledge enhances the need for parties. For many voters a long-established personal party label serves as a general guideline for political action. Party identification for a voter often serves as "a point of reference for making his choice" (Crotty, 1984, p. 17) in electoral decisions. The role of the party lies in making sure such "party-based" voters are registered and that they get out to vote.

Few elections are based on the support of party identifiers alone. The party, particularly in an age of increased nonparty-line voting, can help the candidate activate and appeal to the independent voters. Convincing independent voters is more complex than simply having to remind voters of their party ties and getting them out to vote, as is the case with party identifiers. One must make independent voters aware of their own interests, link the candidate and his or her stands with those interests, and convince the voters that it is worth their while to take action on the basis of these new realizations.

To the degree that parties can control the kinds of candidates nominated and elected and make candidates feel beholden enough to act in concert with party stands, party labels will mean that voters will get what they expected out of their vote.

Although the parties contribute to all of the above functions to some degree, the level of success varies, and the situation is changing. Some of the key functions are currently being challenged by other groups in society.

PARTY ORGANIZATIONS AND THEIR COMPETING MEDIATING GROUPS

As organizations, political parties are increasingly being challenged by a wide variety of groups attempting to involve themselves in traditional party activities. To the degree that other organizations can gather resources and carry out the tasks better than the parties, the days of the party organization are numbered.

The most significant challenges have come in the areas of conducting campaigns and informing voters. Few other organizations can consistently challenge the parties' contributions to democracy, but by striking at the heart of party activity—the control of the election process—the growing importance of other mediating groups weakens the parties in general. As indicated in Chapter 2, the opening for other groups comes about because of changes in society and the largely unanticipated consequences of changes in the legal environment, rather than from a frontal assault on the parties. The purpose of this section is to alert you to some of the players who are encroaching on party territory.

Groups challenging the role of parties come in three forms. Increased campaign activity by traditional interest groups offers candidates alternative sources of support. Personalized organizations loyal to the candidate alone provide much of the financial and human resources for campaigning that were once the exclusive domain of the parties. Business organizations in the form of the media and specialized consultants offer candidates alternative methods of campaigning for a fee.

Interest-Group Challenges

At one time interest groups in the United States largely waited until the elections were over to press their demands on the newly elected officials. Until recently, elected officials were much more likely to first hear after the election from the lobbyists from the National Rifle Association, the Chamber of Commerce, the Teamsters, or the vast array of other groups. Today the introduction comes much earlier in the election process. Currently, the most successful interest groups, and their legally separate political action committees (PACs), have taken on some of the functions traditionally performed solely by the parties.

> PACs are clearly attempting to usurp functions of the two parties and establish themselves as substitutes by recruiting and training candidates and creating pseudo-party organizations of their own. (Sabato, 1985, p. 151)

> If the definition of electoral alternatives has been the mark of the American party, and if control of the nomination is the key to control of elections, then some PACs have begun to take a party-like role in elections. (Sorauf, 1984, p. 79)

Whereas candidate recruitment, training, and selection by PACs is less known, considerable attention has been paid to their increased role in providing campaign resources. PAC contributions have increased significantly as a proportion of total campaign resources, generally far overshadowing party contributions (see Chapter 6).

Beyond the general weakening of the party through loss of control over nominations and elections, the challenge of the PACs rests in the fact that, unlike parties, they narrow political outlooks and develop elected officials dependent on the largesse of groups with a specific agenda. Few interest groups enter campaigns to affect the full public agenda. Many of the most potent groups focus on a single issue (gun control, abortion, and so on) and select candidates to support solely on the basis of that issue. Candidates failing to pass the litmus test of these single-issue groups arouse their wrath. They often find themselves opposed by a candidate supported by the offended group who attempts to focus the campaign on the group's pet issue. Although PAC activists tout them simply as mechanisms for increasing the power of the individual citizen, the fact is that not all groups are organized, and the varying levels of resources among those that are organized diminish their democratic impact.

> Individual PACs take over some but not all of the role of parties. Some PACs mobilize voters and pick candidates; some try to mobilize legislatures, though only on an issue or two.... But no individual PACs begin to approach the totality of the party role.... In their aggregate, but uncoordinated way, the PACs do some of the things the parties no longer do. They furnish a replacement, but not a substitute, for the parties because they have

found no way to build majorities or even large minorities in the electorate. The very changes in American electoral politics that made it difficult for the parties to fill their classic roles make it even more difficult for their competitors to do so. (Sorauf, 1984, p. 80)

Candidate-Centered Organizations

Traditionally, candidates for office depended on the party to gather the necessary resources and run their campaigns. The party served as the intermediary link between a candidate and the voters. The advent of methods by which candidates could communicate with voters independent of the party through the media, the decline of party-line voting, and candidate dissatisfaction with party activities on their behalf encouraged candidates to form organizations loyal to them personally. In some cases these organizations were developed to compete in a primary—often against the candidate of the party organization—and simply continued to exist. Although common at all levels, independent candidate-centered campaign organizations flourish at the congressional level. Since congressional districts often have no distinct party organizational unit and congressional campaigns become a stepchild not getting full support from either the local or the state organization (Crotty, 1984, p. 203), candidates are almost forced to create an entity loyal to their interests.

After gaining office without party support and generally feeling satisfied with the future potential of reactivating the personal organization for the next election, elected officials comfortable with their personal organization do not feel very beholden to the party.

In some areas, personal candidate organizations have gone beyond promoting the interests of a single candidate and have taken on the characteristics of a direct competitor to the parties. In Los Angeles, congressmen Howard Berman (D-Calif.) and Henry Waxman (D-Calif.) lead a liberal political organization that seeks out candidates, trains them, finds campaign resources, and provides campaign services—the traditional activities of parties—almost completely independent of the party.

> The Waxman-Berman alliance was born in the loosely structured world of California politics; it fills a vacuum in a place where parties are feeble and potent organizations are an anomaly. . . . By helping allies get elected or appointed, the leaders create obligations they can later capitalize on in attempting to achieve political and legislative goals. . . . If the new political machines do come to power in the next few years, they will probably follow the Waxman-Berman model. (Watson, 1985b, p. 1620)

As one local party official reflected, "Sure they have been effective; the problem from the party perspective, though, is that we can't control them, and they have shafted some Democrats along the way" (author's interview).

The Media

It is appropriate that the terms *media* and *mediate* stem from the same Latin term—*medius*, meaning "middle." The media have always stood as an "inter-*mediary*" between actual events and the information received by the public. This role involves selectivity. In the selection and presentation of news, the media can be used to either bolster or undermine the political parties.

The contemporary news media, unlike the blatantly partisan press that dominated the first century of U.S. existence, challenges and often denigrates partisanship in all of its guises. The shift toward objectivity has now become a philosophical commitment but was largely motivated by economic concerns. In the era of competing newspapers serving the same local area, all papers could either reflect the dominant local biases or carve out one partisan segment of the clientele. As more and more markets were served by one paper, and each paper attempted to reach a larger and more diverse clientele, overt partisanship became a detriment to growth. The nationalization of the mass media with the development of news services (UPI, Reuters, and so on) discouraged partisanship. The growth of the electronic broadcast media, which not only had a broader and more heterogeneous audience to serve but were under strict licensing limitations attempting to promote objectivity (the equal time and fairness doctrines), increased the danger of participating directly in partisan battles.

> News and information became more richly available and less influenced by partisan perspective; the heavily partisan fare of the past was replaced by more varied content, with the probable consequence that the concern of readers and listeners was distracted from the purely political. (Clubb, Flanigan & Zingale, 1980, p. 284)

Although each change in the technology and usage of media changed politics, television made the most dramatic impact. Television proved to be an advantage to certain kinds of candidates and organizations, especially those that could play to television's emphasis on visuals and personalization. As the main source of political information,

> television has replaced the political party as the principal network of political communication . . . giving that access to anyone who can afford to buy television time, or who is shrewd enough to gain notoriety without buying it. (American Assembly, 1982, p. 5)

From the candidates' position, given the ability to bypass party influence and communicate directly with the voters, "why should they choose to give up their independent control of their message to the parties?" (Salmore & Salmore, 1985, p. 237).

> Television has seemed to make one of the party's old functions irrelevant—
> that of serving as a bridge between the candidate or officeholder and the
> public. The parties developed, in part, to fill in the gap between the citizen
> in his home and the official in his office, and to provide the audiences for the
> campaigning aspirants. Now, through television, the candidates and the
> officials can come directly into the home. (Broder, 1972, p. 239)

The impact of television on politics and parties led Austin Ranney to conclude
that "anything that increases the role of TV in national campaigns, diminished
the role of parties" (quoted in Cantor, 1984, p. 155).

Consultants

Until recently, politics in America was largely a nonspecialized avocation
carried out largely by volunteers with relatively little experience. What expertise did exist resided primarily in the parties. With the dramatic growth in the
technologies and strategies of information gathering and communications,
there developed a significant void of experts available to translate the skills of
polling, television production, public relations, and so on into the political
realm. Paid consultants, often working part time out of their advertising
agencies, initially stepped in, later to be followed by full-time political consultants (see Sabato, 1981). Initially, consultants limited their activities to high-
cost statewide and national campaigns, but their services are now available at
all levels. "The availability of professionals for hire to individual campaigns
has been one of the things which has enabled candidates to operate independently of the parties" (David Broder, quoted in Sabato, 1981, p. 286).
Whereas the party must protect the interests of all candidates on its ticket,
consultants are committed only to their particular client's success. Consultants
often urge their clients to go off on their own and explicitly not coordinate
their activities with the party. Consultants "are basically anti-party and contribute one more factor to the eroding base of the party in campaign" (Crotty,
1984, p. 72). With the profit motive as the bottom line, consultants seek to
enhance their win or loss record to increase the demand for their services in
the future. Knowing that they can walk away from a candidate after an
election, the consultants have less commitment than the parties for insuring
that campaigns are run in a responsible manner and that an elected official
lives up to his or her promises.

The increased activity of the above groups serves as a challenge to political
parties. Parties have lost their monopoly over many of the important political
functions they once controlled.

IS THE PARTY OVER?

Probably the widest held piece of political wisdom during the second half of
the twentieth century was the assertion that American political parties were
dying, if not dead. As Cornelius Cotter and his associates (1984, p. 168)

expressed it, "For at least twenty years, political scientists and journalists have been conducting a death watch over the American parties." The evaluation of the scholars gained public credence and popularity when political journalist David Broder boldly asserted in the title of his book that "the party's over" (1972).

Decline in Party Functions

The evidence of party decline and plausible causes were not difficult to find. One by one, the parties lost many of their key functions in the political process. The introduction of the direct primary and state laws or traditions restricting preprimary endorsements removed the party's ability to control access to political office. The civil service system robbed the parties of their primary basis for motivating workers. Changes in communications technology, particularly the advent of television, provided candidates with direct access to the voters and reduced the role of parties as sources of political information. The labor-intensive campaigns dominated by envelope stuffers and block workers—performing tasks the parties were ready and able to handle—gave way to expensive mass communications and targeted mail operations. Unable to get the technical expertise from the parties, candidates turned to professional campaign or marketing consultants.

Finding parties unable to pick up the additional costs, candidates turned to political action committees to underwrite their campaigns.

> Very simply, PAC contributions help candidates retain the costly services of opinion pollers, campaign consultants, and the media itself. It is in effect, possible to "rent" a political party surrogate, but the price is dear. (Frank Sorauf, quoted in Cantor, 1984, p. 156)

In the era of candidate-centered campaigns, the parties had less and less of a role in campaigns.

> Parties traditionally provided the avenue by which candidates reached voters. What we've done with media, what we've done with polling, and what we've done with direct organizational techniques is that we have provided candidates who have the resources (and that's the important thing, the resources), the ability to reach the voters and have direct contact with the electorate without regard to party. (Pollster Pat Caddell, quoted in Sabato, 1981, p. 286)

The Decline of the Party in Office

Playing a reduced role in campaigns, parties also had reduced influence over elected officials who owed few debts to their party. The party in office still existed as a convenience for organizing legislatures and establishing linkages for bargaining, but the feeling of indebtedness to the party and the loyalty that it precipitated declined dramatically. Elected officials from the local to the national level knew that the party needed them more than they needed the party. Although legislative voting in the United States has never been highly cohesive, fewer and fewer votes resulted in a majority of Republican legislators opposing a majority of Democratic legislators on a particular vote. The proportion of such party votes in Congress fell from 46 percent in the 1950s to 39 percent in the 1970s. During the same period, average individual member support for Democrats fell from 69 percent to 64 percent and for Republicans from 71 percent to 66 percent (Crotty, 1984, pp. 253–254).

Even at the highest levels there seemed to be an estrangement between officeholders and party leaders.

> The Nixon presidency exemplified the degree to which the president and his party can be disassociated. Nixon dumped the RNC [Republican National Committee] chairman, refused the advice of its leaders, failed to campaign for party candidates, and set up a reelection committee almost totally divorced from the national party. When Senator Robert Dole, RNC chairman, asked to see the president, a White House aide in an obvious put-down said, "If you still want to see the President, turn on your television set at 7:00. The President will be on then." (Cronin, 1980, p. 179)

The Decline of the Party in the Electorate

Party weaknesses were most clearly documented for the party in the electorate. Party identification, normally very stable, declined dramatically with more than 72 percent of the electorate expressing a party affiliation in the 1960s and only 63 percent a decade later. Fewer and fewer voters expressed confidence in the parties, with the parties being seen as unimportant actors in the political process.

It was when voters entered the voting booth that the weakness of the political parties became most dramatically evident. Although it was once typical for the vast majority of voters to have a party identification and to vote a straight party ticket, the modal post–World War I voter increasingly became a split-ticket voter. Whether one uses opinion-poll responses or aggregate data comparing votes for different offices, the results are the same; the party does not constrain voters to the degree it did in the relatively recent past. The patterns do show a somewhat curvilinear relationship with the party falling to its lowest level of constraint during the 1970s, although there has been an increase in straight party voting during the last few elections. (See Chapter 5.)

The Decline of the Party Organization

Assessing the over-time strength of party organizations provides a significantly greater challenge than measuring declines in party functions, the party in the electorate, or the party in office. There is not necessarily any relationship between party organizational strength and the other components of the party. Since party leaders have greatest control over organization building, it would not be surprising to find the emergence of renewed organizational effort as an attempt to counteract real or perceived weaknesses in the other two party sectors (see Gibson, Cotter, Bibby, & Huckshorn, 1983, p. 194). Much of the criticism of contemporary parties stems from comparing them with a glorified benchmark. Although well-oiled and effective party machines did exist, they were neither as monolithic nor as widespread as conventional wisdom seems to imply (see Arterton, 1982, p. 125). Most party organizations have had to fight constantly to fill key offices with volunteers. Few state and local parties had permanent headquarters, paid staff, or reliable resources (see Broder, 1972, p. 223). The universal consensus of political observers until very recently was that to the degree that parties were well organized and effective players in the political game, state and local parties were significantly more important than the national parties. The national parties performed very constrained functions such as organizing the national presidential conventions and receded into almost total nonexistence during the nonelection period. During the 1960s, no one seemed to challenge Cornelius Cotter and Bernard Hennessy (1964) when their book title *Politics without Power: The National Party Committees* proclaimed their conclusions about the national parties.

Although hard data are elusive, there seems to be a consensus that by the 1970s the national parties and especially the state and local parties were certainly no stronger as organizations and probably weaker than they had been during any other time in recent history. Numerous participants in the party process remembered very lean years when it was hard to fill party offices and get volunteers for tasks that seemed to have little effect on election outcomes and were not sought out or appreciated by the candidates (see Gibson et al., 1983, p. 206).

A NEW ERA FOR THE PARTIES?

Although David Broder's (1972) obituary for American political parties was viewed as a death sentence, it really was more of a Scrooge-like portrait of a nightmare that the parties would face if they did nothing. As Broder argued:

> It is my conviction—and the central argument of this book—that if we engage ourselves in politics, and particularly concern ourselves with the workings of those strangely neglected institutions, the political parties, that we may find the instrument of national self-renewal is in our own hands. (Broder, 1972, p. xi)

Somewhere between our glorified image of some long-gone party era, the idealistic hope for the parties spawned by the American Political Science

Association's treatise *A More Responsible Two-Party System* (1950), the emerging conventional wisdom of party failure, and the ash bin of history, something happened. The parties refused to die and, in the opinion of many observers, began the long road to renewal.

As explained in more detail in later chapters, the parties faced the hostile environment and indicated some signs of resurgence. In some cases they recaptured functions lost to other mediating groups or defined new functions. Directly challenging the infringement of other groups, the parties have increased their *service role*, directly providing goods and services needed by voters, candidates, and elected officials. Echoing the sentiments of a number of key state party activists, one state chair said:

> We have given the private consultants and the PACS fair warning that we are out to get them. They have had a heyday at our expense, and we are going to move back into the territory. We can provide the same services, better, and without the profit motive getting in the way. In those areas where we need the help of others, they won't have free rein anymore. We plan to coordinate the services we can't directly provide. (Author's interview)

In those areas in which the parties do not directly provide the services, they have interposed themselves between candidates and other mediating groups as *brokers* (see Herrnson, 1986, p. 8). In fund raising for example, the parties are becoming "marriage brokers," informing PACs and candidates of their mutual interests and bringing them together for mutual benefit.

In an attempt to create a more hospitable environment, the parties have worked hard to maintain favorable election laws and create new ones that would secure their positions.

The consequences of party resurgence can be seen by a strengthening of the party in the electorate, a growth in activity and vitality of the party organization, and some renewed coherence in the party in office.

It seems clear that the parties today are not as anachronistic as the prophets of doom might lead us to believe or as vibrant and indispensable as their apologists would claim. It does seem, though, that contemporary social and technological conditions have given them a second chance to do something more than limp along, diminished in power and functions, until they collapse of their own weight. The potential to control their own destiny seems to be in the hands of the party organizations. The age of the "new parties" is not fully here, but the evidence of that potential is increasing. It is this assumption of party potential that guides the remainder of this book.

THE ROLE OF TECHNOLOGY

Aside from asserting that the parties continue to have the potential for playing a significant, if changed, role in American politics, this book argues that realizing that potential will largely be based on the ability of the parties to recapture control of the technologies of politics and reemerge as the providers of campaign services for candidates and sources of information for voters.

For a number of years, the parties concentrated their efforts on the labor-intensive activities of personal contact and were bypassed by more cost-effective and efficient communications techniques. Although new technologies initially threatened the very survival of the parties, many of those same technologies can be used by the parties to solidify their position.

> New technologies for campaigning and raising money have enabled a larger number of organizations other than parties to position themselves so as to influence the outcome of elections.... We are convinced that within the same forces which have put pressure on the parties there are many seeds of strength for the parties. (American Assembly, 1982, p. 3)

CONCLUSION

Above and beyond understanding the admittedly dry definitions and theories, it is important to realize that political parties have the potential for determining who will represent our interests in the very real political decisions concerning war and peace, the levels of taxation, and the services provided by government. Some set of mediating groups is going to recruit candidates, frame political conflicts, manage campaigns, and organize policy-making coalitions. Political parties in America once dominated these processes, but have lost a significant portion of their control to other groups. More than at any other time in recent history, the parties now have the potential to fight back and regain what many believe to be their rightful and desirable place. The remainder of this book describes and analyzes the contemporary and potential role of the unique brand of American political parties in a technological environment.

2

The Origin and Development of the American Party System

The nature and competitive environment of American political parties have changed over the years. Since many of the contemporary characteristics trace their origins to the past, analyzing these developments helps set the stage for understanding the current party system. Although it is possible to divide the history of the parties a number of ways, most scholars recognize five distinct periods. The dividing line between the periods includes major party realignments. A *realignment* involves major changes in the types and numbers of voters supporting particular parties, the birth or death of specific parties, and major changes in party organizational structure and activity. During a realignment new issues divide the electorate in new ways, and voters reorient themselves to the parties in relation to those new divisions.[1]

THE FIRST AMERICAN PARTY SYSTEM (1770s – 1824)

Establishing a date or place to mark the beginning of American political parties is not as easy at it might seem. Fixing such an origin depends largely on interpretation and definition. The earliest division of like-minded individuals seeking to affect the course of politics came during the colonial period and concerned the degree of cooperation owed the British-appointed colonial governors. The Tories, or Loyalists, saw themselves as British citizens and generally supported British rule. The Whigs, or Patriots, opposed British rule

---

1. Historical material for this chapter draws heavily on Sorauf (1984), Huckshorn (1984), Gitelson et al. (1984), and ABC-Clio (1983).

and eventually became the primary supporters of the Revolution. These early factions represent the types of cleavages in attitude that bring people together in organized political ventures, but these committees of correspondence and other informal groups lacked the permanent organization and activity we normally associate with a political party.

With the Revolution completed, the stage was set for the development of modern political parties. Despite the radical break with England and the crafting of a new political system, the ghost of past attitudes and conflicts carried forward. The Founding Fathers carried with them a negative image of the British parties of their day, exaggerating conflict and serving as divisive bastions of "cliquish corruption" (McWilliams, 1980, p. 55).

> Political parties had to battle the personal prejudices of the Founding Fathers in order to establish themselves in the political life of popular government; Jefferson considered them "the last degradation of a free and moral agent"; for Madison they loomed as "dangerous organizations that needed to be discouraged and controlled"; and Monroe denounced them as "the curse of the country." (Orren, 1982, p. 4)

In the *Federalist Papers* James Madison argued that a major advantage of the proposed Constitution was its potential for breaking and controlling the "violence of faction." By the term *faction* Madison meant "a number of citizens . . . who are united and actuated by some common impulse . . . adverse to the rights of other citizens, or to the permanent and aggregate interests of the community" (*Federalist #10*). Madison saw the potential of political parties as working for such selfish interests and discouraged their development.

Despite the hesitancy of the Founding Fathers, many of these same individuals helped organize the first real parties in the United States. When the first surge of excitement over the ratification of the Constitution had passed, it became clear that despite a carefully crafted document, reasonable people could differ on the thrust of government activity. Initial conflicts developed around two members of President Washington's cabinet. Alexander Hamilton, the secretary of the Treasury, spoke out for business interests, centralization of governmental decision making, and a strong executive branch. Taking on the name of "Federalists," Hamilton and his supporters prevailed within the Washington presidency. Initially battling as a factional leader within Washington's administration, Thomas Jefferson left the cabinet in 1793 and became the first party organizer. Opposed to the elitist and monarchical tendencies of the Federalists, Jefferson brought together more than three dozen state and local organizations by 1794 under the Republican label. Joined by an anti-Federalist faction in Congress, the Jeffersonian Republicans (or Jeffersonians, as we will call them to avoid confusion with contemporary parties) sought to limit governmental power and enhance the role of the people. The state and local organizations began to look more and more like parties as they endorsed candidates, met for debate, and communicated with elected officials. In the Congress, the Jeffersonians developed a caucus to nominate leaders from the presidency down to the internal leadership of Congress.

Whereas issues served as the basis for dividing the parties, the practical necessity of appealing to an expanding electorate served as a prime motivation for creating a party organization. Relatively early, the right to vote was extended to most white males, a very atypical approach for the period. "As necessity is the mother of invention, modern parties evolved to meet the need for a political mechanism for organizing, educating and mobilizing a mass national electorate" (Gitelson, Conway, & Feigert, 1984, p. 27). Although the right to vote was relatively widespread, this was not a period of open democracy. Parties were dominated by the economic and social elites.

The development of permanent parties was not greeted with enthusiasm by all. Perhaps reflecting on the battles within his cabinet coalescing around Hamilton and Jefferson, George Washington left office in 1796 warning against the "baneful effects of the spirit of party."

Winning the presidency on his second try in 1800, Thomas Jefferson ushered in two decades of Jeffersonian dominance. The Federalists limped along for a few more elections but disappeared totally by 1816. With the dominance of the Jeffersonians, the battles reflected more intraparty factionalism than party competition. By the election of 1824, they had divided into two factions, which set the stage for the emergence of the Jacksonian Democrats in 1828 and the end of the first American party system.

THE SECOND AMERICAN PARTY SYSTEM (1824–1860)

Led by Andrew Jackson, one faction of the Jeffersonians became the Democratic party. Reflecting the views of its more southern and western bases of support, the Democrats promoted the interests of its less privileged voters by expanding popular democracy through increasing the number of elected positions, rewarding political effort with jobs (the "spoils" system), opposing high tariffs, and encouraging foreign immigration.

Opposing the Jacksonians was an unstable and changing coalition of smaller parties and factions that went under the label of Whigs. Responding to Andrew Jackson's use of presidential power, the Whigs opted for legislative dominance. Substantively, the Whigs favored the interests of business and commerce and limiting immigration.

The alternating success of the Democrats and the Whigs between 1840 and 1856 set the stage for the development of continuing party organizations that nominated candidates, ran campaigns, and encouraged mass membership. During this period presidential nominations shifted to national conventions;

and the Democrats created the first national committee to carry out party activities between elections.

THE THIRD AMERICAN PARTY SYSTEM (1860–1896)

The issue of slavery cut across the party structure and upset old coalitions. The Republican party emerged in 1854 as a response to the northern opposition to slavery. Although the Democrats were able to win in 1856 against an array of antislavery parties, antislavery proponents coalesced around Republican Abraham Lincoln in 1860 and ushered in almost 75 years of Republican domination of presidential politics. Initially in almost total agreement over the issue of slavery and the need to maintain the Union, the Republicans continued to win elections despite internal divisions over economic issues since campaigns focused on memories of the Civil War. The Democrats were not able to shed their tarnished image emerging from the war and capitalize on the divisions within the Republican party between the northern industrial interests and those of western farmers and urban workers. This was a period of militant politics with moralistic positions on issues such as prohibition and charges of conspiracies by the monied interests against the farmers.

> People were motivated by commitments to issue stands that became moral crusades, stimulated by strong, vigorous party organizations, and often mobilized by political movements and minor parties. As a result, mass political involvement and voting turnout reached heights not since equaled. (Gitelson et al., 1984, p. 31)

THE FOURTH AMERICAN PARTY SYSTEM (1896–1932)

The fourth party system reflected less of a shift in voter loyalties than a shift in attitudes toward the political parties as organizations. By the 1890s Republicans could no longer win by "waving the bloody shirt" and reminding voters of the Civil War. A new divisiveness on the basis of economic interests was changing the basis of support for the two parties. The Republicans opposed active government involvement in managing the economy, whereas the Democrats supported regulating monopolies, lowering tariffs, and imposing inflationary monetary policies. The South maintained its Democratic bent stemming from the Civil War. The political battlegrounds became the North and Midwest. Republican policies appealed to the business interests and northern workers who saw protection of business as the route to job security. Midwesterners found the Democratic party's support for moralistic issues and lower tariffs more to their liking. Electorally, the advantage went to the Republicans, who won every presidential election during the period, except for

Woodrow Wilson's victory in 1912, when the Republicans split into two factions, and his narrow reelection in 1916.

From the perspective of the parties, the significant occurrences of this period involved a disenchantment with the parties themselves. Disgusted with the corruption of many strong urban political organizations (machines) and the exclusive political wheeling and dealing in smoke-filled rooms, the parties were faced with new procedures and constraints. Voter registration was forced on the parties to help clean up elections and insure that only eligible voters cast ballots. The parties lost their exclusive right to name party candidates through conventions with the introduction of the direct primary. With less control over the nomination stage, the parties increased their efforts at persuading voters "through the use of newly developing mass advertising techniques to support a party and its candidates" (Gitelson et al., 1984, p. 32). In Congress, party members rebelled against the strong partisan leadership of the Speaker of the House and stripped him of many powers.

THE FIFTH AMERICAN PARTY SYSTEM
(1932–)

The closer one moves to the present, the less one is able to make broad generalizations, for the complexity of political life within our personal experience does not lend itself to easy generalizations. Although there is common agreement on the beginning of the fifth party system, its conclusion—if we have reached it—is still a matter of debate.

We can state precisely that the precipitant of the fifth party system was the stock market crash of October 1929, and typical inertia and the system of fixed elections delayed compelling evidence of a national realignment until the 1932 election. The clear indication of realignment that gave Democrat Franklin Roosevelt the presidency in 1932 and transferred control of Congress to the Democrats for the first time in sixteen years involved a dramatic shift in voter behavior but was not without its precursors. The candidacy of Al Smith in 1928 began the affinity of urban areas for Democratic candidates. "Between 1928 and 1932 Democratic pluralities in the big cities became substantial, and between 1932 and 1936 they grew to overwhelming proportions" (Crittenden, 1982, p. 42).

By 1932 Herbert Hoover's philosophy of limited government response to economic problems appealed to fewer and fewer voters. Roosevelt's growing success with the economy created a "New Deal" coalition based on urban workers, racial and ethnic minorities particularly hard hit by the economic downturn, and the solid Democratic South. It proved to be an unbeatable combination. Occasional Republican presidential victories were not matched by comparable success in Congress or state and local elections and must be viewed more as personal rather than party victories. The Democratic party emerged as the clear majority party, both in terms of the party identification of voters and through its ability to capture electoral victories.

Organizationally, the parties during this period "institutionalized" by creating permanent organizational structures guided by explicit bylaws. They carried out extensive campaign and organizational activities with a growing set of resources. Using a combination of labor-intensive local organizational activity and some forays into the world of mass-media communications, the parties were the key players in the political process as this period began. In time, though, candidates and voters found other more useful methods of gathering information and communicating their message. As a result of these developments, the parties went through a period of soul searching as they attempted to redefine their roles.

THE DEATH OF THE PARTIES OR A NEW PARTY SYSTEM?

By the 1970s, a wide variety of observers came to the conclusion that American political parties were weakening at best or archaic relics existing as little more than empty shells at worst. Different observers used different yardsticks to chart the decline. The decline of party functions outlined in Chapter 1 served as the basis for asserting that parties were irrelevant.

The Party in the Electorate

The steady decline of citizens willing to identify with the parties, particularly among younger voters who represent the future, convinced many observers that the kinds of voter realignments used to demark previous party systems would be either unlikely or impossible in the future. Rather than having *realignment*, whereby new, relatively permanent voting blocs develop, much of the talk was about *dealignment*, whereby voters either rejected party labels or failed to vote according to those labels. Although no absolute consensus has emerged, the most recent analyses reported in Chapter 5 indicate a slight return to partisanship both as self-identification and as a guide to voting, with the Republican party, for the time being, receiving most of the benefit. Not only are there major generational shifts in party attachments, but there are regional ones as well. The traditional Democratic South has given way to a two-party South, especially on the presidential level.

The Party in Office

With the rise of candidate-centered campaigns and the decline of party-line voting, it should be no surprise that elected officials accustomed to getting nominated and elected on their own would show less loyalty to the party once in office. Changing a pattern based on decades of development is likely to be slow, but there is some evidence (detailed in Chapter 7) indicating that candidates experiencing somewhat more dependence on the parties are beginning to behave in ways more supportive of party positions.

The Party in the Campaign

Since the loss of control over naming candidates through the adoption of the primary, and their loss of monopoly over running campaigns to consultants, political action committees (PACs), and the media, the parties have been trying to fight back.

Probably the most significant aspect of the current party era is the difference in approach and success of the two parties in their attempts to play a more significant role in the campaign process. To use Stephen Salmore and Barbara Salmore's (1985, pp. 212–213) distinction, party reform can focus either on the goal of "expressiveness" or "competitiveness." *Expressiveness* reflects the extent to which political parties fairly and accurately represent the ideas of their constituents. This criterion emphasizes the openness and opportunities for realistic citizen participation in the party decision-making process and sees the party in the electorate as a supportive constituency that, although not acting as card carrying members, has a right to be taken into account to the greatest degree possible. During the 1970s the Democratic party emphasized its expressiveness through extensive reforms in the presidential nominating process such as opening up the delegate-selection process and creating mandatory quotas for black, young, and female delegates.

The *competitive* criterion for measuring party effectiveness stresses the winning of elections and thereby affecting public policy as the primary goals. The party democracy sought by proponents of expressive goals may be pursued but only to the degree that it strengthens the party organization in its ability to control the electoral process. Rather than seeing every party supporter as a potential active player, party leaders with a competitive approach view themselves like managers of a baseball team. In its attempt to get supporters (fans), the team management does not let the fans manage. It makes management decisions and then presents them for support or refusal by the fans. Using the competitiveness criterion, a party is effective to the degree that it can identify favorable candidates, marshal resources, and help them win office. During the 1970s and up to the present, the Republican party has emphasized these "service-vendor-broker" roles most successfully and has established the model that the Democrats are now copying. By providing services directly or serving as a broker between candidates and service and resource providers, the parties can recapture at least some of their previous strength, even if performing somewhat different functions.

The Party Organization

In assessing the nature of political parties in any era, we often assume that there is a unidimensional scale with parties being "strong," "weak," or somewhere in between, no matter what aspects we measure. In reality, strength in one area may be used to compensate, and potentially revise, weaknesses in other areas. This is particularly true of party organization, the aspect of the parties over which their leaders have the most control. As parties lost some of their legal roles in the nominating process and saw voters deserting them in the electorate, they had two choices. They could declare defeat and abandon the political battlefield, or they could redouble their organizational efforts. After some delay parties at all levels chose the second route. After a comprehensive study of state and local parties, James Gibson and his colleagues concluded:

> Perhaps it is the very weakening of partisan attachments that has made it necessary for parties to become better organized, to become more effective at voter mobilization and persuasion. (Gibson, Cotter, Bibby, & Huckshorn, 1985, p. 140)

Part of our surprise in finding somewhat more institutionalized and stronger parties in light of other evidence of weakened parties may well stem from a mistaken image of some golden age when party components were universally strong and dominated the functions to which they contributed. As one analyst observed:

> The parties are certainly not lifeless, and the requiem masses sometimes said for them are a bit hasty. . . . too much of the nostalgia for strong vibrant parties is a product of poor memory or creative imagination, since historically American parties in most regions only fitfully performed the Herculean roles often attributed to them retrospectively. (Sabato, 1981, p. 284)

Like Mark Twain, who responded to his premature obituary by stating that "the reports of my death are greatly exaggerated," the death knell for party organizations fails to match reality.

A New Party Era

It is always easier to describe the past and predict the future than it is to analyze the present faithfully, for the closer the analyst is to something, the more difficult it is to generalize beyond the idiosyncrasies. Despite the difficulties, this book asserts that American political parties are in a transitional period that will be looked back upon as a new party era. In the electorate, close party competition rather than a single dominant party will become more evident. Party members in office will look more often to the party for help and direction. Most importantly, the parties that were blindsided by new techniques of resource accumulation and political communication have begun to marshal many of the same technologies for their own renewal rather than accepting their predicted demise. Party organizations have become stronger as organizations, especially on the Republican side, by moving themselves back into the electoral process by performing a service-vendor-broker role. The remainder of this book expands upon these themes.

THE LEGAL ENVIRONMENT OF AMERICAN POLITICAL PARTIES

Until the late 1800s American political parties existed like most political parties around the world today, unfettered by governmental regulation. Political parties were viewed as private organizations—extralegal and extra-constitutional—responsible to no one but their internal leaders and activist supporters. As the political parties grew in their influence over political affairs, their internal operations and general activities drew the attention of government reformers. Initial regulations focused on ensuring honest elections and making the parties more responsible to the general public rather than to their membership. Later reforms took on the parties more directly and threatened their very existence as prime players in the political game. Today the United States has the most pervasive body of statutory law concerning political parties and elections of any nation in the world (see Epstein, 1980, p. 44). Since the Constitution gives the states primary responsibility over the electoral process, the change was neither immediate nor uniform. Serving the laboratory function envisioned by the supporters of federalism, different states tried out new rules, and those that seemed to work well were adopted by other states. Until relatively recently, when the interests of the national parties and the states came into conflict, the courts ruled in favor of the states. More recently, premised on principles such as the "right of association," and the recognition of a need for nationally consistent procedures, the courts have begun siding with the national parties in their desire to control their own destiny (see Mileur, 1986, passim).

Ensuring Fair Elections

The Mechanics of Voting
During the colonial period, voters usually appeared before election officials and orally indicated their preferences. Gradually, the ballot box was introduced, with the parties having responsibility for preparing the ballots for their party. The practice of printing distinctively colored ballots and having party workers observing actual voting increased the potential for voter intimidation and fraud. Votes could be bought, and a party could make sure that voters

lived up to their end of the bargain (see Advisory Commission on Intergovernmental Relations, 1986, p. 124).

The introduction of the secret ballot beginning in the late 1800s, provided by state or local governments, reduced the potential for corruption but forced a number of decisions about ballot format and content. States with strong party organizations resisted state government control but, when forced, chose the *party-column ballot*, which lists all candidates of a party in a vertical column, encouraging voters to think of a party team and making it easy to vote according to party. Two-thirds of the more than 30 states using the party-column ballot make it even easier to support the party by providing a single mark or lever in order to vote for the entire ticket at one time.

The remainder of the states use the *office-bloc ballot* form in which all candidates for one office are listed together. This requires voters to peruse the entire list of candidates for an office to determine their choice. Party-line voting is thus discouraged. (Figures 2.1 and 2.2 illustrate the basic types of ballots.)

Research on ballot types supports the conclusions of party leaders in preferring the party-column ballot and indicates that this ballot form is especially important to less-partisan voters and for lower-level offices. Strong partisans will seek out the candidates of their parties. Highly visible contests for president or governor are not as affected by ballot type as are the many lower-level offices. Here, lacking information from the campaign or a cue from the party, many voters will simply skip over the offices on an office-bloc ballot (see Walker, 1966, pp. 448–463).

Nearly all ballots identify state and national candidates by party, although some states have experimented with nonpartisan elections. Lack of party designation on the state legislative ballot protected Minnesota Republicans for decades, allowing them to control the legislature while the state voted Democratic nationally. When the shift to partisan identification on the ballot occurred in the 1970s, the Republicans lost control of the state legislature. Nebraska remains as the only state electing state legislators without party designation. Virginia does not indicate party identification for state offices.

Nonpartisan elections are much more common in local elections. Many of the major cities, as well as most of the smaller ones, in the United States, are ruled by officials whose party label did not appear on the ballot. Although some of these elections are truly nonpartisan, in many areas candidates are endorsed or supported by the parties, or quasi-party groups have developed under the guise of "good government associations" to fill the void. The assault by the Progressives on the parties around the turn of the century promoted as an article of faith that, unencumbered by their ties to the party, elected officials would express their loyalty to the public at large and serve them better. Although the conclusion that better government would develop is debatable, a number of other consequences are more clear. Nonpartisan elections tend to result in lower turnout and by necessity hinge on popular issues or the personal characteristics of the candidates. From the perspective of the parties, the spread of nonpartisan elections eliminates the main reason for the local parties' existence and allows candidates to begin their political careers divorced from the party. Once in office, they owe little to the party and may well feel uncomfortable asking for party help even if they do seek higher partisan offices (see Kayden & Mahe, 1985, pp. 42–43).

Verifying Voter Eligibility

In small communities and rural areas with interacting citizens there was little need to verify eligible voters, but as the political units increased in size and society grew in anonymity the evidence of voting corruption increased. Squads of bought voters went voting from precinct to precinct, and it was not uncommon for many more votes to be cast in a precinct than there were residents. Between 1890 and 1920 states adopted voter-registration laws. As is often the case, the reform was backed by an odd combination of supporters. The Progressives sought to delete one campaign strategy from the parties, reduce corruption, make sure that elections represented the legal residents, and "institutionalize within the electorate the middle-class virtues" (Crotty, 1984, p. 19) of responsible citizenship and fair elections that they represented. Party leaders generally accepted the reforms as a method of identifying their supporters and developing an identifiable electorate to which they could appeal. The parties preferred systems that required voters to identify their party, thus making supporters more accessible. As described in Chapter 5, by inserting an additional step in the voting process, registration requirements change the nature of the actual electorate, and considerable effort has been taken by the parties to influence the details of the registration process.

Identifying Candidates

The American emphasis on representative government reveals itself in the way we link our elected officials to the public they are expected to represent. We require candidates to be locally eligible voters, and we have established most electoral districts so that a single elected official would be selected from that district. We have generally avoided multimember districts for which a party might develop a slate and proportional representation systems, such as that in many European countries whereby the individual votes for the party and the party vote are accumulated to determine the percentage of seats won. In Germany, for example, supporters of the Christian Democratic party place a mark by the party name as an indication of their preference for the party's list of candidates. If the party receives 60 percent of the vote in a district with 10 representatives, the top 6 candidates on the list are elected.

In the American system, the parties must contest election districts one by one. With varying electoral district boundaries, this requires the parties to combine and recombine at different levels. One combination of precincts

GENERAL ELECTION, TUESDAY, NOVEMBER 6, 1984

MACOMB COUNTY, MICHIGAN

INSTRUCTIONS—To vote a straight party ticket make a cross (X) in the circle under the name of your party. Nothing further need be done. To vote for a candidate not on your party ticket, make a cross (X) in the square ☐ before the candidate's name.

NOTE: Candidates for president and vice president must be voted for as a unit, and the vote cannot be split.

If two or more candidates are to be elected to the same office, and you desire to vote for candidates not on your party ticket, make a cross (X) in the square ☐ before the names of the candidates for whom you desire to vote on the other ticket, and strike out an equal number of names on your party ticket, for that office.

If you do not desire to vote any party ticket, do not make a cross in the circle at the head of any ticket, but make a cross (X) in the square ☐ before the name of each candidate for whom you desire to vote.

If you desire to vote for a candidate not on any ticket, write or place the name of such candidate on your ticket opposite the name of the office and make a cross (X) in the square before the name.

Before leaving the booth, fold the ballot so that the face of the ballot is not exposed and so that the numbered corner is visible.

NAMES OF OFFICES VOTED FOR:	DEMOCRATIC PARTY ⬤	REPUBLICAN ⬤	TISCH INDEPENDENT CITIZENS PARTY ⬤	LIBERTARIAN PARTY ⬤
PRESIDENTIAL ELECTORS OF PRESIDENT AND VICE PRESIDENT OF THE UNITED STATES VOTE FOR NOT MORE THAN ONE	President and Vice President ☐ WALTER F. MONDALE GERALDINE A. FERRARO	President and Vice President ☐ RONALD REAGAN GEORGE BUSH	President and Vice President ☐	President and Vice President ☐ DAVID BERGLAND JAMES LEWIS
CONGRESSIONAL UNITED STATES SENATOR VOTE FOR NOT MORE THAN ONE	United States Senator ☐ CARL LEVIN	United States Senator ☐ JACK LOUSMA	United States Senator ☐ ARTHUR RICHARD TISCH	United States Senator ☐ LYNN JOHNSTON
REPRESENTATIVE IN CONGRESS, 12th DISTRICT VOTE FOR NOT MORE THAN ONE	Representative in Congress ☐ DAVID E. BONIOR	Representative in Congress ☐ EUGENE J. TYZA	Representative in Congress	Representative in Congress ☐ KEITH P. EDWARDS
LEGISLATIVE REPRESENTATIVE IN STATE LEGISLATURE, 74th DIST. VOTE FOR NOT MORE THAN ONE	Representative in State Legislature ☐ JOHN M. MAYNARD	Representative in State Legislature ☐ MICHAEL J. SCOGLIETTI	Representative in State Legislature	Representative in State Legislature
STATE BOARDS MEMBERS OF THE STATE BOARD OF EDUCATION VOTE FOR NOT MORE THAN TWO	Member of the State Board of Education ☐ GUMECINDO SALAS Member of the State Board of Education ☐ JOHN WATANEN, JR.	Member of the State Board of Education ☐ DOROTHY BEARDMORE Member of the State Board of Education ☐ CHERRY JACOBUS	Member of the State Board of Education ☐ LOIS MELLBERG Member of the State Board of Education ☐ MARJORIE F. MORRIS	Member of the State Board of Education ☐ HAROLD M. BOOG Member of the State Board of Education ☐ GWENDOLINE STILLWELL
MEMBERS OF THE BOARD OF REGENTS OF UNIVERSITY OF MICHIGAN VOTE FOR NOT MORE THAN TWO	Board of Regents, University of Mich. ☐ MARJORIE LANSING Board of Regents, University of Mich. ☐ ROBERT NEDERLANDER	Board of Regents, University of Mich. ☐ NEAL D. NIELSEN Board of Regents, University of Mich. ☐ VERONICA LATTA SMITH	Board of Regents, University of Mich. Board of Regents, University of Mich.	Board of Regents, University of Mich ☐ BETTE ERWIN Board of Regents, University of Mich ☐ WILLIAM B. KREBAUM
MEMBERS OF THE BOARD OF TRUSTEES OF MICHIGAN STATE UNIVERSITY VOTE FOR NOT MORE THAN TWO	Trustee of Michigan State University ☐ JUNE KRETZSCHMER Trustee of Michigan State University ☐ CHARLES C. VINCENT	Trustee of Michigan State University ☐ KATHY WILBUR Trustee of Michigan State University ☐ DEAN PRIDGEON	Trustee of Michigan State University ☐ CHARLES SEVERANCE Trustee of Michigan State University	Trustee of Michigan State University ☐ THOMAS W. JONES Trustee of Michigan State University ☐ KURT T. WEBER
MEMBERS OF THE BOARD OF GOVERNORS OF WAYNE STATE UNIVERSITY VOTE FOR NOT MORE THAN TWO	Bd. of Governors, Wayne State Univ. ☐ WINIFRED D. FRASER Bd. of Governors, Wayne State Univ. ☐ DENISE J. LEWIS	Bd. of Governors, Wayne State Univ. ☐ GARY ARTINIAN Bd. of Governors, Wayne State Univ. ☐ GEORGE BASHARA	Bd. of Governors, Wayne State Univ. Bd. of Governors, Wayne State Univ.	Bd. of Governors, Wayne State Univ. ☐ WILLIAM M. HOLLANDER Bd. of Governors, Wayne State Univ. ☐ HAROLD LICHTENBERG
COUNTY PROSECUTING ATTORNEY VOTE FOR NOT MORE THAN ONE	Prosecuting Attorney ☐ CARL J. MARLINGA	Prosecuting Attorney ☐ C. MICHAEL KIMBER	Prosecuting Attorney	Prosecuting Attorney
SHERIFF VOTE FOR NOT MORE THAN ONE	Sheriff ☐ WILLIAM H. HACKEL	Sheriff ☐ STEPHEN E. THOMAS	Sheriff	Sheriff
CO. CLERK - REGISTER OF DEEDS VOTE FOR NOT MORE THAN ONE	County Clerk - Register of Deeds ☐ EDNA MILLER	County Clerk - Register of Deeds	County Clerk - Register of Deeds	County Clerk - Register of Deeds
COUNTY TREASURER VOTE FOR NOT MORE THAN ONE	County Treasurer ☐ ADAM E. NOWAKOWSKI	County Treasurer	County Treasurer	County Treasurer
PUBLIC WORKS COMMISSIONER VOTE FOR NOT MORE THAN ONE	Public Works Commissioner ☐ THOMAS S. WELSH	Public Works Commissioner ☐ TED ODROBINA	Public Works Commissioner	Public Works Commissioner
COUNTY COMMISSIONER DISTRICT VOTE FOR NOT MORE THAN ONE	County Commissioner ☐	County Commissioner ☐	County Commissioner ☐	County Commissioner ☐

Printed by Authority of the County Election Commission.

Figure 2.1 Party-Column Ballot (Michigan)

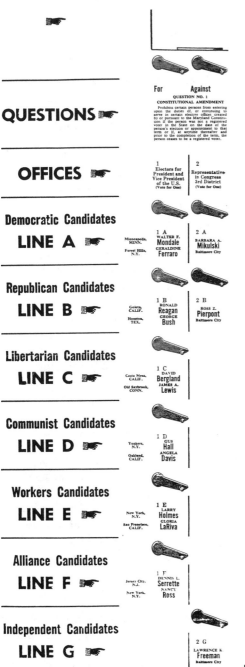

QUESTIONS ☞

For | Against
QUESTION NO. 1
CONSTITUTIONAL AMENDMENT
Prohibits certain persons from entering upon the duties of, or continuing to serve in certain elective offices created by or pursuant to the Maryland Constitution if the person was not a registered voter in the State on the date of the person's election or appointment to that term or if, at anytime thereafter and prior to the completion of the term, the person ceases to be a registered voter.

OFFICES ☞

1
Electors for President and Vice President of the U.S.
(Vote for One)

2
Representative in Congress 3rd District
(Vote for One)

Democratic Candidates
LINE A ☞

1 A
WALTER F.
Mondale
Minneapolis, MINN.
GERALDINE
Ferraro
Forest Hills, N.Y.

2 A
BARBARA A.
Mikulski
Baltimore City

Republican Candidates
LINE B ☞

1 B
RONALD
Reagan
Goleta, CALIF.
GEORGE
Bush
Houston, TEX.

2 B
ROSS Z.
Pierpont
Baltimore City

Libertarian Candidates
LINE C ☞

1 C
DAVID
Bergland
Costa Mesa, CALIF.
JAMES A.
Lewis
Old Saybrook, CONN.

Communist Candidates
LINE D ☞

1 D
GUS
Hall
Yonkers, N.Y.
ANGELA
Davis
Oakland, CALIF.

Workers Candidates
LINE E ☞

1 E
LARRY
Holmes
New York, N.Y.
GLORIA
LaRiva
San Francisco, CALIF.

Alliance Candidates
LINE F ☞

1 F
DENNIS L.
Serrette
Jersey City, N.J.
NANCY
Ross
New York, N.Y.

Independent Candidates
LINE G ☞

2 G
LAWRENCE k
Freeman
Baltimore City

Figure 2.2 Office-Block Ballot (Maryland)

becomes a state legislative district, and part of the district and a number of others make up a congressional district, and so on. Added to the district boundaries is the expectation that the candidate will have meaningful ties to the local area. New residents or locally born individuals having spent a great deal of time away from the district start with a distinct disadvantage. Unlike a Winston Churchill who was moved from district to district by his party for strategic purposes, American parties must compete within the constraints of a localistic emphasis.

As discussed in more detail in Chapter 4, contemporary parties have lost significant control over even the naming of candidates who carry their label. Through the caucus-convention system, the party leaders simply anticipated voter interests and developed a party slate in their own interest. With the widespread adoption of the direct primary system, parties lost their monopoly of the nominating process. Although some states formally allow preprimary endorsements, and others allow selective party support in primaries, primary victories by candidates not favored by the party leaders opened the door to additional successful challenges. The party thus moved from being *the* player in the nominating game to just one of the players. In the presidential nominating process, significant reforms during the 1970s increased the openness and democratic nature of the nomination process while decreasing party control and reflecting the image of the party as a "public utility," to use Leon Epstein's (1986) terminology. Just as the telephone and power companies are considered public utilities responsible to the public at large, rather than just to their stockholders, and therefore subject to increased regulation, political parties began to be seen as responsible to more than just a small group of organizational activists.

Controlling the Party Organization

The shift in perspective from viewing a political party as a private club to seeing it as a public utility is reflected in the laws that define party organizational activity and structure. Although the U.S. Constitution never mentions political parties directly or indirectly, many state constitutions include significant sections on the parties and all have considerable legislation affecting them. More indirectly, a number of federal statutes affect the parties, particularly in the realm of gathering and using resources. Most of the constitutional and legislative provisions are aimed at controlling and limiting the parties rather than enhancing their position.

Organizational Structure and Activity
State laws generally determine the nature of the party organization, how leaders will be selected, the procedure under which official decisions will be made, and the resources available for party activity.

Although most of the legislation and state constitutional provisions regarding political parties serve as limits, public policy in general performs a *party-maintenance* function.

> Public policy performs party maintenance functions. The law ordains that there shall be at least the shell of a party organization and generally invests the officers of this organization with functions of public significance. Public policy assures the minority party in the states of continued existence even at very low levels of electoral success. Stringent ballot access laws [making it difficult for nonparty candidates to get on the ballot], for example, work to prevent the replacement of the minority party by new parties, and the consequent destabilizing of the existing party system. Therefore, public policy invests the two major parties with important systemic functions while protecting their longevity. (Cotter, Gibson, Bibby, & Huckshorn, 1984, p. 149)

One of the earliest challenges to the parties came with the passage of the Pendleton Civil Service Act in 1883 and the similar state laws that followed. Traditionally, party activity was rewarded with *patronage*, favorable treatment of supporters when filling government jobs. Once in office, patronage appointees had the motivation to keep their party in office and willingly gave of their time and resources to support the party organization. The parties argued that the patronage system guaranteed them the resources to motivate campaign workers and build an effective team once in office. Opponents of the patronage system argued that it led to favoritism in the application of laws and inefficiency since political positions required dealing with more complex issues demanding continuity and expertise. The spread of a civil service system emphasizing qualifications and providing job security significantly reduced party access to human resources. Laws forbidding "macing the payroll" (requiring party contributions from appointees) similarly undermined the parties' working capital.

A second wave of reform following the Watergate scandal of the 1970s chipped away at the parties' freedom to support candidates financially in elections. Taking a variety of forms including contribution limits, expenditure limits, public reporting of contributions and expenditures, and public financing of campaigns, each step made it more difficult for a party to support its candidates in the way it wished (see Chapter 6).

As private organizations, political parties could make decisions as they wished. Initially, the caucus or convention system of managing the party and naming candidates was carried out without governmental interference. In the attempt to protect the public, and often as part of a strategy by political activists perceiving their interests ill served by current rules, more and more laws were passed to specify methods of party decision making. It is difficult to separate the abstract goals of reformers using the rhetoric of general principles ("democracy," "equality," "fairness," and so on) and the practical desires of the reformers to strengthen their political position. While crying out for more party democracy, for instance, Robert M. La Follette launched the adoption of the direct primary after the Wisconsin State Republican convention had denied him the party's gubernatorial nomination (Ranney, 1979, p. 219), and Hiram Johnson presided over the development of some of the most stringent constraints on parties in California after recognizing that his supporters did not do well in the smoke-filled-room political decision-making process.

The degree of state involvement in party activities varies dramatically. Some state laws cover parties in a few paragraphs, and others go into great detail specifying dates and places of official meetings as well as decision-making procedures. All states specify procedures for getting party nominees on the ballot, and most outline the composition and duties of permanent state party committees that speak for the party and manage its operations between elections (see Chapter 3).

Traditionally, state party laws have had more effect on how the national parties operate than vice versa. With the Democratic party reforms in their nomination process after the 1968 convention (see Chapter 4), the direction of influence reversed. By favoring specific delegate-selection procedures and threatening to deny recalcitrant parties seats at the convention, the national Democratic party set the tone and impetus for changes in state party electoral laws.

Although state parties vary considerably in resources, structure, and activities, the trend has been toward more and more legislative determination of their character. Even when state laws do not seem to work as intended, the remedy is new legislation rather than freeing the parties to control their own destiny. For example, the highly controlled California parties have long desired to play a more active role in nominations and are currently battling for new legislation giving them the right to endorse candidates before the primary. Wisconsin parties have just succeeded in getting new legislation allowing local party leaders to be selected on the ballot rather than by a less participatory caucus selection. Parties have clearly moved from being private organizations supported and controlled by their activists to state-monitored adjuncts to the governmental process.

THE POLITICAL ENVIRONMENT

The Two-Party System

With minor lapses, the history of American political party competition is one of two relatively equal parties competing for office. Although particular parties have revealed an ebb and flow in their support and have sometimes been replaced, and although some areas of the country have gone through significant periods of one-party control, there is little meaningful party activity outside of the Republican and Democratic folds today. A number of different explanations have been put forward for the relatively uncommon American two-party system.

Structural Theories

The most immediate explanation for the domination of the Republican and Democratic parties in American politics stems from the nature of American electoral law. The system clearly favors a two-party system. Single-member districts in which elections are won by gaining a plurality of votes do not allow sharing of electoral victory among a number of parties. Unlike a proportional representation system, each party must compete on a district-by-district basis. This makes room for one winner and a meaningful opposition but discourages an opposition splintered among many parties. The electoral college system of selecting the president makes presidential elections like 50 single-member districts. To win the electors from a state, a presidential candidate must win a plurality of the votes. There is no benefit to coming in second or third. Furthermore, the presidential system, with a single chief executive and its state-level gubernatorial variant, disallows the kind of coalitional government of including a number of parties possible in a parliamentary cabinet. Election laws make it relatively easy for existing parties to get and stay on the ballot but require extraordinary efforts such as petition drives and conventions for third parties and independents to secure a position. In recent years, third-party presidential candidates George Wallace (1968) and John Anderson (1980) exhausted much of their resources through petition drives and court cases to get on the ballot in all 50 states. The right of their parties to stay on the ballot required a minimum level of voter support from one election to the next, and neither organization maintained the right to stay on the ballot for more than two elections in any state. Current state laws force the maintenance of a shell of the two parties and ignore third-party maintenance. Governmental financing of campaigns favors the official candidates of the two parties and either ignores or disadvantages independents and third-party candidates.

While disagreeing on many substantive issues, political party leaders find a great deal of common ground in their attempts to perpetuate their dominance. Through their control of government and the fact that current elected officials entered political life through the current rules, the two parties strive to maintain the existing system and to enact laws perpetuating two-party domination.

The Nature of Voters

Despite the decline in party identification and party-line voting during the postwar period, political party identification is still one of the best predictors of the vote. Although voters might give lip service to their dissatisfaction with the parties, they tend to vote for major-party candidates over independent and third-party candidates even when they have those options. Knowing that only one candidate can win apparently discourages voters from wasting their votes on the unlikely possibility that a third-party candidate will succeed.

Seeing traditional voting patterns, the most viable candidates generally pursue the major-party route to electoral office, although increasingly they see party support as only one component in their campaigns. Similarly, the providers of campaign resources—individual contributors and political action committees—shower their support on these likely winners rather than on long shots.

Breaking the hold of the two parties involves simultaneously changing the behavior of large numbers of voters, candidates, and campaign supporters—not an easy task as many defeated third-party hopefuls can attest.

Less Immediate Causes

The above factors explain much of the current domination of the two-party system but do not completely explain its origin. The more recent structural adaptations and the behavior patterns adopted by voters and the strategies pursued by political activists may be the result of more basic factors that led to the development of a two-party pattern. Although it may not be possible to identify *the* one causal factor of the two-party system, a number of societal factors have been conducive.

The nature of political conflict in America makes two-party domination possible. One-party systems require almost complete consensus or the ability to coerce compliance from opponents. Multiparty systems thrive in settings where deep cleavages divide society into relatively intransigent groups, each of which hold on to some beliefs on which they will not compromise. By limiting the options, two-party systems require enough conflict to insure the need for competing parties but also enough common ground for compromise.

Many observers, frustrated with the lack of distinctiveness of the American parties, look longingly at European parties manifesting competing ideologies. Transporting political institutions into different social settings is very difficult and may be impossible.

> The differences in political milieu on the two sides of the Atlantic suggest that lessons from the Old World may have little relevance in the New. European parties operate within much smaller geographic confines, usually unitary states, unlike the federated American parties; therefore, they have always been highly centralized, with authoritative central policy-making and candidate selection processes; they have had distinct ideologies from the beginning reflecting cleavages of class and religion deeper than any this country has known; and they exist, usually, not in a two-party but in a multiparty setting, which permits each party to cover a relatively narrow portion of the ideological spectrum and thus to maintain more easily its consistency and distinctiveness. (Sundquist, 1982, p. 55)

American citizens—and therefore their parties—show relatively high consensus on basic beliefs and do not perceive themselves as being divided clearly on class, regional, or other lines. American politics focuses more on differences in selecting means, rather than basic conflict over the desired ends of politics. While revealing a heterogeneous set of interests, most Americans identify with a number of societal groups and find themselves torn in a number of opposing directions when it comes to policy preferences. Combined with the fact that most Americans are not consumed with winning or losing in politics, the lack of absolute references allows the kind of compromise a two-party system requires.

Although not as clear as the *natural dualism theories* (see Duverger, 1954), which asserted that all basic political battles divide between two alternatives (the ins versus the outs, the pros versus the cons, and so on), some of the cleavages in American politics have manifested themselves in two abiding camps. The initial battles over the Revolution and the Constitution set the stage for two opposing groups. With the initial battles out of the way, early sectional battles between the eastern financial interests and those of the western frontiersmen again manifested themselves in two relatively equal groups. The battle over slavery and the resulting Civil War provided a clear issue on which to identify supporters and opponents; that issue dominated politics for decades. Based on the socioeconomic divisions of society the Democrats took up the banner of the common people, with the Republicans appealing to the more affluent citizens.

Despite the inability to isolate a discrete set of causes of the two-party system, and the concurrent difficulty of exporting our preferred arrangement to other countries, the fact remains that the United States has had, and will continue to have a two-party system. The two-party system and the current parties that comprise it represent the oldest party system among democratic political parties in the world. Although our familiarity with a two-party system may heighten our respect for it, a number of clear advantages stand out in the eyes of most observers (for a dissenting view see Lowi, 1983, passim). The existence of two relatively competitive parties enhances the position of citizens by guaranteeing realistic competition for virtually all offices and encouraging inclusive politics in which opportunities for participation are increased. One-party systems have little need to be open and generally provide for little citizen impact. Multiparty systems often fall victim to the sharp societal cleavages that spawned them. Individual parties in a multiparty system have the tendency to become exclusive, requiring absolute belief in a narrow set of principles, which discourages participation. As long as all parties in such a system practice such exclusionary tactics, there is little incentive to reach out to new participants. The extreme factionalism leads to too much conflict and possible immobilization of the entire political system. The bitterness of political conflict and the difficulty of maintaining stable government in multiparty systems such as the one in Italy reflect these problems.

Historical Anomalies:
Third Parties and One-Party Areas

Third Parties

Despite the domination of the Republican and Democratic parties for more than 120 years, a variety of third parties has emerged. Only a handful of third parties have carried even a single state in a presidential election, and none has come close to winning the presidency. Third parties have had some selected success in state and local elections but have not been a major factor. Given their dismal record, one must search for reasons for their persistence. The fact that one current major national party and at least one state party can be seen as having emerged as third parties may have given false hope to these movements. Convinced of their correctness on the issues, leaders of such movements might be able to convince themselves that lightning could strike again. A better understanding of the motivations of third-party organizers stems from the realization that they can be differentiated on the basis of their origin and their goals.

The Origin and Motivations of Third Parties.   The constraints of the two-party system on issues and personal political ambition sometimes rupture and spawn *major-party-bolting* parties. These parties are generally the vehicle of an individual or issue that was not accommodated by the major party. They often enter a campaign to win or, at least, in an attempt to establish themselves as a political force to be reckoned with. The Progressive ("Bull Moose") party split from the Republican party in 1912 when Teddy Roosevelt tried to get back in the White House after giving up the office to his vice president, William Howard Taft, in 1908. His personal appeal was largely responsible for accumulating 88 electoral votes and nearly 30 percent of the popular vote, taking enough support from Taft to guarantee Democrat Woodrow Wilson the presidency. The State's Rights Democratic party (Dixiecrat) ran Strom Thurmond in 1948 after the Democratic party rejected its conservative racial-segregationist positions. Running as the Democratic party in some of the South, it managed to acquire 39 electoral votes without defeating Harry Truman's presidential bid. George Wallace's American Independent party put a scare into the major parties in 1968 and received 46 electoral votes. Although privately not expecting to win, Wallace hoped to force the election into the House of Representatives (required if no candidate gets a simple majority) where he could then strike a bargain for his support. Although Wallace was a Democrat, it is not clear that the votes he siphoned off would have gone to Hubert Humphrey had he not run. Because of the ballot-qualifying laws, in 1980 John Anderson ran more as a nonparty candidate than one from a third party. Frustrated with his lack of support in the Republican presidential primaries, Anderson shifted strategies in midcampaign and received almost 6 million votes but won the electoral votes of no states. Major-party-bolting third parties tend to be closely tied with a particular issue or candidate. Once that issue or candidate departs from the scene they have little staying power.

A second set of third parties expresses little realistic hope of winning elections but rather sees itself as a *protest movement* desiring to publicize its cause. These third parties tend to be more homogeneous and ideological in their views. Some of them, such as a variety of Communist and Socialist parties, are European imports; others like the Grangers, Prohibition, Peace and Freedom, and Right to Life parties express indigenous protests against inequality or a stand on a narrow issue. Some of these parties have shown considerable local strength. The Socialists did well in urban areas with many European immigrants such as Milwaukee, Wisconsin, and New York City. The Farmer-Labor party of Minnesota went on to challenge successfully both parties in statewide elections and eventually combined with the Democrats to form the Democratic Farmer-Labor Party (DFL) in the 1940s, the name by which it still contests elections.

The less common, but perhaps more important, type of third party is the *coalitional* party. In states such as New York where the laws allow candidates to run on more than one ticket, minor parties like the Liberal and Conservative parties have had limited success since the 1960s. By allowing candidates to have their names listed on more than one line of the ballot, these parties bargain for concessions by selectively endorsing major-party candidates and promising to deliver the margin of victory. Figure 2.3 illustrates some of the third-party candidates and causes as depicted on their campaign buttons and other material.

The Disadvantages of Third Parties.   The fact that only the Republican party moved from being a third party to a major national force, that the Minnesota DFL stands out as the prime state example, and that individual third-party victories have been few reflects the disadvantages that third parties face. The election and campaign-funding laws work against third-party movements by denying them things such as election judges and up-front campaign money (see Chapter 6). The process of getting on the ballot requires third parties to expend much of their resources fulfilling the legalities of being listed. With a minimum percentage of votes required to stay on the ballot from one election to the next, the efforts of one year may be wiped out by an election with a minimum showing.

The problems of third parties do not end with getting on the ballot. The habitual support of a large percentage of the electorate for one of the major parties means that their candidates start out with a basic reservoir of support, while the minor party must seek to dislodge voters from their original intentions. Even with an appealing approach, the hesitancy to waste one's vote on a likely nonwinner encourages many voters simply to support the lesser of two evils rather than support the third party. Even among their supporters, third parties have a disadvantage. They tend to draw a disproportionate amount of

Figure 2.3 Third-Party Campaign Material

their support from individuals known neither for their political resources nor their political participation levels. They have a hard time raising money and getting workers. Their failure to gather adequate campaign resources becomes a self-fulfilling prophecy. Lack of resources and the likelihood of success make them unlikely recipients of money from either PACs or uncommitted individuals. Lack of resources dooms electoral prospects, which in turn discourages contributions the next time around. Additionally, since the American political system is open, a third party striking a responsive chord with its approach or issues is likely to discover that its uniqueness has been stolen by one of the major parties. In 1968, for example, George Wallace's political success, partially based on his opposition to school busing, drew both Richard Nixon and Hubert Humphrey to more tentative positions than they initially held. Longtime Socialist presidential candidate Norman Thomas liked to look back on his career in terms of the major social programs, such as the income tax, medicare, and equal rights amendment, that figured prominently in his campaigns and were later adopted by the major parties.

The Importance of Third Parties.   If one defines the *importance of third parties* in terms of winning elections, electorally, third-party impact is limited but not insignificant. As Gary Mauser concluded:

> The entry of minor candidates into a normal two-party electoral contest can influence the outcome of the election in any of three distinct ways: by influencing who turns out to vote, by altering individual voters' preferences for candidates, or by splitting one or more of the major candidates' vote. (1983, p. 113)

From a broader perspective, though, their existence makes some unique contributions. The very existence of a broad range of parties reflects the freedom of expression in the American system and serves as a peaceful outlet for some unique perspectives. In some cases, third parties have served the role of articulating interests and introducing new ideas into the political system. The Wallace challenge in 1968 clearly moved both major-party candidates toward a more conservative stand on issues such as busing. Although such issue development does happen within the major parties and through outside groups and the media, parties look seriously at movements that can motivate individuals to sustain organizations and voters to support candidates.

> There is compelling evidence that third parties do affect the outcome of some elections and that the ideas associated with them are sometimes later reflected in public policy. (Mazmanian, 1979, p. 305)

One-Party Areas

Although the United States has a two-party system nationally and increasingly so on state and local levels, bastions of one-party domination have existed and continue to exit. For decades after the Civil War, the Democratic party dominated southern politics. Democratic candidates faced with Republican challenges regularly reminded voters of the past by "waving the bloody shirt." Generations of southerners learned the acceptability of being a "yellow dog Democrat" (willing to vote for a yellow dog wearing the Democratic label) rather than voting Republican. Ambitious activists found themselves well advised to enter the Democratic fold, which reinforced the recognition where the real political game is played. In a number of states numerous and abiding factions gave the one-party system the look of a two or multi-party system on the state and local levels.

Lest one conclude that one-party systems with abiding factions are just as good as competitive two-party systems, V. O. Key asserted that one-party factionalism "fosters discontinuities of leadership, confuses voters, encourages the recruitment of self-serving demagogic leaders, increase political instability and induces political favoritism" (1949, p. 303). Factions developed around individual politicians or were based on regional interests. With opportunities for competition at that level, local politicians had little motivation to use the Republican party as an alternative route to power. With the shift of the national Democratic party away from southern views on civil rights since the 1940s, the influx of many nonsoutherners and more recent Republican attempts to capitalize on a fertile area led first to split-ticket voting in presidential elections and eventually to the spread of two partyism in the South (see Chapter 5).

In other areas of the country concentrations of voters strongly supportive of a particular party based on voter self-interest or historical tradition maintain that party as dominant. Elsewhere, a traditionally strong party organization in one party and weakness in the other set the stage for one-party dominance.

The increased heterogeneity of the American electorate in most areas, the decline of party identification, the increase in candidate-oriented campaigns eschewing party labels, and the increased efforts of parties to appeal to all voters have worked to reduce the number of one-party areas. Despite very limited support in the past, the national Republican party maintains a well-financed program to appeal to black voters, and the Democrats have tried a number of specific appeals to the business community. As one experienced national party operative put it: "There is hardly a state, city, district, or precinct that we write off anymore. There are significant pockets of our supporters among almost every social and regional grouping" (author's interview).

Although two-party competition is spreading, the shift is not as uniform across offices as it is across jurisdictions:

> In each successive generation during the twentieth century the proportion of one-party states has dropped. By the same measure we can see that the

---

A TALE OF TWO CONTEMPORARY THIRD PARTIES

The Libertarian Party

Origin
Founded in 1971

Basic Principles
The Libertarian party cuts across traditional party and ideological lines advocating conservative themes such as scaled-down government, individual liberty, and a free-market economy combined with traditional liberal themes of reducing the military and ending the draft.

Electoral Record

1972: 4,000 presidential votes after qualifying for the ballot in two states
1980: 92,000 presidential votes and places on the ballot in all 50 states
1984: 235,000 presidential votes and 1,000 candidates running (see Cook, 1984)

Lyndon LaRouche and The National Democratic Policy Committee

Origin
LaRouche's organization would be seen as little more than a personality cult around former Marxist Lyndon LaRouche who shifted dramatically to the right, if it were not for the amount of money it raised and the number of candidates it fielded. LaRouche began by running as a presidential candidate under the U.S. Labor party label in 1972. He then created the National Democratic Policy Committee, a kind of "party within a party," attempting to fill the right-wing vacuum in the Democratic party. He runs in presidential primaries and fields hundreds of candidates for party and lower-level offices, as well as opposing big name Democrats in congressional races. In recent years, LaRouche complained of a conspiracy against him as he battled the Federal Elections Commission challenges to his campaign financing and the criminal investigations of his fundraising techniques.

Basic Principles
While accepting many basic conservative principles, LaRouche has made headlines with support for a laser defense system, quarantining of AIDS victims, and the return of Ferdinand Marcos as Philippine president, and by charging Great Britain with a conspiracy to undermine the United States through international drug trade.

Electoral Record

1972: LaRouche ran for president under the U.S. Labor party and received 40,043 votes.
1980: LaRouche ran in the Democratic primaries and received 177,784 votes.
1984: LaRouche ran in the Democratic primaries and received 121,226 votes and fielded more than 2,500 candidates. More than 200 candidates won, largely for lower-level party positions, school boards, and so on.
1986: LaRouche candidates made national headlines by winning the Democratic nominations for lieutenant governor and secretary of state in Illinois. Democratic gubernatorial candidate Adlai Stevenson III resigned the Democratic nomination and ran as an independent to avoid running with them. Stevenson's campaign was crippled in a state where party-line voting is a longtime tradition. Democratic leaders in other states began to scour their candidate lists to expose LaRouche candidates. (See Cook, 1986.)

proportion of volatile constituencies . . . has risen for president and governor, whereas it has steadily declined for the lower house of Congress. The result was to sharpen the distinctions among party systems around various political offices. (Schlesinger, 1985, p. 1158)

Explaining the differences in types of elections is more difficult than discovering them. The vast media attention to presidential, gubernatorial, and senatorial races reduces the role of traditional party-line voting and opens the door for more competitive races. Races for the House of Representatives, on the other hand, provide fewer opportunities for media domination, but rather than a continuation of party control, we see individual candidates developing their own organizations and using modern means of communication to strengthen their political positions. In both cases, technology has intervened to change the political landscape and threaten the role of the parties.

THE SOCIAL AND TECHNOLOGICAL SETTING

Because political parties are customary, permeable, and highly adaptive institutions formed about elections and not reinforced by law, there has characteristically been a very close fit between parties and the societies in which they exist. (Kirkpatrick, 1978, p. 19)

Political parties do not exist in a vacuum. They draw from and must work within the social and technological fabric of the times. How people use their time, the nature of their social commitments, how they gather information, and their general life-style serve as a backdrop defining the workable strategies and potential of the parties.

Although an exhaustive analysis of the social and technological climate of the United States as we approach the 1990s is well beyond the scope of this book, developing a sensitivity to some key characteristics will help put party activity in context.

The Social Structure

Social Commitments
Without looking back longingly at some former era, it is clear that contemporary society is vastly different from that experienced by the Founding Fathers or existing during the various earlier periods of political party development and reform. In the past few decades,

increasing urbanization and improvements in transportation completed the destruction of the system of isolated "island communities" of earlier years. . . . Issues of national scope multiplied and decision-making increasingly shifted from local and state governments to the national level. . . . Trade unions, professional and trade associations, and other secondary groups of potential relevance to politics multiplied. Thus group pressures upon political behavior and attitudes also multiplied and became more complex and conflicting. (Clubb, Flanigan, & Zingale, 1980, p. 284)

On the individual level, voters moved from existing in "communities of total commitment" to "communities of limited commitment." In the former, most individuals lived, worked, shopped, sent their kids to school, recreated, and the like within relatively narrow geographical confines and with the same people. This type of life-style was conducive to forging deep and lasting social and political commitments. Fewer and fewer people live in such communities today. The more typical contemporary communities of limited commitment are exemplified by the suburban resident living in a bedroom community; commuting to another political jurisdiction to work; shopping in a number of malls around the freeway; taking off for the weekend to recreate at the lake, mountains, or shore; and associating with a wide variety of individuals from a number of communities. Perhaps the ultimate sign of this lack of attachment to a local community is the difficulty many people have answering the basic question, "Where are you from?" Even if a person wanted to get involved in party politics, it is often hard to decide which political community one has the greatest stake in. Having to choose between local politics to have some say on schools; county politics, which affects the roads on which you commute; and state politics, which affects both, but only indirectly, introduces frustration. With such a wide variety of political targets and concerns, the political party is ill equipped to provide help, even if the party organization is alive and well and can be found.

The dilution of the average citizen's commitment to one particular community at any time is increased by the over-time mobility of much of the population. Although it was once common to be born, educated, married, employed, and to die in the same area and often the same house, most Americans now make a number of job-related and preference-related moves. Many corporations test the commitment of employees to the corporation and facilitate having "interchangeable human parts" by requiring moves for upward mobility. New residents in a community generally do not know the political ropes and have some difficulty in getting politically involved. If future moves are anticipated, the lack of permanence may be a good disincentive for not getting involved. Both the complexity of modern life and impermanence of individuals work against the ability of a local political party to recruit a stable core of workers and supporters.

Responsibility for political parties has always been tied to their nature as electoral organizations—to their presence on the ballot and to their organizational presence in the physical constituency. . . . To some extent the decline of political parties is rooted in the decline of those constituencies: no longer do we live, work, play or derive our political lives from the homogeneous local community or neighborhood. (Sorauf, 1982, p. 36)

Social Involvement

Political parties and other mediating groups have traditionally depended on a large cadre of volunteers to carry out their tasks. Although volunteerism is still impressive in America, the increased number of mediating groups vying for citizen support and the changing time commitments provide increased challenges to the parties.

The tremendous growth of interest groups, especially those with relatively narrow single interests ranging from stopping abortion and drunk driving to protecting the freedom to own guns or smoke marijuana, tap many of the same people who might work for the parties. As interest aggregators rather than interest articulators, political parties generally must take broader and less strident stands, often based on compromise, which makes them less appealing as organizations worthy of support.

Traditionally, much of the legwork of political parties during the earlier part of this century was done by housewives. The women's movement demeaned many of the typical volunteer jobs, while the dramatic increase in the percentage of women working outside the home placed severe limitations on their availability for volunteer efforts on any level.

Social Attitudes

Traditionally, political involvement has not been held in the highest esteem in America, but the series of scandals such as Watergate, Abscam, Koreagate, and their local and state versions, while not directly indicting the political parties, have further eroded support for them. A web of cynicism has gripped public evaluation of our major institutions. "Loss of confidence and trust in political and social institutions in the last decade should not be ignored and in fact suggest a contemporary crisis" (Clubb et al., 1980, p. 292).

When asked to evaluate the contributions of the parties according to specific criteria, there has been a steady decline in public confidence. In 1968, 46 percent of the public believed that the "parties are only interested in people's votes, but not in their opinions." By 1980, 59 percent supported the same statement. Similarly, in 1964, 42 percent of the people thought that the parties did a good deal to "help make government pay attention to what the people think," an opinion that dropped to 18 percent by 1980 (Lipset & Schneider, 1983, pp. 386–388).

> Faith in the parties has diminished sufficiently that, by 1983, an ACIR-Gallup poll found that almost half of the population (45%) believed that organized interest groups best represented their political interests, compared with only 24% who believed that either of the political parties does so. (Conlan, 1985, p. 35)

Using time-series data, Jack Dennis (1986) argued that public support for the parties may have reached its low point and be on its way up, but it is difficult to sort out long-term trends and the "era of good feeling" that dominated politics at least during the initial stages of the Reagan presidency.

Reduced support for the parties as institutions may not be so much a negative evaluation as an "increasing sense that parties just don't count for much anymore" (Wattenberg, 1985, p. 1).

> It would perhaps be better for the parties if the public had become more negative rather than more neutral toward them. Negative attitudes could easily be turned into positive attitudes by better performance or a change in policies. To make people care about political parties once again may well be more difficult. . . . It is increasingly difficult for Americans to see the relevance of political parties in this candidate-centered age of mass media. (Wattenberg, 1984, p. xvi)

Taking a somewhat different approach, Russell Dalton (1984) argued that expanding political skills and the information resources of the contemporary electorate change the way in which citizens relate to the parties. When citizens were relatively poorly educated and political information came only at a high cost, party labels and partisan information served a very important purpose. In contemporary society, a larger percentage of the electorate understands the issues and can be mobilized through "cognitive" rather than party means.

> Cognitive mobilization implies that citizens possess the skills and resources necessary to become politically engaged with little dependence on external cues. In addition, cognitive mobilization implies a psychological involvement in politics. (Dalton, 1984, p. 267)

Using over-time data from the United States and a number of advanced industrial democracies, Dalton projected a decline of "ritual partisans" activated by traditional party symbols and supportive of party organizations, and an increase in "apartisans" less supportive of the party per se but aware and involved in the political process (see Dalton, 1984, passim).

Other social attitudes more indirectly affect the parties' ability to carry out their traditional functions. Increased fear of crime makes it more difficult to recruit volunteer block workers to carry the party message and less likely that voters will open their doors to strangers. Increased self-centeredness ("looking out for number one," the "me" generation, and so on) as opposed to selflessness makes it more difficult to forge compromises and get partisans to volunteer their efforts for the good of the party.

The social structure serves as the backdrop for political party activity, and technology serves as the means by which parties carry out their activities.

The Technological Setting

Information transfer is the core technology of politics and the bread and butter of political parties. The parties must develop an effective two-way communications process with organizational activists as well as voters. The degree to which parties can define their audience, craft an appealing message, and activate supporters does a great deal to determine their success.

For many generations, the transfer of political information in the United States was very labor intensive with face-to-face communication dominating. The classic voting studies of the 1940s identified a "two-step flow" of information (Lazarsfeld, Berelson, & Gaudet, 1944) in which political activists would gather information from the media and the parties and would disseminate it to the less politically involved citizens. In the process of transferring political opinions from one person to another, the social context affected what was transmitted. Information was judged as much on the basis of its sources as its content. In this context, the political parties were served well by precinct leaders and block workers who kept in close touch with their local voters and provided them with selective information.

Although the mass media existed, it was less "mass" than today. Early newspapers were often vehicles for particular parties. Later, most cities supported a variety of papers, each taking a definite point of view. With the challenge of the electronic media competing for the attention of the interested citizen, newspapers folded, and the remaining ones took on a more objective flavor. Today, few cities support competing newspapers, and the remaining ones tend to present more balanced news requiring more analysis on the part of the reader to get political directives.

Increasingly, the electronic media, particularly television, predominates as a source of political information. By 1980 more than 75 percent of the public credited television as their primary political news source. Based on the premise of a public stake in distributing a scarce resource such as transmission frequencies, the electronic media finds itself under strict limits encouraging objectivity. The "equal time" provision requires television stations to give or sell time to all candidates if they offer it to any. The "fairness doctrine" is less specific and currently is not being enforced by the government, but reminds broadcasters of their responsibility for objectivity.

Early television stations were largely local "mom and pop" operations catering to the tastes and political views of their local audiences. The economies of scale making large broadcasting operations more profitable by not having to duplicate fixed costs in a number of settings encouraged local stations to join with the national networks, but increasingly the bargain included depending on the networks for most programming.

The national network news programs have become almost an institution in American households around which travel and dinner plans are made. Because of the nature of its audience, network news must present more of a national twist, and because of the size of the audience, it can influence national attitudes and the political agenda. State and local parties can seldom use the national news or advertising potential, and until relatively recently, the national parties had not capitalized on the potential of national advertising.

Messages from the media also affect the bases on which politicians appeal to their supporters.

Before the television networks created their massive audiences, parochialism of the past was primarily rooted in geography, generating diversity that our representative institutions were specifically designed to ameliorate. Segmented communication may facilitate the organization of political interests that transcend geography, politics may be organized horizontally across political boundaries. The result is likely to increase the pressure on our elected legislators as they attempt to satisfy the interests that cross geographic boundaries, while preserving their support among constituents back home. (Arterton, 1983, p. 66)

The political parties are likely to come under the same types of pressures, to eschew localism on the one hand but to be dependent on local concerns on the other hand. Being caught between two competing pressures has increased the difficulty of the party in speaking with a coherent and politically acceptable voice. The most obvious current example is the Democratic party. Its liberal stands on a variety of issues have been driven by a national agenda facilitated, if not caused, by the media. But local party organizations, particularly in the South, believe that the party increasingly does not speak for them. Their attempts to distinguish the local party position from that of the national party has had mixed success. As explained in Chapter 5, one of the causes of increased two-party competition in the South has been the alienation of voters from the stands of the national Democratic party.

The availability of electronic media with its efficient coverage of the information market has challenged the parties in another way. Candidates have discovered that they can circumvent party-information channels and go directly to the people.

Television, and later the video player, made the home an entertainment and information center. Whereas political rallies once served as both entertainment and political activating events, it has become more difficult to get people out of their homes to attend political events.

Other technological advances such as the computer have made traditional party intelligence gathering obsolete. Informal "checking around the circuit" with local political activists to measure the "political pulse" paled compared to sophisticated polling techniques using computerized telephone dialing and data analysis. The ability to tap massive banks of sociopolitical data to predict intended voting patterns was much more impressive than the guesstimates of the polls. Political parties were slow to use such techniques and largely left the field open to consultants and other nonparty activists.

Revolution in transportation deprived the parties of their role as surrogates for candidates who could not be present for every local event. Now even the congressmen from the West Coast can fly to the coast to represent themselves virtually every weekend and return to Washington on the late-night "red-eye special" for the next week's session, perhaps suffering from jet lag but able to carry out official responsibilities. In presidential campaigns, we will never see the kind of "front-porch" campaign of William McKinley with the party carrying out the campaign while the candidate stayed home. Modern candidates jet from state to state making public appearances, hoping to be seen by the local media markets. They plan at least one major television event per day designed to catch the fancy of the national media.

Faced with social and technological changes affecting life-styles and information-gathering techniques, the political parties throughout history have been confronted with the need to adapt or wither.

In the following chapters the discussion focuses in more detail on how the parties have confronted these challenges in their various realms of activity. This information will help readers develop an awareness of the current contributions and future potential of U.S. political parties.

3

Political Parties as Organizations

In the search for American political parties, the most visible component is the party organization. The formal organization manifests itself in the form of lists of officers, scheduled meetings, paid staff, and party headquarters that run the range from seedy one-room operations with a few filing cabinets to opulent executive suites and high-tech media centers complete with television studios and computer centers. To find the political parties in major cites and particularly state capitals, one has only to pick up the telephone directory. Finding the party in less-populated areas is more difficult.

The degree and nature of party organization vary significantly around the country and from one level of government to the next. Traditional organization charts (see Figure 3.1) are often more misleading than enlightening, since they reflect the hopes of party activists or the requirements of state law more than reality. In discussing the party organization, there must be a clear distinction between the national parties existing as a cadre of professional paid staff, guided but not controlled by a volunteer board of directors (national committees), and the state and local organizations representing a mix of paid professionals directing a shifting variety of volunteers.

Despite its elusiveness, the party organization is a key factor providing continuity and direction to party activity and serves as the only locus for party renewal. It is important to remember, however, that although the goal of all major party organizations is winning elections and gaining political power, there is not a direct relationship between a strong organization and attainment of political goals, at least not in the short run.

Determining the impact of organizational vitality of state and local parties on election outcomes poses a problem since it is hard to distinguish cause and effect. Although the simplest argument is that organizationally strong parties

58

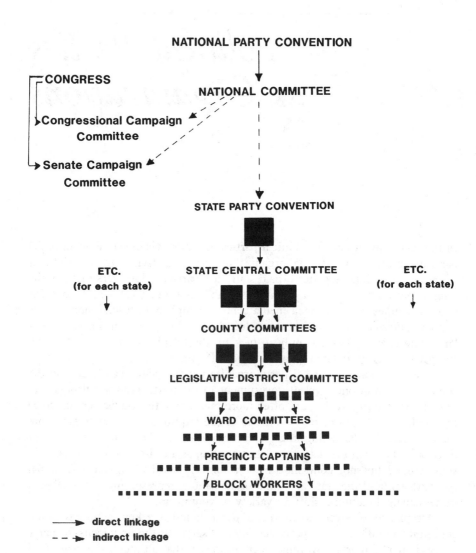

Figure 3.1 Traditional Party Organization Chart

will win more elections, it is less clear which is the cause and which is the effect. Organizational strength may lead to electoral success, or success at the polls could invigorate the party organization. Alternatively, parties with a weak electoral record may try to compensate by beefing up their organizational strength. Despite the competing explanations, John Bibby (Bibby, 1981, p. 104) concluded that party organizational strength does lead to electoral success.

Not all aspects of a party's organizational strength involve its conflict with an opposing party. Often the party organization competes with party supporters or nonparty organizations seeking to control party decisions. The degree to which the organization can win such battles either in head-to-head struggles or, more indirectly, through recruiting, training, supporting, and encouraging favored candidates serves as another measure of organizational strength.

Even if party organizational strength does not lead directly to either intramural or external political success, the parties still affect the electoral process. With their continuing interest in the process, the parties monitor each other and election laws to protect their interests, while attempting to ameliorate antiparty moods and legislation (see Cotter, Gibson, Bibby, & Huckshorn, 1984, p. 34). At times the effects are more direct. The Democratic National Committee through its reforms of the presidential nomination process precipitated major changes in the election laws of 30 states, affecting candidates at all levels from both parties (see Havlicek, 1982, p. 70).

Although measuring the "batting average" of the party in its various battles serves as a direct measure of organizational strength, more indirect measures are easier to come by and focus more directly on the party organization per se. As with all organizations, the parties must gather and organize resources to carry out their activities. The amount, utility, and consistency of these resources determine the nature and variety of activities the parties can carry out.

As James Bryce commented in 1888,

> The greatest discovery ever made in the art of war was when men began to perceive that organization and discipline count for more than numbers.... Americans made a similar discovery in politics. (quoted in Crotty, 1979, p. 33)

ORGANIZATIONAL RESOURCES

Party resources fall into three basic categories. The *human resources* include the volunteers and staff. The *material resources* begin with money but also include the physical facilities, equipment, and information controlled by the party. The *organizational resources* include the legal advantages granted the party as an entity, the advantages of an organized decision-making process, and the public image attributed to the organization.

Human Resources

The Cost of Party Activity

Attracting, training, and motivating individuals to carry out party tasks consumes a great deal of party effort. Political party activity represents a cost to individuals. With a finite number of hours in the day and a variety of demands on one's time, the *time* spent in party activity takes away from the time available for other activities. *Psychological costs* also play a role. Committing oneself to party activity expands one's vulnerability, since the victories and losses of the party now become the individual's victories or losses. Finally, political parties take stands on controversial issues that divide people based on their policy preferences. Active commitment of a party can have a *social cost* alienating friends and family. Individuals gravitate to and away from political party activity for a number of reasons.

The Volunteers

The Options for Participation. Walking into a state or local party headquarters and expressing an interest in involvement will almost always unleash a barrage of opportunities. The traditional party machines often involved participation "by invitation only"; however, modern political parties need a wide variety of volunteers and are quite inclusive. Although the increasing difficulty in getting volunteers and the professionalization of politics have led to an increase in paid staff, political parties without a strong volunteer base lack an important resource and source of vitality.

Volunteers carry out a wide range of tasks, from short-term projects such as stuffing envelopes and maintaining mailing lists to continuing participation as a precinct, ward, or state party official. Representing the perspective of parties as extensions of the public, major-party policy-making is vested in the hands of state party committees, state and local conventions, and the national committees, all manned primarily by volunteers. Even though lateral entry of prestigious individuals to higher-level positions occurs, the route to higher positions usually involves lower-level activity. Aside from maintaining the basic party organization, parties support a number of auxiliary groups such as the Young Republican League, College Democrats, and National Federation of Republican Women, which serve as training and recruitment organs. With the proliferation of competing groups and the emphasis on opening regular party activity to all groups, most of these auxiliaries have fallen on hard times. As one former youth auxiliary activist put it: "Why play sandbox politics when the party leaders were willing to put me on the state central committee?" (author's interview).

Political parties expend their greatest organizational efforts on filling the formal leadership positions required by state or party rules. Neither party has much difficulty developing a full slate of national or state committee members.

The prestige of the position and the opportunity to interact with the "movers and shakers" guarantees interest. A recent survey of county party chairpersons indicates that the vast majority (more than 90 percent) report complete sets of officers at the county level and filled slates for most local parties (Gibson, Cotter, Bibby, & Huckshorn, 1985, p. 149; Gibson, Frendreis, & Vertz, 1985, p. 20). Despite evidence that party organizations are stronger than they were a decade ago in terms of volunteer leaders (Advisory Commission on Inter-governmental Relations, 1986, p. 110), there is still a great deal of variation from one state to the next. Parties in competitive areas are better able to recruit volunteers than were those in one-party areas. Republicans have done a better job of organizing their smaller base of supporters both because of more effort and the fact that the socioeconomic characteristics associated with sup-port for the Republican party are also associated with increased political activity. As discussed in more detail later, individuals with higher education and income tend to involve themselves more in politics, and these same types of individuals are drawn more heavily toward the Republican party.

Contemporary parties may be better off in terms of volunteer leaders than in the recent past, but party activity is still the domain of relatively few individuals. Recent surveys indicate that fewer than 4 percent of the U.S. citizens worked for a party or a candidate during the election period (Crotty, 1984, p. 11).

The Motivations of Volunteer Participants. A number of factors move citizens from inactivity to party involvement. Old-line party organizations dispensing patronage and favors relied primarily on *material* incentives. The ability to reward faithful party workers with government jobs guaranteed a stable core of volunteers.

> When American political parties were strongest, in the latter decades of the nineteenth century, what held them together was not ideology or program—they had precious little of either—but patronage. Yet no cement is more binding than patronage, for making a living is at the center of everyone's concern. (Sundquist, 1982, p. 47)

Although civil service reforms reduced direct rewards and material incen-tives have grown out of favor, they are not dead. The indirect benefits of contacts and preferments still motivate some party workers. As one recent state party chairman explained from his plush executive suite in a premier location overlooking the city: "Sure I was a nonpaid chairman, but I got my rewards. I would not have this law firm or my other business if it were not for the contacts I made through politics" (author's interview).

Uncomfortable with the crassness of material benefits, critics of the polit-ical parties applauded the decrease in professional politicians and political hacks in favor of the more amateur political activists motivated by the intangible *purposive goals* such as pursuing a particular ideology, or a set of policies or cleaning up government. It was assumed that introducing a greater proportion of individuals with less selfish goals would raise the level of political discussion but that the amateurs would be less tenacious in their support of the party organization. As observed by one high-level party activist:

> In the Republican party, the takeover by fundamentalist religious groups in some areas brings a special problem. They enter politics to articulate issue stands, but don't want to take on the nuts and bolts of leadership. They are often not around when the doors need to be knocked and the calls made. (Author's interview)

The well-organized influx of issue-oriented party activists may be the exception. Recent research questions the degree to which the motivation of amateurs more by issues than material rewards currently dominates the parties. The conclusion is that such phenomena are widely separated events and that outcroppings of blocs of issue-based activists are not the cause of weakened party organizations (see Cotter et al. 1984, p. 156; Bell, 1985, p. 21).

For many party activists, involvement serves a social need. With the decline of family interaction due to mobility and the increasing anonymity of life in the modern industrial world, party work serves as a place to meet friends and develop a sense of belonging and self-worth.

An extensive study of local Michigan party leaders covering almost 20 years (Eldersveld 1964; 1982) found that although precinct leaders were initially motivated to get involved by policy concerns or a sense of community obligation, they quickly began to appreciate the social contacts, fun, and excitement. It was these personal social goals that then became more important in keeping them involved.

The increased technological sophistication of party activity has challenged the ability of the parties to absorb volunteers and make them feel useful. Virtually anyone can stuff envelopes, update a card file, or go door to door dropping literature. Teaching volunteers the intricacies of computerized voter files and programmable typewriters makes it seem like it is more work than it is worth, but party leaders are beginning to change their minds. As a successful state chairman reflected:

> We almost forgot about our volunteer base at the state level, and we would have been the losers for it. It is amazing what volunteers can do. It is exciting to see a little old lady in tennis shoes who gained political maturity in the age of the Model T working in front of a computer terminal updating the mailing lists. Not only does it give her a sense of worth, but it also helps maintain the real strength of a party, its people. We can afford a few mistakes for that. (Author's interview)

Who Are the Volunteers?   Volunteer party activists reflect the unique subset of those active in politics generally. They are more likely to be well educated, relatively affluent, and from politically active families. Such individuals tend to perceive more of a stake in the political process, exhibit attitudes conducive to participation, and possess the resources of time and money to facilitate participation (see Conway, 1985, p. 140).

The political attitudes of activists are also more extreme. Activist Democrats tend to be more liberal and activist Republicans more conservative than either party identifiers or the public at large (McClosky, Hoffman, & O'Hara, 1960; Jackson, Leavitt, & Bositis, 1982).

Paid Party Staffs

An increasingly important human resource for state and national parties is the cadre of professional paid staffs. A few decades ago the idea of a specialized party staff between elections was unheard of. Currently, very few county-level or lower party organizations have the resources or perceived need for paid workers. State parties generally have at least a small full-time professional staff, with some state parties having large paid organizations. The most obvious presence of a full-time staff is at the national level. The two national parties divide responsibilities between a national committee serving the needs of the party as a whole and two congressional committees (one House and one Senate) focusing on the particular needs of congressional candidates. The national committees are run on a day-to-day basis by an elected party chairperson. The party's presidential candidate generally has a large say in who is elected as chair at the national convention. The chair is responsible to a national committee representing each state and ultimately reports back to the national convention. The congressional committees are controlled by the party members in Congress and have a member of Congress as chair. As Table 3.1 clearly indicates, the past decade has seen tremendous overall growth in national party staff, with a dramatic Republican advantage. The origin of the Republican advantage is not hard to explain. With more party resources with which to work (see next section of this chapter) and clear evidence of being in the number two position electorally, Republicans had the resources and motivation to emphasize organization. Not only have the sizes of the staffs increased, but so have the qualifications and opportunity to specialize. Traditionally, party staffs swelled dramatically during election years and ebbed to very low levels in the off year, but such dramatic shifts are a thing of the past. The current national parties provide a consistent base of professionals on which other party levels and candidate organizations can draw.

As recently as the 1960s, many state party organizations existed as almost totally volunteer operations, often run out of the state party chairman's home or office. Professional staffing, particularly in nonelection years, was the exception (see Bibby et al., 1983, p. 76).

By the mid-1980s the situation had changed dramatically. Virtually every state chairperson in a national study reported having some paid staff, and 15 percent reported more than 10 full-time employees (Advisory Commission on

TABLE 3.1. PERMANENT NATIONAL PARTY STAFFING LEVELS

	1972	1980	1984	1987[a]
Democratic Committees				
Democratic National Committee	30	35	130	120
Congressional Campaign Committee	5	16	45	75
Senatorial Campaign Committee	4	20	22	30
Republican Committees				
Republican National Committee	30	220	600	275
Congressional Campaign Committee[b]	6	40	130	60
Senatorial Campaign Committee[c]	4	30	90	70

Source: Estimates provided by committee staffs; 1980–1984 reported in Herrnson, 1986, p. 40.
[a] The 1987 figures indicate the normal decline in staff during a nonelection year.
[b] Official name, National Republican Congressional Committee.
[c] Official name, National Republican Senatorial Committee.

TABLE 3.2. STATE PARTY STAFFING LEVELS

Number of Full-Time Professional Staff	Republicans (%)	Democrats (%)
Two or less	8	44
Three to ten	79	41
Over ten	16	15
	(n = 39)	(n = 27)

Source: Advisory Commission on Intergovernmental Relations, 1986, p. 113; based on 1984 survey.

Intergovernmental Relations, 1986, p. 113). As on the national level, state Republican party organizations have larger staffs than their Democratic counterparts (see Table 3.2). Although this differential can be explained partially by the resource and motivational differences applicable on the national level, an additional factor also looms large. In the late 1970s the Republican National Committee (RNC) under the direction of chairman Bill Brock made a concerted effort to build state parties. The RNC trained party staff and, more importantly, directly funded from national coffers state party staffs. A decade later, the Democratic National Committee (DNC) began a similar program in a few targeted states.

Nationwide, there has been an emergence of a generation of party staff members who see politics as a business that rewards effort, skills and creativity more than political contacts. They often begin in campaign or lower-level state party jobs, join the national committees for a while, and then often return as state party executive directors. The emergence of a cadre of professional staff members not only helps the parties but also has benefits for the staff themselves.

The professionalism of party staff has been a real benefit. We can share our successes and failures. Having a group of compatriots to share our frustrations with helps keep us sane. Running a state party can be a delightful job, but it can also be a pain in the ass. Going off to national meetings of executive directors and finding out they have the same problems gives one a whole different perspective. (Author's interview)

The Material Resources

A major component of organization is mobilizing material resources to get a job done. These resources include everything from office equipment to mailing lists, with by far the most useful material resource being access to an adequate and a reliable financial base. Because of money's utility for purchasing all other goods and services, political parties with a solid financial base exemplify the most viable organizations.

One of the greatest difficulties in analyzing the financial base of party organizations comes from the intermingling of resources that keep the organization going and those directly targeted for electoral campaigns. Funds to retain a permanent staff, pay the utility bills, and maintain the organization make it more likely that the party will be ready for the next campaign, but these funds are different from those specifically earmarked for a particular set of campaigns. In this chapter, our interest concerns organizational money rather than campaign finance.

Raising the Funds

When national parties were minuscule operations, especially during nonelection years, and when state and local parties were almost universally run as volunteer efforts out of a chairperson's business office or family room, the organization required few material resources. At that time, state and national parties, as is the case today for local parties, relied almost exclusively on a few big donors and a variety of special events from bean feeds to bull roasts to keep the organization going. Many of the fund-raising techniques build on the desire of givers to feel important and "rub shoulders" with the powerful members of society. As one campaign consultant explained:

> There is no such thing as generosity in politics. People don't give money. They want to know, "What is in it for me?" . . . They trade money for various gratifications. The big ones are ego, patriotism and the desire to belong to something. You're a big deal in your community if a senator or governor stops by your house. It's neat to say you went to dinner with Ronald Reagan, even if 3,000 people were there. That's leverage and we use it. (quoted in Peterson, 1986a, p. A6)

The national parties used a similar approach during the middle of this century by creating a few prestige donor clubs of backers giving large contributions. Contributors received briefings on "behind-the-scenes" insights into Washington events through which they could wangle invitations to White House events for themselves and their friends. At convention time, the national parties sold overpriced advertisements in the national convention programs and party publications to finance other operations. With growing financial needs, and changes in the election laws, the parties, especially at the national level, had to find additional ways to finance their activities.

Direct Appeals to the Voters. The National Republican party took a more businesslike approach in the 1960s with its "Neighbor-to-Neighbor" drives. Coordinating with the state parties, the RNC trained organizers and encouraged them to divide their supporters into manageable units, make face-to-face solicitations, and keep contribution records that could be used in subsequent years. Although the amounts raised were not large by today's standards, this was the first attempt systematically to tap grass-roots financial support. The Democratic party's "Dollars for Democrats" program copied the approach but never experienced as much success.

The labor-intensive personal contact approaches gave way to more efficient targeted direct-mail techniques during the 1970s. Working from lists of previous donors or likely contributors, the Republican party and then the Democratic party sought to broaden their base of contributors (see Broder, 1986b; Edsall, 1985a). By 1980 Larry Sabato had concluded that "direct mail has brought the Republican party from near bankruptcy...to a financial position unrivaled in its history" (1981, p. 294). Direct mail fund-raising works on the theory that you can identify likely contributors on the basis of the magazines to which they subscribe or the organizations to which they belong. You can then motivate them through clever letters exclaiming dire consequences if something is not done immediately and indicating that their donation will contribute to the solution. The *first-generation* letters sent to a more heterogeneous list of likely contributors generally has a relatively low return rate, but the *second-generation* list made up of contributors to the first wave of letters can be solicited over and over again, generally with great success. Fund-raising letters work best with extreme language and credible perceived threat. After taking over the White House in 1981, the Republicans had less of a threat to point to. As a top campaign consultant observed, "you raise money against things. There aren't any devils for the Republican Party to write about....There is no Democratic threat" (author's interview). See Figure 3.2 for some examples of direct-mail solicitations by parties and candidates.

The Republicans combined direct mail and the prestige-club approach to revitalize the large contributor base.

By enrolling their contributors into clubs...the Republican committees appear to have succeeded in making their contributors feel as though they really are a part of the Republican organization. The G.O.P. committees clearly have succeeded in adapting to, and helping to foster, an emergent

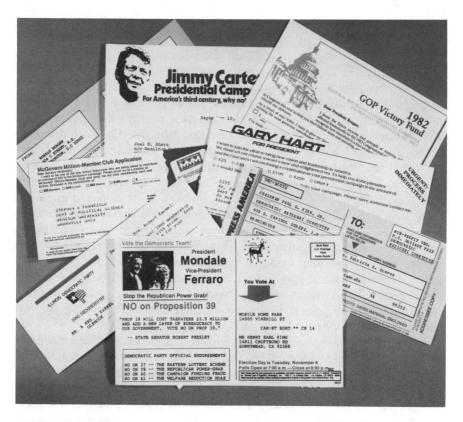

Figure 3.2 Direct-Mail Examples

style of political participation and organizational membership, that of "checkbook activist." (Herrnson, 1986, p. 4)

By the early 1980s the Republican National Committee had a mailing list of more than 1.7 million names (Hershey, 1984, p. 122) and a small contributor (less than $50) base of more than 350,000 people contributing more than $5 million, with smaller, but significant, programs being run by the congressional committees and state parties. The Democrats started smaller and later but have dramatically increased both the number and dollar amounts of their direct-mail contributions (see Herrnson, 1986, p. 4). The Democratic donor list grew from fewer than 3,000 in 1978 to more than 100,000 in 1984 (Salmore & Salmore, 1985, p. 215). As a recent Democratic party treasurer put it: "We have to learn to conduct our party like a business. We have to get the American voters to invest. . . . The Republican Party does this four or five time better than we do" (quoted in Broder, 1985a, p. A15).

Although direct-mail fund raising will serve as a mainstay of party finance for the foreseeable future, the days of dramatic growth seem to be past. A number of factors support this conclusion. The vast untapped reservoir of potential Democratic party contributors may well be less amenable to direct mail than its Republican counterpart, since Democrats generally have less wealth and lower participatory tendencies. More generally, direct mail has lost its uniqueness. Most of us are inundated with contribution requests. The Republicans jumped in early and acquired the most likely contributors, leaving those with less disposition to give or those more difficult to reach.

The use of direct mail has had a significant effect beyond the provision of resources. It forges a bond between millions of small givers and the party (Reichley, 1985, p. 188) that is likely to manifest itself in increased interest in party affairs, the willingess to volunteer time and resources, and the likelihood of enhanced support at the polls. Furthermore, the sophisticated technology and economies of scale in direct mail have provided an opening for the state and national parties to provide training and material for their subordinate units. State and national party computers generate mailing labels and targeted letters for local party units and candidates. The need to coordinate mailings from different party units and the utility of comparing and swapping lists have led to coordinated activity by the different levels of the party.

A logical follow-up to direct mail has been *telemarketing*. Using the established lists and banks of volunteers, and more often paid solicitors, the parties have begun personalizing their appeals over the telephone. Using a prepared speech and a "chatty" tone, the solicitor asks for the target by name, exchanges a few pleasantries, asks for an opinion on current issues, and suggests that the person could help make the political goals a reality by supporting the party financially. Using the telephone as a slight twist in technique from the mails, party leaders are finding that they are reaching a new type of contributor and can now activate some of those on which the direct mail had been wasted.

Government Financing of the Parties.   Although the parties are largely on their own when it comes to financing their activities, some government financing is evident. In the wake of questionable Republican National Committee activities involving corporate contributions to finance the national conventions, and in an attempt to sweeten the post-Watergate campaign-financing reform pot, the federal government provides the parties with a significant part of their national convention costs.

On the state level, various attempts to subsidize the parties have been tried. The California tax checkoff system allows voters to contribute to a wide variety of groups, including parties, on their tax form. The state party budgets in Florida are enhanced by the fact that all election filing fees go to the parties. As explained later, a number of other states route campaign-financing funds through the parties.

TABLE 3.3. FINANCIAL RESOURCES OF THE NATIONAL PARTY COMMITTEES

	Amount Raised in Millions of Dollars					
	1976	*1978*	*1980*	*1982*	*1984*	*1986*
Democratic Committees						
Democratic National Committee	13.1	11.3	15.0	16.4	46.6	17.2
Congressional Campaign Committee	1.0	1.0	2.1	6.5	10.4	12.3
Senatorial Campaign Committee	1.0	1.0	1.6	5.6	8.9	13.4
Republican Committees						
Republican National Committee	29.1	36.0	76.2	83.5	106.1	83.8
Congressional Campaign Committee	12.2	14.1	28.6	58.0	58.3	39.8
Senatorial Campaign Committee	1.8	10.9	23.3	48.9	81.6	86.1

Source: Federal Elections Commission; Malbin, 1984, p. 292.
Note: The 1984 figures do not include the $5.8 million raised by the Association of Democratic State Chairs, and the 1986 figures do not include the $7.6 million they raised.

The Amount of Material Resources Available to the Parties

As Table 3.3 clearly reveals, total *national party* income has increased dramatically in recent years, with all of the Republican committees raising more funds than did their Democratic counterparts. These funds are used to maintain the party organization, to provide the resources to raise additional money, and to give both direct and indirect support to party candidates. Past success in raising money breeds the potential for future success since it allows the hiring of addition staff and the acquisition of printing, mailing, phone bank, and word processing equipment.

In considering sources of party money, most of it comes from individual contributions. Democrats depend on political action committee (PAC) contributions to support the organization significantly more than do the Republicans, with almost 10 percent of the Democratic total coming from PACs in 1984 compared with less than 1 percent for the Republicans (Federal Elections Commission data). Republican success with direct mail accounts for much of the party's more limited dependence on PACs. Although the Republican advantage in overall material resources remains, increased Democratic efforts have narrowed the gap. Compared with the five-to-one or more Republican advantage of the not-so-distant past, the current three-to-one advantage looks less impressive.

The variation in *state party* material resources and fund-raising methods is significant, but total resources generally have shown dramatic increases since a decade ago. Rather than the shoestring operations with budgets in the average of less than $50,000 that predominated as recently as the mid-1960s, by 1984 the median state party budget had risen to $340,000, with a sizeable number of states regularly spending more than twice that amount. Parties in the midwestern states consistently have the larger budgets, with significantly more varia-

TABLE 3.4. ANNUAL BUDGETS OF STATE POLITICAL PARTIES, 1984

Average Annual Budget	Republicans (%)	Democrats (%)
Under $250,000	26	63
$250,000–$750,000	39	2
Over $750,000	34	17
	(n = 38)	(n = 30)

Source: Advisory Commission on Intergovernmental Relations, 1986, p. 113.

tion in other regions (Advisory Commission on Intergovernmental Relations, 1986, p. 113). The Republican advantage evidenced on the national level repeats itself in the states as can be seen in Table 3.4.

A great deal of the party differential can be accounted for by the concerted effort of the Republican National Committee to help state parties directly. By 1984 more than 70 percent of the Republican state chairs reported direct financial aid from the RNC, and 75 percent received fund-raising assistance. The RNC has particularly targeted the South and, secondarily, the Northeast—traditionally areas of weaker Republican organization—for such help. During the same period, only 7 percent of Democratic state chairs reported direct aid, and only 20 percent received fund-raising assistance (Advisory Commission on Intergovernmental Relations, 1986, p. 120; Smith, 1984a, p. 12). Although recent new Democratic initiatives have increased the fund-raising help, the differences are still significant. With Republican state party organizations generally on a sound financial footing, the RNC launched a program similar to its state initiative and now targets financial aid and expert advice to selected county organizations, an effort the Democrats do not have the resources to duplicate.

Differences in fund-raising techniques for state and local parties go beyond variations in national party support. Democratic organizations still rely primarily on the time-honored methods of special events such as dinners and social gatherings, whereas Republican organizations shifted greater emphases to the more technologically sophisticated techniques such as direct mail and telephone solicitation.

The differences in state party material resources show up in the nature of their party headquarters. A nonrandom but extensive set of visits to many state headquarters revealed a range of state party operations from those that operate out of one-room, seedy offices to those with magnificent office suites and a space-age complement of computers, print shops, in-house direct-mail operations, and media centers (see box, "State Party Profiles"). Unlike their national counterparts, state and local party organizations still have a more tenuous existence when it comes to material resources. There is considerably more variation from the election year to the off year. Although the move toward permanent headquarters, stable staffs, consistent budgets, available equipment—institutionalization—is evident, it is not universal.

STATE PARTY PROFILES

Although clothes do not the man make, nor physical facilities fully describe the capacity and vitality of organizations, they do present a clue. During the past year I had an opportunity to visit state party headquarters around the country. In most cases, the observations about their physical characteristics revealed some telling points about the parties: their status, their operations, and their potential for effectiveness.

★ ★ ★ ★ ★

The small white clapboard cottage with a metal roof that serves as the Republican state headquarters in Louisiana exudes the image of the old South. The image is heightened as one looks around the neighborhood with its well-manicured lawns and moss-covered trees. The small "headquarters" sign on the front porch sits where the rocking chair or porch swing could be placed. Entering the front door, one might expect a dish of pecan pralines or a pitcher of mint juleps to highlight the sitting room. One peek through the screendoor shatters the image. Computer terminals are clicking and the main furnishings consist of piles of computer printouts and computer-generated mailing labels. One might conclude that this represents the symbolism of the new parties in the South. A façade of courtly Old South characteristics camouflage a technologically sophisticated business operation. It is a clear case of "new wine in old bottles."

★ ★ ★ ★ ★

Located in a large, new, two-story building in a buffer area between fashionable large homes and a seedier section of Tallahassee, the Republican party of Florida dispenses its array of high-tech campaign and party building aids. A visitor is quickly given a tour of the new "digs," which includes its own telemarketing offices, print shop, computer center, radio and television studio, and traditional offices. With a budget of $4.3 million and a full-time staff of 25, Florida Republicans boast the largest state party staff in the country, despite their minority-party status in terms of party registration and elected officials. Banking on a continued influx of new voters of whom they traditionally capture more than 60 percent, the Republicans are planning for majority status by the end of the century. Strongly favored by the Republican National Committee, and blessed with an impressive fund-raising base, the party wants for few resources and aggressively prepares for the day when *yellow-dog Democrats* (the term for southern Democrats who although out of touch with their party would vote even for a yellow dog if it carried the Democratic label) will join the ranks of incoming Republicans to give them a majority.

★ ★ ★ ★ ★

Residing in the historic Towle House Mansion with its six columns and moss-covered trees, the Democratic party of Florida seems to fit into the fashionable neighborhood a few blocks from the state capital in Tallahassee. The 25 foot-high ceilings, fancy chandeliers, and antique furniture serve as a perfect setting for the wall filled with political trophies—pictures of the state constitutional officers who are thoroughly Democratic. No click of computers disrupts the genteel, but businesslike, atmosphere. The primary hint that this is the new South and not the old is the biracial staff. Recognizing the increasing diversity of Florida Democrats, and the recognition that Florida has become a two-party state in national elections with Democrats still advantaged when it comes to state and local races, the party is showing a new urgency to catch up with the Republicans technologically and organizationally. Although the development of a new statewide voter data base is being done by outside contractors, terminals will soon be entering between the front columns to help Florida Democrats keep pace with the hard-charging, if outnumbered, Republicans.

★ ★ ★ ★ ★

The Minnesota Democratic Farmer Labor (DFL) party's move from its longtime party-owned headquarters in south Minneapolis to a fashionably renovated urban shopping area in downtown St. Paul was somewhat traumatic. As one of the first state parties to own its own building, the shift to being renters, even if it meant plusher and more convenient quarters, took some getting used to. In a climate where walking outdoors for many months of the year holds little appeal, a network of second-floor skyways linking key downtown buildings offered new freedom of mobility and a change in traffic patterns. The move to a second-floor location on a main skyway walking route gave the party more public visibility while the move to St. Paul put it close to the state legislature "where the action is." The headquarters boasts a full-service capacity from computer terminals to an in-house print shop and telemarketing. This well-organized and endowed operation looks more like the typical Republican party headquarters than its Democratic counterparts, a real compliment as the Democrats rush headlong to replicate Republican efforts at party building. While as modern as the latest computer technology, the DFL shows its roots. Almost a decade after the death of its most famous partisan, Hubert Humphrey, the Humphrey legacy lives on. From prominently displayed statues to posters and the announcements of the upcoming Humphrey dinner, the Humphrey presence remains. Although the current state chair, the youngest in the country, is the first chair not to have known Humphrey, she was quick to point out that "while we can't live in the past, it is good to know from where we have come." Hubert could not have said it much better.

★ ★ ★ ★ ★

Working out of a cluttered suite of offices in the basement of a union-owned building (American Federation of State, City and Municipal Workers) on the edge of downtown Madison, the Wisconsin Democratic party fights for its existence in a state known for antiparty attitudes and laws. Consistent with its progressive "peoples party" tradition, the party literature features endorsements from average citizens rather than the more typical big-name endorsements urging party involvement. State law does not provide party registation lists, and campaign finance laws keep state and local campaigns running on a shoestring (a $16,000 limit for state legislative candidates), but the party strives to provide campaign services such as voting lists at limited cost, rather than making significant financial contributions.

★ ★ ★ ★ ★

Entering the spartan, but functional, five-office suite of the California Democratic party in a fairly fashionable section of downtown San Francisco, one could be in just about any city of the world if it were not for the plaintive clanging of the cable cars wafting in through the open windows. The staff takes pride in letting the sounds enter as a treat to callers from outside the city. The limited furnishings tip off the visitor to the ephemeral nature of the operation, which will almost disappear when by state law the chair position rotates to the southern half of the state after two years.

★ ★ ★ ★ ★

After years of picking up stakes and moving to locate its operations close to the newly elected state chair (a person who changes every other year and a position that rotates between someone from northern and southern California), the Republicans finally bought a permanent headquarters. Located in Burbank (a more acceptable location than liberal Los Angeles), the office houses all of the state party staff except the political director, who remains in Sacramento, close to state government action. The headquarters entrance along a strip of small appliance, record, and service shops is unmarked and nondescript. A crudely lettered sign on the door states that "Republican party headquarters are upstairs next door." Walking by the security camera and up the stairs, one finds a large suite of offices with plush carpet and heavy wooden carved doors. Although the occupants are almost embarrassed by the furnishings ("We got a good deal and bought it this way"), the setting exudes the corporate headquarters image for which the party is reaching.

★ ★ ★ ★ ★

Recognizing that Vermont has the smallest capital city and building in the United States, and one of the smallest state populations, one should not be surprised at the scaled-down political party operations in that state. Located in small basement suites in a hotel/shopping complex across from the state capitol, the two parties are separated by fewer than 100 yards. The approach to party politics and issues is only slightly more divergent than their physical proximity. Both parties reflect the Vermont tradition of independence and respect for entrepreneurs that is not captured by the traditional ideological divisions. Geri jackets, duck shoes, and L. L. Bean sweaters reflect both practicality and a statement of independence. Funded by national committee largesse, the Republicans run a sophisticated computerized party. Flushed with their success in 1984 (the governorship, the state house of representatives, and control of the state senate, despite lacking a clear majority), the Democrats have increased their technological lead over most other state Democratic parties.

★ ★ ★ ★ ★

Residing in an office building with the symbolic street number of "1776," the Georgia Republican party located itself among its constituency in one of the classier neighborhoods well out of downtown Atlanta. The offices are nice but not classy, with much of the room taken up by a sophisticated telemarketing telephone bank system with which the party is successfully building a permanent donor base. The offices are populated by young, clean-cut preppies who view politics as an honorable and lucrative profession for those who can master modern technology and techniques. There is a mood of optimism that they are riding the wave of the future and have a significant head start on the Democrats, who are just awakening to the threat.

> ★ ★ ★ ★ ★
> Close to the state capitol, on the edge of the downtown area, the converted "Chicken Shack" restaurant that serves as the public headquarters for the Colorado Republicans exudes an image of suitable functional utility. But this is only part of the story. In an unmarked set of offices next door, one goes through security cameras and locked doors to find the real heart of the operation. Two computers churn out lists not only for the party but at a fee for candidates and on a vendor basis for Republican parties in eight other states. By becoming a vendor to other party organizations, they have developed a source of continuing income as well as providing a service to fellow Republicans at a cut rate. The state party staff spends much of its time giving headquarters tours to visiting state party leaders, who hope to emulate the technological lead of the Colorado Republicans.

Fund-raising at all levels of party organization has become a major organizational activity and source of problems. It can become a vicious circle as new fund-raising initiatives require increased staffs and equipment, only to see that most increased receipts having to be plowed back into maintaining the additional human and equipment overhead. In the view of one activist, "The party structure tends to eat up political money by committing resources to raising it and then spending it on its own internal operations. Parties do a poor job of exporting as much as they could and having it mean electoral gains" (author's interview).

No matter how much money is available, parties traditionally seek more and almost always have a cash-flow problem. Although the continuing nature of the party makes it the obvious choice to perform long-term analysis and preplanning for the election period, many potential contributors have little interest until the heat of the battle is on. Thus when the money is needed, it is not available. The two national parties, especially the Republican party, have dealt with this problem much more effectively than their state and local counterparts. (See Table 3.4.)

Nonmaterial Resources

Although the human and material resources of organizations stand out because of their visibility, organizations carry with them a set of resources that, though not directly observable, can be very important. The nature of party supporters in the electorate and the differential advantage in party image are two key examples.

The Nature of Party Supporters
The primary goal of political parties is activating voters to support their candidates. The parties begin this process with different advantages and disadvantages. (Chapter 5 discusses in more detail party identification and dif-

ferential participation rates.) The nature of the electorate to which a party can most successfully appeal often determines its success. Although there are more self-identified Democrats nationally, Republicans are more likely to turn out and vote and are more loyal to their party candidates. Whereas the Democrats must attempt to hold on to their larger vote base and get the voters through the hurdles of political participation (registration drives, get-out-the-vote drives, and so on), the Republicans must find ways to appeal successfully to independents and wavering Democrats.

Party Images

Politics has always been deeply affected by perceptions that may or may not fit perfectly with reality. Each of the parties carries with it historical "baggage" consisting of the evaluations of the public. Although these evaluations shift with changing performance and the replacement of generations of observers, they show considerable stability and serve as the basis for voter support or opposition. Each new generation does not see the political landscape afresh but has it presented and interpreted by parents, teachers, and other representatives of the previous generation. Although this *socialization* is not complete, leaving room for the impact of contemporary events and new interpretations, there tends to be more continuity than change.

Major historical events leave an indelible mark on organizations. It took the parties many generations even to erase partially the memory of the conflict of the Civil War, with the Republican party still blamed in many sectors of the South. Periods of scandal from Teapot Dome to Watergate besmirch a party's reputation, although the organization tends to bounce back more easily than the individuals involved. Through a pattern of action and rhetoric, the Democratic party has been given the mantle of supporter of the "little guy," with the Republicans more hesitatingly acknowledging their role as protector of the "haves" in society. Within the memory of much of the current electorate, the Democratic party focused its efforts on unemployment during the Depression and led the way for social and civil rights programs. Republicans, on the other hand, asserted support for policies that strengthen the business base of the economy and cautioned against the giveaway aspects of social programs.

Table 3.5 shows the broader contours of party image. Historically, as the party controlling government at the onset of most major wars, the Democratic party tends to get lower marks on preserving peace, whereas Republican control before depressions and recessions makes the public more wary of its capacity to manage the economy effectively. The pattern is clear into the 1970s, except for the war image given the Republican party through the Goldwater nomination in 1964. The peace image again gets somewhat confused during the Vietnam period. The Republican disadvantage in the economic realm does not shift until the Reagan years, but even this perception of success was quickly tarnished along with the more modest Republican gains on the issue of peace with the cloud of the Iran-Contra affair. An important factor in

TABLE 3.5. COMPARATIVE IMAGES OF THE PARTIES AS BEST FOR PEACE AND
BEST FOR PROSPERITY (REPUBLICAN PARTY ADVANTAGE)

	Party Best for Peace	Party Best for Prosperity
1952	+19	− 4
1954	+ 7	—
1956	+ 2	− 1
1958	+ 6	−23
1960	+12	−15
1962	0	−23
1964	−25	−55
1966	+ 4	−21
1968	+15	− 1
1970	+ 6	−15
1972	+ 8	0
1974	− 8	−30
1976	3	−14
1978	− 6	−18
1980	−10	− 4
1982	−13	−10
1984	0	+12
1985	+ 6	+16
1986	+ 2	+14
1987	−10	+ 1
Average	+ 1	−10

Source: *Gallup Report*, nos. 256–257, January/February 1987, pp. 23–26. Figures represent yearly
averages of national public opinion polls asking respondents to indicate which party they believed
would best handle the economy or preserve the peace.
Note: Entries are the percentage of respondents indicating the Republican party minus those indicating the
Democratic party. Plus totals indicate a Republican advantage; minus, a Democratic advantage.

future Republican success will be the degree to which the current Republican
advantage in the economic realm remains after Reagan's term of office.

PARTY STRUCTURE

In our attempt to forge order out of apparent chaos, it is common to represent
visually the structure of parties by relying on an organization chart something
like Figure 3.1. Although such a representation identifies the basic units, it
reveals little about their activities, vitality, or interrelationships. Furthermore,
such a formal model may imply a neatness and power structure both unintended
and unrealistic. Some writers have argued that the party organization is not a
hierarchy but rather a *stratarchy*,

> an organization with layers, or strata, of control rather than one of central-
> ized leadership from the top down.... The party develops this pattern of

relationships—stratarchical rather than hierarchical—because of the necessities of collaborating with and recognizing local echelons for votes, money and personnel. (Eldersveld, 1982, p. 99)

As one state party leader put it:

> The image of the party as a nice clear hierarchy just ain't so. The national committees, state central committees, and county parties have different constituencies and respond to them. In California, national committeemen are chosen by the delegates to the national convention, so the candidate groups that win out in the primary control them. The state central committees are appointed by candidates and elected officials from all over the state. The county committees are chosen by party supporters in the primary. There is little to hold these groups together. The most a state party can try to do is coordinate the efforts of the three to avoid duplication and stepping on each other's toes. (Author's interview)

The Local Parties

There is more variation in the structure and performance of parties on the local level than on the state or national level. Ideally, the parties have a grass-roots base of organization at the lowest political unit (usually the precinct), with coordinated units at the ward, legislative district, county, and congressional district levels. In reality that is often not the case. First, the neatness of the organization chart breaks down early when one realizes that governmental units (counties, cities, townships, and so on) are not coterminous with political constituencies (city council, legislative and congressional districts). Loyalties and efforts are split when parts of the same ward or county are in one electoral district, and other parts are in a different one. Second, with a shortage of volunteers and vacant offices at many levels, it is hard to get people to fill the lowest party offices when they could realistically aspire to higher ones. In many cases the existence of local party organizations does not alone imply strong local interest. Laws in a number of states require precinct caucuses at which time local leaders are chosen, resolutions passed, and delegates chosen to ward, congressional district, or state party conventions. These local leaders may do little for the party after their election.

After an extensive survey of local parties, Cornelius Cotter and his colleagues concluded that "local parties are highly personalized, with little or no bureaucratic structure" (1984, p. 44). Joseph Schlesinger asserted that local political parties "are the creatures of the office-seekers who use them to gain power" and that specific offices provide the nuclei around which effective parties form (1985, p. 1154). If county races are partisan and competitive, two strong party organizations will be maintained. In noncompetitive jurisdictions, the party will largely be a shell and have little motivation for activity or cooperation with organizations at other levels. Typically, the weaker of the two parties in a potentially competitive jurisdiction will emphasize filling out its organization chart and heighten its activity level as a way of increasing its likelihood of attracting votes (Cotter et al., 1984, p. 50).

The national parties have begun to recognize the importance of the local parties. On taking over the national Republican party chair after the 1964 defeat, successful Ohio state chair Ray Bliss talked about "building the party from the basement up, not from the roof down" (quoted in Reichley, 1985, p. 186). After the Republican defeat in 1976, new national Republican party Chair William Brock reemphasized local organizations by creating a separate division to recruit local candidates and leaders, provide field staff, and channel funds. In his words,

> We didn't need to change our fundamental positions; we had to provide a place for people to argue their ideas out, to hone and shape their ideas. We had to build that base at the local level. You've got to have something for people to join within each community. The most fundamental human need is the need to belong, to join with others in a group you can identify with. If you can satisfy that need and build at the local level, the national level will follow. (quoted in Aldrich, Miller, Ostrom, & Rohde, 1986, p. 238)

Renewal of local party organizations is evident in many areas of the country. After reviewing the major recent studies of local parties, Samuel Eldersveld concluded:

> Local party organizations EXIST, they are ACTIVE and combative, they are ADAPTIVE, and they are linked to electoral success . . . [Local parties] are not empty shells. They are in many, many communities dynamic structures, performing significant functions, and linking citizens meaningfully to the political system. (1984, pp. 17–18)

The Party Machine

Although local parties are currently the "weakest link in the party organization chain" (Kayden & Mahe, 1985, p. 105), they have not always been so, and such a concept still seems alien in some areas of the country. Playing on the image of a well-oiled mechanism with a clear purpose and efficient operation, political party *machines* exemplify the height of party organization. Flourishing largely in the urban areas of the Northeast during the late 19th and early 20th centuries, party machines dominated politics by controlling candidate access to the ballot and most major campaign resources. The party presented a slate of candidates loyal to the organization, offering the candidates effective door-to-door campaigning by party activists loyal to the party because it was the source of their government jobs. Voters used their vote not only to support party positions but also in thanks or hope for party help in times of need. The most effective machines prospered in cities with a large influx of immigrants who needed jobs, help with legal problems, and often basic living necessities. A variety of reforms and changes weakened the machine, including the reduction of patronage jobs with the adoption of the civil service laws, a reaction against the corruption of some machines, the introduction of nonpartisan elections, increased public education, and the advent of government-run welfare programs. Once the norm in urban areas, party organizations meriting the label "machine" are now the exception. For example:

> Nassau County (has) a national reputation as one of the last bastions of old fashioned organization; the county's politics are a relic in an era in which elections seem increasingly a function of television and computer technology. . . . The Nassau GOP is a rigidly structured, multilayered hierarchy bearing all the markings of a major corporation. . . . The county party takes pains to recruit young activists; local GOP committeemen often help teenagers land their first summer jobs at the local park or neighborhood swimming pool. Many young people go on to make the organization the basis for an entire career. (Watson, 1985a, p. 1623)

State Party Organizations

Although the titles and methods of selection vary, state party organizations are guided by a state central committee representing the various areas of the state, with the day-to-day activities generally carried out by a volunteer chairperson, an executive director, and the staff. The state central committees usually meet only a couple of times a year to give general direction. A number of state party executive directors agreed that the state committee does not do much as a committee. It has one large meeting a year, largely to fulfill state election law requirements. It is hard to find a way to use it as a group. More importantly, it taps the members as individuals to perform important tasks, but it is more because of their abilities and willingness to work than because they happen to be on the state committee.

The state party organizes the state convention, stimulates organizational activity on lower levels, and increasingly has become the repository for data, mailing lists, and expertise that can be drawn on during the campaign period. Xandra Kayden and Eddie Mahe concluded that "state parties are more like small versions of the national parties than they are like the local parties beneath them on the organizational ladder" (1985, p. 100). In some states, party caucuses within the legislature rival the state party in terms of staff, financial resources, and the ability to service the needs of incumbent or aspiring members of the legislature.

Variations in state party activities, organizational structure, and strength reflect both historical trends and the nature of current leadership. As one national party staff member charged with revitalizing the state parties put it:

> A number of factors explain the wide variation in state party activities and resources. Personal leadership still counts for a great deal. Effective state

chairmen can tap the resources for an effective state party. Political potential and past success also play a role. Few states which have never had a Republican governor have strong state Republican parties. Without a shot at the governorship there is little reason for the existence of the state party. (Author's interview)

In competitive situations, all organizations tend to counterorganize and take on the character of the opposing group, particularly if it has been successful (Cotter & Bibby, 1980; reported in Kayden & Mahe, 1985, p. 91). A state with one well-organized party will tend to see both parties stress organizational activity. Given personal ambitions and divergent policy goals, one-party states tend to break into internal factions.

The state parties are intertwined in another way. Since parties are regulated by state laws that are made uniform for both parties, reforms initiated by one party affect the other. The reforms in the nomination process stimulated by the national Democratic party after the 1968 election resulted in a number of state laws affecting both Republicans and Democrats alike. Traditional methods of party decision making and the selection of state central committee members fell victim to expectations of intraparty democracy enforced by the Democratic party.

The National Parties

The Convention and National Committees

The supreme authority of the national parties is the presidential nominating convention, held every four years. Although conventions approve the basic party rules and state nominees for national committee membership, the emphasis at the conventions is on adopting a platform and determining the presidential and vice-presidential nominees; organizational concerns generally take second place. Between conventions, the national parties are guided by national committees, which in turn select a national chairperson and executive committee to oversee the professional staff.

In recent years, the two parties have taken different approaches to determining the membership of the national committees. The Republican party includes the state party chairperson, a national committeeman, and a national committee woman from each state and the territories for a total of 162 members. As a part of their emphasis on the "expressiveness" and internal democracy of the party, the Democratic party expanded its national committee to more than 300 members in 1972, including not only state chairpersons but also members apportioned to the states based on voting support for the Democratic party, as well as representatives from groups such as the Democratic Governor's, Mayor's, and County Officials' Conferences and the congressional leadership. Although the national committees remain primarily white, male, and middle-aged (see Table 3.6), the changes in Democratic rules and

TABLE 3.6. COMPOSITION OF THE NATIONAL COMMITTEES (PERCENTAGES)

	Democrats		Republicans	
	1970	*1975*	*1968*	*1972*
Age				
29 or younger	0	2	0	0
30–39	12	18	7	9
40–49	37	37	44	39
50–59	26	31	30	32
60 or more	25	12	19	19
Race				
White	92	81	100	100
Black	6	13	0	0
Other	2	6	0	0

Source: Longley, 1980, p. 77.
Note: Columns do not all total 100 due to rounding.

emphasis increased the number of women, minorities, and youth. No such shift was evident in the Republican party (Longley, 1979, pp. 364–367).

The national committees meet only a few times a year but do set the general direction of the party and select the chairperson. Until recently, the national party chair was generally a political ally of the presidential nominee and won office based on that tie. Although chairpersons are still expected to serve the president of their party and are in a tenuous position if the nominee loses, there is increased emphasis on selecting a chairperson, especially for the party out of power, with strong management and political credentials and interest in building the party organization. One campaign manager for a successful chair candidate explained:

> Campaigning for national chair is like most campaigning, only the electorate is smaller and more is known about each member. Much of the campaign is personal, looking for that particular "hook" which might create a supporter. The hooks include such things as who supported you in the past, what issues might you build credit on, who wants the party to do what, etc. A fair amount of the campaign involves preemption, trying to scare off or discourage potential opponents. Most campaigns involve travel, targeted mail, numerous phone calls and social events. We spent over $100,000 to get a non-paying job. (Author's interview)

The party chair presides over a growing staff (see Table 3.1) of professionals divided into a number of functional areas such as research, public relations, fund raising, organizational support, candidate training, and political strategy. Each party, especially the Democratic party, has established a number of liaison offices with specific minority groups such as women, Hispanics, and blacks. Traditionally, both parties encouraged the development of various subsidiary groups such as women's federations and youth groups, but interest in these organizations has declined in recent years as the parties have opened their doors to direct participation.

Congressional Campaign Committees

Responding to their unique needs and resources as well as a feeling that the national committees were not created to serve their interests, incumbents of both parties in Congress had created active campaign committees by the 1960s. Initially, the congressional committees primarily served the fund-raising and political strategy needs of the incumbents who made up their membership. Increasingly, with their success at fund raising, the Republicans have taken the lead, with the Democrats in hot pursuit, in providing training, contributions, expertise, and services to both incumbents and challengers. Although housed in the same national party headquarters and committed to coordinating their efforts, the congressional committees emphasize their distinctiveness, recognizing that their strength insulates the congressional party from national committee dominance and makes members of Congress more beholden to the congressional committees than to the national committee.

PARTY ACTIVITY LEVELS

In recent years the parties, particularly on the state and national levels, have increased the variety and extent of their activities. While continuing to fulfill the *legal requirements* of selecting leaders, nominating candidates, and holding conventions, the party organizations have increased the *organizational maintenance activities* of fund raising, volunteer recruitment, voter registration, and attempts to guarantee election laws favorable to the party. The national parties have expended considerable effort and resources in organization building through training and direct provision of resources or staff, with some state parties doing the same for their component units. As the parties have become more and more permanent units, they have become involved in continuing *research*, establishing data bases of voting trends, mailing lists, polling data, and the like. The *campaign activities* of the parties are extensive, from identifying and training candidates to offering campaign resources and running get-out-the-vote drives (see Chapter 6 for a more detailed discussion). In an age when parties have lost some of their positive image and must compete with other mediating groups, many have attempted to improve their image through *public relations activities*. These efforts involve everything from standard advertising and the provision of speakers for nonpartisan events to harnessing organizational resources for community activities. For example, the Republicans in Missouri have a program to build low-income housing, and the Colorado Democrats' "Donkey Project" allows individuals to help fight world hunger by buying a donkey to be sent overseas.

Table 3.7 and 3.8 outline over-time changes in state and local party

**TABLE 3.7. OVER-TIME COMPARISON OF STATE PARTY ACTIVITY
(PERCENTAGE OF STATE PARTIES REPORTING ACTIVITY)**

Activity	1960–1964[a]		1975–1980[a]		1984[b]	
	D	*R*	*D*	*R*	*D*	*R*
Organizational Maintenance						
Voter registration	35	42	58	80	—	—
Research						
Polling	12	33	30	70	50	78
Campaign Activity						
Services to candidates[c]	53	63	87	96	76	100
Contributions to state candidates	—	—	—	—	70	90
Public Relations						
Regular newsletter	71	63	70	82	—	—

[a] Cotter et al., 1984, p. 33. The data are based on a national survey of party chairs. Historical data rely on the recall of previous chairs.
[b] Advisory Commission on Intergovernmental Relations, 1986, p. 115. Data are from a national survey of state party chairs.
[c] Highest percentage for a single service (campaign seminars) provided. This figure may overestimate performance of any individual service by a party.

**TABLE 3.8. OVER-TIME COMPARISON OF COUNTY PARTY ACTIVITY
(PERCENTAGE OF COUNTY PARTIES REPORTING ACTIVITY)**

Activity	1979		1984	
	Democrats	*Republicans*	*Democrats*	*Republicans*
Organizational Maintenance				
Voter registration	56	45	78	78
Research				
Polling	11	16	23	25
Campaign Activity				
Distributing campaign literature	79	79	89	91
Organized campaign events	68	65	88	88
Contributed money to candidates	62	70	69	77
Organized telephone campaigns	61	65	78	78
Bought newspaper ads	62	62	62	66
Sent mailings to voters	47	59	66	75
Bought television or radio time	33	33	36	35

Source: 1979: Gibson, Cotter, Bibby, & Huckshorn, 1985, p. 151; 1984: Gibson, Frendreis, & Vertz, 1985, p. 20.

activity levels. Two patterns stand out: The over-time increase in party activity and the general Republican lead in activity level. A number of factors account for this lead including the fact that Republicans have more resources, that their minority party position in most areas has necessitated greater organizational effort, that the Democrats have been able to rely more consistently on outside groups such as labor unions to carry out some activities, and that state and national Republican organizations have taken a greater interest in increasing the organizational capabilities of their constituent parts.

ORGANIZATIONAL CHANGE AND THE RELATIONSHIP AMONG PARTY LEVELS

The Tradition of Party Decentralization

As E. E. Schattschneider wrote 40 years ago,

> "Decentralization of power is by all odds the most important single characteristic of the American political party." Schattschneider described national parties as merely "a loose confederation of state and local bosses for limited purposes." Similarly, writing just before a wave of rules changes altered forever the selection of convention delegates, Frank Sorauf, the most influential contemporary party scholar, observed, "Despite all the appearances of hierarchy in the American party organization, in no important way does any national party unit limit the autonomy of the state and local party organization." (quoted in Arterton, 1982, pp. 102–103)

A decade later, one of the major texts concluded that "there is no point on which writers on American politics are so . . . agreed as that our state and local party organizations, taken collectively, are far more powerful than our national organizations" (Ranney & Kendall, 1956, pp. 160–161). Currently, one would be hard-pressed to find anyone asserting such an evaluation. Today, the degree to which we see revitalization of the party organizations, it is primarily, but not exclusively, led by the national parties. The interesting question is not whether the national parties were able to reverse the situation of being little more than loose confederations of, and led by, state and local organizations but the routes the national parties took to assert their new dominance.

A wide range of observers affirm the increased centralization and nationalization of the parties:

> In the second half of the twentieth century, a "new" party has been emerging, one that is more national in scope, more active, and with clear signs of greater linkage among its nuclei. (Schlesinger, 1985, p. 1162)

> Where parties have successfully modernized and reversed their organizational decline, reforms have often been led by the NATIONAL parties. Especially in the Democratic Party, this appears to have reduced the relative degree of decentralization in the party itself. (Conlan, 1986, p. 10)

> The decentralization and weak organizational structure characteristic of American parties at the national level are changing, and will continue to change until the parties . . . become national bureaucracies with hierarchies, divisions of labor, and so on. (Kayden, 1980, p. 276)

Perhaps based on the presumption that state and local parties better supported democracy, few observers bemoaned the conclusion of Cornelius Cotter and Bernard Hennessy's 1964 book *Politics without Power: The National Party Committees.* Twenty years later, after observing the state of the parties, the American Assembly was quick to conclude: "The national parties must invest their expertise and resources to nourish growth of stronger state parties, but in so doing, they must not extend their political control to eliminate local authority, initiative, and prerogatives" (1982, p. 9).

By the terms *nationalization* or *centralization* we do not imply the disappearance of state and local parties—far from it. In many cases state and local parties possess more organizational resources and carry out more activities than they did at other any time in history. The change involves an increased uniformity in how state and local parties carry out their tasks, a uniformity stimulated by the national parties through rewards and, to a lesser extent, sanctions. It also reflects the degree to which the national parties can act on their own to affect political outcomes, without the support or cooperation of state and local units. In one sense it is possible to conclude that the nationalization of the parties during the second half of the 20th century is simply another example of the nationalization of other social institutions. It is common to talk about the "age of executive ascendency" that vaulted presidents and governors into predominant positions over their respective legislative bodies and to reflect on the homogenization of public information and outlooks due to the replacement of local news sources by the national media. Although such trends make it easier to understand the nationalization of the parties, much of the movement in that direction resulted from conscious choices by party leaders. Although the full range of consequences was not always clear, the national parties did not stumble into their current role.

The two major parties embarked in the 1960s on two very different roads to nationalization. The Democratic party emphasized the establishment and enforcement of national convention delegate-selection rules, and the Republican National Committee made itself indispensable by providing resources and services to state and local affiliates.

The Routes to Party Nationalization

The Democrats: Nationalizing the Rules
The Democratic party responded to its conflictual 1968 convention and ensuing electoral defeat with the so-called McGovern-Fraser Commission (named after its succession of chairpersons) and followed this with roughly a dozen

subsequent national party commissions. These commissions emphasized the "expressive" role of the party with the goal of democratizing the presidential nomination process and increasing the roles for women, blacks, and youth. (See Chapter 4 for the substance of the changes.) While changing the face of party leadership, in some ways the importance of these structural changes was not in the substance but in the ability of the national party to prescribe state and local rules. Once the masters of their own procedures, state and local parties found themselves pushed in directions many of them did not want to go. Despite the lack of any clear precedent or specific authority, the McGovern-Fraser Commission was "able to emit an aura of authority which led to virtually complete success" (Steed, 1985, p. 5).

Combined with a moral presumption that insuring proper representation of minority groups was the right thing to do, the Democratic party's ultimate sanction was to challenge the credentials of delegates from unrepresentative delegations at the next national convention. State legislatures in many states proceeded to change laws relating to elections and party structure to bring them in line with the new rules. Occasionally, opponents of the new rules went to the courts. After reviewing the cases, Charles Longley (1980, p. 75) concluded that the national party organization "won three and lost none." The federal courts have taken the position that national party rules supersede state laws and state party regulations. Although some states, particularly in the South, opposed the infringement on state's rights, the Democrats in general felt comfortable in applying their historical pattern of requiring national conformity in public policy to their own internal operations. Aside from attempting to structure the nominating process to increase expressiveness, the Democrats experimented with midterm conventions at which they would hash over platform positions. Each of these conferences cost more than $1.5 million and perhaps even more in terms of organizational conflict. As a midwestern state party executive director argued: "This was money that could be better used to provide campaign and party building services to repair some of the bloodletting from the issue and ideological battles at the last national convention" (author's interview).

The Republicans: Nationalization through Service

Largely ignoring the Democrats' concern for the expressive goals of parties, the Republicans responded to disappointing performance by focusing national efforts on enhancing organizational capabilities as the route to becoming more competitive in elections. The national Republicans did not awaken one morning and decide to redirect past efforts, marshal resources, and attempt to dominate state and local parties. To some degree, Republicans had always compensated for their smaller following in the electorate with superior organizational and campaign efforts. The story of the contemporary Republican party is not one of change in *kind* of efforts but rather in the *degree* and *location*. During the 1970s the Republican party redoubled its efforts in applying the newest organization-building technologies and using the national party as the primary stimulus and provider of services. As Leon Epstein characterized it, "The Republicans have nationalized their party effort by a method analogous to the federal government's grant-in-aid system" (quoted in Conlan, 1985, p. 40). As in the federal analogy, few grants come without some strings attached. Direct strings included changes in organization structure, standardization of procedures, sharing of resources such as voter and mailing lists, and coordination of efforts. More indirectly, to the degree that the state or local party felt beholden to the national party, it would avoid challenging national party policy initiatives (see Cotter & Bibby, 1980, pp. 1–2). Furthermore, candidates who once deferred to the interests of the local party organization and then went through a period of bypassing the party and establishing their own organizations were drawn back to the national parties because of the new resources they could provide. The national parties now have some say in the messages its candidates express:

> Recent party activities have encouraged the campaign communications of many contemporary congressional elections to become more nationally-oriented, more generic, and more professional. They also indicate that the national party organizations now have the capacity to function as agenda setters. (Herrnson, 1986, p. 21)

Realizing the importance of state and local party organizations, the Republican party attempted to perform a delicate balancing act, simultaneously strengthening the national organization through the provision of services and expertise while providing state and local organizations resources and help for party building. During the late 1970s the RNC began sending field staff at no cost to state parties, giving them organizational advice and access to national party resources such as mailing lists, computer software, research, training, and expertise. Initially focusing on the state parties, more recent efforts are on building certain local units through similar methods. Unleashing significant resources both directly and indirectly to state and local parties has taken much of the bite out of concerns over local party autonomy.

For those who question the utility of state party-building activities by the national parties, the Party Transformation Study gives a clear answer. Shortly after Republican efforts on the state level, the study showed a significant increase in party organizational strength (as measured by factors such as programmatic capacity and organizational complexity) and consistent differences between the Republican and Democratic parties that had not been there a few years earlier. State Republican party organizations were much more likely to engage in programs such as training candidates, contributing to candidates, and polling voters while evidencing more active party organizations with permanent staff and significant budgets. Similar party differences were not evident on the local level since Republican efforts had not yet begun (Cotter et al., 1984, p. 16; Gibson, Bibby, & Cotter, 1983, pp. 198–204).

The Democrats: A Belated Response

While expressive and competitive reforms are not necessarily in conflict, the Democratic pursuit of expressive instead of competitive goals used up party energy and resources reforming and enforcing the rules, which meant that there was less energy and fewer resources for building the national party through services. As one key party activist complained:

> While we were fighting among ourselves, alienating good Democrats, and repeatedly wordsmithing the same rules, the Republicans were getting a decade of experience in the new tactics of modern campaigning and organization building. We just shot ourselves in the foot. Standing on the side of democracy provides us good rhetoric, but does not seem to win elections or strengthen the organization. (Author's interview)

As AFL-CIO chairman and loyal supporter of the Democratic party Lane Kirkland put it:

> The serious problems facing the Democratic Party are rooted not in its ideology, but in its inability to work as a unified "delivery system" of money and organizational structure on behalf of Democratic candidates. (quoted in Perl, 1985, p. A9)

If imitation is the sincerest form of flattery, the modern Democratic party has begun to flatter its national Republican counterpart. From providing specific services to organizational building programs, the DNC almost literally took the pages out of the Republican book, only delaying its application by a few years (see Table 3.9). Using the same "carrot-and-stick" approach as that of the RNC, the DNC has recently done things such as providing field staff to selected states and supporting direct-mail campaigns, but only after state chairs have signed pledges to comply with DNC standards and take over the programs once they were in place.

Although the RNC has already developed the national party as a service provider, the DNC has come a long way in recent years in the eyes of its state and local affiliates. Humor often reveals real feelings. Until recently, party activists in the states were less than enamored with the support provided by the DNC. A joke that kept popping up at party meetings asserted that there are three classic lies in the United States: "The check is in the mail," "I will still respect you in the morning," and "I'm from the Democratic National Committee and I'm here to help you." While state and local party activists still enviously compare their national organization with that of the Republicans, the most recent DNC initiatives have narrowed the gap.

Stepping back from the emphasis on expressive goals was most clearly manifested when the Democratic party under the direction of chair Paul Kirk abolished the scheduled 1986 midterm convention to save resources for competitive activities and to "lower the decibel level" (Broder, 1985b) of party

TABLE 3.9. COMPARATIVE PARTY ADOPTION OF TECHNOLOGICAL APPLICATIONS AND PARTY SERVICES

Application/Year	Republican Party	Democratic Party
Direct Mail (campaign)	1964	1972[f]
Permanent National Headquarters[a]	1970	1984[g]
In-House Television Advertising	1970	1984
Direct Mail (fund-raising)	1978	1980
Local Party Organization Effort[b]	1978	1981[h]
Institutional Advertising[c]	1978	—
Young Community Leader Program[d] (Concord Program)	1978	1981[i]
National Staff Assigned to State Parties	1978	1984[j]
Preprimary Endorsements[e] (national party)	1978	—
Electronic Mail Network	1982	—

[a] Broder, 1972, p. 236.
[b] Bibby, 1981, pp. 110–113.
[c] Kayden & Mahe, 1985, p. 76.
[d] Ibid., p. 74.
[e] Ibid., p. 77.
[f] McGovern campaign.
[g] Salmore & Salmore, 1985, p. 205.
[h] State Party Works Program.
[i] Lexington Program.
[j] Salmore & Salmore, 1985, p. 215.

conflict. Despite pressure from the liberal activist contingent the current national party leadership has emphasized party organizational building and the provision of campaign services.

Explaining the Partisan Differences

In some ways it is intriguing that the Democratic party, noted for its innovativeness in the policy realms and its willingness to deemphasize local interests to national control, should abandon its innovative bent when it came to party organization building only to rely on a very localistic approach to party activity. A number of factors stand out in explaining the Republican lead in the realm of providing services.

One factor is *motivation*. Being the majority party, dominated by incumbent officeholders generally satisfied with the traditional party-activity patterns with which they won office, dampened enthusiasm for wholesale change within the Democratic party (Jacobson, 1985, p. 171). Decades of Democratic electoral success created enough frustration to encourage Republicans to look for alternatives. With Democratic incumbents well financed as individuals due to the propensity of contributors to favor current officeholders, they had little motivation to share some of the largesse through the party (see Herrnson, 1985, p. 16; Erickson, 1982, p. 4; Arterton, 1982, pp. 109–110).

The Democratic party's ability to draw on resources and services such as the Committee on Political Education of the AFL-CIO union and on the resources of incumbent congressional office staffs lulled them into "organizational complacency" (Sabato, 1982, p. 82).

The Republicans, on the other hand, knew they "were number two and had to try harder." More of their local activists saw party-provided technology and services as an opportunity rather than a threat.

Another factor is *resources*. Providing services costs money, time, and staff. Although Democratic incumbents tend to outspend Republican challengers, the Republican party organization has traditionally had more resources with which to work than its Democratic counterpart. From the 1930s, when the Republicans "started businesslike, broad-based finance solicitations... some twenty years ahead of the Democrats" (Cotter & Bibby, 1980, p. 9), to the present, the Republicans have had more to spend and fewer campaign debts to retire.

Starting out with fewer organizational resources, the Democratic problem was exacerbated by the diversion of significant time and financial resources into the process of procedural reform. Early in the reform process an underfunded national Democratic party was spending almost all of its resources on reform commissions and the operation of various caucuses representing women and minorities.

A number of significant *attitudes and outlooks* differ across the parties. The major difference pervading the parties during the 1970s was a disagreement over the role of the party. Whereas the decision makers in the Democratic party, responding to the umbrella nature of an organization beholden to many battling factions, focused on the expressive goals of making the party more democratic, the Republicans accepted the competitive goals. With its more homogeneous membership and agreement on electoral goals, the Republicans were more willing to accept the centralization necessary to provide services efficiently (Sorauf, 1980, p. 77). The reduced tenor of factional battles within the party also allowed the Republicans to maintain a continuity of leadership that facilitated long-term planning and programmatic continuity.

Some would also argue that the pragmatic business background of many Republican leaders has made them more willing to experiment with new approaches (Sabato, 1981, p. 296). Given the greater number of areas of Republican electoral weakness, it could also be that Republicans were willing to take a chance since they had very little to lose.

Whatever the complex of causes, the movement toward the service-vendor party most clearly began within Republican party organizations on the national level and to a large degree on the state and local levels.

Some Applications of Innovation Theory

Political parties are not the first organizations attempting to recapture their places in light of a hostile environment. Unless one assumes that political parties are completely unique organizations, one can compare the process of party change to changes in other realms.

The Motivation to Change.   The history of political parties moving toward the service-vendor model verifies the common pattern that organizations are shocked into change when traditional techniques fail to satisfy their goals. Discussions with party decision makers clearly indicate that they credit election defeats as the stimulus for innovation. On the national level, the 1964 Republican defeat brought about the first wave of organization building, and the defeats in 1974 and 1976 shook the party's foundations and ushered in the modern service orientation. For the Democrats, the double shock of losing the presidency and the Senate in 1980 redirected their efforts. As a basic rule, winners seldom innovate.

The Role of "Change Agents."   The presence of "the right person at the right time" stands out as crucial for most of the significant applications of new services. For the Republicans, national chairmen Ray Bliss (1965–1969) and Bill Brock (1975–1980) deserve much of the credit for redirecting party efforts. Democratic party chairman Charles Manatt (1980–1984) served as a similar innovator. On the state and local levels, far-sighted chairpersons were often pointed out as being determinative for the introduction and successful application of specific approaches. The timing of specific initiatives is important. State and local parties need to establish their resource base before embarking on ambitious service programs. As a national party staff member charged with promoting state and local party change explained it: "The adoption of technology is still driven more by far-sighted individuals, rather than available resources or organizational structure. When those individuals leave the scene, technological advances often lie dormant" (author's interview).

Overall the national party has served as a primary change agent, although as a national party staff person outlined the process, "some of the new technology was tried out at the state level and then came to Washington to be redistributed back to the states by the national parties" (author's interview). In many cases, innovation has been facilitated by a "carrot-and-stick" approach with the national party offering services with some strings attached.

The national parties' stimulation of increased communication between party activists and staff, both through electronic mail networks and face-to-face meetings, has also spread new ideas. In the words of one state party executive director:

There is nothing like sitting down with a colleague facing similar problems and picking his mind as to what works and what doesn't work. I would trust a tested approach from someone on the firing line over a textbook model any day. The catharsis of sharing our frustrations is only slightly more important than sharing our ideas. (Author's interview)

In some areas of the country, particular state parties have built a reputation as models. The Colorado Republican party entertains a constant parade of party leaders wishing to observe and copy its sophisticated package of candidate services. Above and beyond serving as a model, it has become a computer service center for a number of western states that use its computers at a fee for voter list creation and targeted mail creation and management. The promise of the states in a federal system as a "laboratory for new ideas" is alive and well when it comes to political services.

Innovation and Competition.   In a competitive realm, participants are always looking for the factors that provide a competitive advantage. The move toward the service-vendor party verified Cornelius Cotter and John Bibby's (1980) assertion that "parties tend to counter organize." Seeing the emerging Republican organizational advantage, the Democrats on all levels began to copy the Republican initiative. Those areas with more limited Republican effort saw more limited Democratic efforts by and large (see Gibson, Frendreis, & Vertz, 1985, p. 15).

In comparing political party entrance into the age of service-vendor parties, it is clear that the similarities between the parties as innovators and the innovators in other realms are more significant than the differences. Parties go through many of the same processes and are subject to many of the same forces.

Remaining Organizational Conflicts

While shifting to the provision of services and reducing the emphasis on issues and ideology, political parties have not avoided conflicts over policy preferences and individual aspirations.

As relatively open and democratic institutions with well-established processes for the periodic expression of common interests (conventions, nominations, precinct caucuses, and so on), the parties are ripe for factional battles. Conservatives took over the Republican party in 1964, and liberals did the same on the Democratic side in 1972. The contemporary Republican party has an uneasy alliance with the "New Right" groups that have a definite agenda including opposition to abortion and support for other family issues. The most obvious contemporary factionalism has emerged in the Democratic party, which has spent a great deal of time and effort mollifying and appealing to a wide variety of factions and caucuses from blacks, Hispanics, and women to lesbians and gays. As a recent top party official lamented:

> The term "the Democratic Party" is a misnomer to the extent that it implies a national commitment. In reality, the Democratic party is little more than a coalition of factional representatives who speak self-evidently for the interests of their members. They don't come to their positions as Democrats, but as hyphenated-Democrats. (Author's interview)

Many of the reform movements within the parties have been thinly veiled strategies on the part of particular candidates or issue adherents to structure the decision-making process so as to promote their candidate or cause. An old political dictum asserts: "Beware of reformers bearing gifts." Few people get excited about the value of changing rules and procedures in the abstract. In most cases they see a direct benefit for their goals.

The Democrats face a growing problem with the restiveness in many of their state parties. Loyal to the Democratic party since the Civil War, a large segment of southern party supporters have become increasingly dissatisfied with the liberal stance of the national party, particularly since it embraced the civil rights cause in the late 1940s. Southern party activists, especially in recent years as the Republicans made organizatinal and electoral inroads, publicly call the national party "a bunch of liberal nuts," "an albatross around our necks," and "them" rather than "us." In many southern states, Democrats run on Republican principles under a Democratic banner, a strategy that becomes trickier and trickier as the Republicans increase their ability to publicize the tactic, and an emerging bloc of blacks and white liberals fight to keep the state parties true to national Democratic principles. Reflecting the views of many of his counterparts, one southern Democratic state chairman explained:

> We can't build or maintain a viable party based on the national Democratic party with its far out stands and ties to every radical group. The O'Neills, Kennedys and Ferraros just don't sell. We must start with the grassroots and build a party which represents our people. The trickle down approach from the national party will not work here. We will gladly accept their money and their help, but not the radical baggage. (Author's interview)

ORGANIZATIONAL VITALITY AND STRENGTH

Until relatively recently, observers of the political parties have assumed that weakening of the party in the electorate and in office would also be reflected by a weakening of the party organization. Implicit in their arguments was the assumption that there was a set of external factors uniformly acting on all components of the parties to decrease their vitality and importance. Increasingly, there is evidence that "party organizations are themselves independent forces in the process of party system change" (Gibson et al., 1985, p. 1). In fact, enhanced party organizational strength may well be the way in which parties compensate for decreased support in the electorate and to strengthen their potency once in office. The move by the party organizations to become providers and coordinators of services for voters, candidates, and other party units is a creative response to an otherwise bleak organizational promise. Adaptation in the light of changed conditions is the hallmark of a vital organization, and the parties have adapted with a vengeance. Whether this renewed organizational strength translates into political success or not is an important, but different, question—a question on which many of the subsequent chapters will focus.

4

Political Parties and the Naming of Candidates

> I don't care who does the electing, as long as I can do the nominating.
> —*Boss Tweed of Tammany Hall*

The concept of elections brings to mind signs, television commercials, speeches, and all of the hoopla associated with the competition between two nominees. Political party activists and candidates have learned through experience that the winners and losers are often determined before the first lawn sign goes up or the first speech is given. Designing the districts from which candidates run and determining the nominees establish the context in which the campaign will take place, and it is those issues we will discuss first.

ESTABLISHING THE ELECTORAL DISTRICTS

Candidates run *for* office by running *from* a district, and it is that district which serves as a frame of reference for campaign strategy. A commitment to localism pervades much of American political thought. Although somewhat hesitant about government control of our lives, Americans are more amenable to political decisions made by friends and neighbors who supposedly have a better feel for local concerns. American election laws establish minimal criteria for candidates, requiring that they be residents of the state from which they are running (although not necessarily of the district) for the same period required for voting. The informal expectations are more strict, threatening candidates without long-term local affiliations with being seen as "carpet-baggers" (originally a derogatory term for northerners seeking private gain in the post–Civil War South). The late Senator Robert Kennedy, whose family was tied most closely to Massachusetts, ran into considerable trouble when he ran for the Senate from New York. More recently, former basketball star Tom McMillan (D-Md.) angered some party activists by announcing his candidacy for the House after living only three years in the district. His eventual defeat of hometowners in both the primary and general elections put the issue to rest. Fred Grandy (R-Iowa), with a reputation as an actor on the television series "Love Boat" and Hollywood connections, seemed especially remote from his rural Iowa district, but he overcame the lack of deep local ties. While local ties are still useful, the geographic mobility of the American population today allows more flexibility than was true in the past.

Localism also reflects itself in the way established geographic districts from which elected officials are selected were established. Some states have experimented with *at-large elections* for Congress, in which a statewide district chooses more than one member, and some cities have voters choose a number of city council members from a citywide list, but most elected officials are drawn from single-member districts. An elected official is expected to pay special attention to the needs and interests of the local constituency, and voters in the constituency have a special claim on the efforts and positions of "their" representative.

Local orientation in politics is so ingrained in most of us that we find it odd to discover the more national orientation of other systems. In the British parliamentary system, for example, the parties often help their key leaders switch districts to ensure them a safe election. A prime case was Winston Churchill, who ran and won from a number of districts during his career. Electoral districts in the British system are more an administrative convenience than are the more identifiable political entities to which voters are accustomed in the United States.

Drawing the District Lines

Given the political and legal aspects of American localism, the process by which district lines are drawn becomes part of an important political strategy in which the political parties attempt to play an active and determinative role. Drawing the lines in particular ways determines the types of voters to which the party must appeal and to whom the potential candidates must claim local ties.

The Constitution gives the states, rather than Congress, primary responsibility for determining most election laws and procedures, including the drawing of district lines. The state legislatures retained the right to determine their own electoral districts and those for Congress, while delegating the establishment of district lines for lower offices to those levels. On the national level, after each census Congress uses a formula essentially dividing the number of residents by the number of seats in Congress (now 435) to apportion the number of seats allowed to each state. The state legislatures must then draw the district lines within their boundaries. Until relatively recently, the state legislatures had to answer only to the political forces within the state in drawing the lines. Redistricting plans followed the same route as all legislation, requiring passage by the legislature and a signature by the governor. The less robust the party competition in the state, the more likely that a legislature dominated by one party with a governor of the same party could control the process. The parties attempted to get away with as much as they could to draw lines that would help them in the next elections. In a democracy, it is assumed that all procedures should work toward maximizing the individual voter's control over the political process. As the redistricting process developed under state control two related problems emerged: the relative population of districts and the actual nature of districts.

Relative District Population

Although it has always been generally assumed that districts within a state or local jurisdiction should have relatively equal populations, the realities of political interests interceded. Political parties and other interests doing well under an existing plan, and particularly the incumbents not wishing to jeopardize a district in which they had become comfortable, joined to thwart redistricting in many jurisdictions. Population shifts from the rural areas to the cities and suburbs, combined with the maintenance of old district lines, led to dramatic inequalities in the population of districts. Voters in some urban districts found their representative responsible for two to three times as many citizens, thus reducing the impact of the urban citizen's vote. Existing elected officials and party leaders had little motivation to change the system. Legislatures were dominated by rural legislators who had little desire to redraw the lines that guaranteed their positions. Freedom from the population-equality expectation allowed party leaders to pursue more partisan districting plans.

For many years, the Supreme Court refused to rule on redistricting cases, defining them as purely political questions outside of the Court's purview. Eventually, arguing on the basis of "unequal protection of the laws," the Supreme Court agreed in *Baker v. Carr* (1962) that districts must be as equal as possible to ensure the power of the individual voter. With the *one-man, one-vote* ruling, the states were required to redistrict after each census. Since census data allow only a certain degree of precision, and competing values (such as maintaining recognized boundaries of localities) can be supported, the courts have spent the past three decades more precisely defining the limits of equality. The parties have been active in the battles through the courts looking out for their own interests.

Since every electoral system embodies some form of bias—intentional or unintentional—it is impossible to come up with a criterion on which there is no disagreement. Although goals such as one person, one vote; equality; and fairness are bandied around in almost every discussion of redistricting, each of the parties accepts a different operational definition of those terms perceived as being more beneficial to their partisan goals. Republicans have generally argued that there should be a relatively close relationship between the percentage of votes a party receives in legislative contests and the percentage of legislative seats won by the party. Thus a party receiving 60 percent of the overall vote in legislative contests should end up with 60 percent of the seats. On the surface that seems ultimately fair. But Democrats are quick to point out that given lower participation rates of their party members, they often win safe Democratic districts with relatively few votes, and that overall, seats versus vote ratios provides a distorted measure of fairness. If the two parties cannot agree on what the overall outcome of redistricting should look like, it is no wonder that they disagree on the district-by-district decisions that affect the outcome of actual races (see Cain, 1985, pp. 563–564).

The Composition of Districts

The various court rulings increased the amount of redistricting activity and guaranteed population equality but did little to diminish partisan strategies for drawing the lines. Although the requirements of population equality, con- tiguousness of district parts (the district must be made up of areas that geographically touch), and the preference for compact districts that maintain established boundaries limited the freedom of the participants in redistricting, they were not without their strategies.

Gerrymandering refers to the process of drawing district lines to minimize the political strength of one political group while maximizing the strength of another. The term comes from a cartoon by Thomas Nast depicting a redis- tricting plan signed by Massachusetts Governor Elbridge Gerry in the early 1800s combining Republican precincts in such a way as to resemble a salaman- der (see Figure 4.1). For a party with a clear majority in the electorate—party A, say—gerrymandering consists simply of designing each district with a majority for party A. In more competitive areas a "pack-and-crack" strategy is used. Areas with strong majorities for the opposition party—party B—are "packed" together in one district ensuring that party B will waste many votes in winning that district; meanwhile, party B's votes in other areas are "crack- ed" into small blocs and combined with areas of party A's strength so that party A will win comfortably but not wastefully (see Figure 4.2).

Traditionally, redistricting was as much a matter of "guesstimation" as empirical analysis, given the massive data and the unlimited ways in which districts could be structured. In recent years, the parties have relied on computers to sort through the data and design alternatives based on the criteria they specify. As political scientist and plaintiff in the first successful redistricting case Gordon Baker concluded:

> The recent development of widespread and pervasive gerrymandering is the result of judicial preoccupation in the late 1960's and after with one facet of fair representation—equipopulous districts. . . . The adaptability of computer technology during the same period of time brought a new degree of sophis- tication to boundary manipulation. The results were likely to be far more durable than the comparatively crude guess-work that formerly characterized even the most professional efforts at political cartography. (1985, p. 551)

Figure 4.1 The Original Gerrymander
Political cartoonist Thomas Nast coined the word *gerrymander* after looking at the redistricting
plan devised by Massachusetts Governor Elbridge Gerry in 1812. His cartoon portrayed the
partisan district plan as a salamander and named it a "gerrymander."

When faced wtih a strong incumbent or potential opponents, gerrymandering may involve forcing two incumbents of the opposition party into
one district, requiring them to move, retire, or face a head-to-head contest. In
other cases lines can be drawn so that incumbent or potential candidates are
faced with an almost entirely new district, divorcing them from their traditional base of support. In either case it may be possible to create an opening for
your party (see Grofman, 1985, p. 544).

In determining the existence of a gerrymander, a number of considerations must be taken into account. In the purest sense, a gerrymander is limited
to a plan whereby one party is extensively discriminated against *before* the
election takes place, and the election outcome is not simply the result of
ineffective candidates or campaigns. Since the Supreme Court rule in *City of*

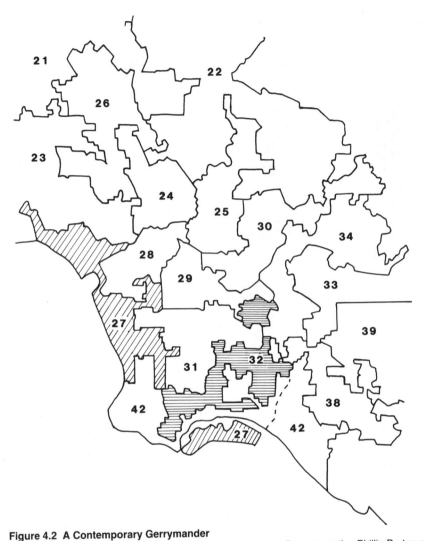

Figure 4.2 A Contemporary Gerrymander
The 1983 California redistricting plan devised by Democratic Representative Phillip Burton not only made the most of partisan line drawing but also ended up in the courts. In an attempt to strengthen the Democratic position, bizarre lines were drawn. In the 32nd district, for example, the political architects created a virtual Republican "island" in the middle, combining stronger Democratic areas into one district. The 27th district was similarly created to tie together Democratic areas and simply jumped over the Palos Verdes Peninsula, leaving an elongated district with unconnected portions.

CONFLICTING PARTISAN MOTIVATIONS
AND REDISTRICTING

Conflicting political motives clearly make strange political bedfellows in redistricting battles. When the Indiana Democratic party took the Indiana Republican party to court over a redistricting plan that it believed discriminated against its candidates (*Davis v. Bandemer* [1986]), the Republican National Committee found itself supporting the local Democrats, and the Indiana Republican party found the California Democratic party filing a brief and hiring a publicist on its behalf. No matter how concerned the national Republican party was about Indiana, it was more concerned about California. There, a Democratic plan led to 1984 election results in which, despite receiving a majority of the congressional votes, the Republicans received only 17 of the 45 congressional seats. (See Taylor, 1985b, p. A4.) In a decision less than satisfactory to either side, the Court ruled that political gerrymandering was unconstitutional but could not agree on criteria for determining when a proposal met constitutional requirements. It is clear that the courts have not seen the last of political redistricting cases.

Mobile v. Bolden, those claiming discrimination have had to prove a clear intention on the part of public officials.

Given the mix of party and personal goals, the parties do not always stick together on redistricting plans (see box). State legislators often support plans generally hurting their party but better meeting their personal political ambitions. The process of building a coalition behind a redistricting plan involves publicly selling the plan on the basis of fairness, selling the plan to fellow partisans on the basis of its benefit to the party, and, if opposition party votes are needed either for passage or public relations, sweetening the plan to help out a few members of the opposition by making their seats safer.

Parties often eschew bragging about their gerrymandering successes, preferring to present an image of public service and concern. More recently, however, some party leaders have attempted to reinforce the importance of the parties in this process by bragging of their success. After a particularly partisan and successful Democratic plan in California, one Democratic leader explained:

What we did to the Republicans was to fully use the powers which go along with controlling the governorship and both houses of the Assembly to create the most favorable redistricting plan ever. They would have stuck it to us if they had the chance. Fortunately, we were in control. (Author's interview)

The importance of redistricting can be seen in the effort the parties are making in anticipation of the 1990 census. The stakes in the 1991 congressional redistricting process are high. Almost 40 seats are likely to change states. The estimated big winners will come from the Sun Belt, with Florida (+4), California (+3), Texas (+4), and Arizona (+2) leading. The big losers from the Frost Belt include New York (−5), Pennsylvania (−3), and Michigan and Ohio (−2) (Broder, 1985c, p. 14). The Republican National Committee (RNC) has established a long-term lateral attack by attempting to elect more state legislators and governors to increase the likelihood that it will control the redistricting and by running a more targeted campaign to elect state legislators in districts of vulnerable members of Congress. This not only puts in place a set of likely candidates with track records and established organizations but also gives these potential line drawers the motivation to draw Republican districts in which to run.

The redistricting after the 1990 census may well be partially premised on the desire to use technology to the fullest. The Indiana plan leading to *Davis v. Bandemer* (1986; see box on page 101) stemmed from a computer-generated plan commissioned by the state Republican party. Using returns from previous elections and census tract information, the consultant created a plan that resulted in the Republicans gaining 57 percent of the state legislative seats while garnering only 48 percent of the legislative vote (Taylor, 1985b, p. A4).

Although redistricting is important, the parties have lost some of their control for three reasons. First, the line drawers are less willing to buy into the purely partisan plans since they were more likely to have won without party help and feel that they owe the organization less. Second, the decreased tendency of voters consistently to support the same party makes the prediction of the future behavior of a district less precise. Finally, incumbent office-holders show great resiliency against attempts to carve up or expand their constituencies. Many incumbents, especially when the legislative body doing the redistricting was in the hands of the opposition party, have been forced to run in districts composed of an almost entirely new set of voters and yet survive politically (see Born, 1985, p. 305).

RECRUITING CANDIDATES

Although few candidates are forced to the campaign trail, few decide to run for office without some sign of implicit or explicit support from politically active groups. Traditionally, the only groups that really counted were the parties. After working one's way up through the party by performing needed tasks loyally and conscientiously, a person was contacted by the party leaders and given the opportunity to think about running for office. Without such a nod a candidacy was seen as meaningless. Today a multitude of groups and organizations compete with the parties as recruiters, and an increasing number of candidates are self-recruited, placing themselves in positions where others will think of them as possibly viable candidates. Interest groups, both local and national, urge candidates to carry their banner. The press makes or breaks potential candidates depending on whether or not they are mentioned among those who should be considered for an opening. As two top media analysts expressed it:

> Being a viable candidate depends less on support from a party organization than on the ability to sell oneself in a media campaign. . . . The greater the disarray of the parties, the more important is television as a means to short circuit what used to be normal political channels . . . television gives outsiders with sufficient resources a better chance than even before to enter the fray. (Lang & Lang, 1984, p. 220)

In high-visibility races, the campaign consultants as well as the media become "pre-selectors. . . encouraging and discussing candidacies often with the mere announcements of their choices of clients in a race" (Sabato, 1981, p. 34).

Although the decision to run for office is highly personal, encompassing a mix of political, economic, and personal considerations, the parties still play an important, but more limited, role. Paul Herrnson (1986, pp. 9–13) distinguished between three types of candidate recruitment: "passive," "active," and "negative." *Passive recruitment* involves party efforts to make candidates aware of election opportunities and the services the parties can provide. Many potential candidates show up at party-sponsored training sessions and candidate schools still undecided whether or for what office they might run. The perspectives provided allow them to determine the kind of candidate they might make, the general political climate, and the nature of modern campaign techniques.

Active recruitment involves the party aggressively seeking out potential candidates. Although more common in relatively hopeless districts and by local parties, the Republican National Committee began using its field workers for much more active recruiting in 1978. Likely winners were given primary support. Although there were some clear successes, after a few cases in which nationally supported candidates lost to those backed by local leaders, the rules were changed to require local party approval before party backing in the primary would be forthcoming. For many ambitious potential candidates, active party recruitment may require only a few supportive comments. In other cases, promises of significant support, at least in the general election, are required.

Recently, Republicans, particularly in a number of southern states, took the recruitment process further by urging incumbent Democratic officeholders to switch parties. Recognizing that it is easier to get a proven winner reelected than to mount a doubtful challenge, party leaders showed targeted Democrats detailed demographic charts of their district to prove that it was winnable by a Republican. Using a classic "carrot-and-stick" approach potential switchers were told that if they became Republicans the party would give them money for constituent mailings to explain the switch and full backing in the next election; if they did not, they were threatened with a serious challenge the next time they ran (Taylor, 1986a, p. A14). By carefully choosing districts whose voting patterns and opinions did not match the Democratic party identification of their elected officials, the Republicans got a number of officials to switch and successfully increased the size of their state legislative delegations in a number of states.

Negative recruitment involves attempts to dissuade potential candidates from running and creating a disruptive primary race. The party may simply provide evidence that another candidate has a better chance of winning, or it may smooth the way for the undesired candidate to run for another office. Such discouragement may be difficult. As one party activist pointed out: "It comes down to a problem of egos. You have two or more young ambitious politicans and only one seat. Each person has his group of supporters, and each person thinks he can win the primary" (quoted in Herrnson, 1986, p. 13).

More indirectly, the public favor with which the party is held affects who is likely to run. Although local party support and strength are important, national trends also have an effect. Potential candidates become serious the autumn of the preelection year. If the party is well respected more candidates are willing to take a chance (Watson, 1985c, p. 2049). In the wake of Watergate, many potentially strong candidates decided not to take the risk in 1974, and the Democrats won in districts that could have gone Republican with a stronger candidate. Similarly, many potentially strong Democratic candidates looked at Jimmy Carter's ratings and decided not to run in 1980, relinquishing some Democratic seats to Republicans. In 1986, even with control of the Senate in the balance, a number of potentially strong Democratic candidates did not want to risk secure positions to challenge Ronald Reagan's popularity, which had rubbed off on the Republican party and its candidates. Conditions changed dramatically by the time candidates were making their decisions for 1988. Ronald Reagan's decline in popularity after the Iran-Contra revelations rubbed off on the Republican party and gave a number of potential congressional candidates pause.

The parties have a stake in fielding candidates for all offices to show the vitality of the party and to take advantage of atypical events (the death of a candidate, a late-breaking scandal, and so on) that could deliver an unlikely district to their control. The less favorable the district, based on past voting trends or the popularity of the incumbent from the opposition party, the more active a role the party must play. In the most favorable constituencies, the problem may well be too many candidates all fighting for the same campaign workers, funds, and voters and in the process tarnishing the eventual winner. In such cases the party may get involved in "negative recruiting." Insuring an adequate group of competent candidates is important above and beyond the impact on the parties. The parties seem best suited to seeking out potential competent candidates, subjecting them to a degree of "peer review" and presenting them to the electorate. Without an active group with continuing involvement in this process, guaranteeing the desirable options is questionable. In the long run "the quality of the people's verdict depends on the quality of the options from which they choose" (Keech & Matthews, 1979, p. 203).

NOMINATING NONPRESIDENTIAL CANDIDATES FOR OFFICE

American election laws are based on the premise that voters can make a meaningful choice only among a relatively constrained set of options. The nomination procedures were designed to narrow the field of candidates to make the choice possible. In the sections that follow a distinction is made between nominations for the presidency and all other nominations. Although the processes and procedures are intertwined, presidential nominations in America are unique enough to merit separate consideration in the later portions of this chapter.

The Historical Development of Nomination Procedures

The long-term trend in nominating procedures reflects a broadening of the base of individuals involved in the process and increased autonomy of the candidates. This process reveals a great deal about the nature and composition of the parties.

Early nominations were made by the elected officials of the day through legislative caucuses. The party as a separate entity was not anticipated by the framers of the Constitution, and the existing parties were limited largely to groups of elected officials sharing common political outlooks. As the electorate was expanded and the nominees had to appeal to a broader set of voters, the role of the party organization outside of government began to increase. Party caucuses and conventions became the forum to nominate candidates, although the ultimate decisions were less democratic than it might seem when deals were cut in the infamous smoke-filled rooms. With the legal right to place individuals on the ballot, the party during that period used its power to broaden its appeal, balancing the ticket by including representatives of various ethnic and political groups and spreading the political benefits around.

The power of the party over the individual candidate graphically emerged in the 19th century with the common practice of rotating congressional seats. Abraham Lincoln served only one term in the House of Representatives before bowing to the party practice of shifting candidates from one county to the next after each election. The party rewarded its faithful with a term or two in office before transferring the nomination to another party loyalist. Although the incumbents might chafe at such treatment, they had little recourse but to follow the party's wishes, for not to do so would mean electoral defeat (see

Price, 1971, p. 19). Such party control carried over into the 20th century only in those areas with strong party machines and virtually vanished with their demise. On the congressional level, organizational changes affected the nomination process. With the development of the seniority system, which gave members with the longest continuous service the leadership positions, local parties found it increasingly unwise to keep sending newcomers to Washington, and the practice of almost automatic renomination of incumbents arose.

By the end of the 19th century, growing public distrust of parties and strategic choices by candidates and groups not favored by the existing procedures led to the adoption of the primary system as the major method of party nomination. Primaries dramatically redefined the nature of political parties, from a small group of activists to a much broader group of affiliates with much less obvious commitment to the party.

The Direct Primary

Although conventions, and in many cases hand picking of party nominees by a small group of party leaders, dominated the nomination process during the first century of the American system, the entrance into the 20th century unleashed a dramatic revision of the nomination process—the direct primary. Reflecting distrust in the party leaders, Wisconsin's Robert M. La Follette captured the democratic motivations of the Progressives and the major journalists of the day when he asserted:

> Abolish the caucus and convention. Go back to the first principles of democracy: go back to the people. Substitute for both the caucus and convention a primary election. (1913, p. 198)

Within two decades of the first primary law in 1902, all but four states had adopted some form of primary for most offices, with Connecticut eventually making it universal in 1955. Although state laws in some states still allow nominations for some offices to be made by convention, direct primaries clearly dominate as the favored nominating method.

Types of Primaries

With election laws in the hands of the states, it is no surprise that primary laws vary dramatically in terms of voter eligibility, timing, and candidate impact. Each of the laws reflects the strength and perceived self-interests of the parties at the time of their adoption. Although generally fearing primaries, the parties found it hard to thwart them initially and impossible to abandon them once in place. Thus the parties took the more realistic stand of attempting to structure primaries in the least threatening manner.

Although premised on the belief that primaries would return control over nominations to party members, there is less agreement about how to define *membership* and the right to participate. One can conceive of arraying the various types of primaries on a continuum with one end representing the most constrained participation, where the potential participant must make a true public commitment to the party, to the other end of the continuum, where the primary is simply a two-step election open to any eligible voter at either stage. The party organizations in general support a more constrained primary electorate giving them some sense of the party constituency and a more predictable bloc of voters to pursue.

The *closed primary* provides the most constraint on voters, and most states (38 plus the District of Columbia) have opted for a restrictive definition of voter eligibility, requiring potential participants to register their party affiliation publicly, often a significant period before the primary. In some states registration with a party requires signing a sworn statement that one has supported the party in the past or intends to in the future. Although not enforceable by law, such an affirmation gives true independents some pause and serves to reinforce a voter's sense of affiliation. On primary election day the voters registered by party can vote only for the candidates contesting a nomination in their party, and independents must sit out the primary.

The *open primary* gives voters a choice of party primary. Nine states (Hawaii, Idaho, Michigan, Minnesota, Montana, North Dakota, Utah, Vermont, and Wisconsin) have taken this more expansive view of party membership, allowing voters secretly to decide in which primary they wish to participate. Unencumbered by registration with a particular party, voters in these states show up on election day and are secretly given access to both party ballots (the systems vary from separate ballot boxes for used and unused ballots to voting machines that lock out voters once they begin voting within a party's primary). Although the procedures vary, the voter can choose the party primary in which to participate but is limited to that party's primary.

Aside from denying the parties an identifiable list of party adherents, the open primary opens the nomination to *crossover voting* by members of the other party. Dramatic shifts in the number of voters participating in a party's primary from election to election may occur naturally as voters gravitate to the primary of the party having more interesting contests, or they may be the result of organized "raiding" whereby a candidate or party encourages its followers to participate in the opposition party's primary in order to affect its outcome.

Blanket primaries, held in three states (Alaska, Louisiana, and Washington), provide the voter with even more choices. Relieved of registering by party or expressing a party preference on primary day, voters in these states can skip from one party to the next during the primary, voting in different party primaries for each office. In such a system the voter might help choose the Democratic candidate for governor but skip the Democratic contest for the congressional nomination in favor of the Republican contest. Under such a plan, neither the party organization nor the candidates have a firm feel as to the primary electorate. Even if they get "their" candidates to the polls, there is not any assurance as to who will vote in each separate primary contest.

With the growing Republican strength in the South, Louisiana Democrats adjusted the primary rules to their benefit. Facing the more and more frequent situation of a divisive Democratic primary with the Republican candidate avoiding a primary and waiting in the wings fresh for battle and backed by a unified party, the Democrats pushed through a primary plan whereby all candidates of both parties would run in the primary, with the top contenders going on to the general election. This diminished the Republican advantage to the degree that Democrats have controlled the governorship ever since.

No matter what the eligibility requirements, the primary electorate is not a faithful sample of party voters or of voters in general. Closed primaries automatically exclude independents who generally end up voting for the candidates of one of the parties in the general election, whereas the more open primary electorates continually change in composition. In general, compared with the general election electorate, the primary electorate is smaller (except in those one-party areas where the primary is in reality the election), better educated, better off, more ideological, and more partisan (see Polsby, 1983b, p. 697).

The Timing of Primaries

State laws vary widely concerning the time between the primary and the general election. Given the existence of a primary system, party leaders are of mixed mind about scheduling. Most party leaders seem to prefer an early primary, giving them enough time to heal the wounds, marshal resources, and go into the general election prepared, but some leaders echo the words of their colleague from Wisconsin, that

> our late primary provides the party with an indirect benefit. With only seven weeks from the primary to the general election, after winning the primary most campaign organizations collapse in a heap for a few weeks out of exhaustion. We step in to fill the gap, reunite the party, pick up the pieces, and help plan a strategy for the general election thrust. (Author's interview)

The Impact of Primaries on the Candidates

Replacing conventions dominated by a small identifiable group of party activists with primaries dramatically changed the way in which candidates went about seeking a position on the ballot. Long-term commitment to party activity gave way to personal candidate organizations. Ambitious candidates exploited the shortcomings of fellow partisans and attempted to position themselves to discourage their candidacies or challenge them in a primary. Lacking the financial and technical support from the party during primaries, candidates became accustomed to seeking outside help from consultants, nonparty volunteers, and interest groups, establishing a pattern that soon carried over to the general election campaign. As Jeane Kirkpatrick argued, the primary allows the candidate "the capacity to directly appeal to the voter [making] it possible to bypass not only the party leadership, but the dominant political class. . . .Primaries also tend to personalyze politics by focusing attention on disagreements within parties" (1978, pp. 6–7).

The definition of winning or losing in a primary varies from state to state. Although most states declare the candidate receiving the most votes the winner, nine southern states require a runoff primary if no candidate receives more than 50 percent of the vote, and Iowa and South Dakota send the nomination to a convention if no one receives more than 35 percent of the vote.

Losing a primary means more in some states than in others. Twenty-six states have "sore loser laws" prohibiting primary losers from running in the general election as independents or under another party's label. Primary winners not only acquire an uncontested place on the ballot, generally including party designation, but also are officially in line for both the material and symbolic help the party can give.

The Impact of Primaries on the Party Organization

With the adoption of direct primaries, the party organizations went from having almost complete control over who had the right to run for office to only one player in the game—a player besmirched by perceived past infractions. Virtually everyone saw the primaries as intentionally punishing the parties and warning them against attempting to gain too much control in the future. Jeane Kirkpatrick concluded that "primaries are the institutional embodiment of the persistent American suspicion of organizations" (1978, p. 7). Attempting to rid the nomination process of boss control, the primaries rid it of party control also (Ranney, 1975, p. 129).

Lack of control over the nominees campaigning under the party label can create a major embarrassment for the party. In recent years, a member of the Ku Klux Klan won the Democratic congressional nomination in San Diego, and all the party leaders could do was to encourage voter support of the Republican candidate (Lane, 1983). In the 1986 Illinois primary, two candidates associated with Lyndon LaRouche's extremist policies won the Democratic nominations for lieutenant governor and attorney general. Adlai Stevenson, winner of the gubernatorial primary, was forced to run as an independent, rather than on the Democratic ticket with individuals whose views he abhorred. Stevenson and the state Democratic party had to ask voters to split from the party to support Stevenson and a set of newly chosen candidates for lieutenant governor and attorney general and then go back to party-line voting for the lesser offices. In a state long dominated by the Cook County (Chicago) Democratic machine, which made party-line voting an article of faith, such a request sounded heretical and invited derisive evaluations of a party that could have let such a thing happen. The courts came to the aid of the Alabama Democratic organization in the 1986 gubernatorial primary. The attorney general, a former Republican, encouraged Republicans to support him in the runoff primary and approved a letter warning local election officials that they would face prosecution from his office if they did not allow Republicans to vote as Democrats. The court ruled that he had abused his office as attorney general and allowed the state party to award the nomination to his opponent (Peterson, 1986b, p. A4).

Lacking control over nominations after the adoption of the direct primary, the party retained fewer incentives for organizational activity. Potential candidates realized that the party was only one arena of civic activity in which they could make their name. Less ambitious volunteers more often found state and local party conventions rather hollow activities once the power of nominating candidates was withdrawn. For volunteers, the lure of more personalized involvement in a candidate's quest for office often seemed more appealing than more anonymous toiling in the party organizational vineyards. Thus the party not only lost one of its primary rationales for existence but also found some of its incentives for volunteer support reduced.

Before primaries existed, the parties more successfully managed conflict, at least in public. Potential candidates were encouraged or discouraged, and before being given the nod to run, an attempt was made to balance the party ticket, taking into account ethnic, racial, religious, and ideological factors. Incumbents with satisfactory performance records and party loyalty automatically received the nomination unless there was a party interest in rotation, and new potential candidates were evaluated for party loyalty. With the adoption of the primary, conflict increased in two arenas. Outside of party control, the battle for the nomination became an open game. Fierce primary battles erupted for more positions. Primary competition became most likely for open seats with no incumbent and when party loyalties or the weakness of the incumbent of the opposition party predicted a good chance of electoral success in the general election. It is not only the direct loss of party control that hurt the parties but also the fact that a competitive primary leaves the candidates depleted of resources, having to face the general election with party supporters who hurled insults and charges against one another during the primary. The conflict does not end on election day. Individually battling their way onto the ballot, successful primary nominees making it through the general election enter office feeling less beholden to the party. They realize that the party did not guarantee them a position on the ballot in the past and is unable to do so in the future. They must thus establish a personal political strategy, which may or may not coincide with the party's desire for loyalty to the organization and its principles.

In another sense, primaries decreased competition. Before primaries existed, the parties took clear responsibility for ensuring that there were candidates for all offices, and the primaries facilitated abdication of this role. In 1900, before there were primaries, fewer than 5 percent of the congressional districts failed to have candidates from both parties. During the first half of this century, this percentage stayed around 20 percent, with the Democratic primary in the South being tantamount to election and accounting for some, but not all, of the uncontested general elections. Renewed efforts by the parties and the growth of the two-party South began to emerge in the late 1906s when the percentage of uncontested races dropped to about 10 percent, where it remains (see Schlesinger, 1985, pp. 1159–1160).

The Party Fights Back:
Preprimary Endorsements and Services
The frustration and implications of having to wait until after the primaries to get involved directly in the campaign encouraged party organizations to involve themselves formally in the primary process. Although informal help and encouragement of favored candidates by party leaders has occurred since the adoption of primaries, party organizations sought ways to affect primary outcomes directly and to establish themselves as important actors. Two methods stand out, preprimary endorsements and the provision of campaign services.

Preprimary Endorsements.   The earlier the party gets into the nomination game, the more important its role is likely to be. Even with the direct primary, the party organization's right to endorse a candidate formally before the primary may encourage the unendorsed candidate to drop out, affect voter decisions by giving them additional information, or allow the party to marshal organizational resources such as contributions, volunteers, and services to the benefit of the endorsee. One or both parties in 17 states use or are legally permitted to use a state convention for endorsing candidates for statewide office. Only two states (California and Florida) forbid such endorsements, and in the remainder of the states the practice is not used (Conlan, 1986, Chapter 4, passim).

On the national level, the Republican congressional committees began very selectively supporting primary candidates in the late 1970s and the Democrats followed suit a few years later. In both parties endorsement now requires full approval of state and local party officials and is the exception rather than the rule.

Part of the hesitancy in using preprimary endorsements stems from the lack of party control over primary outcomes. Preprimary endorsements are a double-edged sword. To the degree that endorsees win the primary and the endorsement is seen as a key factor, they strengthen the party's hand in the eyes of the candidates and the public (see Mann, 1981, p. 51). On the other hand, a number of state parties such as those in Minnesota and Wisconsin have suffered the embarrassment of having their endorsed candidates lose in the primary, thereby damaging the party image more than lack of endorsements might have done. As one state party officer put it, "We have become more and more wary of endorsements for the high visibility state offices such as governor. There are just too many chances to be overriden" (author's interview).

Preprimary Services. Less threatening to the party, and somewhat useful for making candidates feel beholden, is the provision of party services to primary candidates. Although state and national parties have always made their candidate schools (see box) open to any potential party candidate for a fee, a number of state parties now offer a wide variety of services from mailing list creation and polling to the creation of advertising materials. In the words of one state party executive:

> We can't have the party just sitting around twiddling its thumbs until the nomination is made. By that time the candidates would have found the services they need elsewhere. We put out a list of services, offer them to any candidate, and establish a business arrangement with them. The winners will come back to us during the general election and enhance the services, and they will remember that we were there to help when they needed it once they get in office. (Author's interview)

The Continuing Role of Caucuses and Conventions

Only eight states allow or require the use of party conventions to nominate candidates for all statewide offices, and another four states do so for at least some statewide offices (Conlan, 1986, p. 73). Although party caucuses and conventions in most situations (other than on the presidential level) no longer have the formal right to nominate, they still carry out a number of important functions. State and local party conventions serve as forums for issue development and candidate testing, guide the administration of the party organization, provide party activists with an opportunity to interact and enthuse over one another, and in a number of states marshal party support and resources behind particular candidates by giving them preprimary endorsements.

Generally, local caucuses or conventions meet at least yearly and from their ranks select delegates to the conventions of the broader political jurisdictions (ward, congressional district, state, and so on). A number of states hold regular precinct caucuses, open to any individual feeling an affiliation to the party. Both parties' caucuses are generally held on the same night to disallow the same voters from participating in both. Minnesota, for example, had close to 300,000 Republicans and 600,000 Democrats participate in 1986. Xandra Kayden and Eddie Mahe reported an increase in the number and participation in local party caucuses that has "gone a long way toward breathing life into the local party" (1985, p. 113).

Although caucuses and conventions provide an avenue for direct involvement by the most interested citizens, they may not represent the population or

HANDSHAKING 101: CAMPAIGN SCHOOLS

Although many aspects of running for office are either common sense or the product of native skills, thousands of candidates, campaign managers, finance directors, and spouses attend special courses sponsored by the political parties to learn the fine points. Often including role-playing simulations, frank capability assessments, and videotaped performances, the training mixes lectures and hands-on experience. Topics include media skills, fund-raising tactics, campaign computer software, presenting yourself to the public, avoiding embarrassment from one's family, managing volunteers and staff, and establishing issue positions. After the one-to-five-day courses at the Republican Campaign Management College, or the more recently established Democratic training academy, participants will have been exposed to the best advice available from incumbent politicians, party staff, and campaign consultants. Training segments and typical advice include:

Handshaking 101

- Smile.
- Look your target straight in the eyes.
- Don't slouch.
- Let them remember a firm handshake without bruising their bones.
- Provide high-volume handshaking without damage.

Television Appearances 410

- Dress for television. Dark suits convey a more powerful image and light blue shirts photograph better.
- Never say "no comment." Deal with an embarrassing question by either ignoring it or responding to the question with another question.
- From the moment you get in the studio consider yourself "on the air." Don't say anything you would not want thousands of people to hear.
- Television is a conversational medium. Pretend you are talking to a good friend in your living room.
  Don't get angry.
  Don't scream.
  Don't look back and forth between the camera and the interviewer. You will either look nervous or look like a spectator at a tennis match.
- Try to know as much as possible about your interviewer and his or her audience's interests before you arrive.

These and the many other techniques taught will not guarantee success, nor are they amenable to the personalities, skills, and specifics of any candidate's race. But they alert key campaign personnel to what has worked in other settings and which major errors to avoid. (See Granat, 1984.)

CONTROLLING THE CONVENTION FLOOR

A longtime Republican party activisist in Minnesota recounted the increased role of fundamentalist Christians on the state convention floor in this way:

> There was a young man who stood in one of the aisles and had on one of those straw bowler hats. When he had his hat on, everybody voted yes, when he took his hat off, everybody voted no. It was an amazing thing to watch, the votes went exactly the way his hat went. We had less than 100 votes out of more than 300. They were in total control. (Edsall, 1985c, p. 9)

---

the party members as a whole. Conventions are easier to control by factions than are primaries. (See box, "Controlling the Convention Floor.")

PRESIDENTIAL NOMINATIONS: A SPECIAL CASE

Although most nominations for office involve only one stage—the direct primary—nominations for the presidency involve a number of stages and a variety of processes.

The Party and the Emergence of Candidates

Since incumbent presidents are almost guaranteed renomination and have considerable control over the national party, the party becomes a vehicle for their renomination battle, should there be a battle. Contests with no party incumbent better represent the role and potential of the parties.

Defeated party nominees, particularly if they were not humiliated at the polls, have first claim as "titular head" of the party. Party nominees are usually given the opportunity to select the chair of the national committee and top staff members. Having their people running the national committee facilitates their role as party spokesperson.

Repudiated nominees and those expressing little interest in renomination evidence weaker control over the party and may find that challenges to "their" party chair become battles between potential nominees. Contests over the post of party chair between elections often serve as initial tests of candidate strength.

Between elections, the party has the opportunity to showcase candidates. Party leaders in Congress gain exposure and legitimacy as party spokespersons, an increasingly important factor with both houses now available "gavel to gavel" on cable television (C-SPAN). Party-encouraged conferences for governors and other elected officials provide a forum in which potential candidates might emerge. The Democratic National Committee (DNC) sent Jimmy Carter around the country to speak for the party at a series of bean feeds and bull roasts well before the 1976 nomination process formally began. These trips spread his name and established the contacts he wove into a campaign organization. Aspiring presidential candidates line up to present the party response to major presidential speeches. Opportunities to chair party and convention committees or to serve as convention keynote speakers provide an early test for future candidates. Hubert Humphrey's 1948 civil rights speech on the floor of the Democratic convention indelibly marked him as presidential timber, as did New York Governor Mario Cuomo's performance 36 years later. Campaign duties can perform the same function. Ronald Reagan's party-supported election-eve plea for support of Republican candidates in 1964 established the legitimacy of Reagan as a political force.

Amassing Convention Delegates

Presidential nominations are made by the quadrennial conventions of each party. The delegates to these conventions are selected in a number of ways. Traditionally, selection as a delegate served as a reward for long and faithful party service, and delegates owed their loyalty to the state party organizations selecting them. Gaining the nomination involved dealing with delegation leaders, generally governors or other high-ranking elected officials, and building a coalition of delegations. Conventions "brokered" by a handful of large-delegation leaders were the norm, with individual delegates often having little say, although the brokers did have to take into account the popular support of candidates.

Expanded citizen control of presidential nominations progressed more slowly than the direct infusion of democracy provided by the direct primary for lower-level offices. A number of states substituted the primary for state conventions to choose delegates to the national conventions quite early, but during the first half of this century fewer than 20 states and fewer than one-half of the delegates were selected in primaries. Public and press preference for primaries and the pressure caused by the Democratic party reform commissions after the 1968 election led to a dramatic increase in the number of primaries and the percentage of delegates selected in that way. Even more importantly, this period saw a dramatic increase in the percentage of delegates formally committed to one of the candidates through the primary process (see Table 4.1).

The Primary Process

The role of the primaries has changed dramatically in the presidential nominating process. Until recently, with relatively few delegates chosen in primaries and the vast majority of them having no legal commitment to support a particular candidate, the primaries were not very important as a direct method

TABLE 4.1. GROWTH OF THE PRIMARY AS A METHOD OF SELECTING NATIONAL CONVENTION DELEGATES

	Year	Number of Primaries	Number of Delegates	Percentage of Delegates Chosen in Primaries	Percentage of Delegates Committed in Primaries
Democratic Party	1952	17	1,230	46	18
	1956	21	1,372	50	38
	1960	17	1,521	45	20
	1964	18	2,316	51	41
	1968	17	2,623	49	36
	1972	23	3,016	66	58
	1976	29	3,008	75	66
	1980	31	3,331	71	71
	1984	25	3,933	55	51
	1988	31	4,160	77	61
Republican Party	1952	15	1,206	46	24
	1956	18	1,323	47	43
	1960	15	1,331	41	35
	1964	17	1,308	48	35
	1968	16	1,333	45	36
	1972	22	1,348	53	41
	1976	28	2,259	66	54
	1980	33	1,993	75	69
	1984	24	2,235	57	52
	1988	33	2,277	77	58

Source: 1952–1980: Polsby, 1983a, p. 64; 1984–1988: *Congressional Quarterly Weekly Reports*, 1984–1987.

of amassing supportive delegates. Presidential primaries served more as public testing grounds of candidate popularity and legitimacy. Candidates overcoming tremendous odds (such as Dwight Eisenhower, who won a write-in victory in the 1952 Minnesota primary) are taken much more seriously, whereas candidates doing less well than expected (such as Lyndon Johnson, who lacked a clear mandate in the 1968 New Hampshire primary) found their candidacies seriously questioned. Candidates often used the primaries to test the waters or to overcome a perceived weakness (such as Kennedy's youth and Catholicism in 1960 or Nixon's loser image in 1968).

The strategies for using and interpreting presidential primaries are tricky. In many states the candidate can choose whether or not to compete. Taking one's name off the list of candidates and avoiding the competition is usually better than getting beat, but bypassing a primary in which significant support could be generated can be just as damaging. Incomplete matchings between candidates also exacerbates a variety of problems associated with interpreting presidential primaries. Winning or losing a presidential primary is as much a case of perception as reality. Although garnering a plurality of the votes is usually defined as winning, a small plurality is not good enough for a candidate perceived by the press and public to be strong; likewise, something less than a plurality is viewed as "winning" for a candidate starting out with many disadvantages. Ronald Reagan did as well in the New Hampshire primary against an incumbent president as George McGovern had done in 1968 (42 percent), but Reagan was expected to do so much better that it was not perceived as a "win." The perception factor turned around in 1980, when George Bush coming from a caucus victory in Iowa claimed "Big Mo" (momentum) only to do worse than expected relative to Reagan in New Hampshire, and the Bush campaign began to fold. The "expectations game" killed off a number of candidates on both sides in 1988.

Above and beyond the number of votes, the timing of certain primaries enhances their importance, and the nature of the particular state invites questions about what the results represent. New Hampshire's continuing battle to hold the first primary guarantees considerable press coverage, and the results have made or broken a number of candidacies. But numerous questions remain about whether the results of a few voters in each party, in a state that clearly does not mirror the national or party composition, should have such an inordinate impact. The traditional timing of the California primary for maximum impact in sorting out the final few candidates late in the primary season raises similar questions, although in recent years the nomination has been decided well before the California contest. Unable to guarantee either first or last position, a large number of southern states joined together in 1988 to hold a "Super Tuesday" regional primary to enhance their influence and the attention candidates pay them.

Although primaries are still important as testing grounds, the fact that almost three-quarters of the delegates are now chosen in primaries and virtually all of them are selected by a process in which they are committed to a particular candidate encourages candidates to focus on the primaries.

Successfully competing in a primary state requires considerable effort and resources. The federal election law provides candidates having raised significant amounts of small contributions in a number of states with matching funds to carry out their campaign. By accepting federal funds, candidates agree to limit their expenditures in each state based on a formula that takes into account the size of state's electorate. Lacking the typical base of party support available in the general election, candidates must create their own organization and contact voters directly. In small states like New Hampshire, face-to-face contact is both possible and expected. Reflecting the attention candidates give to New Hampshire's first-of-the-season primary, it is not uncommon for voters realistically to state, "I would never vote for a president whose hand I have not shaken and who has never looked me in the eye." Given the state-by-state expenditure limits for money provided through the federal matching fund in primaries, the emphasis on New Hampshire can be seen by the fact that late in the campaign when money gets tight, candidates and their entourage often dash over the border to Vermont late at night for motel rooms in order to conserve their limited New Hampshire allowance. In larger states, primary campaigns rely heavily on the mass media and targeted mail-campaign techniques rather than face-to-face contact. Under these conditions, money becomes even more important.

State Caucuses and Conventions

The national convention delegates not chosen in the primaries emerge from a combination of state and local conventions. In certain states some national convention delegates are chosen at regional conventions with the remainder at the state convention; in other states all delegates emerge from state conventions or state central committees. The large number of local, regional, and state conventions places a great burden on candidate organizations that must monitor and organize large numbers of volunteers. The complexity and number of conventions make anything but local press coverage unlikely except in unique cases. Iowa jumped into the spotlight in 1976 with an early set of precinct caucuses selecting delegates. Press attention on Jimmy Carter's win and Ronald Reagan's strong showing against incumbent president Gerald Ford changed the perception of the campaign, and the Iowa caucuses have now become an accepted major battleground for ambitious candidates. The nomination calendar was pushed back even further for 1988 when Michigan instituted a caucus process for selecting candidates beginning more than two years before the election. When asked why his as-yet-unofficial campaign organization had spent millions in that process, Vice President George Bush argued: "I had to do well there. The press expected it. If I had not done well the headlines would say "Bush campaign falters." We just did not have a choice given the attention the press was going to pay" (NBC-TV, "Today," August 1986).

Although party caucuses initially served to gather the party faithful and facilitate arriving at compromise solutions that would strengthen the party, the opposite is often the case today. With the increased attention paid to caucuses as battlegrounds among presidential contenders, the caucuses now often foment factionalism. An extreme example is Minnesota's "walking subcaucus" rules. After the precinct caucus is convened, the supporters of each candidate form a separate subcaucus and then divide the delegates to be chosen to the next level of convention using a complicated formula. No attempt is made to find common ground or to hammer out a compromise.

The National Conventions

The national convention is the legal decision-making body of the national party, legitimizing rules, nominating candidates, establishing policy positions, and giving direction to party efforts. Aside from generating formal contributions, the convention serves as a reward for activists, provides a setting

TABLE 4.2. REPRESENTATION OF TOP ELECTED OFFICIALS AT NATIONAL PARTY CONVENTIONS

	Year	% of Senators as Delegates	% of House Members as Delegates	% of Governors as Delegates
Democratic Party	1956	90	33	100
	1960	68	45	85
	1964	72	46	61
	1968	68	39	83
	1972	36	15	80
	1976	18	15	47
	1980	14	15	76
	1984	62[a]	67[a]	94
	1988	80[b]	80[b]	100[b]
Republican Party	1968	55	31	88
	1980	63	40	74
	1984	49	43	81

Source: 1956–1980: Polsby, 1983a, p. 114.
[a] Reflects increase due to reserving "superdelegate positions" for elected officials.
[b] Based on 1988 superdelegate provisions.

for building party enthusiasm, and, particularly in the age of mass media, provides the party with a forum for making news.

The Delegates

Each party controls the process of delegate apportionment and selection (subject in many cases to state laws). The apportionment formula determining the number of delegates allowed each state varies significantly by party. The Democratic apportionment formula is based directly on population, and the Republican formula gives bonus delegates to areas of Republican voting strength (see Huckshorn & Bibby, 1983, pp. 659–666). The Democratic convention is significantly larger than the Republican convention (more than 3,000 versus fewer than 2,000 for the Republicans). Recent Democratic reforms (see discussion later in this chapter) have led to dramatic increases in the percentage of blacks, women, and younger voters, but the representativeness of the Republican conventions has increased more slowly. After the first wave of reform that dramatically reduced the number of elected officials at the Democratic conventions (especially in 1972), supplemental special delegate positions for top-level elected officials (governors, members of Congress, and so on) have reversed the trend somewhat (see Table 4.2). Despite increased representativeness of groups targeted by the Democratic party reform commissions (blacks, women, and younger voters), neither the Republican nor the Democratic party convention delegates mirror the population as a whole. After comparing the surveys of delegates to the 1984 conventions, Thomas Edsall concluded that:

TABLE 4.3. CHANGING NATURE OF NATIONAL CONVENTION DELEGATES

| | | Percentage of Delegates in Each Category | | |
	Year	Women	Under 30	Blacks	College Degree
Democratic Party	1968	13	4	7	63
	1972	40	22	15	56
	1976	33	15	11	71
	1980	49	11	14	66
	1984	51	9	17	72
Total Population Democrats in category	1980	56	27	19	12
Republican Party	1968	17	1	2	—
	1972	35	7	3	—
	1976	31	7	3	65
	1980	29	5	3	—
	1984	49	—	4	63
Total Population Republicans in category	1980	53	27	4	18

Sources: Crotty, 1983, pp. 129, 137; Jackson, Brown, & Brown, 1980, p. 208; Keefe, 1987, p. 108; Mitofsky & Plissner, 1980, pp. 37–40; Sussman & John, 1984, p. A6.

In terms of income and education, Democratic and Republican delegates are far better off than the electorate at large. But in terms of ideology, the delegates at the Democratic National Convention... were more liberal, and the Republicans... are more conservative, than voters nationally. (1984a, p. A7)

Table 4.3 reveals the general demographics of the national convention delegates as well as indicating some of the over-time changes. Although revisions of the rules clearly changed the composite picture, convention delegates clearly stand out as a unique group of citizens. Obviously more politically involved, they also tend to come from the higher socioeconomic groups in society. Although the ideological orientation of delegates depends on the success of various presidential contenders, delegates tend to be more extreme in their political views than the average citizen or party adherent.

The Process

The history of political conventions is one of numerous conflicts over the membership, rules, platforms, and nominations. Delegates traditionally came representing state party organizations for a week of enthusiastic speeches, partisan stimulation, and partying, with much of the decision making done by delegation chairpersons wheeling and dealing with their bloc of delegates. Some nominations were swung by enthusiastic floor demonstrations sweeping the crowd, but most were made by decisions far from the public eye. Conventions retain the right to validate their own memberships through their credentials committee. Traditionally, candidates and ideological groups used credentials committee battles to deny opposing delegations the right to participate. (For a historical view see David, Goldman, & Bain, 1960.)

Contemporary conventions are mild compared with their predecessors. There has not been a nomination fight requiring more than one ballot for three decades. The news media find it more and more difficult to spot a legitimate story in the typical predetermined and scripted conventions. Even the "spontaneous" candidate demonstrations are scheduled and controlled. A number of factors account for the change. The heavy reliance on primaries means that an obvious front-runner tends to emerge earlier. The very presence of the electronic media discourages partisans from "washing their dirty linen" with the whole country tuned in. For the first time since television covered conventions, the major networks failed to cover the 1984 convention gavel to gavel. The delegate-selection process has taken its toll. "The convention is now a body dominated by candidate enthusiasts and interest-group delegates who meet to ratify a choice made mostly through primary elections" (Polsby, 1983a, p. 76).

The Platform

Political party platforms are some of the most maligned documents in American politics. As the embodiment of acceptable compromises among groups with relatively widely diverging opinions, they are bound to include significant ambiguity, but they are not meaningless. The process by which the platform is created through preconvention hearings, draft proposals to the convention, and floor votes educates the party in areas of consensus and disagreement, and the list of individuals and groups testifying before the platform committee indicates something about to whom the party listens and wants to appeal. To the degree that the nomination is undecided or the nature of internal party conflicts are unclear, platform votes both within the committee and on the floor serve as tests of strength.

Although long on rhetoric and short on new ideas and explicit controversy, the substance of the platform does signal the general policy preferences of the majority controlling the convention. Subtle and not-so-subtle shifts in party platforms can be significant. When the Republicans backed away from advocating the Equal Rights Amendment in 1980 after support in previous years, it provided a clearer picture of the Reagan majority.

Platforms are designed as documents from which to campaign and not necessarily to govern. They include numerous commitments to goals and causes unlikely to engender much dispute and capable of verifying the party's commitment to what is "good" and "right" (see box). Despite the predominance of campaign rhetoric, there are differences between the stands taken by the two parties. Although only 8 percent of the party pledges between 1944

1984 NATIONAL PARTY PLATFORMS—SELECTIONS

Democratic

A fundamental choice awaits America—a choice between two futures. It is a choice between solving our problems and pretending they don't exist; between the spirit of community and the corrosion of selfishness; between justice for all, and advantage for some; . . . between arms control and an arms race; between leadership and alibis.

America stands at a crossroads.

Move in one direction, and the President who appointed James Watt will appoint the Supreme Court majority. . . . The President who launched a covert war in Central America will determine our human rights policy. . . . The President who opposed every nuclear arms control agreement since the bomb went off will be entrusted with the fate of the earth.

We offer a different direction.

Republican

This year, the American people will choose between two diametrically opposed visions of what America should be. The Republican Party looks at our people and sees a new dawn for the American spirit. The Democratic Party looks at our nation and sees the twilight of the American soul. . . . The Republican Party's vision of America's future . . . begins with the basic premise:

From freedom comes opportunity; from opportunity comes growth; from growth comes progress.

The Democratic Party understands none of this. It thinks our country has passed its peak. It offers Americans redistribution instead of expansion; contraction instead of growth, and despair instead of hope. In foreign policy it asserts the rhetoric of freedom, but in practice it follows a policy of withdrawal and isolation.

Today we declare ourselves the Party of Hope—not for some but for all.

Not every problem cries out for a federal solution. . . . The great tasks of compassion must be accomplished by people who care and by policies which foster economic growth.

★　★　★　★　★

The Reagan Administration measures military might by dollars spent. The Democratic Party seeks a prudent defense based on sound planning and a realistic assessment of threats. . . . We need a President who will understand that human rights and national security interests are mutually supportive.

The supreme purpose of our foreign policy must be to maintain our freedom in a peaceful international environment in which the United States and our allies and friends are secure against military threats . . . we shall keep the peace by keeping our country stronger than any potential adversary.

★   ★   ★   ★   ★

For the 1980's, the Democratic Party will emphasize two fundamental economic goals. We will restore rising living standards in our country. And we will offer every American the opportunity for secure and productive employment.

Free enterprise is fundamental to the American way of life . . . Economic growth enables all citizens to share in the national great physical and spiritual wealth, and it is maximized by giving them the fullest opportunity to engage in economic activities and to retain the rewards of their labor.

★   ★   ★   ★   ★

A top priority of a Democratic administration will be ratification of the unamended Equal Rights Amendment.

The Republican Party is the party of equal rights. From its founding in 1854 we have have promoted equality of opportunity. The Republican Party raffirms its support of pluralism and freedom.

★   ★   ★   ★   ★

We support the tough restraints on the manufacture, transportation and sale of snubnosed handguns, which have no legitimate sporting use and are used in a high proportion of violent crimes.

Republicans will continue to defend the constitutional right to keep and bear arms. When this right is abused and armed felonies are commited, we believe in stiff, mandatory sentencing.

★   ★   ★   ★   ★

The Democratic Platform affirms its support of the principle of religious liberty, religious tolerance and church/state separation and of the Supreme Court decisions forbidding violation of those principles.

The Republican Party supports voluntary prayer in the schools and urges that the federal role in education be limited to reverse the disastrous experiment with centralized direction.

★   ★   ★   ★   ★

The Democratic Party recognizes reproductive freedom as a fundamental human right. We therefore oppose government interference in the reproductive decisions of Americans. . . . The Democratic Party suppports the 1973 Supreme Court decision on abortion rights.

The unborn child has a fundamental individual right which cannot be infringed. We therefore affirm our support for a Human Life Amendment. . . . We oppose the use of public revenues for abortion.

and 1976 were in direct conflict, there has been an over-time increase in differing positions (Pomper, 1980b, pp. 168–170). Far from being pure rhetoric, a significant portion of platform commitments find themselves acted upon by the winning candidate. As Gerald Pomper asserted:

> The most important conclusion to be derived from the mass of figures is that pledges are indeed redeemed. . . . During the last decade of government action, almost two-thirds of all promises were fulfilled in some fashion, with 30 percent directly enacted through congressional or executive initiations. . . . We should take platforms seriously—because politicians seem to take them seriously. (1980b, pp. 161, 176)

Public Relations

With the nomination generally a foregone conclusion before the convention begins and the convention largely accepting the nominee's choice for vice-president and party chairperson by acclamation, the parties have increasingly attempted to script the convention for maximum positive public exposure. The most galvanizing and symbolic speakers are sought to portray the party to the nation as much as to excite the crowd in the convention hall. Slick visual presentations heralding past party heroes and current nominees serve as the first media barrage of the campaign. Each party attempts to troop out not only its political stars but also luminaries from the sports and entertainment realms who support its cause. With the introduction of television, the convention became the ultimate media event. Everything from "spontaneous" demonstrations to speeches are meticulously crafted and scheduled for prime time. George McGovern's willingness in 1972 to allow the platform debate to drag on until the middle of the night and thus force his acceptance speech to be given in the wee hours of the morning was generally regarded as exemplary of his bumbling media campaign, rather than lauded as an expression of open debate and democracy.

Speaking for the party, the national convention presents the country with a presidential nominee having the right to wear the party label and in line for federal campaign funds allocated to the party candidates. From the perspective of the party organization, though, presidential nominations have strayed far from being party activities. The party serves as a host for an event for which the guests are "invited" by others through the primaries. Although the party affects the rules under which invitations are secured, it is a far cry from the party-controlled process that preceded it.

In assessing the role of the parties, the American Assembly concluded that:

> the "reformed" nomination process, particularly on the Democratic side, has weakened the parties and their national conventions . . . that tide should be stemmed and . . . the role of the primary should be increasingly seen as a safety valve if other regular party nominating processes go awry, rather than as the dominant nominating processes which they have become. (1982, p. 8)

Although the point is well taken, it has largely been lost on the party leaders and presidential contenders. The 1988 race shows no abatement of the role of primaries in the process.

The Democratic Party Nomination Reforms

Political parties, like most organizations, respond to failure with introspection and an openness to change. For the Democratic party, the disastrous 1968 convention with riots in the streets and acrimonious conflict on the convention floor (see box, page 126), not only led to a less-than-wholehearted campaign for Hubert Humphrey but also spawned the first in a series of reform commissions. Responding to charges that the 1968 convention failed to represent major components of the Democratic party numerically, the Democrats took a major step in redefining the party. Although the idea of party "membership" has always been a vague concept, it generally has been viewed as those individuals expending the effort to get involved in primaries, caucuses, and conventions. The McGovern Commission (officially the Commission on Party Reform and Delegate Selection, later to be called the McGovern-Fraser Commission when Senator George McGovern's presidential ambitions led him to relinquish the chair to congressman Donald Fraser) began a much broader definition of the party by formulating rules that would increase the opportunities for convention participation by blacks, women, and young people. Driven by a distrust of the old-time party machines, exemplified by the Daley machine that exacerbated the conflict at the 1968 convention in Chicago, and philosophically opposed to almost any form of party organization, the reformers argued that emphasizing the expressive goals of fairer representation not only was the right thing to do but that it would pay off in electoral benefits. The McGovern-Fraser Commission spawned roughly a dozen subsequent commissions, each one usually following an electoral defeat, which formulated and reformulated the rules affecting delegate selection (see Steed, 1985, p. 4).

The McGovern-Fraser Commission (1968–1972)

The McGovern-Fraser Commission began the major departure from past delegate-selection processes that allowed candidates to bypass the primaries, that clearly failed to represent numerically significant portions of the population at the conventions, and that included undeniable patterns of intentional political discrimination. Subsequent commissions largely responded to its initiatives.

The 15 guidelines promoted by the commission emphasized opening the presidential nomination process to the grass-roots party member by requiring open meetings and procedures for delegate selection, requiring potential delegates to state openly their candidate preference, discouraging the selection of delegates by state central committees, and encouraging more local level delegate selection (see Crotty, 1984, pp. 50–51). The most direct and well-

THE DEMOCRATS SELF-DESTRUCT:
THE 1968 CONVENTION

The 1968 Democratic Convention in Chicago shocked the party into beginning a series of structural reforms as it left deep wounds in the party and seared into the memories of millions of Americans dramatic visual images of conflict, repression, and irony. Among the most dramatic images were:

- A CBS television reporter being slugged and beaten to the floor on national television by one of Mayor Richard Daley's security guards; Walter Cronkite, "the most trusted newsman in America," breaking out of his typical objectivity to denounce "Daley's Goons."

- Scenes of students, poor people, radicals, and crazies taunting the police and being beaten over the heads with nightsticks and doused with tear gas—images that would turn the "Yippies" (Youth International party) from a giant put-on into a real political force and that, for years to come, would indelibly label the police as "pigs."

- Richard Daley being cheered on the floor of the convention by his faithful followers while being denounced not only by the people in the streets but also by large segments of the press and the public.

- Senator Abraham Ribicoff (D.-Conn.) denouncing Mayor Daley and the "Gestapo practices on the streets of Chicago" while Richard Daley sits in the front of the auditorium giving the television "cut" signal.

- Hubert Humphrey, on his night of great victory, accepting his party's presidential nomination with a speech extolling the "politics of joy" while the band played "Happy Days Are Here Again," only to have the television networks cut to scenes of marchers in the street, civil disobedience, and what became known as a "police riot."

The above images, and many more like them, taught the Democratic party many lessons, and primary among them was the feeling that somehow what was happening on the floor of the convention was out of touch with what was happening in the streets and, more importantly, out of touch with the concern of many Democrats. This lesson smoothed the way for making the delegate-selection process more democratic and ensuring a wider representation of the population.

publicized rule established quotas for women, blacks, and younger voters. A more indirect consequence arose from the fact that states choosing a primary-election method of selecting delegates would have the composition of their delegation subject to less evaluation. This stimulated a virtual flood of states to move to the presidential primary system (see Table 4.1).

As surprising as the extent of the reforms was the fact that the commission was able to bring about compliance. Boldly asserting its right to force compliance, the consequences of the commission were impressive. State parties revised their own rules and spearheaded efforts to change applicable state laws. Fourteen states adopted the presidential primary in direct response to the commission's guidelines (Huckshorn & Bibby, 1983, p. 661). The 1972 convention saw more than 98 percent of the delegates selected in primaries or open caucuses and conventions, the percentage of black and women delegates tripled, and the percentage of younger delegates increased fourfold over the comparable 1968 figures (Crotty, 1983, p. 62).

Although the results were directly applicable only to the Democratic party, the Republicans felt the fallout from the McGovern-Fraser Commission. Informally, finding their selection procedures compared to the Democrats, the Republicans became more sensitive to the issue of discrimination but did not change the formal rules. More directly, to the degree that the Democratic reforms required legislative action, the Republicans found themselves under the same new state laws requiring primaries and open decision-making processes.

The Mikulski Commission (1972–1974)

The 1972 convention was largely a success according to the McGovern-Fraser Commission guidelines: yet the Democrats suffered one of the most massive defeats in American electoral history. The openness of the convention occurred largely at the cost of reducing the opportunities for participation by the party "regulars" (elected officials, party officials, labor leaders, and so on) who had dominated previous conventions (see Table 4.2). In the wake of defeat they were quick to say "I told you so" and endorsed the establishment of a commission headed by Congresswoman Barbara Mikulski (D-Md.) to undo the changes.

The Mikulski Commission failed to achieve the goals of the party regulars. It basically endorsed the reforms of the McGovern-Fraser Commission and made modest adjustments to mollify the most vocal criticisms (Steed, 1985, p. 7). The quota system was replaced with a less stringent and more vague nonmandatory affirmative-action program. State party committees were given the opportunity to select more delegates in the hope of providing positions for elected officials and minorities. Open primaries were discouraged in favor of selection processes allowing participation by Democrats only. The reformers gained a major victory by including provisions that caucuses and primary decisions allow a proportional division of delegates, rather than a winner-take-all system. Allowing a candidate receiving a threshold of 20 percent of the vote a proportional percentage of the delegates rather than reserving them all for the winner was designed to encourage competition and increase the power of political minorities (see Crotty, 1983, p. 71). The concerns of those interested in more party discussion of issues led to the creation of a midterm party conference.

The Winograd Commission (1975–1978)

Dissatisfied with the extent of the changes promulgated by the Mikulski Commission, and particularly disturbed by the increased importance of primaries that weakened control of the party organization over the nomination process, the party regulars encouraged national chair Robert Strauss quietly to appoint the Winograd Commission to check the influence of primaries.

Although unsuccessful in reducing the number of primaries or reversing much of the effort to open the nomination process, the Winograd Commission did satisfy some demands of the party regulars by reserving 10 percent of the state delegations for public and party officeholders. The commission also promulgated a rule binding delegates to the candidates for whom they were pledged for at least one vote at the convention. After losing out in the delegate-selection process in 1980, Edward Kennedy challenged the binding of delegates, arguing that it reduced the flexibility of the convention, but he lost on the floor.

The Hunt Commission (1980–1984)

The series of reform commissions and the uncertainty of the rules from one convention to the next had begun to take its toll. The press and the public showed less interest, and the reformers and party regulars were getting tired of expending considerable effort on rules. The Hunt Commission discussed a wide variety of issues but limited its recommendations. The rule binding delegates was dropped, but more significantly, the role of the party regulars was increased by creating a larger group of "superdelegates" drawn from the ranks of elected and party officials (governors, members of Congress, and so on) that could be added to each state delegation.

The concept of increasing the number of party professionals was not simply an attempt by the party regulars to ensure their positions but was premised on the argument that their experience allows them to "serve as a voice of reason tempering more extreme proposals" (Cook, 1985c, p. 2159), and the "convention participation would create stronger ties between the party and its officeholders" (Crotty, 1983, p. 98). It was hoped that the superdelegates would remain uncommitted through much of the nomination process, but their early selection "put a great deal of pressure on them to commit early and form a powerful bloc to give potential candidates a psychological momentum" (Cook, 1985c, p. 2159). In 1984 the early commitments made Walter Mondale the obvious winner before most of the primaries had taken place.

The Fairness Commission (1985)

In preparing for the 1988 convention, the opinion was growing that the party had spent enough time on rules and it was time to get on with more productive activity. The Fairness Commission decided to get its work done quickly and deal only with the most onerous unanticipated consequences of previous rule changes. Its recommendations increased the number of superdelegates slightly but delayed their selection to much later in the nomination process, encouraging them to remain uncommitted. It also made minor revisions in reducing the threshold (the minimum percentage required) for dividing numbers of delegates proportionally in a primary and gave up on trying to outlaw open primaries in states such as Wisconsin (see Cook, 1985c, p. 2158).

The Consequences of Democratic Party Reform

In assessing the consequences of reform, one is naturally drawn to an emphasis on the substance of the changes. Although it is clear that particular reforms affected the choice of nominees, and the changes in general affected the composition of the convention, the Democratic party's two decades of emphasis on changing the expressive nature of the party may well be more important for other reasons. Perhaps the most significant direct consequence is not in the substance but in the ability of the national party to dictate rules. Despite the lack of a clear precedent or specific authority, the McGovern-Fraser and subsequent commissions were able to "emit an aura of authority which led to virtually complete success" (Steed, 1985, p. 5).

More indirectly, although *expressive reforms* (those focusing on the degree of democracy in party decision making) and *competitive reforms* (those focusing on the party's capacity to win elections) are not inherently in conflict, the Democratic pursuit of expressive goals over competitive ones between 1968 and the early 1980s seems to have hurt the party competitively. On the one hand, the reforms, even with their belated revisions, weakened party control of the nomination process and "made it easier for issue-oriented enthusiasts and candidate loyalists, rather than party regulars and public officials, to control the party's nominating machinery" (Hershey, 1984, p. 137). Alienated party activists and supportive groups have taken out their disgust by reducing their support for the party and its candidates.

Just as importantly, the energy and resources the Democratic party spent on reforming and enforcing the rules meant that there were fewer resources and less energy for direct support of competitive goals (see Huckshorn & Bibby, 1983, p. 662). Money and effort spent on arranging meetings, doing research, drafting advisory opinions, and ensuring compliance meant money and resources that could not be spent to support candidates.

CONCLUSION

The party's loss of complete control over the nomination stage is one of the major political changes of this century. Once forced to give up control, the party organization has only been able to chip away at the edges to establish a renewed role. On the subpresidential level candidate recruitment and preprimary endorsements provide some, albeit limited, opportunities. The role of the party organization at the presidential level in this candidate-centered age is even more constrained. In a significant number of cases, the party organization accepts the nomination process with fatalism and focuses its effort on the general election.

5

Voters: Intended Targets of Party Influence

Although political parties espouse comprehensive goals affecting all of society, on the day-to-day level where decisions are made, the number one goal remains crafting strategies to catch the fancy of the majority of voters. The major political parties are above all electoral organizations seeking to control the personnel of government through elections. Given the prime role played by voters in this process, the parties expend considerable effort to control the size and composition of the electorate, understand the motivations of voters, and frame strategies likely to result in majorities on election day. The concept of "the voters" or "the electorate" implies more stability than is really the case, since the size, composition, and motivations continually change. Although there have always been generational shifts in composition and to a lesser degree motivations as older voters leave the electorate and young voters enter, recent years have seen both amplifications of traditional shifts and a new set of forces particularly affecting the size and motivations of the electorate. To some degrees the parties remained observers of this process, unable to control the societal and technological changes accounting for the shifts in voting participation and behavior, but in a number of key areas the parties have found ways to channel the changes to their benefit.

WHO VOTES? THE SIZE AND COMPOSITION OF THE ELECTORATE

Although wrapped in the rhetoric of democracy and citizen duty, the act of consistently casting one's vote is carried out by only a minority of eligible citizens. The title of Arthur Hadley's book *The Empty Voting Booth* (1978) expresses the problem. In the wake of day-to-day requirements to pay the mortgage, keep the house in good repair, nurture the children, and pursue one's profession and avocations, taking the time to prepare for voting and actually casting the ballot find stiff competition. Legal barriers thwart some potential voters, but the vast majority of nonvoters choose not to participate.

The Level of Voting Participation

By now most of us are accustomed to being embarrassed by the relatively low voter turnout evidenced by American voters. Since 1945, an average of 58.5 percent of the eligible voting-age population have voted in national elections, and the comparative figures for other Western democracies reveal a much stronger commitment to voting (Australia, 95 percent; West Germany, 87 percent; France, 79 percent; United Kingdom, 77 percent; Canada, 77 percent; Japan, 73 percent; and so on) (see Orren & Verba, 1983, p. 13; Powell, 1982). Eligibility requirements and the frequency of elections vary from country to country. Longer residency requirements, higher age requirements, and less frequent elections all contribute to higher turnout. Although cutting back on residency requirements and lowering the age requirement and the relative frequency with which Americans are called to the polls all account for some of our lower participation rates, they do not fully explain them. Even more discouraging than outright levels of participation in national elections are the significantly lower levels of participation in nonpresidential elections and the overall downward trend in voting participation. As Figure 5.1 reveals, midterm congressional elections draw less than 40 percent of the electorate, and since the 1960s, participation in both presidential and congressional elections has dropped more than 10 percentage points.

One factor in the decline of voter turnout over time is the increased alienation citizens show toward politics in general and toward particular political institutions and processes (Conway, 1985, p. 54). Part of the most dramatic decline during the middle of the period can be accounted for by the infusion of the less participatory 18–21-year-old age group in 1972, but other age groups have also experienced significant declines. A number of factors account for the slight reversal of the trend during the past few elections. Reducing legal and social discrimination for southern blacks and the stimulus of increased two-party competition in the South played a role in increasing the motivation and rewards for participation. An even more optimistic sign comes from the evidence that participation rates are not beyond our control. As described later in this chapter, extensive voter-registration and get-out-the-vote drives by the parties seem to be bearing some fruit.

Overall patterns in turnout mask a number of significant variations from one election to the next. In general, participation levels decline from the high-visibility presidential contests to the lower-stimulus local contests and primary elections. The more hotly contested the election on any level, the more voters that are likely to turn out. Part of this can be accounted for by

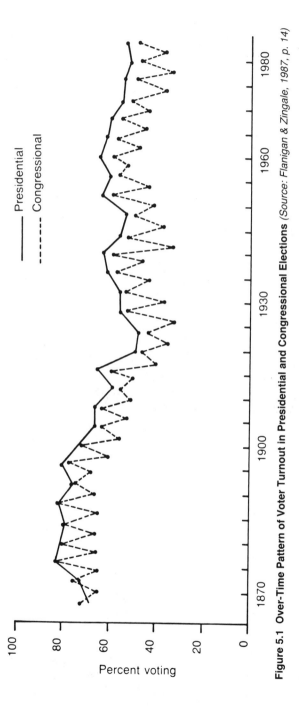

Figure 5.1 Over-Time Pattern of Voter Turnout in Presidential and Congressional Elections *(Source: Flanigan & Zingale, 1987, p. 14)*

increased citizen interest and knowledge and the very nature of a hotly contested race in which candidates and parties expend considerable resources getting people to the polls. Although primaries generally draw a minuscule proportion of the electorate, primary turnout in remaining one-party areas of the South often exceeds that of the general election, since the primary victory is tantamount to election.

The Composition of the Electorate

State laws place relatively few limitations on voting, with virtually everyone over 18 years of age and not a convicted felon having the right to vote. Most states limit voting to those having resided in the state for a certain period (often 30 or 60 days). With the increased physical mobility of American citizens, waiting periods for legal residency have been made significantly lower than they were in previous years.

Although some groups in the population (i.e., more mobile voters) find it more difficult to meet the legal requirements, most of the variation in voting participation involves information and motivation.

The Social Demographics of Voters and Nonvoters

The most general pattern distinguishing voters from nonvoters is *socioeconomic status*, a composite of one's education, income and occupational status—three highly interrelated factors (see Figure 5.2). In general, the higher one's socioeconomic status, the more likely one is to vote. A number of explanations stand out. Education increases understanding of political issues, teaches the procedures for participating, and enhances the realization that one's vote will count. Increased financial well-being gives one a more perceived stake in tax and spending decisions by elected officials, as well as often providing the flexible work schedule and leisure time facilitating participation.

The pervasiveness of socioeconomic status in explaining variations in voting participation masks a number of other factors (see Figure 5.2). Blacks and other minorities vote at much lower rates than whites, but this reflects lower average socioeconomic status rather than some racial component. In fact, in recent years, with increased black awareness, blacks have voted somewhat more than whites of similar socioeconomic status.

Younger voters participate less than older voters for a number of reasons. Although increased physical mobility due to education and job transfers makes registration more difficult, limited experience and resources reduce their perceived stake in political outcomes. After middle age, participation declines again as older voters find it more difficult to vote due to physical problems, and they lose some of their interest in future political decisions.

Differential turnout rates are of more than academic interest since political parties and candidates use this data for planning strategy. Recognizing that demographic groupings have different propensities to support different parties leads the parties to take an interest in increasing participation among their supporters. For example, lower participation rates among blacks sends a signal to Democrats who depend on black voters for support significantly more than do Republicans. Recognizing the potential problem, Democrats carry out strategies to increase black participation to compensate for their lower general tendency to vote. The general unreliability of the black vote, though, reduces the influence of blacks in the Democratic party below their numerical proportions.

The Political Demographics of Voters and Nonvoters

Political Socialization.   For many potential voters, the propensity actually to vote can be traced to their political *socialization*, the informal process in which one informally learns from family and friends appropriate behavior patterns. Children from families in which voting was done as a matter of course are more likely to develop the pattern than children learning early that political activity is either irrelevant or even undesirable (Conway, 1985, pp. 47–48). It is clear that attitudes associated with political participation are not randomly distributed either among the population or among the supporters of the two parties. Lower socioeconomic groups manifesting lower participation rates are less likely to provide their children with attitudes supportive of participation. From a long-run perspective, since such attitudes are passed from one generation to the next, small changes in attitude effectively transmitted can have a mushrooming effect as subsequent generations come along. After studying groups of age cohorts in the population, V. Lance Tarrance concluded that younger voters socialized during periods with lessened family and community pressure to participate will pass these perspectives on and that we should thus expect nonvoting to increase in the future (1979, p. 83). Breaking the cycle of nonparticipation will require the intervention of new influences such as the media and/or the parties.

Party Identification and Participation.   The indirect result of the above direct causes of varying rates of political participation is a pattern of partisan differences that generally disadvantage the Democratic party. The Democratic party, as discussed in greater detail later in this chapter, draws support disproportionately from the less participatory segments of the population such as minorities, the less educated, and generally those on the lower end of the socioeconomic scale. The data in Table 5.1 verify Margaret Conway's general conclusion that "there has also been a consistent pattern across the years of both strong and weak identifiers with the Democratic party being less likely to vote than strong and weak identifiers with the Republican party" (Conway, 1985, p. 133).

The pattern is even more evident in nonpresidential election years when

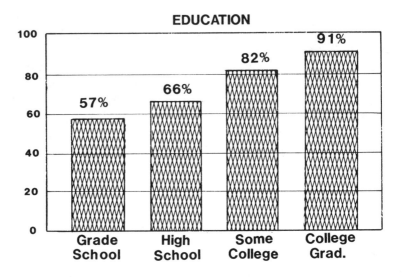

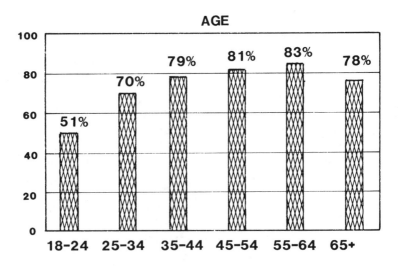

Figure 5.2 Comparative Reported Voter Turnout, 1984
Note: Reported voting levels are somewhat higher than actual voting levels. Higher socioeconomic groups are somewhat more likely to overreport voting (see Hadley, 1978, p. 28), but the differential in honesty does not fully account for the differences among socioeconomic groups. *(Source: 1984 American National Election Study Data, Center for Political Studies, University of Michigan. Data made available through the Inter-University Consortium for Political and Social Research.)*

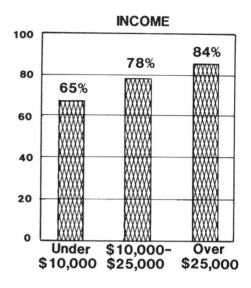

INCOME

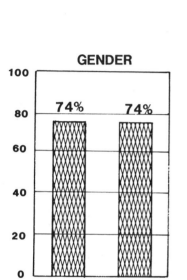

GENDER

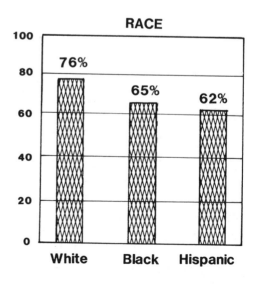

RACE

TABLE 5.1. COMPARATIVE TURNOUT OF PARTISAN GROUPINGS IN PRESIDENTIAL AND OFF-YEAR ELECTIONS

	Percentage of Eligible Voters Voting				
Party Identification	1876 (Pres.)	1978 (Off Yr.)	1980 (Pres.)	1982 (Off Yr.)	1984 (Pres.)
Strong Democrat	83	55	86	76	92
Weak Democrat	70	36	67	60	69
Independent	63	27	54	36	64
Weak Republican	76	51	77	60	78
Strong Republican	93	65	90	80	89

Source: 1976–1984: adapted from Conway, 1985, pp. 131, 134.
Note: Data exclude southern states.

the lack of publicity and stimulation leads to a significantly greater drop in voting by Democrats than voting by Republicans. Democratic candidates find themselves faced with a significantly greater task in getting their voters to the polls, whereas Republican candidates can almost assume turnout of their partisans and can focus their efforts on converting and activating the more undecided voters.

The Partisan Mix of Different Elections.   Both the number and type of voters vary as one moves from primaries to presidential and nonpresidential elections. Primaries are legally limited to formally registered partisans in most states and involve individuals with more interest in politics and more extreme policy positions. Most primaries draw little media attention and do little to stimulate expanded participation. Presidential election campaigns, on the other hand, disseminate considerable information and receive extensive media coverage leading to more excitement and a surge of voting by the more peripheral and less partisan voters. Such less-committed voters are drawn disproportionately to the party of the most popular presidential candidate, swelling his or her vote total and helping the lower-level candidates of the party. The decline in information and excitement in midterm congressional and local elections leads to participation by the most motivated activists and returns the partisan division to normal (Campbell, 1985, p. 25). The electoral implications of this surge and decline of voters reveals itself in the fact that winning presidential candidates normally boost the number of their fellow partisans in Congress, whereas during the past seven midterms the president's party lost an average of nearly 29 seats in House. The more general implication of the surge-and-decline pattern is that parties and their candidates must use different strategies depending on the type of election. Primaries, with the lack of a party cue, and limited to motivated party activists, are fought more on the basis of issues or the personal traits of the candidates. Presidential elections reintroduce the party as a voting cue, but include a much higher percentage of weak partisans and independents. The off-year elections provide the most likely forum for candidates to battle along partisan lines.

Surmounting the Legal Impediments to Voting

Voter Registration

Campaigns attempt to activate and motivate voters, and one of the most effective campaign techniques involves directly manipulating the composition of the eligible electorate. Voting participation in most states involves a two-step process, registering as a voter well before the election and voting on election day. Getting people registered is the key hurdle in getting them to vote. Whereas only 68.0 percent of the eligible voters registered in 1984, 88.0 percent of those registered eventually voted, for a reported turnout of 59.9 percent of all eligible voters. The percentage registered and percentage voting figures are inflated since they are based on reported behavior from public opinion polls, and respondents tend to inflate their levels of participation to make themselves look like better citizens. Actual turnout in 1984, based on election figures, was 53.0 percent (U.S. Department of Commerce, 1985). State laws vary considerably concerning the ease and process of registering. The parties and candidates support those registration procedures they perceive as most beneficial to their partisan cause.

The trend in recent years is toward less-restrictive registration requirements and procedures. The period of residency required to register has generally declined, with some states allowing election day registration. Many states allow mobile registrars to set up shop at county fairs and shopping centers, rather than requiring potential registrants to come to government offices during business hours. Some states allow party workers to be deputized as registrars to register supporters selectively. Other states simplify the process by allowing registration by mail or "voter-motor" procedures enabling voters to register when they apply for a driver's license. Traditionally, registration lists were purged of voters who had not participated in a set number of elections, but a number of states have shifted to permanent registration whereby voters are not automatically stricken from the current rolls by not voting. In the process of opening the registration process, two patterns stand out. The majority party in a state generally shows considerable hesitancy to change a registration pattern under which it has prospered, whereas the minority party looking for a new breath of life embraces change. Recognizing that about two-thirds of unregistered voters would generally vote Democratic, Republicans have generally opposed plans to make registration easier. Although politicians almost universally act on the premise that increased turnout helps the Democrats, some research argues that the situation is more complex (DeNardo, 1980; Tucker, Vedlitz, & DeNardo, 1986). Minority parties that can stimulate large defections from the majority party could benefit more from a large turnout than the majority party in a constituency.

Whatever the procedures, the two parties approach registration drives in different ways. Accustomed to being the minority party among nonregistered voters, Republicans tend to use "rifle" approaches, targeting likely Republicans and approaching them individually to register. This may involve a party worker taking a "poll" on party preference either by telephone or at the door, with a follow-up visit or call only to the identified Republicans to encourage or carry out registration. The efficiency of this process has been greatly enhanced by the capacity of computers to create and monitor contact lists. Democrats, on the other hand, recognizing the generally larger pool of nonregistrants likely to support their cause, use a "shotgun" approach, encouraging registration through the media and setting up registrars in high-traffic areas, knowing that they will get more than their share of Democrats naturally. In 1984 the Reagan administration challenged registration programs in state agencies when they discovered that welfare offices were being used. "They assumed—and probably rightfully so—that most voters who were also welfare clients would register as Democrats" (Cain & McCue, 1985, p. 5).

The year 1984 became a banner year for emphasizing voter registration. The Jesse Jackson campaign registered thousands of black voters, particularly in key urban areas. The Republican party countered with a multimillion dollar national registration and get-out-the vote drive, although "to some extent the GOP registration surge was spontaneous and self-generating . . . only 33% of the newly registered whites had been signed up by organizations, as opposed to 47% of newly registered blacks" (Cavanaugh & Sundquist, 1985, p. 48).

The effect of increased registration in 1984 reversed the downward trend in presidential election participation, increasing turnout to 53.3 percent after the historical low of 52.6 percent in 1980. The Republican success in the registration battle can be seen by the fact that Ronald Reagan did better among new registrants in 1984 than among voters in general, and new registrants gave 54.0 percent of their votes to Republican candidates for the House of Representatives, despite the Democratic success among all voters for those offices (Reichley, 1985, p. 194).

Buoyed by their success in 1984, the Republicans launched an aggressive registration drive in 1984 designed to lure lifelong southern Democrats into the Republican party, which now stood for the principles in which they believed. Operation "Open Door" received mixed reviews. Aiming for 100,000 switchers in targeted states, the Republicans fell short but showed some impressive gains. More than 54,000 voters actually switched their registration to the Republican party, and another 43,000 indicated a commitment to do so (Peterson, 1985, p. A3). The Republicans pointed to the thousands of newly registered Republican voters, and Democrats pointed out that the Republicans did not reach their stated goal and that many of the newly registered voters were new residents and not former Democrats.

TABLE 5.2. EXPRESSED REASONS FOR NONVOTING BY REGISTERED VOTERS, 1980 (IN PERCENTAGES)

Motivational Factors	
Not interested/Don't care	11.2
Didn't prefer any candidate	16.0
Subtotal	27.2
Voting Mechanics	24.4
No way to get to the polls/Out of town on election day/ Could not take time off work/etc.	
Incapacity	
Sick/Family emergency	17.1
Other Reasons/No Reason Specified[a]	31.3

Source: U.S. Department of Commerce, *Current Population Reports*, "Voting and Registration in the Election of November 1980," Series P-20, no. 370 (1980): 7.
[a] Due to funding cutbacks in the Census Bureau, this question was not asked after 1980.

In a more ill-fated project, the Republican National Committee embarked on a "Ballot Security" program in anticipation of the 1986 elections. Publicly justified as purging the voting lists of voters who had not kept their voting records up to date, letters were sent to voters in precincts where Ronald Reagan had received less than 20 percent of the vote in 1984. If the letter came back as undeliverable at that address, it became the basis for asking that the voter's name be purged. After becoming public, the focus on Democratic and particularly black precincts caused a great deal of embarrassment, and the program was eventually dropped (Taylor, 1986b, p. 11).

In many areas, the parties have recaptured their party-building role by taking on tasks, such as registering voters, that they had let fall to the candidates by default. An in-depth study of registration in Los Angeles showed that the party organization registered most new voters, Republicans out-registered the Democrats, and contrary to previous assumptions, these newly registered voters were very likely to vote (Cain & McCue, 1985, p. 16).

Getting the Voters to the Polls

It does little good to field strong candidates and convince voters of their worth if the voters never get to the polls to cast their ballots. Table 5.2 outlines the reasons nonvoters gave for failing to vote in 1980. Although individuals may be somewhat hesitant to outline honestly their reasons for nonvoting, the figures cause some concern. Whereas about 30 percent of the nonvoters expressed a lack of motivation to vote and reflect a failure of the campaign to have its intended impact, close to 25 percent of the nonvoters specifically identified problems with voting procedures and mechanics. Many of the reasons given suggest strategies the parties may attempt to increase participation. Although both parties are plagued with nonvoters among their ranks, the problem of nonvoting tends to affect Democrats more than Republicans (Conway, 1985, pp. 130–133; see DeNardo, 1980; and Tucker, Vedlitz, & DeNardo, 1986, for a conflicting opinion). Three separate aspects of voter mobilization concern the parties and their candidates: easing the process of voting, getting their supporters to the polls, and capitalizing on the absentee-ballot provisions.

Facilitating the Voting Process.   Although few political activists openly condone placing increased impediments to voting, the parties espouse conflicting rhetoric to justify the political strategies most advantageous to their cause. Democrats indicate their belief in democracy by supporting increased and more convenient voting precincts (often located in areas of party strength such as low-income neighborhoods or publicly supported senior citizens apartments), longer voting hours, and simplified procedures—all of which are gauged to increase Democratic turnout. Democrats go beyond public voting legislation to encourage turnout by encouraging corporations to allow their hourly employees paid leave time to cast their ballots. In some cases this becomes part of a union contract. This emphasis makes sense since hourly employees are more likely to vote Democratic, whereas a higher percentage of salaried employees are Republican and already have more freedom in setting their schedules. Although supportive of democracy, Democratic leaders seem to take a contradictory position by opposing frequent elections focusing on different levels of government, realizing that the more times they must troop out their voters, the more difficult it will be to get them to the polls each time. The Democrats would much rather combine federal, state, and local elections on the same day and focus their efforts on getting their voters out less frequently.

Whereas the Democrats emphasize democracy, the Republicans exclaim the rhetoric of voter responsibility. Knowing that their supporters are much more likely to turn out, Republican leaders argue that citizens should not be forced to the polls against their will. Republicans smugly assert that by making voting too easy, the overall quality of the electorate and its decisions will decline. Voters with enough responsibility to take some effort to vote will, according to the Republican case, take the effort to inform themselves and vote more responsibly. Building on the rhetoric of voter responsibility, Republicans add the theme of fiscal responsibility, arguing that proliferation of voting precincts and added hours use tax dollars unwisely and that Democratic encouragement of time off for voting and proposals to make election day a holiday would reduce American productivity. Taking a seemingly inconsistent approach, Republican leaders are much more likely to support separating federal, state, and local elections, requiring voters to come to the polls (and requiring added expenditures) more frequently and ensuring that more local races not get lost in the hoopla of the major races.

Although a feasible case can be made for maximizing either democracy or responsibility, these rhetorical volleys mask the true motivations. Each party supports voting laws designed to ensure a mix of voters most likely to support its candidates. In states with two relatively strong parties, the competing forces result in election laws that are advantageous to neither party exclusively, but in one-party areas this may not be the case. For example, majority parties in one-party states tend to encourage approaches such as mobile registrars (not requiring potential voters to come to government offices to register), postcard registration, or election day registration. Under such rules they are likely to garner more new voters than the minority party.

Get-Out-the-Vote Drives.   The act of voting for most citizens competes with numerous other responsibilities: working late at the office, picking up school-children in the car pool, hurrying to a second job, finishing projects around the house, experiencing the inability to get to the polls, or simply forgetting about the election. Although competing responsibilities impinge on the supporters of both parties, Democrats feel a greater brunt of the impediments and respond with more intensive effort on election day. A greater percentage of Democratic party and campaign expenditures involve telephone banks to remind voters to vote, poll watchers to identify nonparticipants, and transportation projects to get people to the polls.

Absentee Ballots.   Many voters find it impossible to cast their ballots in person due to travel or health problems. Until recently, the parties only sporadically took advantage of the role they could play, stimulating absentee-ballot voting. The Republican absentee-ballot strategy in the 1982 California governor's race was seen as the margin of victory and serves as a pattern for other party organizations. Using the computer and party mailing lists to identify likely voters in need of absentee ballots (older voters, sales people, military personnel, and so on) and in Republican areas, the party distributed thousands of absentee-ballot applications. Those returning the application were registered and sent a ballot. A follow-up telephone bank followed to make sure they actually voted. On the basis of a very narrow margin that could be fully accountable by the Republican advantage in absentee ballots, George Deukmejian became governor of California, a state that has recently elected a majority of Democrats to state and local office.

UNDERSTANDING THE AMERICAN VOTER

Democracy places a great deal of responsibility on the average citizen. Rather than being a loyal subject taking direction from a presumably wise and assuredly powerful leader, a citizen in a democracy is expected to define his or her preferences, gather extensive information on the capabilities and positions of potential leaders, and assess the utility of choosing one candidate over another in an election. Although observers were always aware of the unrealistic expectations placed on voters to analyze rationally and exhaustively each electoral decision independently, it was not until the advent of modern polling techniques in the middle of this century that we began to get a firmer picture of how voters actually made up thier minds.

The Initial Profile of Voters: Identifying Voter Shortcuts

Recognizing the unrealistic expectations of voters, early studies looked for shortcuts by which voters could simplify voting decisions. Two interrelated but separate research paths developed. One focused on the process by which voters acquired and used information to direct their voting choices. The other looked more deeply at the motivations behind voting choices. Within each focus there developed similar alternative images of the voter as he or she went about making a voting decision. The most common early image portrayed a *dependent voter* (see Pomper, 1975, pp. 5–9) approaching each election with a relatively fixed set of social and political characteristics, established well before the election, relatively immune to change and serving as both a predictor and explanation of electoral behavior. Research focused on determining those fixed factors best able to predict the electoral behavior of most voters. Studies concluded with statements that "blacks tend to vote Democratic" or that "people in business usually support the Republican candidate." Although fixed factors such as social status and party loyalty provided the general contour of the electorate, they implied a static model, not accounting for change over time or dramatic changes in voting behavior from one election to the next. Focusing on the volatile aspects of elections, the *responsive-voter model* emphasizes the conditions under which more short-term factors such as issues and candidate images can overcome long-term patterns and begin the processes by which long-term patterns break down. Studies were more likley to conclude that "voters dissatisfied with the handling of the Iran hostage situation abandoned Jimmy Carter for Ronald Reagan" or that "the public trusted Ronald Reagan more than Walter Mondale."

Although researchers are far from agreement about which model best represents reality, the discussions that follow on the two major focuses (information processing and voter motivations) agree on two aspects. First, the methods of research affect the nature of the results. Asking certain kinds of questions of certain types of voters determines the ultimate findings. The earliest studies of individual voters used small samples of narrow geographic areas to gather extensive information on the background and behavior of voters (Lazarsfeld, Berelson, & Gaudet, 1944; Berelson, Lazarsfeld, & McPhee, 1954) or emphasized fixed social and political factors (Campbell, Converse, Miller, & Stokes, 1960). Later studies more extensively analyzed those voters breaking away from their predicted moorings. Second, a consensus grew that since the earliest studies in the 1940s and 1950s, the nature of the American electorate and the technology of political communication had changed significantly to increase the necessity or opportunity for more responsive voting.

Information Processing and the Vote

Recognizing the tremendous information costs associated with voting, the early studies assessed the ways in which the typical voter gathered the information needed for voting decisions. Despite relatively wide availability of political information through newspapers, magazines, and the radio, research discovered a "two-step" flow of information (Lazarsfeld et al., 1944; Berelson et al., 1954) in which the more-aware segments of the population passed on political cues to their less-informed acquaintances, often accompanied by their biased evaluation. Perhaps because the primary researchers were sociologists working in the political realm, the process of "opinion leadership" emphasized the social setting. Since individuals with similar outlooks tended to associate over long periods, opinion leaders affected large blocs of voters and imbued them with relatively consistent outlooks. Voting could be explained by the demographic variables (i.e., education, income, occupation, race, and so on) that tended to group blocs of voters. Local opinion leaders often served as party officials such as precinct or ward chairpersons and did not hesitate to extol the virtues of their party while belittling the other party. Newspapers, the prime information source for the opinion leaders, often took a partisan stance, and voters paid attention to opinion leaders who selectively disseminated partisan views in a more palatable form.

Not only do the information sources reflect a biased selection and presentation of information, but the information recipients (the voters) also develop selective patterns for gathering and evaluating information. Armed with vague candidate or party loyalties, voters seek out (*selective attention*), respond favorably to (*selective perception*), and remember (*selective retention*) information supportive of "their" candidate or party (Stokes & Miller, 1962). Thus a vague preference is bolstered by supportive information, which in turn solidifies the preference and encourages increased selective information acquisition that can be used to justify the stand to oneself and others. Far from being the most objective analysts, voters with the most information are likely to have acquired it in the most biased manner. A shortcut clue as to one's political preferences becomes a listing of the information sources one chooses to use. Loyal readers of the *National Review* or listeners of "Paul Harvey News" are generally conservatives, not open-minded seekers of a broad range of views, whereas readers of *The New Republic* or *Ramparts* use the material to bolster their liberal views. During political campaigns, Republicans tend to read Republican candidate literature and listen to Republican advertisements, and Democrats do the same for material generated by their party or candidate. Even in situations such as candidate debates in which selective attention cannot be brought into play, partisans tend to remember more of what their candidate said (*selective retention*) and to view their candidate as the "winner" of the debate (*selective perception*) (see Abramowitz, 1978, passim). The ultimate determination of the winner of presidential debates is deeply affected by the media itself. Although early polls showed Walter Mondale "winning" the first debate against Ronald Reagan in 1984, the more the media covered the story, the larger the percentage of the public that saw Mondale as the winner (Light & Lake, 1985, p. 101).

Changes in the availability and technology of communications affect the process by which voters acquire political information. Face-to-face communications between friends or between a party worker and voter gave way to less personal media that is less likely to provide consistent partisan cues.

With the development of the electronic media (primarily television) fewer citizens needed their information channeled through opinion leaders. More than 75 percent of voters reported television as their primary source of political information. The hapless party precinct worker interrupting a television program "must either stay and watch in silence or else excuse himself and quickly move on" (Banfield & Wilson, 1963, p. 122). Although television is not immune to partisan and ideological biases, the "massness" of the emerging mass media worked against extreme positions. For a television newscast or entertainment program to be acceptable to its diverse audience and satisfy the licensing requirements of the Federal Communications Commission, the goal, if not the reality of objectivity, came into focus. Unlike many of the newspapers owned or heavily influenced by a particular party, television stations and networks eschewed partisan labels and presentations. In every election year between 1956 and 1980, more than 75 percent of major newspapers endorsed the Republican presidential candidate (Hennessey, 1981, p. 244). Although television stations do not formally endorse candidates, there has been a lingering belief that they have consistent partisan biases. Careful analysis of campaign coverage fails to reveal a consistent pattern of partian bias favoring one party or the other in television news (see Hennessey, 1981; Patterson, 1980). The voter depending on television news was faced with more information but fewer direct voting cues. Research on voter biases in selecting, interpreting, and remembering political information transmitted via television news programs indicates that it is the volume and nature of the coverage more than voter choice that determines what is communicated (Patterson, 1980, pp. 84–86). Along with the shift to less-partisan news came easier access to state and national news relative to coverage of local candidates and issues. Although a local newspaper could afford to focus on community politics, the extensive equipment costs of broadcasting encouraged television stations and networks to capitalize on economies of scale by covering larger media markets that had more heterogeneous audiences. The broader and more diverse geographic areas encouraged stations to emphasize those political aspects common to the largest portion of the audience.

Not only did the shift to television as the primary source of political news change the geographic emphasis, it also changed the substance of news coverage. Recognizing the difficulty of portraying the nuances of issues in a medium emphasizing visual images and excitement, news coverage of campaigns focused on the "horse race" aspects of politics—Who's winning? What strategies are being used? What is the true story of the conflicts within the campaign? (see Patterson & McClure, 1976; Patterson, 1980).

Earlier research on selectivity of voter-information processing and extensive evidence (and criticism) of the mass media's failure to provide voters with the kinds of issue and candidate-performance information necessary to make voting choices reinforced the conventional wisdom that campaigns do not change voting intentions. At best, the campaign was seen as reinforcing prior intentions and activating voters to the degree that they would actually cast their ballots. Up to this point, research on campaign information processing largely supported the dependent voter model, whether it was opinion leaders structuring campaign information or voters assimilating political information in ways designed to support preexisting preferences. By initially rejecting the mass-media coverage of politics as a viable explanation for causing voting decisions, the information-processing focus did little to explain the increased voter volatility beginning in the 1960s and reaching new heights in later decades.

One information-associated explanation grew out of a careful look at the varieties of mass media, even within the constrained realm of television. Although television news may be too general and nonissue oriented to shift voter outlooks, paid television advertising, particularly short spot advertising not subject to the selective attention of viewers, accounts for significant information acquisition (Patterson & McClure, 1976; Patterson, 1980; Joslyn, 1984, p. 216). Viewers are accustomed to advertising spots so that they do not turn them off (the selective inattention that does plague longer political advertisements), they see them seldom enough to make them interesting to watch, and they can present dramatic differences between the candidates and parties in a simple, easy-to-comprehend way. Although spot advertising is only feasible in well-financed campaigns for major offices, and the amount of information that can be presented is limited, "even a tiny morsel of meaningful information gleaned from campaign communication can be important because it may be all the voter has to work with" (Joslyn, 1984, p. 216).

Voter Motivations

The act of voting represents a complex process. The voter may or may not be able to verbalize or even recognize the process he or she went through to make a voting decision. The concept of "motivation" implies a basic assumption that human behavior is goal oriented. The act of voting is viewed as contributing to one or a number of goals. It also assumes that voters are at least subjectively rational. *Subjective rationality* means that voters can satisfy themselves that their votes made sense. Few, if any, voters leave the voting booth saying, "Boy did I just do a stupid thing." Most can give an explanation for their act. However, the explanation may not satisfy the criterion of *objective rationality* imposed by an outside observer. Voters supporting Ronald Reagan under the misperception that he wanted to increase government spending would not be seen as objectively rational but, until convinced that their perceptions were wrong, would view their votes as subjectively rational. Any other perspective on the vote implies that voting is a reflex reaction or an idiosyncratic behavior devoid of a reasonable pattern. A variety of possible motivations may help explain an individual's vote. Although the motivations are interrelated, voters can be viewed as deciding on the basis of instrumental, social, or psychological goals.

Voters who approach their electoral decision from an *instrumental perspective* view their voting decision as a way to affect the policies and performance of government by determining governmental personnel. The instrumental voter best fits the democratic ideal of the voter facing each electoral choice anew with a firm view of his policy goals and relevant information on the policy stands and likely performance of the candidates. Unbound by previous personal voting decisions, the instrumental voter combines an assessment of past candidate performance with current promises for each candidate and votes for the one most likely to help the voter reach his or her policy goals. The assessment involves both the policy perspectives of the candidates and their potential for performance in office. Performance in office could mean anything from the ability to pursue preferred policies successfully to getting the voter individual help by intervening with the bureaucracy. For example, committee chairs in Congress openly flaunt their power positions as a measure of their performance potential, whereas more junior members assert their willingness to satisfy the casework demands of their constituents.

Incumbents encourage voters to reward their past performance by encouraging them not to "change horses in midstream" or to "stay the course," and challengers proclaim "I will not lie to you" or ask, "Are you better off today than you were when the incumbent was elected?" Factors such as the candidate's party give clues to potential performance. Morris Fiorina (1981) asserted that a candidate's party label associates him with a cumulative remembered assessment of the party's successes and failures. The candidate's previous political experience and current endorsements by political and community leaders contribute additional evaluative information to the voter's decision, but none of these factors is individually determinative for all voters. If the winners perform satisfactorily and pursue the policy interests of the voters, they are likely to be supported again in the next election, but it, too, is a new contest, and voter support is contingent upon the relative stands and performance potential of an opponent. The instrumental voter is a clear case of "responsive" voting. As personal preferences, candidate stands, and assessments of performance change, voters respond to the new set of choices.

Social voters are motivated by the impressions of others. Human beings exist as participants in a complex set of social interactions from primary groups such as the family to secondary groups at work or school to a sense of membership in ethnic, religious, regional, and other groupings. Considerable research reveals that through the socialization process we develop our basic outlooks, values, and attitudes, some of which are political. Young children informally emulate the outlooks of friends and family, and social groups attempt directly to teach their members "appropriate outlooks." Agreeing with those around us makes life more pleasant and serves to compliment the wisdom of those whose values and outlooks we have acquired. Individuals breaking from the group perspective run the risk of dirty looks, specific scolding, or even ostracism. Traditionally, newly socialized individuals could look forward to a long period of interaction with people of similar outlooks, and members of social groupings went through similar life experiences and had similar political needs. Given these similarities in outlook and the likelihood that social groups would transmit information supportive of the conventional group wisdom, it was understandable that they would vote in similar ways. Reliance on social factors led to viewing voters as "dependent" on the forces that shaped their outlooks well before the current election and which would be informally enforced by the social group.

Although no theory of group socialization assumes a perfect transfer of attitudes and outlooks, recent societal changes have affected the traditional socialization process. The impact of friends and family has been challenged by alternative sources of outlooks, especially from the mass media (Conway, 1985, p. 48). The increased physical mobility interrupts group interaction, and the social mobility gives younger group members a wide variety of new life experiences combined to diminish simple patterns of socialization. In contemporary society, where mass media has replaced information interchange within social groups, where approximately one-fifth of the population moves each year leaving behind friends and family, and where more open education and career patterns allow more individuals to break with the past, the social bonds that made prediction simpler no longer apply. Individuals still seek the guidance and approval of social groupings, but for individual voters, the particular groups to which they look vary over time. Increasingly, individuals find themselves torn in a number of directions by their various social affiliations. The son of immigrant working-class parents who goes off to college and a career in business may well be under cross-pressures when it comes to voting, and there is no clear evidence whether early outlooks or current associations will generally prevail.

In the voting booth, the unique characteristic of "social voters" is their attempt to please others with their vote. Although the original circumstances leading to a particular political orientation may not be remembered, this type of voter carries out a pattern of voting traceable to either early socialization or the influence of contemporary associates.

Some voters are motivated by *psychological identity*. Each individual goes through life with an image of who he or she is both in politics and in other realms. Although the search for one's identity is a never-ending process, increasing age and experience tend to solidify one's self-image. These images include both the labels by which we describe ourselves (Republican, liberal, Democrat, moderate, Independent, conservative, and so on), the causes with which we identify (the Republican party, the Democratic party, environmentalists, anti-Communists, and so on), and the behavior patterns we attempt to emulate (i.e., honesty, consistency, thoughtfulness, intellectualism). Politics provides us with the opportunity to verify our own self-image, an important activity for psychological well-being. Thus the self-identified Republican voting for the Republican candidate feels good for verifying his own label as a Republican, for supporting the Republican party cause, and for maintaining consistent behavior.

By now it should be clear that the same behavior may result from a myriad of different motivations. Party-line Republicans may have made a judgment independently in each election that the Republican candidates best serve their policy goals. Or they may be attempting to curry the favor of family or friends. Or they may be following a self-image with a distant source no longer having a direct influence. To the degree that psychological voters are captives of their self-images, they are dependent voters.

In the voting booth, the psychologically motivated voter supports a candidate because of a match between the voter's and the candidate's labels. These labels may have initially developed through a process of group socialization or a judgment about which party or cause would help the individual serve his or her policy needs, but those motivations have receded to the background with psychological identity coming to the fore.

VOTING RESEARCH AND THE PARTIES

Extensive analysis of voter behavior began with the presidential elections in the 1940s. Although focusing on information flow and opinion leadership, their findings emphasized other social components of the vote (see Lazarsfeld et al., 1944: Berelson et al., 1954). Using demographic variables such as education, income, and occupation, Paul Lazarsfeld created the "Index of Political Predispositions" designed to predict the voting behavior of various groups within the population. Extensive effort was placed on tracing the voting patterns of blocs of voters such as Catholics, blacks, and various educational groups. Research moved more directly into the hands of political scientists with the continuing series of surveys done by scholars at the Survey Research Center at the University of Michigan. Beginning with the publication of *The American Voter* in 1960, results of these surveys give us the first long-term look at the change and continuity of voting behavior.

The earliest studies confirmed the intuitive assumptions that few voters carefully based each vote on an analysis of all information and alternatives. Rather, most voters approached the election with a "standing decision" (a dependent voter approach) largely linked to their own sense of the best party to promote their interests. Although specific short-term forces such as an issue, candidate personality, or historical event might have swayed a few voters from their partisan moorings, most of them stayed with their party.

In the study of the 1956 election, very few voters (11.5 percent) explained their preference for one party over another in ideological terms. A larger number (24.0 percent) supported the party in power when times were good for them and shifted when times were bad. The largest percentage (42.0 percent) associated the interests of the key groups to which they belonged to one party or another, and the others (22.5 percent) either blindly followed the party or voted on the basis of no issue or ideological position (Campbell et al., 1960, pp. 216–265).

The Primacy of Party Identification

Although voters were seen as varying in their motivations, an underlying theme of early empirical voting studies emphasized the cardinal position of the individual's self-indentification in partisan terms. The concept of party identification pervades much of our knowledge about both the electorate and political parties.

> Labeling attachment to a political party as "identification" rather than "membership" or "affiliation" was an intentional attempt to clearly identify the limits and nature of the relationship. When one identifies with a group or organization, it is a psychological linkage rather than a physical one. The party identifier sees party stands worthy of emulation and thereby accepts their orientation to the political world and sees political matters as other party members see them. Party identification simplifies decisions in the political realm by filtering out information and interpretations of political events and giving the person the preferred way to act. (Wattenberg, 1984, p. 12)

Party identification is seen as having *direction*, as in response to the question "Do you consider yourself to be a Republican, Democrat, Independent, or other?" and in some cases *intensity*, in the degree to which one feels attached to one party or the other.

> In its social-psychological sense, [party identification] means "feeling part of" or "akin to." Individuals *consider themselves* part of organizations with which they have no formal attachment. It is on the basis of identification that we usually speak of people as Democrats or Republicans. (Wasby, 1970, p. 313)

The importance of party identification lies less in its measurement than in the assertion that psychological identification serves as a precursor to behavior. In the most explicit models, party identification *causes* one's voting choices, and in the less strict view, party identification at least *predicts* voting and may be based on either social or instrumental motivations.

The Origins of Individual Party Identification

In its most precise definition, party identification is a psychological attachment devoid of other motivations, but no one is born a Democrat or Republican.

TABLE 5.3. SOCIAL TRANSMISSION OF PARTY IDENTITIES, 1980

	Parties of Mother and Father				
Party Identification of Child	Both Democrat (%)	Both Independent (%)	Both Republican (%)	Father Democrat/ Mother Republican (%)	Mother Democrat/ Father Republican (%)
Democrat	64	14	11	29	29
Independent	26	80	29	39	34
Republican	9	6	60	30	21

Source: Adapted from Sorauf, 1984, p. 142.
Note: Table omits individuals who did not answer or who did not specify Republican, Democratic, or Independent party identification for themselves or their parents.

Two general processes serve to develop a sense of attachment in voters. Children born in a particular *social setting* emulate the identification of their family and friends and find that espousing the appropriate identifications stimulates approval of those whom they wish to impress. Five-year-old Johnny parroting his parent's partisan stance is patted on the head and told, "What a bright little boy you are." The child making inappropriate partisan statements is either ignored or chastised. The nature and consistency of social cues vary. Children born into families in which both parents have strong and consistent partisan attitudes are considerably more likely to be partisan and follow the parental outlook than are children from households with weak partisan outlooks or in which parents disagree in their party commitments. Although conventional wisdom suggests that fathers serve as political role models more than mothers, empirical evidence indicates that this was true only for less-educated children in the past (Jennings & Langton, 1969), and the situation has more recently been reversed, with mothers becoming slightly more likely to influence partisan choices (see Table 5.3). Parents may be the earliest and most effective agents of political socialization, but they clearly are not the only force. At any age, the desire to please others can intervene, but the earliest social forces tend to have more staying power.

In regard to *instrumental motivations*, partisan identification can also stem from a voter's calculated evaluations of the parties and their traditional stands on the issues. The policies of each party appeal to different groups in the population. Voting consistently with one's self-interest over a number of elections and finding that it leads one to consistent support of a particular party eventually leads one to develop a sense of loyalty to that party and a willingness to use a candidate's party label as a shortcut cue for voting. The conventional wisdom shared by various population groupings among the electorate as to the party best serving their interests is reflected in the partisan loyalties of these groupings. In contemporary politics, blacks heavily favor the Democratic party, and union members and lower-income individuals are somewhat more

Democratic than the population as a whole. Individuals associated with business and wealthier individuals provide stronger support to the Republican party. Such continuing allegiances make sense given the types of policies each party supports.

Few voters develop a party identification solely on the basis of social or instrumental motivations; in real life, there is an *interaction of motivations*. Children socialized to support a particular party tend to interact primarily in later life with people having outlooks similar to those of their parents and have their social motivations reinforced. Furthermore, children tend to develop life-styles and political needs similar to those of their parents and find that a party identification forged by social needs also satisfies their instrumental needs. Individuals choosing a party on the basis of instrumental needs often interact more frequently with people having similar political outlooks and have their identifications strengthened by social forces. No matter the original motivation for a partisan choice,

> once a person has acquired some embryonic party attachment it is easy for him to discover that most events in the ambiguous world of politics rebound to the credit of his chosen party. As the virtue of his party's virtue gains momentum in this manner . . . future events will be interpreted in a fashion that supports his partisan inclination. (Campbell et al., 1960, p. 165)

The reinforcement process is bolstered by the tendency to gather and evaluate information in a partisan manner. Democrats are more likely to read material supporting their party, and the same is true for the Republicans.

One of the clearest contemporary patterns is the decline in the percentage of voters willing to identify with a party and the increase in independent voters (see Figure 5.3), pointing to a *breakdown in the identity transmission process*. Changes in the social and instrumental context of American politics have been dramatic in recent decades.

> During the early part of our nation's history, citizens lived a much simpler life in which they were affiliated with relatively few and mutually supportive groups, and were exposed to limited amounts of information. (Clubb, Flanigan, & Zingale, 1980, p. 283)

The transmission of party identification works well when parents provide specific partisan cues, when children are not exposed to the opinions of social groups widely at variance with that of their parents, when children do not gravitate to life-styles significantly different from that of their parents, and when historical events and new sources of information do not strain the credibility of perceptions supportive of the chosen party. In recent years, each of the above factors has changed in the direction of reducing the effectiveness and predictability of partisan choice and behavior patterns. After monitoring a generation of parents and their children over three decades, M. Kent Jennings and Gregory Markus concluded:

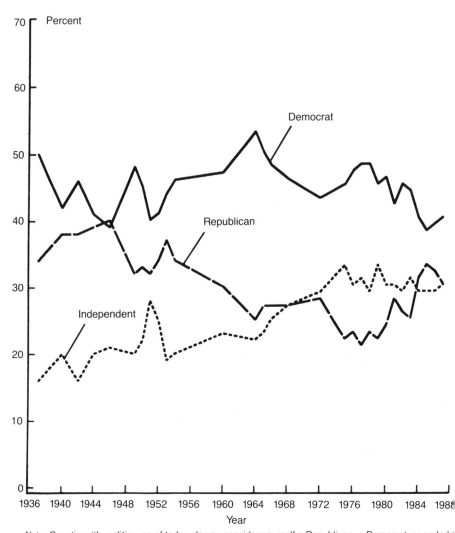

Figure 5.3 Distribution of Party Identifiers and Independents *(Source: Stanley & Niemi, 1988, p. 126)*

The high school class of 1965 . . . began their adult political lives strikingly less committed to political parties than were their parents, and they have remained less committed for nearly two decades. (1984, p. 1015)

Historical events such as Watergate and the Vietnam War have shaken the faith of individuals in the parties in general and in particular parties. The physical and social mobility of individuals makes it much more likely for voters to interact socially in an intensive manner with individuals with widely differing political outlooks than did their parents and early associates. The first-generation college graduate from the small town now raising a family as a management-level employee of government or a large corporation has a very different set of social interactions from the more traditional pattern of former years when individuals were born and educated, raised their families, and worked in the same community with the same group of friends and relatives in close proximity. With a new physical location and life-style, different issues become politically important, and old political identifications fail to serve current needs. With a more inconsistent set of social and instrumental motivations, not only does the individual face the political world with less partisan commitment but, as a parent, gives his or her children a less vociferous set of partisan guidelines. In the society as a whole, as partisan commitment becomes less of a norm, few individuals feel socially pressured to make a partisan commitment. An increasing proportion of the current electorate came of age politically in an antiparty era and, seeing little use for party identification on their own part, were hesitant to pass on a commitment to their children (Kayden & Mahe, 1985, p. 176). The wheel is given another spin as candidates and even the parties explicitly appeal to voters on nonpartisan bases.

The argument that parental socialization determines a child's party identification does not seem to leave much room for partisan change. It is hard to explain why a generation of children brought up in Republican homes during the 1920s and 1930s could become Democrats in the 1940s or how a generation of children brought up by those Democratic parents in the 1960s and 1970s could so easily shift toward the Republican party in the 1980s. Philip Converse (1975) posed an intriguing solution based on the premise that "actions speak louder than words." Observing their Republican parents voting Democratic in the 1930s and 1940s, children might well have missed their lip service to the Republican party, with the same phenomenon happening in the opposite partisan direction during the 1980s.

The Distribution of Party Loyalties

Despite the general decline in party identification during recent decades, the majority of voters still profess a party identification, and the recent evidence hints at the possibility of both a slight increase in the willingness to identify and the possibility of a realignment in partisan advantage. The conventional wisdom that there was an inevitable "onward march of party decomposition," manifested by an increasingly lower percentage of party identifiers in the population, began to be challenged in the mid-1970s as the trend first halted and then began a reversal (Sundquist, 1983, p. 589). Tables 5.4 and 5.5 confirm the conclusion that "a point of no return has not been passed, beyond which heightened identification with the parties is no longer possible" (Clubb et al., 1980, p. 288).

TABLE 5.4. OVER-TIME DISTRIBUTION OF PARTY IDENTIFICATION (PERCENTAGES)

	1960	1964	1968	1976	1980	1982	1984	1985	1986	1987	1988
Democrats	47	53	46	47	46	45	40	38	39	40	43
Republicans	30	25	27	23	24	26	31	33	32	30	29
Independents	23	22	27	30	30	29	29	29	29	30	28

Source: Gallup Poll, 1960–1988.
Note: Entries show yearly averages.

The shift, albeit slight, back to the parties involves more than an in-creased willingness of individual voters to identify with a party, for the increased identification has benefited the Republican party more than the Democratic party. By the mid-1980s Republican identification had almost reached parity with that of the Democrats. This reversed the pattern of Democratic domination among party identifiers beginning in the 1940s when scientific measurement of party identification first began (see Figure 5.3). Even *dealignment* (the movement away from party identification) is a net gain for the Republicans, who have battled for years against a strong Democratic majority (Taylor, 1986a, p. A14). The explanations for the Republican gains and Democrat losses vary widely. Initially, analysts, and particularly Demo-cratic activists, explained the shift in party identification as the result of short-term and transient conditions associated with recent historical events. The combination of a repudiated set of Democratic administrations dealing unsatis-factorily with the war in Vietnam and the Iran hostage situation compared to an immensely popular Reagan administration that "flexed its military muscle, touted patriotism and presided over one of the most robust economic re-coveries" (Norpoth, 1985, pp. 5–6) shifts much of the blame from the party's shoulders. Viewing recent increases in party identification and its shifting distribution as purely a passing phase, likely to evaporate with the departure of Ronald Reagan, does not explain why the Republicans were not as significantly crippled by the repudiation of Watergate and fails to include evidence of longer-term and deeper trends.

Much of the research on party identification views it like religious affilia-tion, as a global commitment to a particular cause or organization. There is growing evidence that voters (Maggiotto, 1986) and even political activists (Hadley, 1985) can make separate calculations about their partisan identity according to the level of government in question. Particularly in the South, the phenomenon of being a national Republican and a local Democrat is widely recognized. Some observers assert that "split-level realignment" has taken place

and that the country now has a normal Republican majority at the presiden-tial level, a competitive system in the Senate, and a system that favors Democrats in the Hosue of Representatives and below the federal level. (Cavanaugh & Sundquist, 1985, p. 40)

TABLE 5.5. OVER-TIME CHANGE IN PARTY DEMOGRAPHICS, 1976–1985

Characteristics	Republican 1985	1976	% Diff.[a]	Democrat 1985	1976	% Diff.[a]	Independent 1985	1976	% Diff.[a]
Total	33	22	+11	40	46	− 6	27	32	− 5
Sex									
Men	34	20	+14	36	45	− 9	29	35	− 6
Women	31	24	+ 7	44	48	− 4	25	28	− 3
Age									
18–24 years	36	15	+21	30	40	−10	33	45	−12
25–29 years	33	15	+18	36	44	− 8	31	41	−10
30–49 years	30	20	+10	40	49	− 9	30	31	− 1
50+ years	33	29	+ 4	46	48	− 2	21	23	− 2
Region									
East	31	24	+ 7	43	45	− 2	26	31	− 5
Midwest	34	24	+10	36	39	− 3	30	37	− 7
South	32	15	+17	43	56	−13	25	29	− 4
West	35	28	+ 7	38	44	− 6	27	28	− 1
Race									
White	35	24	+11	36	43	− 7	29	33	− 4
Black	6	5	+ 1	81	76	+ 5	13	20	− 7
Education									
College	40	27	+13	33	36	− 3	28	37	− 9
High school	31	20	+11	41	48	− 7	28	32	− 4
Non–high school grad.	23	19	+ 4	52	59	− 7	25	22	+ 3
Occupation									
Professional	40	28	+12	32	37	− 5	28	35	− 7
Clerical & sales	35	24	+11	37	40	− 3	28	36	− 8
Skilled workers	32	18	+14	36	49	−13	32	33	− 1
Manual workers	26	15	+11	44	52	− 8	30	33	− 3
Unskilled	27	14	+13	46	53	− 7	27	23	− 4
Religion									
Protestant	36	28	+ 8	39	43	− 4	25	29	− 4
Catholic	30	15	+15	44	54	−10	26	31	− 5
Labor union									
Union	25	15	+10	39	43	− 4	26	31	− 5
Nonunion	35	24	+11	38	44	− 6	27	32	− 5
Income									
$25,000+	38	—	—	32	—	—	30	—	—
Under $25,000	29	—	—	46	—	—	25	—	—

Source: *Gallup Opinion Indexes*, no. 244–245 (January–February 1986), no. 131 (June 1976).
Note: Figures vary slightly from Table 5.4 where yearly averages were used.
[a] Difference in party percentage between 1976 and 1985.

Although historical events certainly affect political perceptions of all kinds, particularly party identification, some long-term trends indicate more fundamental shifts in partisanship. It may well be that Watergate "may have halted what would have been the natural emergence of a Republican majority,...[and] provided for the a false respite" for the Democratic party (Edsall, 1984a, p. 34). The Republican shift can be explained by assessing Democratic weaknesses and Republican strengths. On the Democratic side, the party is

> partly a victim of its own success. The unemployed of the 1930's having been transformed (with their children) into the middle class of the 1980's, it is no surprise to see many of them lose their loyalty to traditional Democratic programs which take their tax dollars. (Hayden, 1985, p. 4)

As 1970s antiwar activist and current California state legislator Tom Hayden said, "the parents of the baby-boomers were garment workers and foundrymen who were helped by the New Deal Democrats, and for that the baby-boomers are thankful. But they themselves cannot be loyal to nostalgia" (1986, p. C4).

Increasingly, the New Deal Coalition forged by Franklin Roosevelt of southerners, blue-collar workers, minorities, urban dwellers, Catholics, and Jews faced divisiveness among its own ranks as the once more monolithic subgroups splintered.

It is not so much that there is a new set of issues dividing society but, rather, that once cohesive subgroups have more divided opinions.

> The quarrel between the parties in 1984 centered on the same set of issues that impelled the New Deal realignment: What is the proper role of government? How big, how active and how expensive should it be? How activist should the government be in redistributing wealth and income and opportunity from the more to the less favored and in protecting citizens against the hazards of life? (Cavanaugh & Sundquist, 1985, p. 36)

The problem for the Democrats was that union members, urban dwellers, southerners, Catholics, Jews, and most other components of the New Deal Coalition (with the notable exception of minorities) divided internally on these issues.

The most stable component of the New Deal Coalition, blacks, are beginning to express some frustration. Some leaders think that "black voters stand to be taken for granted for the rest of this century unless they demonstrate that there is a real 'black' vote, not just a predictable Democratic vote that happens to be black" (Coleman, 1985, p. B5). Whereas Republican leaders argue that blacks have been in bondage for 50 years as "captives of the Democratic Party" (Daniels, 1985, p. A21), black voters act as if they see no alternative, giving increasing percentages of their votes to Democratic candidates.

On the Republican side, a once diverse group of interests including the business community and particularly the Sun Belt entrepreneurs seeking increased freedom from government regulation, the traditional ideological right wing with its anti-Communist and limited government goals, and the religious right interested in opposing abortion and supporting family issues coalesced around the Republican party (see Sundquist, 1983, p. 579; Edsall, 1984a, p. 73). Although failing to make inroads among blacks, the Republican party has not given up on ethnic voters. It has targeted the most economically successful groups in the wave of new immigration (Asians, Cubans, and Eastern Europeans), focusing on their patriotism and anticommunism. The goal is to lock in these immigrant groups early by making a place for them in the party. The hope is that their children and their children's children will carry on their party loyalty just as the Democrats benefited from the attention they paid to the Jews, the Irish, and the Italians in the 19th century. Similar to the Democratic New Deal Coalition of a generation before, the various components of the current Republican coalition are not in total agreement on all issues, but the leaders of each component recognize the mutual benefit and encourage support by their constituents.

The staying power of the current Republican coalition is already being questioned. Moderate Republicans in many areas feel increasingly uncomfortable with the ideologues and the religious Right. The religious Right gravitated to the Republican party out of disgust toward the liberal social and moral values of recent Democratic candidates, particularly at the national level. The excitement of Ronald Reagan's victory in 1980 soon gave way to frustration as the new administration failed to focus on the "family issues" (abortion, school prayer, pornography, and so on) so much a part of the religious Right's political agenda. The entrance of television evangelist Pat Robertson into the 1988 Republican presidential contest signifies frustration with trusting the rhetoric of others and a hope of gaining more direct power. The religious Right may well provide a clear challenge to Republicans.

> The GOP's days of getting a huge conservative Christian voting bloc on the political cheap are probably over. Either fundamentalist GOP support will erode, or it'll come at the steeper price of GOP losses elsewhere in the electorate. (Phillips, 1986, p. B4)

Two pieces of information concerning the nature of contemporary party identification add credence to the argument that the recent shifts are something more than brief responses to historical events. After decades of criticism that the parties stand for the same things, voters have begun to perceive an increased difference. During the 1952–1976 period, a relatively stable 46–52 percent of the voters saw policy differences between the parties. By 1980, 58 percent of the voters saw a difference and the figure jumped to 63 percent in 1984. "This greater public perception of philosophical differences between the parties may well be one of the most long lasting changes in the political system from the Reagan era" (Wattenberg, 1985, p. 5). Also significant is the fact that although identification has declined for the Democrats and increased slightly for the Republicans, the trend of weak identifiers greatly outnumbering strong ones has begun to reverse (Kayden & Mahe, 1985, p. 160).

Changes in the mix of Republicans and Democrats could come about through conversion of voters from independence to partisanship, conversion from one party to the other, or differential rates at which each party mobilizes new voters or loses supporters through death or political inactivity. The consensus of current research points to the differential recruitment of new voters and the mobilization of previously inactive voters as major factors, rather than alternative explanations that Republicans are better at keeping their supporters in the electorate or converting former Democrats (Clubb et al., 1980; Claggett, 1985).

Party identification is heavily dependent on *demographics*, or the characteristics of a population, and the nature of party coalitions dramatically emerges by looking at the social characteristics of Republicans and Democrats (see Table 5.5). Through differential socialization and independent instrumental evaluation of the party most likely to serve one's needs, most social groupings in the United States show a distinctive partisan profile. In general, individuals with lower income, less education, and less prestigious occupations as well as women and minorities are more likely to be Democrats. But with the Republican resurgence in party identification affecting almost all groups in society except blacks, the difference between groups is less today than it was a decade ago.

The data in Table 5.5 reveal a number of significant factors. Individuals responding to these national surveys fall into a number of groupings, often with combinations of individual group association. For example, an unskilled worker is more likely to have limited education and to be nonwhite. If you are interested in using these data to predict individual proclivities, individuals identified with a number of *reinforcing* groupings, all of which show strong support for one party (i.e., the nonwhite, less-educated, unskilled worker), are more likely also to identify with that party than the individual associated with cross-cutting groupings with conflicting partisan predispositions (i.e., the well-educated nonwhite with a professional job). Also, the two polls reported in this table are essentially "snapshots of a moving picture." The same people were not interviewed at two points in time, thus making it difficult to determine the process of change. For groupings based on *ascriptive characteristics* (those factors over which the person has little control such as sex and race) over-time change in party identification comes primarily from shifting political preferences. Changes in groupings based on *achievement characteristics* (those factors that change naturally over time such as age or those characteristics over which the individual has some control such as the decision to get more education or move to a new region of the country) may come about due to changed perspectives of group members or a dramatic shift in the kinds of people associated with that grouping. Thus the dramatic increase in Republican identifiers in the South could be due to native southerners converting to the Republican party, an over-time influx of new residents of the South arriving with predominantly Republican perspectives or some combination of the two.

Although Table 5.5 does not definitively explain the process of change, the political implications are clear. In the past decade, Republican party identification increased among all groupings, whereas Democratic party identification decreased among all groupings except nonwhites. The largest shifts during the period took place among younger voters, Catholics, and southerners. Since an increased number of voters opted for the label of "independent" during the recent past, Republican gains are not necessarily Democratic losses. Conversion from Democratic ranks into the Republican fold versus partisan mobilization of previous independents seemed to apply most often to the middle-age voting bloc that came to political maturity during the antiparty era of the early 1970s. This would include men, residents of the South and West, less-educated voters, nonprofessional workers, and Catholics. For all other groups Republican gains are better explained by a reduced percentage of independent voters.

Traditionally viewed as the party of the well educated, the affluent, and the business professionals, the Republican party has become the favored party of younger voters and is within striking distance of being the favorite of men, midwesterners, westerners, clerical workers, skilled workers, Protestants, and nonunion families (see Table 5.5; Cook, 1985b, p. 1929). Two particular groups in the population, young voters and southerners, reveal dramatic shifts likely to have the most significant long-term implications.

Although never as integral a part of the Democratic coalition as other components, *young voters* entering the electorate distinguished themselves during the 1960s and 1970s as more Democratic and more independent than the electorate as a whole. Partially based on an expected political benefit from these voters, the Democratic party pushed the lowering of the voting age to 18 in 1972. Until the 1980s, the newest entrants into the electorate were somewhat more Democratic than all voters in terms of party identification and considerably more likely to support the Democratic presidential candidate. Since that time both trends have reversed. The youngest voters (18–24 years old) are currently slightly more independent and Republican, significantly less Democratic than the population as a whole, and significantly more Republican, less independent, and less Democratic than previous generations of new entrants.

Explaining the party identification of young voters seemingly challenges the socialization literature that asserts that children will be like their parents in terms of party loyalties. It could be that new instrumental motivations or shifted social ties to new associates superseded family influences. Part of the puzzle may be explained by Philip Converse (1975, p. 143), who reminded us that children socialized during the contemporary period experience more expressed partisan independence among their parents and an increasing percentage of parents whose professed party loyalties run counter to their political behavior. The large number of Democrats contributing to Republican victories in four of the past five presidential elections may prove that "actions speak louder than words" in the political realm as well as elsewhere. With children from traditionally Democratic households not hearing their parents espousing an intransigent partisan label, living in a historical period in which they are encouraged to "do their own thing," and seeing their parents vote for Republican candidates, there is little surprise that they might find the Republican party appealing. Although it is difficult to determine whether instrumental evaluations of the parties lead to a party identification or whether the party label affects one's evaluation, the evidence is clear that young voters view the Republican party as the one most likely to bring peace, prosperity, and a better future (Broder, 1985a, p. A8).

Interpretations of the long-term importance of the partisan shift of younger voters vary. Although younger voters participate less than older voters and thus have diminished their voting power, many see them as a "forecaster group" providing a weather vane of impending trends (Ladd, 1985b, p. 59). Whether or not their perspectives permeate other segments of the electorate, their increased participation in later years and the departure of older generations will increase their role in elections, and to the degree that they retain their partisan distinctiveness, their existence will increasingly affect the overall distribution of party loyalties. The danger of putting too much emphasis on the youth vote lies in its potential volatility. The life-styles, goals, and behavior patterns of younger voters are less fixed if for no other reason than that they have not become comfortable through experience. Evaluations of the political implications of the partisan predispostions of younger voters take on a partisan flavor. Republican National Committee chairman Frank Fahrenkopf views it as a major departure point and, perhaps optimistically, asserted that "people historically have remained in the party that they first registered in throughout their whole life" (quoted in Cook & Watson, 1985, p. 2427). Democratic analysts, while agreeing on the basic figures, "point out that party identification is becoming less and less significant, and that there is a real difference between Republican party identification in presidential elections and voting in state and local elections" (Edsall & Johnson, 1986a, p. A4).

For generations, the adjective *solid* graced virtually every discussion of party behavior in the South. The roots of Democratic party loyalties in the South stem from hatred of the Republicans who were viewed as the instigators of the Civil War and perpetrators of discriminatory reconstruction policies. For generations, southern Republicans found themselves forced to participate in replays of the old battles at election time. The division set in place by the Civil War solidified through the process of socialization and the continuing realization by ambitious politicians that Democratic party politics was the only game in town. A one-party system allowing for intraparty factionalism and often meaningful choices at the primary stage avoided the division along economic lines evidenced in the rest of the country and "preserved white control and supremacy" (Lamis, 1984a, pp. 6–7). Whereas the Depression led the better-off voters in the rest of the country to gravitate toward the Republican party and the working class to favor the Democrats, "in the South this process was delayed over three decades while the racial issue continued to dictate Democratic solidarity" (p. 8). As the national Democratic party forcefully took up the cause of civil rights, the basis for the one-party South evaporated. Southerners first responded by withholding their Democratic votes for the presidency and often supporting the Republican candidate but retaining both their Democratic party identification and local voting patterns. Changing attitudes made life difficult for southern Democratic activists:

> Southern Democratic leaders walk a tightrope. They have to speak and act progressively enough to retain the allegiance of blacks, whose voters are crucial to their election, while not speaking or acting so boldly liberal as to earn the antipathy reserved for northerners. (Cavanaugh & Sundquist, 1985, p. 58)

Although a new, but fragile, Democratic coalition still controls many areas of the South,

> The 11 states of the Old Confederacy are today the most volatile and important battleground of American politics. No other region has such unstable new political coalitions, and none seems more ready to abandon old voting habits. (Broder, 1986c, p. A1)

Increasingly southern voters have realized that the Democratic party was no longer the "repository of traditional southern values" (Steed, 1985, p. 17). Although some of the values are still racial, other economic and ideological perspectives have increased in importance for fueling the conversion of southern Democrats into Republicans (Price, 1984, p. 13).

While conversion of southerners was taking place, the composition of the southern electorate changed dramatically as blacks with a strong Democratic party linkage moved out, and young, well-educated professionals and white-collar workers followed the job opportunities to the southern Sun Belt states. One study found more than one-third of the new Republicans to have migrated from outside the South and brought their party identifications with them (Price, 1984, p. 13). Since 1956, 49 percent of all white migrants to the South have been Republican, roughly double the percentage of Republicans among native whites (Taylor, 1986a, p. A14). As one Florida Republican officer stated:

> The party identification trend line is on our side. Ten years ago we had four hundred thousand Republicans and now we have close to two million. With the influx of close to one thousand new voters per day and our ability to register three out of every five of them as Republicans, we can see the Republican majority on the far horizon. In fact our logo proclaims, "an emerging majority." (Author's interview)

Although the causes are not all known, the fact remains that the South, once a unique bastion of Democratic party identification, now has about the same party divisions as the remainder of the country (see Table 5.5). The result lies not only in the election of more Republicans but also in the willingness of elected officials to switch their own allegiance, a phenomenon seldom accompanied by political success in the past. Through operation "Open Door" the Republican party actively sought out Democratic officials and encouraged them to switch. A relatively large number of officials on all levels took the step. As one southern Republican official put it:

> After years of Democratic control of elected office, and faced with a relatively sparse "bench" of potential Republican candidates, it is much cheaper to get a person with an established backing to switch parties than to try and knock them off. In those districts with basically Republican sentiments and a Democrat in office, we were not afraid to threaten them that unless they switched we could no longer allow them to go unchallenged. After the switch, our ability to sell our position along with the personal support of the converted official often turned a once safe Democratic seat into a toss-up or even a Republican seat. This had the further effect of allowing more voters to conceive of themselves as Republicans. (Author's interview)

Although justified as listening to the will of the people or "putting principles above politics," a careful study of party switchers and their electoral success concluded that party switching may be an act of conscience, but it also appears to have positive electoral benefits. Most instances of party switching "entail BOTH conscience and calculation" (Castle & Fett, 1985, p. 14).

The Democratic party still leads in southern party identification, but it is ripe for considerable change. Old patterns die hard, but the crack in the Democratic façade first seen in presidential voting has begun to inch toward lower-level offices (Broder, 1986a, p. A8).

Party Identification and the Vote
The extensive emphasis on party identification assumes that psychological commitment to a party serves as a precursor to the vote. The mechanisms linking a voter's partisan identification with a voting choice vary. For voters lacking any other information, a blinding, almost visceral, sense of identity compels them to support their party "colleague." More aware voters keep a "running tally of past performance of the parties in office" (Fiorina, 1981) and use a candidate's party as a significant factor in predicting which candidate will best serve their needs. For some voters, party identification serves as a screen by which they filter and evaluate political information, giving more credence to the issues and arguments promoted by fellow partisans. For other voters, the same issue positions and candidate evaluations leading them to a voting choice leads them to a party choice, and their partisan identification enables us to

predict their behavior but not necessarily explain it. The complexity of the human decision-making process insures that individual voters may well be affected by a combination of the above factors and that the individual mix of factors changes over time. Attempts to determine the degree to which a person's party identification *explains* voting rather than *predicts* it fall victim to the difficulty in getting voters to express their true motivations. Few voters willingly admit they vote on the basis of blind party loyalty; rather they clothe their rationale with more socially acceptable references to issues and candidate performance. Although we may not be able to explain precisely the linkage between party identification and the vote, assessing the over-time utility of party identification as a predictor of the vote will tell us a great deal about the importance of the party label.

The earliest studies of voter behavior emphasized the importance and permanence of party identification as both a predictor and explanation of the individual vote. As the *American Voter* expressed it:

> Few factors are of greater importance for our national elections than the lasting attachments of tens of millions of Americans to one of the parties. These loyalties establish a basic division of electoral strength within which the competition of particular campaigns take [*sic*] place. (Campbell, Converse, Miller, & Stokes, 1960, p. 121)

Flush with polling data from the 1950s elections, the assertions of party attachment and loyalty fit the evidence quite well. More than 80 percent of the voters voted for the congressional candidates of their party, and in the presidential races more than 90 percent of the Republicans and 80 percent of the Democrats supported the candidates of their party (see Table 5.6). On the aggregate level, split-ticket voting was relatively rare with fewer than one-quarter of congressional districts or states voting for a congressional candidate or governor of one party and a presidential candidate of another party (see Table 5.7). Three decades later individual party-line votes in presidential elections declined and split-party results in districts and states increased dramatically. During the same period individual ticket splitting increased from 10 percent to more than 20 percent in off-year congressional elections and from 27 percent to more than 50 percent in state and local elections (Price, 1984, p. 15). In the 1984 elections, 54 percent of the voters reported having split their tickets. Those least likely to split their tickest were blacks (30 percent), southerners (49 percent), those with less than a high school education (42 percent), and the lowest-income groups (38 percent). Contrary to previous findings, Republicans (52 percent) reported splitting their tickets more than Democrats (44 percent). As expected, self-identified independents largely acted independently, with 76 percent splitting their tickets (*Gallup Report*, no. 230, November 1984, p. 14). The increased ticket splitting by Repub-

TABLE 5.6. INDIVIDUAL PARTY-LINE VOTING, 1956–1984

	Presidential Elections[a] (% of Party Identifiers Voting for Party Candidate)		House Elections[b] (% of Party Identifiers Voting for Party Candidate)	State and Local Elections[b] (% of Party Identifiers Voting a Straight Ticket)
	Republican	Democrat		
1956	96	85	91	72
1958			90	74
1960	95	84	88	71
1962			90	62
1964	80	87	85	60
1966			85	66
1968	86	74	82	64
1970			85	64
1972	95	67	82	45
1974			82	44
1976	91	82	81	—
1978			79	—
1980	86	69	77	49
1984	96	79	70	46
Average	90	79	83	60

[a] Gallup Opinion Index, 1956–1984.
[b] Adapted from Price, 1984, p. 15, based on data from the Center for Political Studies Surveys, University of Michigan.

TABLE 5.7. AGGREGATE SPLIT-TICKET VOTING, 1900–1984

	Percentage of Districts with Split-Party Results[a]	
	President/House	President/Governor
1900–1908	3.9	10.5
1912–1924	12.7	18.8
1928–1940	15.4	22.2
1944–1956	20.4	24.5
1960–1972	33.9	44.0
1976–1984	34.7	35.0

Source: Congressional statistics from Ornstein, Mann, Malbin, Schick, & Bibby, 1984, p. 56. Gubernatorial statistics from Advisory Commission on Intergovernmental Relations, 1986, p. 55.
[a] Districts or states carried by the presidential candidate of one party and the congressional or gubernatorial candidate of another.

licans may stem from the increased heterogeneity of Republican identifiers accompanying the overall Republican gains. The stereotypical white, upper-middle-class Protestant Republican has been joined by blue-collar southerners, religious traditionalists, and others to create a much more diverse partisan constituency.

Ticket splitting does not necessarily mean that party identification is irrelevant:

Political affiliation is much like church affiliation. Being a Democrat or a Republican, like being a Catholic or a Baptist or a Presbyterian, is part of one's identity. Once acquired, that affiliation is not quickly and easily changed. One may not go to services regularly—may even go to another church on occasion—but will still remain a members of one's denomination. Similarly, a party member may visit another political church on election day, attracted by the music, or the sermon, or the charisma of the preacher, without undergoing conversion and gaining a new political identity. (Cavanaugh & Sundquist, 1985, p. 39)

Although the evidence indicates a slight increase in the importance of party identification for voting in the most recent elections, the general pattern of decreased importance of partisanship stands out. In the terminology of earlier voting studies (Campbell et al., 1960, pp. 40–44), "short-term forces" such as issues and candidate evaluations play a significantly larger role in voter choice today than they did in the past. The more immutable factors such as group and party allegiances leading to a predictable "standing decision" supportive of the same party, election after election, have receded in importance (Huckshorn & Bibby, 1982, p. 87).

Although we cannot fully sort out all factors leading to this increased willingness of voters to abandon party loyalties and support candidates as individuals, a few contributory factors stand out.

One factor is social. Increased physical and economic mobility in the population reduces the influence of traditional *social* interactions that solidified partisan identifications and behavior. Voters transplanted to suburbs with no partisan history and little or no party organization found little to encourage partisan behavior (Sandman, 1984, p. 514). More generally, individuals moving to new geographic or social settings often break their partisan ties with the past with no assurance that new ties will be encouraged by friends and neighbors in the new setting.

Political parties most effectively provide voting cues in the absence of other information sources. Increased *educational levels* make voters more capable of understanding the issues and make it more likely that they will seek out and be able to assimilate and evaluate new sources of *information* (Ladd, 1985b, p. 60; Clubb et al., 1980, pp. 287–288). Voters able to determine their own responses to issues and evaluate candidates are less likely to agree completely with the options provided by their party. Compared with the recent past, more citizens today have consistent *issue* positions and are guided by these positions when they cast their ballots (Crotty, 1984, p. 48).

Partisan cleavages are based on issue cleavages. The partisan cleavage emerging from the Depression and the New Deal period stemmed from differing perceptions on how the American economic system should operate and be managed. These economic perspectives "are part of the personal experience of only the oldest fraction of the current voters" (Hershey, 1984, p. 24). The issues arising out of the 1960s and beyond—race, Vietnam and the "social issue" (law and order, drugs, permissiveness, and so on—cut across the existing lines of party cleavage . . . . these issues blurred the distinction between the major parties and created polar forces that found no satisfactory expression through those parties. (Sundquist, 1979b, p. 349)

Since the less issue-oriented elections of the 1950s and 1960s, research shows that voters have become increasingly aware of issue distinctions between the parties and have begun to cast their ballots in ways more consistent with their opinions on issues. There is less evidence that the parties capture a consistent set of issues preferred by voters (Piereson, 1978, pp. 275–278). Faced with parties that simultaneously support issues with which they agree and disagree, voters must take the good with the bad and support the party that agrees with them on the most important issues. The potential of total voter commitment and decreased voter confusion over where the parties stand will not come about until there is increased consistency between the party and issue cleavages. Although incomplete, the gravitation of conservatives interested in economic freedom from government control, fear of domestic and international threats to our way of life, and definite stands on the contemporary social issues (profamily, antiabortion, control over local schools, and so on) toward the Republican party is a beginning. Combined with less economically advantaged individuals giving a higher priority to social justice and equality moving toward the Democratic party, this process serves to increase the correspondence between party and issue cleavages.

Voters are also influenced by the *media* and *information technology*. In the not-so-distant past, political communication and campaign persuasion happened largely on a face-to-face basis. Candidates counted on parties to provide the workers to communicate messages. The messages promoted by candidates of the same party varied significantly from one area to the next, reflecting the beliefs and values of local residents. The coming of mass media and technologically sophisticated methods of communication encouraged candidates to bypass the political parties and to appeal to voters on their own. The increased access to national media messages made it difficult for a party convincingly to send localized messages without the potential of embarrassment from getting caught saying two different things. Candidates fearful of the national message carefully disassociated themselves from the party message and ran as individuals (see Reiter, 1984, p. 97). The process reinforced itself. Candidates who saw voters giving less salience to the party message appealed in less partisan terms, which reduced the salience of the party even more (Wattenberg, 1982, p. 217). After realizing they were on their own, candidates used the resources at their disposal.

Television by its very nature emphasizes the personal characteristics and forces issues to the background, whereas other techniques such as targeted mailing and narrowcasting on cable television attempt to break through the party label and appeal on more narrow grounds (see Chapter 6). Incumbents, particularly in Congress, found ways to communicate with voters and serve directly, thus reinforcing their personal power base (see Mayhew, 1974; Fenno, 1978; Frantzich, 1986). Rather than relying on party organizations to communicate with voters, congressmen and congresswomen increasingly established mailing lists to distribute their personal newsletters, increased government funding for personal trips to the district, and encouraged requests from voters to help them personally with their problems with government. The fact that much of this activity occurred during the nonelection period and with government funds increased the potency of the message and reduced the resource constraints.

It will take a number of years to determine whether the modest increases in party identification and party-line voting are anything more than a temporary reversal. Until recently, it was assumed that party strength as measured by vitality of the party organization and support for the party in the electorate went hand in hand. The decline of the party in the electorate in the face of the revitalization of party organizations implies that

> it is the very weakening of partisan attachments that has made it necessary for the parties to become better organized, to become more effective at voter mobilization and persuasion. (Gibson, Cotter, Bibby, & Huckshorn, 1985, p. 140)

It is easier for a party to depend on a set of consistent supporters to propel its candidates into office than to have to create a voting coalition one vote at a time. The party organizations willing to do little more than raise the party flag and wait for the party faithful to gather around are doomed to failure in the contemporary political environment. The degree to which organization and the commitment of resources can compensate for declining party loyalty is unknown, but a changing political environment requires political organizations to adapt or face extinction:

> Developing new functions, eliminating old functions, or performing old functions in new ways may be mistaken for decline, when in fact, it is the path to continued success. (Frendreis, Gibson, & Vertz, 1985, p. 11)

A major contributor to a competitive party system is insecurity (Schlesinger, 1985, p. 1167), and the current volatility of the electorate provides the parties with plenty of insecurity. In the words of Xandra Kayden and Eddie Mahe:

> the decline of party identification has encouraged the parties to work harder; like the brokerage house, they are now forced to win the old fashioned way: "They have to earn it." (1985, p. 93)

Despite the trend toward the reduced saliency of party cues in voting, groups in society still take on unique partisan characteristics in their voting.

TABLE 5.8. PARTY VOTING AMONG SOCIAL GROUPINGS IN PRESIDENTIAL
ELECTIONS, 1960–1984 (AVERAGE PERCENTAGE, REPUBLICAN VOTE)

	1960–1972		1976–1984		Difference between Early (1960–1972) and Later (1976–1984) Period Averages
	%	Variation from Total Vote[a]	%	Variation from Total Vote	
Total	49	—	53	—	+4
Sex					
Male	53	+4	54	+1	+1
Female	49	—	52	−1	+3
Race					
White	52	+3	58	+5	+6
Nonwhite	16	−33	13	−40	−3
Education					
College	57	+8	57	+4	—
High School	49	—	52	−1	+3
Grade School	43	−6	44	−9	+4
Occupation					
Prof. & bus.	57	+8	59	+6	+2
Manual	40	−9	47	−7	+7
Age					
Under 30	43	−6	48	−5	+5
30–49	48	−1	54	+1	+6
50 yrs.+	52	+3	54	+1	+2
Religion					
Protestant	57	+8	56	+3	−1
Catholic	33	−16	50	−3	+17
Region					
East	45	−4	49	−4	+4
Midwest	50	+1	53	—	+3
South	51	+2	53	—	+2
West	50	+1	55	+2	+5
Union Households	36	−13	42	−11	+6

Source: *Gallup Report*, no. 230, November 1984.
[a] Difference between group support for the Republican candidate and the overall support. Positive numbers reflect a Republican advantage; negative numbers, a Democratic advantage.

Table 5.8 averages the presidential election results from two periods to diminish the idiosyncracies on any one particular election and compares the partisan preference of different groupings over the past 30 years. Although Republicans have done better in recent presidential elections, among most population groups the differences in voting preferences by and large match the differences in party identification. Women vote more in support of Democratic candidates. Nonwhites show significantly less support for Republican candidates, and the gap between blacks and whites is increasing. College-educated voters and professionals gravitate more to the Republican party, whereas less-educated voters and those in blue-collar jobs support the Democrats, but the Republicans have increased their support among these groups. Some of the most significant Republican gains came from members of union households, although such voters still line up predominantly in the Democratic column. Young voters support Democratic candidates for president more than older voters, with the Republicans making gains among younger and middle-aged voters. The East remains the only consistently Democratic region of the country in presidential elections. The once mammoth difference between Protestants and Catholics has diminished to the point that the two groups vote almost alike. In general, Republican gains among almost all groupings in the population have led to a blurring of the distinctive voting patterns. The social background of voters still provides a clue to their voting behavior, but the labels mean much less.

Has the Realignment Finally Come?

For a number of decades political analysts have waged a realignment "watch," carefully studying each blip on the charts as the possible indication that the long overdue phenomenon was about the appear. Historically, the parties have realigned every 40 years or so (Burnham, 1970). The election of Thomas Jefferson (1800) spelled the end of Federalist party domination. Andrew Jackson (1828) ushered in an era of frontier democracy. The election of Abraham Lincoln (1860) saw the birth of the Republican party as a national force precipitated by the divisions of the Civil War. The election of William McKinley (1896) rejected the agrarian populism of William Jennings Bryan and reflected the growing domination of American industrialism. More recently, Franklin Roosevelt (1932) ushered in the era of Democratic party domination and the welfare-state liberalism we have come to expect of government (see Broder, 1972, p. 189). Although no one expects an automatic realignment to happen without cause, most observers anticipated that by the 1970s a major set of conflicts and new issues would divide the polity in new ways and have a lasting effect on the party division.

The signals are somewhat mixed, partially due to varying descriptions of past realignments and definitions of what a contemporary realignment would look like. In the strict sense, a realignment requires (1) a shift in the way major social groups vote; (2) a significant change in the partisan balance of power, and (3) the emergence of a new majority political party.

The analysis of previous realignments indicates that rather than representing a dramatic and immediate break with the past, realignments involve a number of stages and proceed unevenly across communities (Sundquist, 1979b, p. 342). For many voters, historical events push some voters to a middle ground of partisan independence or political inactivity as a precursor to taking the ultimate step and changing party allegiance (see Claggett, 1985, p. 1; Clubb et al., 1980, pp. 259–260; Ladd, 1985a, p. 18). The availability of considerable data and the ability to interview actual participants focused a great deal of research on the New Deal realignment during the 1930s. Three models to explain the dramatic shifts emerged. The *Conversion* model (Ladd & Hadley, 1975; Erickson & Tedin, 1986; Sundquist, 1983) asserted that "in the 1930's millions of voters shifted their party identification from the Republicans to the Democrats" (Sundquist, 1973, p. 3). The *Generational Replacement* model (Campbell et al., 1960; Jennings & Niemi, 1981) asserted that realignment stems from the entrance into the electorate of younger voters with distinctive political views and the departure of an equally distinctive group of older voters. The *Mobilization* model (Anderson, 1979; Clubb et al., 1980, pp. 259–260) asserted that critical events stimulate relatively inactive and nonpartisan voters and get them to take on a similar partisan orientation and participate. In the 1930s the newly enfranchised women (1920) and immigrants provided such a pool of nonpolitical "immunized" (Anderson, 1979, p. 18) voters captured by the New Deal for the Democratic party. Each of these processes seems to have been at work in the 1930s and are at work today. There have been a considerable number of conversions from Democratic to Republican party identification, particularly in the South. The party switching by elected officials is a significant indicator of shifts in party fortunes, and it occurred systematically during previous partisan realignments (King & Benjamin, 1985, p. 21).

Simultaneously, a generational replacement process with less clear overall implications is taking place. The oldest cohort of voters, largely products of the pre–New Deal era and reflecting a somewhat more Republican orientation than the population as a whole, is being replaced by the youngest cohort of voters expressing a significantly greater Republican orientation. The significance of this shift depends on the permanence of the party preference of younger voters and the degree to which they effectively pass down these orientations to their children (Norpoth, 1985, p. 8). During the 1970s, with decreasing levels of voting participation, significant increases in the percentage of voters unwilling to express a partisan identification and a decline in party-line voting, the catchword was *dealignment* rather than *realignment*. To some, dealignment meant a steady and irreversible decline in the importance of party ties to voters and elected officials. Democratic National Committee chairman Paul Kirk argued that:

> Realignment is a myth. . . . President Reagan has helped the Republicans overcome their 50-year status as the minority party in the American electorate, only to find that partisan ties no longer mean much to the voters. (quoted in Broder, 1986a, p. A1)

Others assert that dealignment may well be the precursor of realignment. Frustrated with the choices and dissatisfied with previous identifications, voters drift away from their partisan moorings but stand ready to be mobilized by another party (Miller & Wattenberg, 1983; Craig, 1985). This was clearly the case before the New Deal realignment (Clubb et al., 1980, p. 275). The slight increase in voting participation and the more significant increases in party identification and party-line voting since the mid-1970s provide a "sign the period of dealignment is moving toward one of realignment" (Clubb et al., 1980, pp. 275–276).

The new technological environment could be credited with affecting the way in which realignments come about. Changing political orientations on the individual level involve convincing voters that their previous preference no longer met their needs. Increased effectiveness in communications changes the efficiency and possibly the potency of political messages:

> To the extent that there has been a realignment of the electorate, it is as much of a conversion based on cash and technology—and the advertising and public opinion that they buy—as it is a diffuse and spontaneous grassroots-originated upheaval of American voters producing the kind of transformed allegiances characteristic of the political revolutions of 1932, 1896, 1856 and 1828. (Edsall, 1986b, p. D2)

The debate among the experts whether a realignment has really occurred rages on with disagreement based on differing criteria, methods of analysis, and personal preferences about the party that "should" be the majority. It is difficult to analyze a process we are so close to and about which there is so much data. Consensus on past critical realignments undoubtedly did not emerge immediately and could not be subject to such complex and precise analysis. If a complete realignment is defined as (1) social groups voting differently than they did in the past, (2) a significant change in the partisan balance of power, and (3) the emergence of a new majority party, there is significantly greater agreement on the first two criteria than on the last (Ladd, 1985b, p. 58). Although some would assert that the shifts in group voting and the decline in Democratic party dominance is temporary, this perspective is harder to maintain as the pattern reasserts itself with minor variation in each new set of data. The failure of a new majority party to emerge challenges our view of past realignments with their more dramatic results of a new party controlling the political scene for decades. To accept the existence of realignment, "there is no necessary reason why one party has to have a clear, persisting edge over its rival" (Ladd, 1985b, p. 60). It may well be that the emerging realignment means the shift from Democratic party dominance with the New Deal Coalition to an era of party parity in partisan identifications and increased electoral competition at all levels of government and across geographic areas (Cavanaugh & Sundquist, 1985)—not a bad scenario for those that believe parties contribute to democracy by contributing meaningful choices from which voters can choose.

6

Political Campaigns: The Ultimate Test

For the candidate and party alike, the acid test of effectiveness comes in the wee hours of election night when the victors collapse elated and the losers slink off to lick their wounds. Despite the protestations of graceful losers that it was worth it to put up a good fight, most campaign participants privately believe the old locker-room aphorism, "Winning isn't everything, it's the only thing." This chapter explores the role of the political parties in the election campaign that precedes the determination of winners and losers.

THE LEGAL CONTEXT

There is a great temptation to begin the analysis in the middle of the campaign process with all of the drama and hoopla of the charges and countercharges, campaign rallies, and public relations that characterize many campaigns. Such an approach, though, fails to recognize that campaigns vary significantly, and it is important to understand the context within which both specific types of campaigns and campaigns in general are run. As explained in Chapter 4, the drawing of district lines gives the candidates from particular parties a better chance of election. The context of campaigns sets the stage for determining the kind of campaign that works and may well predetermine the probable outcome. The political parties often recognize the potential partisan advantages and disadvantages of alternative rules of the game and fight to establish the most favorable laws.

Fixed Elections

No American politician gains prestige by pulling a colleague aside and whispering, "Do you want to know when the next election will be held?" Unlike parliamentary systems in which the scheduling of elections stems from an explicit strategy by the majority party or occurs automatically whenever the government loses the support of a majority of the parliament, American politicians of both parties know exactly when the next election will be. During World War II Winston Churchill, reflecting the parliamentary experience, asked Franklin Roosevelt when he was going to announce the postponement of the 1944 presidential election due to the war, but Roosevelt never considered such an alternative.

Fixed elections have partisan implications. Unlike a parliamentary system in which the majority party can secretly gear up its supporters, call a surprise election, and catch the opposition off guard, the party out of power in the American system can plan for the long run. The gathering of resources, recruitment of candidates, and planning of policy initiatives all occur around a known electoral calendar. In the policy realm, tough and potentially unpopular policy decisions can be made as far from the election as possible, with the popular decisions announced close to election day. It was no mere coincidence that Jimmy Carter cut public works projects and Gerald Ford pardoned Richard Nixon as early in their terms as possible since they anticipated public dissatisfaction. On the other hand, increases in social security benefits and tax cuts engender more interest in election years.

The Single-Member District System

Virtually all of our elected officials are the only individuals selected to represent a particular constituency. This not only fosters localism by candidates but also makes it difficult for parties to coordinate campaigns, especially on the local level. The varying constituency sizes means that for any one election the party is attempting to compete in districts with overlapping boundaries. The congressional districts encompass a number of complete state Senate districts and parts of others. County commissioner districts include a number of state legislative districts and parts of others, and so forth. Party organizations organized around established geographic units (counties, towns, and so on) must compete within other electoral districts having little established identity except on paper. This encourages candidates to go directly to the people individually and discourages a coordinated party campaign.

Minimal Government Interference in Campaign Activity

Although federal and especially state laws have a great deal to say about nominating candidates, financing campaigns, and the administration of elections, candidates and parties are on their own when it comes to persuading and activating voters. Unlike many parliamentary systems, no official date marks the beginning of the campaign. The courts view candidates as exempt from libel and slander charges, trusting the public to police undesirable charges. The electronic media must abide by the "equal time provision," requiring them to give free time to all candidates if it is given to any one, and sell time to all candidates at the same rate offered one. But the government does not provide for, or constrain, campaign public relations. In such a system, candidates compete not only with each other but also with other potential persuaders (commercial advertisers, proponents of various causes, and so on) for the attention and support of voters. Creativity carries considerable weight. To establish legitimacy and gain the attention of voters, candidates in recent years have sent out mailings that look like official government communications, created ads that looked like television news programs, and freely attacked their opponents with questionable factual basis without fear of legal repercussions.

Types of Elections

The antiparty movement around the turn of the century that spawned the primary system also brought with it a move toward nonpartisan elections for many local offices, judicial positions, and two state legislatures (Minnesota and Nebraska). Promoted as improving the quality of public service untainted by partisan considerations and directing political concern to local rather than national issues, nonpartisan elections had two unintended consequences. The parties often found ways formally or informally to endorse particular candidates, and the higher participation rates of Republican voters meant that Republican-oriented nonpartisan candidates won more often than would be expected. After a number of decades of Republican control under a nonpartisan system, the reimposition of party designation on the Minnesota state legislative ballot led to a dramatic increase in Democratic legislators.

Running in nonpartisan election requires a different type of campaign than for a partisan setting. Lacking a partisan cue to simplify the choice, voters are more volatile, and the personal recognition and evaluation factors of candidates loom large.

Election Mechanics

Unable to settle the inherent conflicts over voter eligibility, the Founding Fathers gave the states almost exclusive control over election laws and mechanics, with only major changes such as opening the process to women, minorities, and younger voters etched in federal enactments.

Ballot Types and Voting Procedures

Democratic theory, reveling in the competence of voters, pays little attention to mundane factors such as the design of the ballot and the voting procedures, but these factors can make a difference.

In the early years of the Republic, the tradition of oral voting or the provision of distinctive ballots by the party allowed observers to monitor individual voters and facilitated the buying of votes. In many jurisdictions, the so-called Tasmanian dodge was an established practice. Voters would be given a filled-in ballot and would be expected to return with the blank ballot given them by the election judges to prove they had voted the way the party intended before getting paid. By the turn of the century, the secret ballot provided by the government was universal and, as expected, led to a sharp increase in split-ticket voting with voting beyond the view of party observers (Rusk, 1970).

More recently, the adoption of voting machines and various computer-based punch cards have increasingly replaced paper ballots. While promoted as methods of increasing election efficiency and the reduction of fraud, party organizations in some areas have resisted change for fear that it might affect their supporters adversely. In most cases, Democratic party organizations, cognizant of their larger contingent of less-educated and less technologically sophisticated voters, have cautioned against rapid changes in procedures that might intimidate more of their supporters.

Two methods of organizing names and office seekers on the ballot predominate. The *office-bloc ballot* organizes candidates around the offices they seek, and the prospective voters must seek out their preferred candidate from among each list. The majority of states use a *party-column ballot* listing all of a party's candidates in one column, thus facilitating part-line voting, since the voters simply have to mark all blocs or pull all levers in one column. Even more preferred by the party organizations are the ballot forms in 21 states (*Book of the States, 1982–83*, p. 104), which allow voting a straight party ticket by pulling a single lever or marking a single box. Although the ballot forms encouraging straight party voting have little effect on the high-visibility races for statewide or national office, voters impressed with candidates at the top of the ticket or oriented toward a particular party revert to party-line voting for lower-level contests about which they have little or no outside information.

For the less-visible offices, seemingly irrelevant factors such as ballot position can intrude. When confronted with a list of candidates, voters show a disproportionate tendency to support the first name on the list (Taebel, 1975). The majority party in a state often argues to have incumbents placed first, ensuring them an advantage, with the minority party fighting for the rotation of names across precincts.

Knowing the ballot type gives candidates direction for approaching the voters. The office-bloc ballot, with no provision for straight party voting, encourages an everyone-for-themselves approach, whereas a party-column ballot, especially with a straight-ticket-voting option, encourages coordination of efforts.

The Electoral College

For presidential campaigns, the electoral college system affects major campaign-strategy decisions. Distrusting the competency of the average citizen, the Founding Fathers interposed a group of electors between the voter and the choice of the president. Entering the voting booth, the voter chooses among two or more lists of electors equal in number to the total number of representatives and senators allotted the state. The list receiving a simple plurality of a state's votes casts that state's electoral votes for president. It was initially assumed that electors would use their own judgment and be selected by state legislators for their competency and reputation. Early in the process, the parties and their presidential candidates lined up supporters to run as electors, and these electors publicly committed themselves to support the party candidate. Although electors are not legally bound, the fact that becoming an elector is a reward for active partisans and the threat of political repercussions of opposing the party's presidential candidate have kept most electors in line. The relatively few unfaithful electors failing to uphold their commitment to a candidate have had no effect on the eventual outcome.

The winner-take-all aspect of the electoral college, giving an entire state's votes to the candidate receiving a majority, encourages candidates to write off those states they are sure to win or lose and focus on the states in doubt. Although presidential candidates may make courtesy stops to encourage their supporters in states where voting traditions make affecting the outcome unlikely, most of the campaign effort and strategic decisions on issues reflect the need to win in the more competitive states. Proposals to divide the electoral votes of a state proportionally or to scrap the entire system sound efficient and fair on the surface but run into opposition from a number of quarters. Some opponents assert the basic success of the system and fall back on the dictim "if it ain't broke, don't fix it." Political activists from the large competitive states fear losing influence, whereas strategically located groups fear loss of power. Black leaders, for example, although generally supporting methods of making the political process more democratic, hesitate to change the electoral college since blacks are concentrated in the large competitive states and can use this position to increase their influence within the Democratic party. Party organizations in these competitive states are also lukewarm about change. Currently, they can expect repeated visits by their presidential and vice-presidential candidates; this attention encourages the party organization. Organizing the rallies, distributing the publicity, and providing policy advice give the party organization a renewed purpose, and access to presidential campaign resources provides the wherewithal to carry out both campaign and organizational tasks.

THE POLITICAL CONTEXT

The Partisan Context

Although significant evidence reveals that a majority of voters split their tickets and fewer electoral districts are absolutely safe for the candidates of one party, all candidates begin with a base of loyal party supporters, and most compete in a district where the loyal supporters of one party outnumber those of the other. The specific mix of loyalty and advantage frames the campaign task. The candidate favored with a majority of loyal partisans focuses on solidifying the support and activating the predisposed. The candidate facing an unsupportive majority focuses more on the undecided voters and attempts to make inroads among his opponent's partisan base. Traveling around the country during a campaign, it is generally possible to determine the partisan complexion of various districts by looking at the campaign billboards. In strong Democratic areas, the references to the candidate's Democratic affiliation often overshadow even the candidate's name, and Republicans use the same strategy in their areas of strength. Candidates battling in districts without a partisan majority for their party soft-pedal their own partisan label and emphasize "voting for the person, not the party," or a similar message.

In most cases, areas of strong party competition also have stronger and more active party organizations, although determining whether organizational strength leads to voting support or vice versa remains unclear. The existence of a viable party organization encourages the candidate to rely on it more during the campaign, which in turn encourages a strengthened organization.

The Incumbency Factor

Running for office from that office is considerably easier than taking on the current officeholder or even contesting an office with no incumbent. In 1986 more than 95 percent of incumbent House of Representatives members and more than 75 percent of the senators running for reelection won. House members tend to be somewhat less vulnerable since they run in less visible and less well financed campaigns. Although incumbents must defend their personal records in office and are potential victims of a negative political climate, they possess a series of inherent advantages in a campaign. Incumbents generally begin their campaign in a district where their party predominates already. Through previous campaigns and the continuing glare of publicity, incumbents have much higher name recognition than virtually any challenger, and in the absence of other information voters support the known over the unknown. Incumbents possess a considerably higher motivation to stay in power, vindicating their record, and can draw indirectly on their staffs and the resources of public office for reelection purposes. Drawing the line between the use of government-supplied resources for official representational functions and campaign purposes has proven to be impossible. The *frank*, or free mailing privilege (see box), for example, is necessary to allow public officials to keep in touch with their constituents, but it is difficult to draw the line to determine when such a resource is being used unduly for election purposes (see Frantzich, 1986). On the state and local levels, the right of officials to emblazon public works projects with their names and pass proclamations keep their

THE POWER OF A SIGNATURE:
THE CONGRESSIONAL FRANK

Although most Americans riffle through desk drawers or billfolds looking for a stamp, members of Congress simply have to sign the upper right-hand corner of their envelopes to send them on their way (a process that has even been simplified by printing the signature on envelopes).

The free mailing privilege—the *frank*—has existed since the earliest days of the Republic to allow members of Congress the ability to communicate freely with their constituents—a privilege they used more than 500 million times in each of the most recent years. The operative term for determining what could be freely sent under the frank has always been *official business*, but defining that term has largely been the responsiblility of the individual member.

Indirect evidence of political use of the frank, such as the fact that mailings increase dramatically in election years; that there have been significant increases in the volume of outgoing mail associated with the arrival of computerized mail handling; and that there is flagrant misuse, such as virtually soliciting campaign funds and promoting the incumbent, led to some limitations. Under current rules, members are not allowed to send mass mailings two months before an election, are prohibited from soliciting funds using the frank, cannot send unofficial communications (Christmas cards, sympathy cards, letters of congratulation) under the frank, and have to limit the number of personal pictures and use of the pronoun *I* in their newletters.

Despite the limitations, the frank remains a powerful tool for incumbents. In responding to a suit by Common Cause challenging current uses of the frank, the courts recognized the problem but did not agree to intervene:

> We do not suggest that the franking privilege may never be shown to create such an imbalance in the campaign process as to constitute a cognizable interference with important rights. We hold only that the level of impact has not been shown to be sufficient in this case for us to assume the responsibility of redrafting a statute or promulgating regulations. (District Court decision, quoted in Frantzich, 1986, p. 30)

Although the court decided that the impact of the frank was not significant enough to change the status quo, few incumbents would be willing to give up the privilege or extend it to their challengers. Incumbent congressional offices look like the mail rooms of not-so-small mail-order businesses promoting only one product—the incumbents.

name in the public eye—not an insignificant advantage given the low name recognition of most candidates.

The factors of advantage to incumbents in elections are not limited to those associated with the offices and the incumbents themselves. Realizing the traditional advantages of incumbents, the individuals and groups providing campaign funds favor incumbents and reinforce their superior position, which in turn perpetuates the tradition. Political parties desiring to maintain a presence in public office discourage challenges to their party's incumbents and often conserve their own scarce resources by discouraging contests against entrenched incumbents. For example, in the 1986 House of Representatives races, more than 60 representatives faced no opposition in the general election. Incumbents, often having first gained political office without major party help, and almost guaranteed an increase in personal political support, begin to view the party as one of the many competitors for their attention and support.

PARTIES AND THE GATHERING OF CAMPAIGN RESOURCES

The increased probability of *candidate-centered*, rather than *party-centered*, campaigns emerged after the enactment of the direct primary and accelerated as candidates discovered the mass media and new technology. Although still relevant to campaigns, the party became only one of many organizations affecting their direction and outcome. The discussions that follow outline the general nature of modern campaigns, focusing on—but not limited to—the role of the parties as organizations.

Campaigns are essentially tasks of resource mobilization. In reaching the goal of election, candidates must perform some mix of the following: mobilizing the predisposed, demobilizing the hostile voters, convincing the undecided, and converting the initially hostile. Each task requires designing a persuasive message, communicating the message, monitoring the response, and facilitating the desired behavior. On the practical level this includes things such as canvassing or polling voters, designing campaign advertisements, buying media time, distributing leaflets, and driving people to the polls. Each of these tasks is expensive in terms of time and money.

Organizational Resources

Party organizations were initially created to manage individual campaigns and to coordinate the various campaigns going on under the party label. In many areas the candidate was almost irrelevant to the process, relying on the party organization to marshal its armies of precinct workers to communicate in a labor-intensive manner, one-on-one, with individual voters. Campaign advertising consisted of printed slate cards and party advertisements touting the party "team." But as

> face-to-face media give way to mass media, and the technological sophistication of campaigning increases, candidates are turning elsewhere for assistance and funds, for access to the mass media depends not on party, but on skills and money. (Agranoff, 1979, p. 233)

Certainly, since the 1950s it has become increasingly clear that the party organization is incapable of providing all of the resources needed to win elections. Realizing the inadequacies of the parties, and holding out little hope for a quick redirection, candidates turned inward to create personal campaign organizations under their own control. The spread of candidate-centered campaign organizations varied regionally and across different offices but became the norm. The trend toward candidate-centered campaigns reached the national level in 1972 when Richard Nixon not only reduced the campaign role of the Republican National Committee but also created a totally separate reelection committee with no pretense of relying on the national party. Reflecting his own personal goals, he even discouraged the party from fielding congressional candidates in some southern districts in order not to upset conservative Democratic incumbents (Cook, 1985b, p. 1929).

The one-man–one-vote rulings and the redistricting that followed also contributed to the development of candidate-centered campaigns and campaign organizations. Redistricting under strict numerical constraints meant that new district lines would not be coterminous with identifiable political units. The parties found their traditional country or city boundaries cross-cut by a number of overlapping districts making it more difficult to create a party organization serving a number of candidates. In self-defense, candidates created personal organizations completely committed to their individual political well-being (see Schlesinger, 1985, p. 1163).

By the time the party organizations modernized their approaches and evidenced a commitment to the necessary campaign technology, few candidates were willing to give up independent control over their campaign organization. Candidates began to rely more on the party organizations to carry out routine—albeit important—tasks of voter registration and general get-out-the-vote drives and to serve as a repository for information on potential volunteers and supporters.

Just about the time many observers were writing the party organizations off, they refused to die. Although only rarely recapturing their original role, they are fighting back on a number of fronts. In attempting to regain a more significant role, the party organizations increasingly offer sophisticated campaign services much like any other vendor and serve as a broker between candidates and vendors, between candidates and political action committees, and between candidates for different offices (see Cotter, Gibson, Bibby, & Huckslor et al., 1984, p. 46). The range of services provided tends to increase as one moves from the local to the national level, but recent surveys of local party campaign activity reveal a significant and growing effort. As Table 6.1 points out, local Republican organizations are more active, but the difference between the parties has narrowed considerably during recent years.

The role of parties in campaigns is in a state of flux. It will be a long time—if ever—before candidates will again totally trust their campaigns to the party organizations, but it is far too early to write off the party organizations.

TABLE 6.1. CAMPAIGN ACTIVITY OF LOCAL PARTIES IN THE 1984 ELECTION

	Percentage of Local Party Organizations Performing Activity	
	Democrats	*Republicans*
Distributed Campaign Literature	89	91
Arranged Fund-Raising Events	84	85
Organized Campaign Events (rallies and so on)	88	88
Organized Telephone Campaigns	78	78
Conducted Registration Drives	78	78
Contributed Money to Candidates	69	77
Coordinated County-Level Campaigns	67	72
Organized Door-to-Door Canvassing	67	68
Sent Mailings to Voters	66	75
Purchased Newspaper Advertising	62	66
Purchased Radio or Television Time	36	35
Utilized Public Opinion Surveys	23	25

Source: Adapted from Gibson, Frendreis, & Vertz, 1985, p. 20. Based on data from the Party Dynamics Project, which provides longitudinal survey data on county party organizations.

Human Resources

The Volunteers

Although the mythology of inexperienced volunteers contributing their time to run campaigns and promote candidates of their choice without outside stimulus fits well with democratic theory, it has seldom been the case for anything but the most minor elective offices. In the era of party domination of campaigns, party professionals called most of the shots, and the volunteers often had a stake in the patronage the election would bring. With the increased technological sophistication of campaigns, volunteers seldom had the skills to perform the most important tasks such as polling, computer data entry and analysis, and telemarketing. Although volunteers with appropriate training can still perform important functions, the increased percentage of the population in the work force and the increased variety of leisure-time opportunities reduced the pool of potentially reliable volunteers. Those volunteers remaining are significantly different from their predecessors. Rather than drawing their motivation from a sense of loyalty to the party or a desire to reap the fruits of victory, contemporary volunteers are more likely to have a personal commitment to the particular candidate or find satisfaction in working for an ideological cause or issue.

The Consultants

Realizing that campaigns were changing and not understanding the mysteries of computer targeting, time buying, polling, and the like, candidates have gravitated increasingly toward purchasing these services from campaign consultants. After studying the process, Larry Sabato concluded that "consultants have replaced party leaders in key campaign roles" (1981, p. 7; see also Polsby, 1983a, pp. 73–74).

The rise of the consultants is not an unmixed blessing. Although most provide useful services, their use has increased the cost of campaigns, and there is little guarantee of the quality of the product. The title "consultant" is a self-imposed credential and in the words of a national party consultant: "There are a lot of rip-off artists out there dealing with candidates not having the expertise to judge quality, but so afraid of losing that they don't dare not use them" (author's interview).

Perhaps more frightening is the fact that campaign consultants have little responsibility to anyone. Unlike the party whose reputation can be impugned by an irresponsible candidate, consultants work largely out of the public view and can simply walk away from the "mistakes" they put in office (see Polsby, 1983a, p. 75).

The parties have attempted to confront the challenge of consultants both obliquely and head on. Although the ultimate goal is to "displace and replace the consultants" (Salmore & Salmore, 1985, p. 221) by offering the necessary campaign services less expensively and better, this is certainly unrealistic in the short run and probably in the long run. When replacing the consultants has been unrealistic, the parties have attempted indirectly to control them. In many cases, the parties serve as a *broker*, directing candidates to particular consultants, especially those who limit their support to candidates of one party and who work with the party, rather than running "party-bashing" campaigns. Increasingly, the parties are linking up with consultants on a long-term basis, signing contracts for a number of campaigns at a lower rate and either offering the services at a cut rate or donating them to candidates. Such an arrangement gives the party some control over the consultant's work, provides the party with information for long-range planning, and reduces costs, and the consultants are able to stay employed during the nonelection period (see Herrnson, 1986, p. 8).

In a more direct challenge, the parties, especially at the national level, have created in-house consulting services available at cut rates to their candidates. In 1986 the Republican Congressional Campaign Committee media center involved itself directly in more than 150 campaigns designing, producing, and distributing campaign commercials just like any full-service advertising agency, charging only a fraction of the commercial price. The Democratic counterpart provides a scaled-down version of many of the same services.

Party Field Staff

Party and campaign politics in America, especially at the more local level, have always lacked true professional guidance. Most campaign organizations, especially at the state and local level, are comprised of well-meaning but inexperienced staffs. Increasingly, the national parties have been providing professionally trained field staffs to advise and coordinate campaign activities. As the Republican field staff director put it:

> Until relatively recently, the NRC's field staff were the only party professionals in the field and therefore got involved in everything from party building to campaigning. With the increased quality of state party and campaign staffs we can focus our efforts a bit. (Author's interview)

National party field staff become the corporate memory for campaigns, helping them to avoid past mistakes and providing information such as who will put up lawn signs, serve as volunteers, or host campaign events. They also serve as brokers between candidates and vendors. As one campaign manager put it:

> The field staff are particularly helpful when it comes to contracting for services. They have sample contracts and know what to look out for. They sit right down with us and help negotiate with the vendors. With all the charlatans in the business, we just don't get "took" as often with them around. (Author's interview)

As watchdogs for the national party, the field staff serve as conduits for campaign help to candidates who make a real effort to promote party interests. Their advice is tempered with a bit of a threat, since candidates following the advice are in line for additional contributions of funds and services.

Despite the benefits, local party and campaign organizations—fiercely guarding their independence—do not always welcome the help. A longtime Republican field staff member argued that the relations between the state activists and the field staff often went through three stages:

> Initially we were viewed as "those smart guys from Washington who know the answers." As state party activists became better trained and realized we had no magic answers, some resentment at our power developed. Increasingly we have carved up the responsibilities and have found a niche which is accepted by the locals. (Author's interview)

The superior resources of the Republican party allowed them to use a more extensive team of field staff and to keep them in the states during the nonelection period to build the party organization. In 1986 the Democrats began a pilot program providing paid Democratic National Committee (DNC) staff in 16 states but exacted a loyalty oath from the beneficiaries. The state party organizations were required to guarantee that they would perpetuate the party-building programs after the initial national party support. Candidates benefiting from the program were required to run with, not against, the principles and candidates of the national party (see Broder, 1986a, p. A23).

Campaign Schools

With the increased campaign sophistication in strategies and technology, candidates and their key staff members required training and updating. Both parties offer local seminars and full-fledged Washington courses for candidates, campaign managers, fund-raisers, and even the candidates' spouses. The Republican Campaign Management College brings potential candidates together with some of the best professional consultants in the business. Campaign seminars are far from passive lectures; many involve role-playing sessions and even full-blown campaign simulations or "war games" in which the campaigners rehearse what they have learned (see Hershey, 1984, p. 140). The exposure to ideal campaign approaches allows the national party indirectly to control the approaches used by its candidates and to create a demand for the now-familiar services the party can provide (see Hayden, 1985, p. 10). The national parties view their efforts as having a "ripple effect." As one trainer reflected, "The national party once bore the burden of training, much of this is now done by the state and local leaders we trained. The important thing is not that the national party does the job, only that the party does it" (author's interview).

Despite the growth of candidate-centered campaigns, the parties on all levels, especially the national, are fighting to remain a player in the provision of human resources.

The Material Resources

Activating the predisposed and motivating the wavering voters require a considerable commitment of resources. Although some local races still rely on word of mouth and the efforts of individual candidates, most campaigns depend on purchased advertising and some paid staff.

As astute political observer, Alan Ehrenhalt, expressed it: "there are a number of clearly marked routes to victory in . . . elections. Money is the best" (1985a, p. 1739). Money is the most "transferable" resource, enabling one to buy other resources such as organizational strength, name identification, and public support. Although the most well financed candidates do not always win, underfinanced candidates start with a significant disadvantage. Too much money can often be frittered away, but too little money can seldom be stretched.

It is possible that, at least on the national level, we are reaching a point where money is no longer a major factor since most viable candidates have enough to run a satisfactory campaign. At some point increased amounts of money cannot be used effectively, and it has a sharply declining utility in campaigns (see Will, 1986, p. A19). This has been seen most clearly in senatorial campaigns. Few Senate candidates of either party in 1986 were severely strapped for funds in the general election. Although the national Republican Senatorial Committee spent nearly eight times the amount of money of its Democratic counterpart, contributing to the more than $1.0 million advantage of Republican candidates ($3.81 versus $2.8 million) over their Democratic challengers in the 16 most hotly contested races, the Republican candidates lost 11 of these 16 contests (Edsall, 1986e, p. A46).

The Costs of Campaigning

Without much exaggeration, Christopher Arterton wrote about the "arms race quality of campaign spending" (1983, p. 59). Expensive new campaign technologies emerged as add-ons to traditional methods rather than replacements. Candidates spend many times the annual salary of the office to which they aspire. In 1986, although less than 15 percent of House races were tight (won by less than 55 percent), the average winning candidate spent over $250,000. It is hard to sort out cause and effect precisely. Most often expensive new technologies such as television and computerized mailings are blamed with beginning the upward spiral (Ladd, 1986a, p. 6), but to some degree the availability to extensive money drew the technology vendors toward campaigns rather than vice versa.

The Legal Environment of Campaign Finance

Traditionally, campaign fund raising relied primarily on volunteer efforts. The initial test of a candidate's appeal lay in the ability to convince friends and neighbors to support his or her campaign. Until the 1970s candidates and political parties were largely left to their own devices to raise the necessary funds. True, laws forbade direct contributions by corporations and businesses, but attempts to limit and monitor candidate spending faced little enforcement. Federal efforts began after revelations concerning the immense expenditures of the Nixon campaign in 1968 and were accelerated by the revelations surrounding Watergate, which was so closely linked to too much money raised and spent with no control. Major concern focused on huge interest-group contributions whose activities smacked of buying access and support. The Federal efforts culminated in the Federal Elections Campaign Act (FECA), initially passed in 1971 with significant revisions in 1974. The situation on the state and local levels reveals considerably more variation. By the late 1970s every state had enacted some type of law regulating campaign finance such as limiting contributions and expenditures, requiring disclosure, and, in some cases, providing public financing.

On the national level, congressional and presidential campaigns were treated differently. Congressional campaigns faced increased public scrutiny through precise public disclosure rules enforced by the Federal Election Commission and specified limits on allowable contributions from groups and individuals (see Figure 6.1). In congressional campaigns, individuals are limited to contributing $1,000 for each candidate's campaigns (primaries and the general election count separately). Organized groups, political action committees, can give each candidate $5,000 per campaign. The national parties can provide

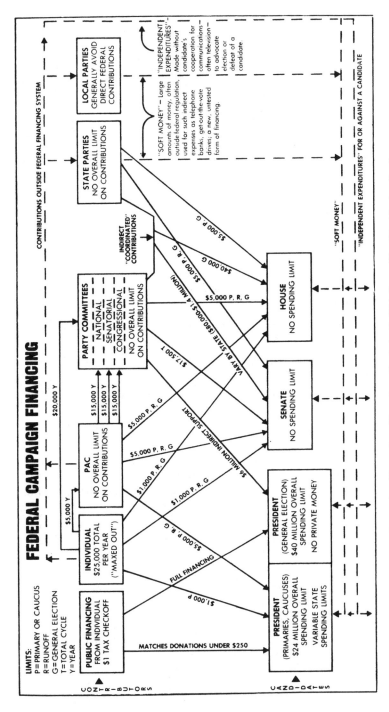

Figure 6.1 Sources of Federal Campaign Financing (Based on charts by Gail McCrory, The Washington Post)

TABLE 6.2. STATE CAMPAIGN-FUNDING ALLOCATION PROCEDURES

	Fund Collection		
Fund Allocation[a]	Party	Party or General Fund	General Fund
Party Only	Iowa Kentucky Maine Oregon Utah	Idaho North Carolina Rhode Island	Montana (1975–78)
Party and Candidate			Oklahoma
Candidate Only		Minnesota	Hawaii Maryland Massachusetts Michigan Montana (1979) New Jersey Wisconsin

Source: Ruth Jones, "State Public Campaign Finance: Implications for Partisan Politics," *American Journal of Political Science* 25 (May 1981), p. 347. Published by the University of Texas Press.

[a] In states where funds are allocated only to parties, party leaders have considerable discretion over the use of public funds, including use in campaigns. The exception is Rhode Island where parties are prohibited by statute from using any public funds for campaign purposes. Where money is allocated to individual candidates, states may be ordered from least inclusive to most inclusive according to the number of campaigns eligible for public funding: Michigan and New Jersey fund only gubernatorial campaigns; Montana, gubernatorial and supreme court; Massachusetts and Oklahoma, all constitutional offices; Minnesota, all constitutional and state legislative offices; Wisconsin, all constitutional, state legislative, and supreme court campaigns; in Maryland and Hawaii, public funds may be used in all campaigns for major state offices as well as many local offices.

House candidates $5,000 and Senate candidates $17,500 in direct contributions, but this is far overshadowed by the indirect contributions they can make (see discussion below). For the presidential campaign, federal matching funds support primary campaigns when a candidate shows initial popular support through the ability to raise funds and support continues as long as the candidate shows continued voter support throughout the primaries. After the conventions, the candidates of the two major parties receive a fixed federal grant to run their campaigns and are forbidden from raising additional funds independently.

Although most states have followed the congressional pattern, relying on public disclosure to affect the nature of campaign funding, 17 states provide some form of public funding for state offices (see Table 6.2). In these states significant debate occurred over the role of the parties in funding distribution. Eight states bypass the parties completely and provide funds directly to the candidates, and the remainder provide the party some role in distribution (R. Jones, 1981, p. 345). Procedures that bypass the parties in the distribution of funds contribute to the development of candidate-centered campaigns rather than strengthen the party role. Since state funding generally comes from taxpayers designating a party to support, the majority party in a state usually receives more money in absolute dollar amounts, but the minority party usually receives more than its numerical percentage of the electorate would warrant (p. 342). States like Wisconsin crafted their public financing laws directly to discourage interest-group contributions through political action committees (PACs). Wisconsin candidates opting for public financing must live under severe expenditure limits but receive matching funds for individual contributions. After the first $5,000 in PAC contributions, additional PAC contributions *reduce* the overall spending limits. Candidates choosing not to go the public financing route have no expenditure limits but grant their opponents the right to no limits while still receiving public financing. Given such an incentive structure, most candidates live within the public financing rules.

The major purposes of the funding laws were to reduce the impact of big contributors, cut the cost of campaigns, and increase the importance of grass-roots support from small contributors. But, many observers believe that the laws have unduly hampered political parties.

> Public funding of the presidential races goes directly to the candidates, further emancipating candidates from the parties. The contribution and expenditure limits of the law encouraged the use of media and direct mail. When the austerity of the spending limits or an inadequacy of funds due to low contribution limits forces candidates to cut back spending, they typically make those cuts in areas like local campaign activities and rallies—areas most susceptible to party influence and partisan flavor. (Orren, 1982, p. 37)

Recognizing the built-in disadvantages to parties, a series of revisions to the FECA in 1979 attempted to undo some of the damage. State and local parties are now allowed to spend an almost unlimited amount of money promoting volunteer activities and are unfettered in their expenditures for get-out-the-vote and registration drives (Colella, 1984, p. 17). The national parties can raise this so-called soft money for state and local parties and channel money not normally allowed in federal and many state campaigns (corporate funds, individual contributions beyond the legal limits, and so on) (see Hershey, 1984, p. 138). Although this revision was promoted as a method of increasing state and local party involvement in campaigns, many observers view the use of soft money as a way for the national parties to get around funding limitations and a process by which corporations and other interest groups can enhance their political power unduly (see Drew, 1983, pp. 14–18).

The Politics of Funding Reform

In no other area of campaign reform do partisan goals loom so significantly as when funding laws are written. In writing the most recent laws, incumbent officeholders from the major parties made sure that third parties and independent candidates would be disadvantaged by not allowing them up-front money. Presidential candidates from the two major parties receive matching funds as soon as they have raised the necessary amount of small contributions in a number of states. Third-party and independent candidates receive money only after they reach the 5 percent of the vote threshold in the general election. Congressional politicians, accustomed to campaigning largely on their own, made sure that party influence over their own electoral fortunes would remain limited by eschewing public financing, which might be channeled through the parties, and limiting party contributions. Although proponents of stronger parties generally assert that the surest way to strengthen the parties would be again to make them a central player in campaign financing (see Pomper, 1980b, p. 16; Eddie Mahe quoted in Havlicek, 1982, p. 177), elected officials deciding their own fate take a more parochial view. Republicans, with a better-financed party organization, are more willing to take the limits off the party, whereas Democrats, fearing an overwhelming Republican advantage, support public financing and severe limits on individuals, the PACs, and parties (see Salmore & Salmore, 1985, p. 238).

> There are a dozen good reasons why the parties' role in financing campaigns should be strengthened ... [but] with the Republican's clear superiority today in party fund-raising, the Democratically-controlled House will not pass a "reform" that lifts the ceilings on party contributions to candidates. (Broder, 1985d, p. C7)

Contemporary Sources of Campaign Funds

The Overall Picture.   A number of clear patterns emerge in the contemporary pattern of campaign finance. The amount of money spent on campaigns increases each year significantly more than inflation. The key variable in the ability to raise funds is incumbency, with incumbents raising the spending twice the amount spent by challenges on the average. Since there are more Democratic incumbents than Republicans, overall totals of expenditures indicate a Democratic advantage, but this is misleading. When comparing similar situations (incumbents with incumbents and challengers with challengers), Republican candidates are almost universally able to raise more funds. Although considerable attention has been paid to the clear growth of political action committee (PAC) funding, individual contributions still provide the majority of campaign funds. Party contributions and expenditures on behalf of candidates make up a very small portion of all campaign funds, with Republican candidates more likely than Democrats to receive significant party funding (see Figures 6.2 and 6.3).

Individual Contributions

The lower the level of the office, the more important are *small contributions* from friends, relatives, and candidates themselves. Although public financing at the presidential level encouraged party organizations and particularly PACs

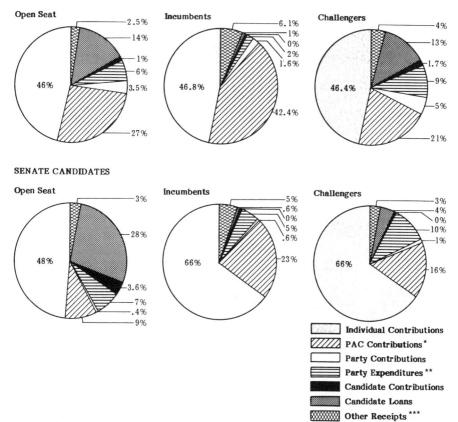

HOUSE CANDIDATES

Open Seat

Incumbents

Challengers

SENATE CANDIDATES

Open Seat

Incumbents

Challengers

Individual Contributions
PAC Contributions*
Party Contributions
Party Expenditures**
Candidate Contributions
Candidate Loans
Other Receipts***

Note: Chart includes all spending (primary, runoff, and general) of all candidates running in the November 1984 general election. Proportions of receipts from particular sources in Senate races may be significantly affected by a small number of campaigns.

* A *political action committee* (PAC) is a political committee that is neither a candidate committee nor a party committee.

** *Party expenditures* are limited expenditures made by party committees on behalf of federal candidates in the general election. 2 U.S.C. 441a(d).

*** *Other receipts* include loans, rebates, refunds, contributions from unregistered entities and other campaign committees, interest, and dividends.

Figure 6.2 Sources of Campaign Funding, 1984 *(Source: Federal Elections Commission, Record 11, July 1985, p. 7)*

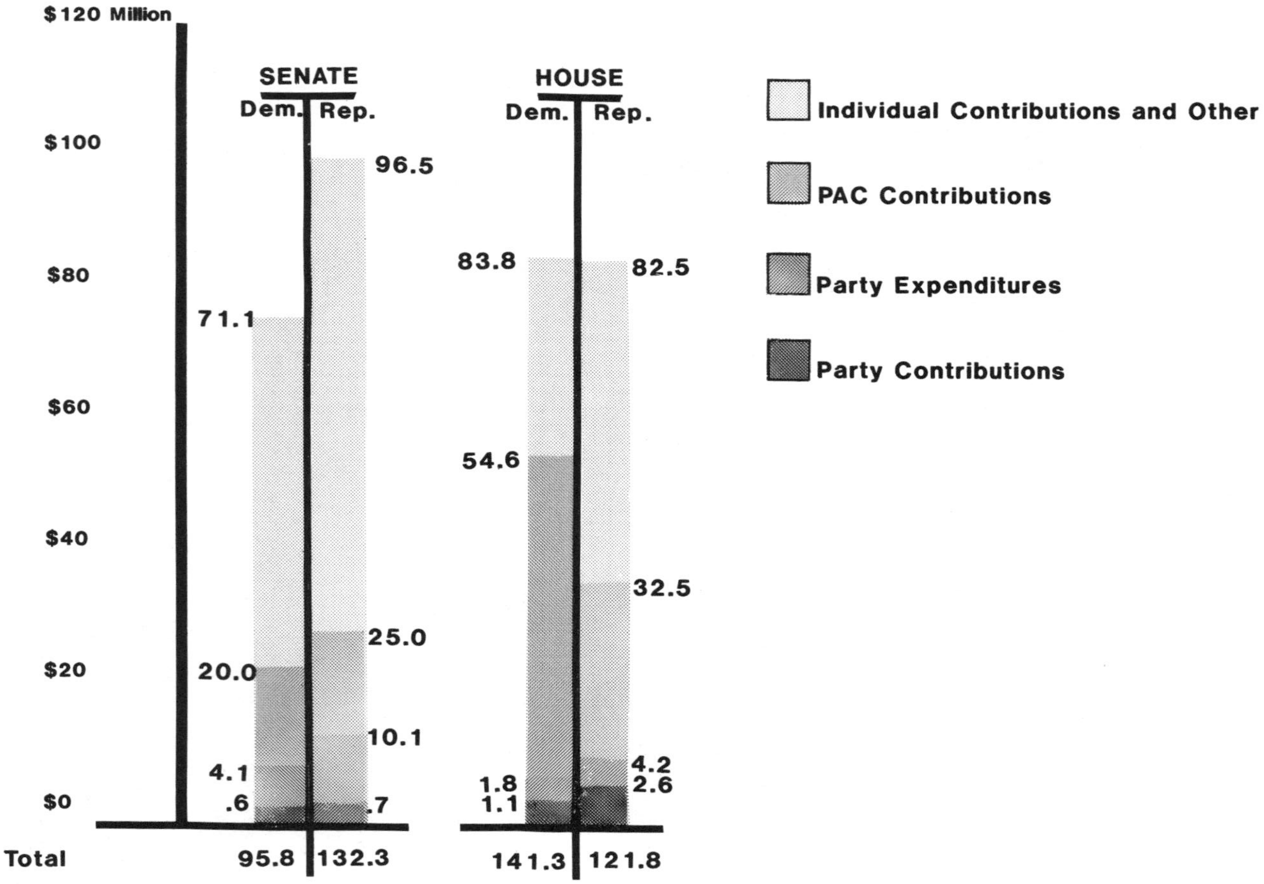

194

Figure 6.3 Sources of Funding for House and Senate Candidates by Party, 1984 (*Source: Federal Elections Commission*)

Legend:
- Individual Contributions and Other
- PAC Contributions
- Party Expenditures
- Party Contributions

$120 Million
$100
$80
$60
$40
$20
$0

SENATE

Dem. / Rep.

96.5
71.1
25.0
20.0
10.1
4.1
.7
.6

Total: 95.8 | 132.3

HOUSE

Dem. / Rep.

82.5
83.8
32.5
54.6
4.2
2.6
1.8
1.1

Total: 141.3 | 121.8

A ROSE BY ANY OTHER NAME

Despite its common use in everyday political conversation, there is no such thing as a "political action committee" according to the laws. The Federal Election Campaign Act defines two types of organizations commonly referred to as PACs.

A *separate segregated fund* is a political committee established by a corporation, labor organization, or incorporated membership organization. It can accept voluntary contributions from a limited class of individuals (members, employees, stockholders, and so on) and can use organizational funds and resources for establishing the separate segregated fund but not for contributions to candidates.

Independent political committees are not connected to another organization and must pay for their own administrative expenses from the contributions they raise. Independent Political Committees are free to raise funds from the general public.

to expend their resources on lower-level offices, most local campaigns fail to capture the attention of outside groups. Increased campaign costs for middle- and upper-level offices make it more cost effective for candidates to pursue larger contributions from both individuals and PACs. In 1974, 46 percent of House campaign contributions and 38 percent of those in Senate races came from donors of $1,000 or less. Ten years later such small contributors made up the funding for only 19 percent of the House and 23 percent of the Senate races (see Anderson & Spear, 1985, p. B15). Although still a significant source of campaign funding, more and more individual contributors are approaching the $5,000 limit in federal campaigns and belie the categorization of grass-roots supporters. Some campaigns have effectively used direct-mail techniques to encourage small contributors, but the approach tends to work better for organized causes and political parties.

Political Action Committees

The Federal Election Campaign Act specified ways in which organized groups could contribute to political campaigns through the creation of a *political action committee* (see box, above). The perceived initial success of some groups in gaining influence through the creation of a PAC encouraged competing groups to jump on the bandwagon. Figure 6.4 outlines the dramatic increase in the number of PACs in recent years with the current total approaching 5,000. The greatest increase has occurred among corporate PACs and the nonconnected groups promoting particular causes and ideologies. In 1986 PAC contributions made almost one-third (32 percent) of all receipts in House and Senate races, with almost one-half (45 percent) of the House winners receiving more than half of their receipts from PACs.

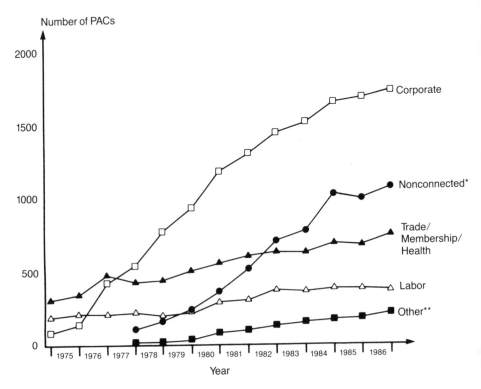

* For the years 1974 through 1976, the FEC did not identify subcategories of PACs other than corporate and labor PACs. Therefore, numbers are not available for trade/membership/health PACs and nonconnected PACs.
** Includes PACs formed by corporations without capital stock and cooperatives. Numbers are not available for these categories of PACs from 1974 through 1976.

Figure 6.4 The Growth of Political Action Committees, 1975–1986 *(Source: Federal Elections Commission,* Record *13, February 1987, p. 6)*

PACs can support candidates of their choice in a number of ways. Direct contributions of up to $5,000 for each stage in the federal electoral process (primary, runoff, and general election) serve as the major method of support by most PACs. Constrained by the relatively low limits on direct expenditures, ideological and cause-oriented PACs have shifted more of their resources toward "independent expenditures" both for and against candidates. As long as expenditures are not coordinated through a candidate's organization there is no limit on purchasing advertising time, sending direct mail, or using other forms of campaign activity to encourage the election of or defeat of particular candidates. Although some candidates publicly disavow negative campaigns against their opponents or strident expenditures on their behalf, few are disappointed by their appearance unless the involvement of the PAC becomes an issue itself. The National Conservative Political Action Committee (NCPAC), after a high level of success in targeting liberal Democrats in 1978 and 1980, has found some of its campaigns counterproductive since then. An attempt to unseat Senator Paul Sarbanes (D-Md.) through early negative advertising in 1982 backfired with Sarbanes getting a great deal of positive publicity and an outpouring of financial and political support. Figure 6.5 outlines the kinds of expenditures made by various types of PACs.

PACs tend to support incumbents since they are most likely to win and focus on the chairs and members of committees dealing with legislation of interest to their membership. Hoping for postelection access, PACs primarily give to sure winners and often back both candidates in close races to hedge their bets. In the 1984 congressional elections, incumbents received 72 percent of all PAC contributions compared with 16 percent for challengers and 11 percent spent in open seats with no incumbent (Federal Election Commission data). Each year incumbents depend on PACs for a larger percentage of their funding. Between 1982 and 1984 incumbents increased their dependence on PAC contributions from 37 to 44 percent of their total receipts. The PAC contribution patterns help perpetuate the self-fulfilling prophecy of incumbent invulnerability. Starting with an uphill battle, challengers receive little of the PAC money needed to communicate their message effectively, whereas their already adequately funded incumbent opponent receives an additional financial boost from the PACs. The David and Goliath battle becomes even more one-sided, with the biblical outcome uncommon. The election results show a renewed incumbent advantage, and PAC managers express satisfaction with their past strategy of focusing on incumbents and plan a similar approach in the future. The wheel is given another spin, with incumbents in the driver's seat.

Although Democrats like to portray themselves as woefully underfunded and disadvantaged by Republican access to the "fat cats" and the PACs, the picture is more complicated. The preponderance of Democratic incumbents at the national level means that overall, Democrats receive a larger percentage (57 percent in 1984) of PAC contributions than do Republicans (see Figure 6.6). When similar types of races are compared, though Republicans hold the advantage in each category (see Figure 6.7).

Different types of PAC employ different support strategies (see Figure 6.6). Labor PACs continue their long tradition of almost exclusively supporting Democratic candidates:

> More than 95 per cent of the money given by labor groups goes to Democrats. Friendly Republicans are more often helped by labor's lack of support for their opponents than by direct assistance. (Crotty, 1984, p. 207)

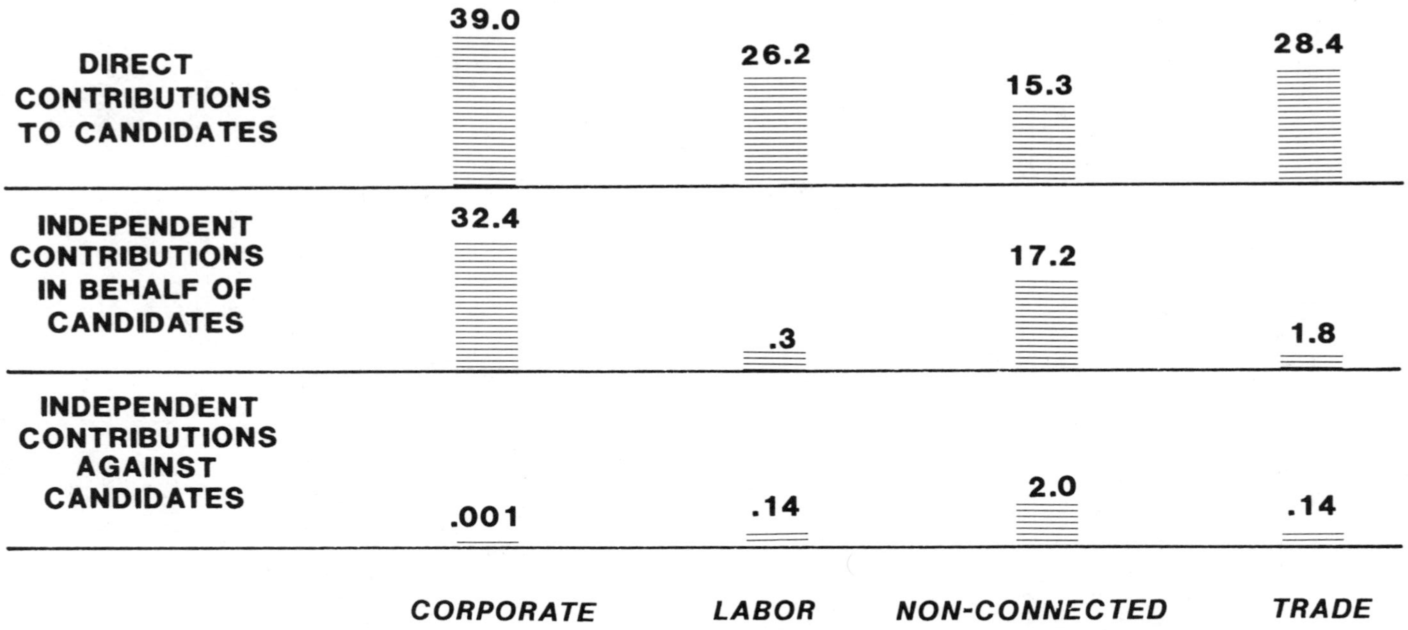

DIRECT
CONTRIBUTIONS
TO CANDIDATES

INDEPENDENT
CONTRIBUTIONS
IN BEHALF OF
CANDIDATES

INDEPENDENT
CONTRIBUTIONS
AGAINST
CANDIDATES

	CORPORATE	LABOR	NON-CONNECTED	TRADE
DIRECT CONTRIBUTIONS TO CANDIDATES	39.0	26.2	15.3	28.4
INDEPENDENT CONTRIBUTIONS IN BEHALF OF CANDIDATES	32.4	.3	17.2	1.8
INDEPENDENT CONTRIBUTIONS AGAINST CANDIDATES	.001	.14	2.0	.14

Figure 6.5 Types of Political Action Committee Contributions, 1984 (in millions of dollars) (Source: Federal Elections Commission, press release, November 1985)

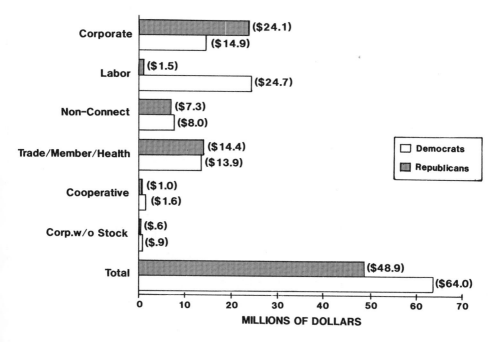

Figure 6.6 Nonparty Political Committee Contributions to Candidates by Party, 1984
(Source: Federal Elections Commission press release, December 1, 1985)

Although more bipartisan in their support, trade and especially corporate PACs increasingly direct their support to Republicans and are less likely to support both candidates in a race than they were in the recent past (see Edsall, 1984a, p. 77; Figure 6.7). At first the ideological and issue (nonconnected) PACs seem to divide evenly in their partisan support, but the picture changes if you include their heavy involvement in independent expenditures on behalf of, or opposing, candidates. The groups most likely to use independent expenditures heavily favor Republican candidates.

Supporters of political action committees argue that in an increasingly complex political environment it is hard to motivate citizens around broad-based issues and that support of narrower coalitions of individuals is the only way to promote citizen involvement in the electoral process (Alexander, 1983, pp. 29–30; see box, "The Case for PACs"). They assert that contributing to a PAC is a legitimate contemporary method of exercising the right to "petition government for the redress of grievances." This position has considerable public support as evidenced by the fact that more people in recent elections claim to have contributed to a PAC than to either a candidate or political party (Cantor, 1984, p. 158).

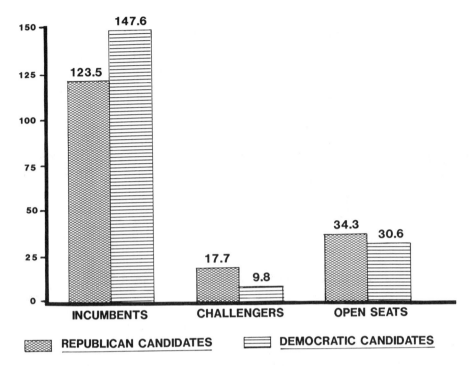

Figure 6.7 Political Action Committee Contributions for Various Types of Congressional Races (average 1984 PAC contributions in thousands of dollars) *(Source: Federal Elections Commission press release, December 1985)*

Although many observers would agree with the above sentiments, especially when it comes to legitimizing the PACs supporting the causes in which they believe, they realize the potential dangers. The PACs pump a great deal of money into campaigns, therefore escalating the cost of running for office (Boren, 1985, p. S16605). The PACs and the interests they represent can have significant influence on elected officials leading to decisions potentially controlled by the highest bidder and the selection of the "best public officials money can buy." On a broader level, debate rages as to the impact of PACs on the parties. Some observers view PACs as the cause of party decline, "making the parties increasingly impotent in performing their traditional role as agents of compromise" (Cantor, 1984, p. 155) and promoting candidates with "little sense of obligation to their state and local parties" (Huckshorn & Bibby, 1982, p. 91). Frank Sorauf (1982, p. 34) suggested that we need to consider PACs, like political parties, as "public utilities" subject to considerable public control. Although no one argues that PACs help the parties, some observers point out that the forces reducing the power of the parties (the increased role of the

THE CASE FOR PACS

Political action committees have almost become dirty words in American politics, representing unfair, unequal, and selfish influences on the political process. Herbert Alexander (1983) added some balance to the discussion by outlining six positive contributions that PACs make to the political system:

1. PACs increase participation in the political process.
2. PACs allow individuals to increase the impact of their political activity.
3. PACs are popular mechanisms for political fund raising because they respect the manner in which society is structured around occupations and interest groups.
4. PACs and the interest groups they represent serve as a safeguard against undue influence by the government or by the media.
5. PACs have made more money available to political campaigns, thereby ensuring that candidates' views are known.
6. PACs have contributed to greater accountability in election campaign financing, replacing subterfuge with an established procedure for reporting business contributions.

media in campaigns, decline in party-line voting, and so on) were in place well before the recent growth of PACs and that the fact that "PACs are getting stronger and parties are getting weaker...[is] coincidental for the most part" (Cantor, 1984, p. 155).

Although the debate goes on, the parties have made some attempt to tame their supposed competitors and capitalize on the PAC phenomenon. As Ann Lewis, political director of the Democratic National Committee, sees it:

> When you look at it on paper, it would seem that PACs and the parties would be rivals. But in practice, we've come to a very important accommodation....Our party has become a broker, a facilitator, and a sometime matchmaker for the PACs. (quoted in Sabato, 1985, p. 141)

The parties send signals to the PACs highlighting races deserving their attention. Indirectly, official endorsement or the commitment of party resources into particular campaigns labels a race as "important and winnable," thus luring increased PAC involvement. As Representative Tony Coehlo, former chair of the Democratic Congressional Campaign Committee, explained it:

> We can turn the PACs off it we don't approve of somebody. We can put the stamp of approval now. In affect, we [the Congressional Campaign Committee] are the party. (quoted in Ehrenhalt, 1985b, p. 2187)

More directly, the national parties send out fact sheets and inform PACs of their targeted campaigns. The Republican Senatorial Committee maintains a toll-free telephone line for PACs to get updates on key races and receive suggestions to improve their giving strategies (Sabato, 1985, pp. 146–147). The Republican Congressional Campaign Committee has established a computerized contribution history for all PACs. Whenever an incumbent Democrat votes against the interests of a PAC that supports him or her, the PAC gets a message stating "Here's how your guy has been voting in the last six months, and are you really sure you want to give him $5000 this time around?" (Edsall, 1984a, p. A7).

Increasingly, party officials serve as "marriage brokers," coaching candidates on which PACs to approach and how to approach them, telling PACs who need what kind of help, and physically getting the PACs and candidates together either individually or at large "cattle shows." In the view of Joe Gaylord, executive director of the National Republican Congressional Committee:

> If we ever were rivals, we're not anymore. . . . We see ourselves as the people in the middle. To the PACs we try to offer ourselves as a service to provide information about Republicans who are running for Congress. For our candidates we try to help match them to the PACs. (quoted in Sabato, 1985, p. 141)

Realizing the political and legal advantage of PACs, some party organizations have directly encouraged or actively participated in the creation of new PACs. The Republican National Committee began GOPAC in 1980 using direct mail to fund targeted races with more than $1.5 million. DEMPAC, the Democratic attempt to use the same approach, literally copying parts of the solicitation letter, lacked the necessary planning and coordination to have an impact (Hershey, 1984, pp. 124–126). On the state level, the Minnesota Republican party created the Minnesota Leadership Council. More than 200 members pledged an average of $1,000 and agreed to support candidates suggested by the party. To get the nod, candidates agreed to follow party suggestions in organizing and carrying out the campaign. This not only gave the party some control over the campaign but also allowed it to claim some credit for winning races.

Although PACs and parties compete for many of the same resources and for the loyalty of winning candidates, the capacity to work together has established an uneasy truce.

> Both parties seem to be resigned to the age of PACs. Like Willie Sutton who robbed banks "because that's where they keep the money," the parties have begun to direct their attentions to the overflowing PAC treasuries. (Sabato, 1981, p. 273)

The Party Role in Campaign Finance

With the dramatic increase in campaign costs and the growth of PACs, the political parties have played a smaller relative role in directly financing campaigns (see Figure 6.2). On the federal level the amount varies between 5 and 17 percent of total campaign expenditures depending on the race (Hershey, 1984, p. 121). The role of the parties takes on additional importance, though, when you take into account the massive amount of money spent by the parties (especially the Republicans) on indirect campaign expenses such as surveys, voter registration, advertising, and staff (see Edsall, 1984b, p. A10). The importance of the party support varies with different races. In recent years, gubernatorial and senatorial candidates find party financial support less important, but there is slightly more party involvement in congressional and state legislative races (see Cotter et al., 1984, p. 22). Republican candidates experience a more reliable base of party expenditures than do their Democratic challengers. As one political consultant analyzed it:

> At least since World War II, the parties have not been very reliable funding sources for the candidate. It used to be that you could only really contribute to candidates through the parties. Now party money is a relatively small percentage of a candidate's total funding. Contributors find it more satisfying to contribute directly to a candidate for a cause. They get their egos massaged by backing a winner. (Author's interview)

Focusing solely on the party contribution as a percentage of all financial donations may unduly diminish its perceived importance. Party contributions often arrive as "seed money" early in the campaign when most needed. The parties are much more willing to support long-shot candidates in their attempt to contest all races. This forces even strong incumbents to carry out a reasonable campaign. Party funding can also help break the "loser cycle" faced by most challengers who need money to prove they have a chance to win (Sabato, 1982, p. 75) but who have difficulty raising such money from PACs or individuals. Party money may also be more "visible" to the candidate than a series of PAC or individual contributions since a variety of party sources (state, local, national, and so on) find their contributions "bundled," at least in the mind of the recipient. The PAC contributions, on the other hand, arrive as limited and discrete "packages" of support. Finally, although party contributions are only one among many sources of support, the variety of forms of party support add up to amounts that are far from trivial.

Campaign fund-raising techniques vary little from general party fund-raising approaches (see Chapter 3). In most areas, especially for the national parties, direct face-to-face solicitation to dependence on campaign events (bull roasts, $100 a plate dinners, bean feeds, and so on) have given way to direct mail and telemarketing (see box, page 204).

Republican party fund raising has always exceeded Democratic efforts, but the explanation lies only partially in the higher average resources of

RING! RING! IT'S
THE PRESIDENT CALLING

The telemarketing "boiler rooms" that sprout up during each election look little like traditional campaign headquarters. The antiseptic rows of telephones and computer terminals are seldom bedecked with red, white, and blue bunting or campaign posters. The little old ladies who volunteered for voter contact in the past have more often than not been replaced by paid workers with no particular commitment to the party or candidate. Unlike the party block worker leisurely going door to door to provide information, solicit funds, and philosophize over politics, telemarketing callers have little time for idle conversation. They launch into their pretested scripts and attempt to complete their 30 calls-per-hour quota. Telemarketing is used to raise funds, identify likely supporters, and get out the vote. In 1986 more than 2 million voters received an automated call from the president saying, "Hi, this is Ronald Reagan, and I wanted to remind you to get out and vote on Tuesday" (see Peterson 1986d, p. 11). In the more sophisticated operations, initial telephone contacts are followed up by computer-generated letters referring to the call and often including information acquired by the operator (financial pledges, position papers on issues of interest, and so on). In some cases, much of the process is automated, with the telemarketing operator pushing a button on the computer during the call to generate the follow-up letter immediately.

Telemarketers begin by accumulating telephone lists from voter rolls, car-registration lists, magazine subscribers, organization members, and elsewhere. After each contact the data base is updated, enabling more careful targeting of messages. Past contributors get contacted again and again, and initial "polls" of voters provide the information needed for get-out-the-vote drives preceding the election.

So who knows, the next time your telephone rings it might be the president taking time out of his busy schedule to find out your views, to encourage a contribution to the party, or to get your help for his cause in the voting booth.

Republican party supporters and the efforts of the party organization. The relative homogeneity of Republican party supporters and candidates makes it easier to raise money:

> Republican donors need not worry about which Republican gets the money, so they are willing to let the party decide. Democratic contributors have more reason to care which Democrat ends up with their donation—candidates range all over the ideological map. (Jacobson, 1985, p. 157)

Although the Republican party continues to dominate in the amounts of money raised and expended, expanded efforts by the Democrats have paid off in a narrowing of the gap between the parties in terms of direct expenditures.

It is becoming more common to pick up your telephone and have a recording of the president or some other national leader saying "We could sure use your help in getting good Republicans (or Democrats) elected to office" and then having an operator remind you of past contributions before asking for your commitment this time.

Using lists of former contributors or of registered voters in precincts strongly supporting the party, the computer automatically dials the number of a prospective giver. As the telephone rings, everything known about the prospect from name and address to previous contributions and organizational affiliations flashes on the screen. Using a breezy, informal script, the volunteer, or more likely paid operator, tells of the current financial need. One approach in 1986 told recipients that there would be an important strategy meeting with a very popular retiring incumbent that evening, and "we need your contribution tonight so that we can report your support to Marjorie (Holt)." Once a commitment is made, the operator pushes a few keys and a "personalized" letter with the promised pledge is printed out by the computer.

Although the positive response rates are relatively low, the low cost per contact makes the technique advantageous. In 1986 the Republican party used 17 telephone centers to contact more than 11 million voters in 25 states, raising millions of dollars in the process (see Peterson, 1986d, p. 11; Edsall, 1984c, p. A6).

Political parties have a number of different routes by which they support favored candidates. Not only can each geographical level of the party play a role, but within each level the parties can contribute in different ways.

Direct monetary contributions are the clearest way in which the party can support its candidates, but such contributions are strictly limited in federal and many state and local races. With their greater resources (see Figure 6.8), Republicans on the national level have been able to support every candidate up to the legal limit of $5,000 for each stage (primary, runoff, and general election) of House races and $17,500 for Senate races, whereas the Democrats have had to be more selective. Until relatively recently, the Democratic party has shown less strategic sensitivity in its contributions:

Much of the Democratic money is wasted on incumbents who hold safe seats. . . . The Democrats' severe tilt toward safe incumbents tends to protect the partisan status quo, but fails to encourage winning new seats by unknown challengers, and leaves marginal incumbents particularly vulnerable when the voters turn against the party. Republicans focus on close races. (Edsall, 1984b, p. A10)

The more than two-to-one resource advantage of the Republicans on the national level also applies on the state and local levels (see Arterton, 1982, p. 111). With both parties "maxing out" in terms of direct contributions in the key races, an increased effort by the Democrats has reduced the direct expenditure gap between the parties in congressional contests, with the major differential now being the Republican advantage in indirect expenditures.

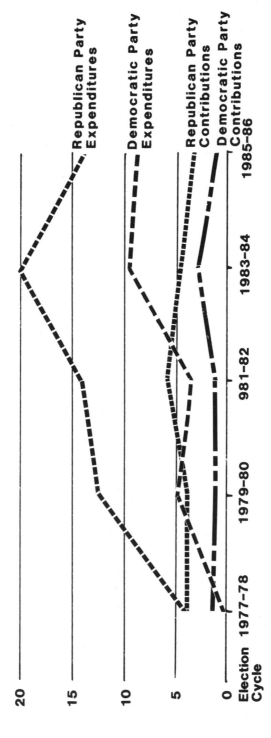

Figure 6.8 Major Party Support Provided to Congressional Candidates, 1977–1986 (millions of dollars) *(Source: Federal Election Commission, Record 11, July 1985)*

Capitalizing on the willingness of Republican givers to trust the party to make good use of their money, and attempting to raise their visibility as a key player in the campaign-financing process, the National Republican Senatorial Committee and some state Republican committees (most notably Minnesota) have exploited a loophole in the campaign-financing laws. After contributing the maximum allowable to each race, the parties set themselves up as conduits for "bundling" contributions. Individual contributors are solicited to give money to specific campaigns through the party committee. The party passes the money on (some $6 million for the National Republican Senatorial Committee in 1986) to the targeted races, and in the process the party's goodwill among candidates increases (see Edsall, 1986d, p. 13).

Above and beyond direct contributions, federal laws allow parties much more leeway in *coordinated or joint expenditures* on behalf of candidates for services such as polling, advertising, voter registration, get-out-the-vote drives, and computer time. The laws allow the party to spend up to $40,000 in House races and $1.4 million in the largest state Senate races for such services (see Smith, 1984a, p. 18). As with direct contributions, in this area also the Republicans have the resources to do considerably more (see Figure 6.8). The value of these expenditures is heightened by the fact that the parties generally price these in-kind services well below the market value and are often able to engage in cut-rate contracts with large vendors.

Since the national parties are relatively well off financially compared with most state and local parties, they have sought ways to increase their expenditure opportunities and roles in campaigns. Increasingly, the national party organizations are making *agency agreements* with state and local party organizations, agreeing to serve as the agent of those parties and thereby spend not only their own legal limits but also that of the lower level parties (see Huckshorn & Bibby, 1982, p. 92). For example, the national party could contribute up to the $5,000 limit in the primary and general election and make $20,200 in indirect contributions to a House race and then do the same for the state party organization. This would allow an overall total of $70,400 in contributions. Using the same technique in Senate races (where party contributions vary with state size), a national party making its own contributions and those for the state party could contribute between $108,300 in the smallest state to more than $1.5 million in the largest (see Jacobson, 1985, p. 155).

Reform of Campaign Funding

Most preferences for campaign-funding reform reflect the partisan goals of the reformers. Republican party officials have exploited the Federal Elections Campaign Act much more creatively than the Democrats. Democrats, with a less reliable resource base, generally support campaign-spending limitations and public financing, whereas Republicans find such approaches less appealing. Although there is considerable public concern about campaign financing, polls indicate a general disapproval for public financing of presidential campaigns and even less support for public financing of congressional races. Among the public, Republicans are most likely to disapprove of congressional campaign funding (Civil Service, Inc., 1985). Consensus on limiting PAC contributions is even harder to reach since the incumbent officeholders controlling reform are advantaged by the current system. Since the Supreme Court decided (*Buckley v. Valeo* [1976]) that campaign contributions are protected as a form of expression, the ability to control spending has been greatly diminished. With the courts' blessing, individuals and particularly PACs can spend any amount they wish, as long as it is independent of the candidates.

Concern over campaign finance is not limited to the national level. A public commission in California, citing figures that since 1958 there has been an increase of more than 3,000 per cent in state legislative race costs with more than 90 per cent of the receipts currently coming from sources outside the district, concluded:

> Sharply rising expenditures and shifting sources of money have distorted the legislative process, changed the nature of electoral competition, and undermined public confidence in the state's legislative institutions. (California Commission on Campaign Finance, 1985, p. 5)

Observers interested in strengthening the parties in general concur that limits on party contributions need to be lifted (Ladd, 1986b, p. 33) and that public funding should be channeled through the parties. But Democrats are hesitant to support such reforms until their fund-raising capabilities are more on a par with the Republicans.

CAMPAIGN TECHNIQUES

The Traditional Approach

Traditionally, political campaigns in America activated the large bloc of partisans and motivated wavering voters through labor-intensive methods. The political party organizations served as effective vehicles for activating loyalists through campaign rallies and communicating information on party candidates using door-to-door block work convincing voters in face-to-face situations. To some degree this personalized and labor-intensive method of campaigning still pervades local level campaigns, with the significant difference that a candidate's personal organization rather than the party often makes the contacts.

Harnessing the Mass Media

With the arrival of mass-communication techniques, especially the electronic media, more candidates have seen its potential for reaching efficiently large numbers of voters with high-quality standardized messages. The efficiency advantages of the mass-media approach also contained the seed of its major disadvantage: messages needed to be so general and inoffensive to any group that they lost much of their impact. Candidates began to sound alike, and most soft-pedaled their partisan ties in hopes of luring independents and partisans of the other party to their side.

Television and other early uses of the mass media undermined traditional Democratic party strategies more than they did for the Republican party. The Democratic New Deal Coalition involved the forging of a set of divergent minorities into an election-day majority. This requires communicating different messages to each group, but "television campaigning directed specifically to any of these groups is difficult, since what is directed toward one group may be seen by all" (Edsall, 1984a, pp. 94–95).

Replying on the free coverage provided by the news media can deeply affect the campaign agenda. Realizing the time constraints, wise candidates expressed major policies in a few sentences hoping to get on the evening news. Candidate schedules increasingly included "photo opportunities" having the candidate doing something visual for the television cameras, whether or not it had anything to do with the capacity to do the job. The media did little to help the candidate express a substantive message. Understanding the public's limited interest in complex issues, an increasing percentage of media coverage focused on the "horse race" aspects of the campaign: Who is ahead in the polls? Who has raised the most money? Whose campaign organization is working well and whose is not? (see Patterson & McClure, 1976; Patterson, 1980). Aside from a limited repertoire of attention-focusing devices, the media controlled the substance of coverage more than the candidates.

Harnessing the New Technology

Although the free mass media—largely uncontrolled by the candidates—predominates, especially in campaigns for major offices, candidates at all levels attempt increasingly to harness the new technology to personalize mass-communication techniques. As a national party strategist put it:

> Technology is most useful in the middle-sized congressional and state legislative races. In local campaigns direct contact with the voters is still possible. In the big campaigns the mass media predominate. It is the middle-sized campaigns, where a candidate's message gets drowned out in the media and traditional personal contact is not possible, that technology has its big impact. Primaries for most offices are also fertile ground for new technology since they allow the candidate to break through the cacophony of competing messages. Sometimes, the very use of new technology becomes a new item portraying the candidate as sophisticated and "with-it." (Author's interview)

Going beyond bland mass appeals, modern campaigns purchase the new technology to send the right messages to the right people in the right way.

With purchased advertising, the candidate and his or her supporters again gain some control over what is communicated to whom. The need for technological sophistication to reach these goals provides an opening for the parties. Paid campaign consultants moved into the political realm more than 30 years ago and began helping candidates design and deliver campaign messages. More recently, the parties fought their way back into the game, asserting that they could beat the consultants at their own game providing the same services in a better and more cost-effective manner. A "turf" battle between the parties and independent consultants to determine the favored sources of such services is currently being played out, with the future of the party organizations held largely in the balance.

Sending the Right Messages

The plural form *messages* is intentional. Modern campaigners realize that citizens approach the voting booth with a variety of motivations capable of being served. The *instrumental issue voters*, exemplifying the democratic ideal of citizens supporting candidates with issue preferences close to their own and having the skills to carry them out, may not be in the majority. *Psychological voters*, using the voting choice to verify their own self-image as a liberal, Republican, southerner, or the like, vote without issues being in the forefront. *Social voters*, deeply affected by the preferences of those they respect, use the vote primarily to reflect this respect. Appealing to each type of voter and the multitude of combinations requires different kinds of messages.

Reaching the Instrumental Voters.   Instrumental voters want their vote to affect ("be instrumental in") the direction of public policy, but policy preferences vary widely. Fewer and fewer candidates fly blind or make educated guesses about voter preferences. Public opinion polling enables candidates to determine the general motivations of voters, get a feel for their own public image, assess the kinds of issues preferred by various types of instrumental voters, and determine how to reach them.

As campaigns became less party oriented, private pollsters were one of the first consultants candidates hired. In recent years, the parties have attempted to regain some control by offering polling capabilities to candidates directly. By contracting for a number of polls with one consultant or by coordinating the polling activities of a number of campaigns, the parties undersell the private vendors. Opinion polling is expensive (with a typical statewide poll costing more than $50,000), and giving the results to a candidate is viewed under the election laws as a contribution, which counts against the total allowable by the party. Recognizing that a major source of value in a poll is its timeliness, the laws allow parties to devalue the cost of a poll over time. The parties can save some of their contribution limit by using the detailed poll results to give general advice immediately (which is not counted against the contribution limit) and wait to give the entire poll results to a candidate until the monetary value is low (see Smith, 1984a, p. 17).

Polls come in a number of forms and perform a variety of functions. Short *benchmark polls* assess opinions and information at a particular time. They are most often used early in the campaign to get a general feel for where the public stands on issues or to measure awareness and opinions on particular candidates. Since polls are a "snapshot of a moving picture," such polls cannot assess trends. *Panel studies* ask the same respondents similar questions over the duration of the campaign. They allow the assessments of trends but are considerably more expensive and suffer from the inherent disadvantage that after numerous waves of questioning the respondents are different from the general population whose outlooks have not been stimulated by repeated questioning. The Republicans lead in the development of *tracking polls*, which use small daily samples to plot campaign trends and allow immediate redirection of campaign strategies. Unlike panel studies, a portion of each sample is made up of new respondents, reducing the impact of repeated polling and reducing the cost of following the same people.

Not only does party provision of professional poll results help candidates make strategy choices, increase their chances of victory, and make them feel beholden to the party, but it also provides the potential for affecting the issue agenda. As one national Republican activist explained:

> In 1982 we wanted to focus the campaign on the economic issues. We offered sophisticated polling capabilities to many campaigns at a greatly reduced cost. We created the basic questions repeated in all districts and allowed candidates a few questions of their own to be asked only in their districts. Our questions heavily emphasized economic issues. When the results came back to the candidates they knew a lot more about their constituents' economic preferences than any other issue. Since candidates like to work from areas of knowledge rather than ignorance, they were drawn to these issues and the national party had a subtle impact on what was discussed. (Author's interview)

Despite the poll results, candidates lack full control over what they credibly can stand for in a campaign. Voters expect some degree of consistency over time, and opponents are only too willing to point out shifts on major issues. Party organizations on all levels engage in *opposition research*. Based on the time-tested strategy "know your enemy," the parties keep records on the public statements, the official decisions, and even the personal characteristics of prospective opponents. The Republican National Committee's sophisticated computer indexing of newspapers from around the country serves as an example of what technology can do. A candidate's comments from years ago can be instantly accessed through REPNET, the Republican electronic mail system, and immediately brought into the current debate.

Candidates are also constrained in their issue stands, at least indirectly, by the process of establishing their personal party identification. The same factors leading a candidate to become a Republican or Democrat lead to fairly predictable issue positions. Although Republican and Democratic candidates cover a wide ideological range, in many cases reflecting preferences of the local electorate, in particular races the Republican candidates are almost invariably more conservative than the Democratic candidates on the majority of issues.

To the degree that candidates must use mass-media approaches to communicate their issue stands and to the degree that general public preferences are known on the issues by both candidates, their stands will tend to be similar—both rushing to the stand preferred by the public. Just as two businesses competing for customers on main street or at the mall choose adjoining locations to reduce the transportation differential, candidates take similar policy positions so that most voters will not have to move too far to accept their positions (see Hotelling, 1929; Mauser, 1983, pp. 140–148). On controversial issues splitting the constituency, the wise candidate attempts to let the opponent take a position first in hopes of capitalizing on a mistake. When voter preferences are not known, candidates gravitate toward the moderate position under the assumption that it will be least offensive to most voters.

Recent years have seen a dramatic growth of negative advertising. Although it was once an accepted strategy never to mention your opponent, modern campaigns use attack ads regularly (see box). As one consultant put it, "People would say they didn't like negative ads, but our polls showed they changed people's minds" (quoted in Peterson, 1984, p. C4).

Reaching the Psychological and Social Voters. Psychologically motivated voters respond to symbols and labels. In the attempt to improve the tarnished image of the party labels, in recent campaigns both national parties augmented candidate advertising with "institutional" ads promoting the party. For example,

[in 1980], the most visible program sponsored by the national Republican party was its televised advertising campaign which urged citizens to "Vote Republican for a Change".... these "institutional" ads were designed to improve the public image of the party as a whole and raise pointed criticisms of Democrats in general.... RNC polls recorded a high level of citizen recall of these ads which caricatured the Speaker of the House.... For the first time, the technology of mass television advertising has been brought into service of a party rather than a candidate. (Arterton, 1982, p. 106)

The national Democratic party followed the pattern, and proparty ads have now become the staple of most election years. The better-financed state parties have taken a page from the national book in this realm. Minnesota Republicans credit their generic ads urging Democrats to support a change in government with their success in capturing the lower house of the state

THE LITTLE GIRL WITH THE DAISY

The classic negative advertisement never mentioned Barry Goldwater in 1964 but successfully linked Goldwater with war and Lyndon Johnson with peace.

Video	Audio
Camera up on little girl in field, picking petals off a daisy	*Little girl:* "One, two, three, four, five, seven, six, six, eight, nine, nine—"
Girl looks up startled; freeze frame on girl; move into pupil of her eye, until screen is black.	*Man's voice, very loud as if heard over a loudspeaker at a test site:* "Ten, nine, eight, seven, six, five, four, three, two, one—"
Cut to atom bomb exploding. Move into close-up of explosion.	Sound of explosion.
	Lyndon Johnson voice-over: "These are the stakes—to make a world in which all God's children can live, or to go into the dark. We must either love each other, or we must die."
Cut to white letters on black background: "Vote for President Johnson on November 3."	*Announcer:* "Vote for President Johnson on November 3. The stakes are too high for you to stay home."

legislature in 1984 for the first time since state legislators ran under a party label.

In an attempt to improve the image of the party label, state and local party organizations have expanded their activities beyond the strictly political realm. Republicans in California have worked on housing and integration of Asian refugees, and other state parties run refuges for the homeless (Colorado), raise money for the starving, and help build senior citizen housing and a pool for the handicapped (New Mexico) (see Kayden & Mahe, 1985, p. 107). All of these public relations and social service activities are designed to strengthen the gut level approval of the individual parties and encourage party-label voting above and beyond the issues.

Voters motivated by *social factors* are more difficult to reach through the campaign. Prestige endorsements encourage some voters to back particular candidates, and the parties provide favored candidates with access to top political leaders for photo opportunities and official endorsements. In the more important campaigns, visits by the president or key elected officials are often coordinated through the party organs. The social influence of friends and neighbors is difficult to control. Campaigns successful in reaching voters based on instrumental or psychological bases receive the added benefit of establishing a pool of voters who may socially influence their friends and relatives. In the long run, parties attempt to make it socially acceptable to support their candidates. For a long time, voting Republican in much of the South was socially unacceptable. "Yellow-dog Democrats" (who would vote for a yellow dog if he were a Democrat) prevailed. Working hard, and favored by national Democratic candidates and policies opposed by many southerners, beginning with presidential contests, the Republican party slowly developed a foothold in the South. Although a pervasive two-party South is far from a reality, voting Republican no longer carries the stigma it once did.

Communicating with the Right People

Casting political communications to the wind in the hope that some messages will fall on fertile ground characterizes fewer and fewer modern campaigns. Rather than using a "shotgun" approach with wide appeal, campaigns increasingly use a narrow "rifle" approach, carefully targeting specific audiences to receive designated messages.

Some General Targeting Considerations.   Although there is no absolute science to campaign strategy, three strategies have become part of the conventional wisdom. First, *focus on the voters who will make a difference.* Not all voters are equal, particularly in presidential campaigns. The electoral college system with its winner-take-all aspect rewards the winner of the popular majority in a state with all electoral votes of that state. Presidential candidates spend little time communicating with the voters in states they are sure to win or lose, since improving one's percentage counts for little. Presidential candidates spend most of their time and focus on issues of interest to voters in "toss-up" states having a large electoral vote. The attention presidential candidates give to areas of deep strength or weakness is largely designed to boost the long-term vitality of the party organization, an activity most presidential candidates eschew unless they are far ahead in the polls.

In primary elections for all offices, wise candidates focus their efforts on voters eligible and likely to vote in the primary. In the majority of states with closed primaries, voters unregistered with a party are ineligible to vote in the primary. It does little good to create a broad base of support among all voters and in the process lose the primary through innattention to party activists. Among the partisans, experience has shown that those of higher socioeconomic status and those with more extreme outlooks will take the time to vote.

Second, *go where the "ducks" are.* When seeking support, candidates target likely voters in current areas of strength. It is easier to increase one's support from 70 to 75 percent than from 20 to 25 percent. Voters surrounded by supporters of a candidate find themselves under social pressures to conform and are more amenable to that message.

Third, *know the voters and meet them where they are.* Voters vary as to the social, instrumental, and psychological factors motivating their votes.

Although it may be possible to change the importance of the various motivations, it is significantly less work to build on their current needs and interests (Arterton, 1983, pp. 43–44). Different targets respond to different messages. There is nothing new about the technique of targeting per se. When former New York City Mayor Fiorello LaGuardia sampled different ethnic foods in various neighborhoods and spoke of their unique needs, he was sending the message that he appreciated each group and had an understanding of their interests. In contemporary campaigns, the strategy remains the same, although the technology of identifying appropriate groups and the means of communication differ.

Mass-Communications Targeting.   Modern voters find themselves bombarded with political information during campaigns. One political consultant estimates that the average individual is faced with more than 3,000 messages a day, and a major activity involves screening out the irrelevant and inconsistent ones (Matt Reese, author's interview). Political stories in the news and purchased advertising by the candidates compete for the attention for voters with a multitude of nonpolitical messages from the news media and advertising. Voters selectively attune to those messages serving their individual interests. Spot advertising of short messages gives the candidate maximum flexibility in gaining the attention of specific groups of voters. Although spot advertising is much maligned as simplistic and misleading, current research emphasizes that many voters receive significant issue-oriented information from such 30- and 60-second presentations and use the information in their voting decisions (Patterson & McClure, 1976).

The design of spot advertising for maximum effect has become a profession of its own, with both national parties operating extensive media-production service centers. As important as the design of the spot is the way in which it is used. Significant effort is placed on targeting the spot to appropriate audiences. This may be as simple as choosing a particular radio station based on its audience (such as discussing social security on the easy-listening station favored by senior citizens) or choosing a specific time spot (discussing mass transit during afternoon "drive time" when communters are stuck in traffic). For television programs, more extensive audience profiles indicate who watches which programs at which times, enabling the targeting of messages to be even more precise. Data collected for the Nielson ratings determine the cost of commercials and enable traditional advertisers to choose their audiences, and similar data are available to political advertisers. Improved polling techniques and improvements in the ability to produce high-quality television advertisements have made it possible for candidates to change course almost overnight, responding to charges from their opponent or attempting to stem a growing estrangement from a particular segment of the electorate (see Ehrenhalt, 1985b, p. 2559). In the larger campaigns, professional *time buyers* ply their trade, charging significant fees:

> Using computers which analyze census data and audience breakdowns for television and radio programs, time buyers are able to project exactly which types of voters are likely to be watching which programs at which times. . . . As one media consultant put it "we're all going into computers. We've had to because television costs have gotten so high and the potential for wasting votes is so great. You just can't operate out of the hip pocket anymore." (Peterson, 1986c, p. A8)

Although broadcasting remains a major communications vehicle, increased emphasis is being placed on *narrowcasting*. Cable television presents programs with more distinctive audiences at a fraction of the cost of commercial television (Arterton, 1983, pp. 16–17). Candidates, parties, and interest groups have begun using satellite transmissions in campaigns. By preannouncing programs of special interest to a small, but important, segment of the electorate, they build their own targeted audience.

> Until now, politicians have used television to send shorter, universally appealing messages to large audiences. The new television will mean longer messages targeted to smaller audiences. (Neustadt, 1982a, p. 220)

For example, the Chamber of Commerce's business network "Busnet" links key business leaders to candidates and their own lobbyists giving them direction on making their contribution and voting choices. Some candidates use cable television to hold state or nationwide meetings to spur on their local supporters. In 1982,

> Nationally . . . Republicans far outstripped the Democrats in applications of new technology. They rented satellite time to distribute footage of GOP senators to local TV stations for late-night use. (Neustadt, 1982a, p. 219)

For many campaigns, extensive use of targeted electronic communications is not cost effective. For example, most congressional districts do not coincide with a particular media market. Those districts covering more than one market find their costs multiplied, whereas those districts making up only part of a media market waste much of their resources communicating with voters who cannot vote for them. In such cases other targeting methods must prevail.

Targeted Mail.   *Targeted mail* provides a less expensive and often more effective method of communicating with voters than that of relying on general news coverage or purchased electronic advertising. Every new generation of campaign activists believes it has invented the new techniques. Direct mail has a relatively long history. Woodrow Wilson sent out more than 300,000 pieces of campaign mail in 1914. Dwight Eisenhower used the *Reader's Digest* experts to design his direct-mail appeals. But it took the introduction of the computer to make direct mail the staple of modern campaigns. Although massive mailings were possible to do by hand, the use of computers had an "unlocking effect," expanding the methods of identifying groups to target and facilitating a volume of communication virtually impossible using traditional methods. As one campaign manager put it, computer targeting allows one to work as a surgeon with a "scalpel rather than with a shotgun . . . . Most local campaigns can't afford mass media, and if they can, their message is drowned out by the flashier campaigns. Targeted mail and phone banks are the preferred alternative for getting to the people we want" (author's interview).

List creation is crucial to successful mailing, and a targeted mail campaign is no better than the lists on which it is based. To some degree the quality of a list rests on mechanical aspects such as its accuracy (names spelled correctly with correct addresses), timeliness (deceased and other ineligible voters deleted), and efficiency (duplicate names deleted), but this is only part of the question. The effectiveness of a list depends on the amount of information it can tell you about voters and their interests.

> In earlier periods, the decentralized party organizations performed this task as part of the solicitation of votes: citizens were contacted by precinct workers who knew them personally. Today, much of the communication and information gathering and retention takes place electronically. (Arterton, 1983, p. 20)

The art of list creation has as many variations as practitioners. Campaigns in states with voter-registration lists already on computer tape start with an advantage. Such lists are enhanced by "merging and purging" them with lists of subscribers to specialized magazines, owners of particular kinds of cars, census information on the kinds of people living in particular zip codes, and so on (see Figure 6.9). Campaigns in areas without statewide registration lists approach the problem of list creation in the same way businesses do. They buy, borrow, or trade lists that seem to contain potential contributors or supporters. The utility of various lists differs depending on the task at hand. Lists designed to solicit contributions must be tested for response rate, since a very small percentage of any list will contribute. The initial first-generation lists are "prospected" using variations in appeal. Both the quality of the list and the appeal are measured on a subset of the lists before a broader mailing is made. Respondents to the first mailing become part of a pared down second-generation list made up of strong supporters. These refined lists are contacted again and again. Fund-raising consultants argue that "the secret of fund raising is that the most likely contributor is someone who has given before" (Smith, 1984b, p. 23). A number of observers argue that the Republican advantage in targeted mail fund raising may never be duplicated by the Democrats. Republicans, with their higher education levels and homogeneity on the issues seem to respond to the written word more than Democrats. Furthermore, the Republican organization got a head start in creating useful

218

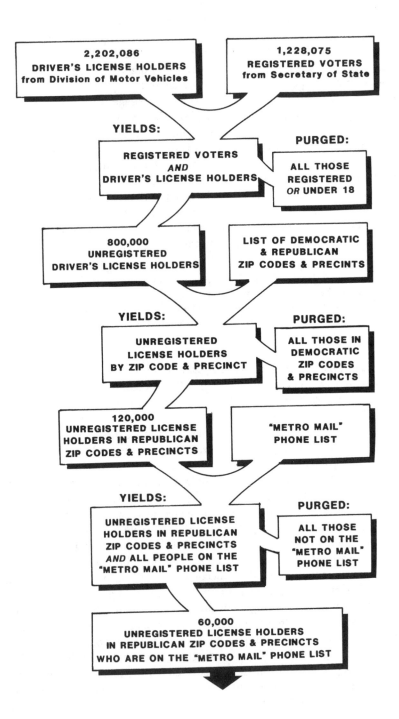

2,202,086
DRIVER'S LICENSE HOLDERS
from Division of Motor Vehicles

1,228,075
REGISTERED VOTERS
from Secretary of State

YIELDS:

REGISTERED VOTERS
AND
DRIVER'S LICENSE HOLDERS

PURGED:

ALL THOSE
REGISTERED
OR UNDER 18

800,000
UNREGISTERED
DRIVER'S LICENSE HOLDERS

LIST OF DEMOCRATIC
& REPUBLICAN
ZIP CODES & PRECINTS

YIELDS:

UNREGISTERED
LICENSE HOLDERS
BY ZIP CODE & PRECINCT

PURGED:

ALL THOSE IN
DEMOCRATIC
ZIP CODES
& PRECINCTS

120,000
UNREGISTERED LICENSE
HOLDERS IN REPUBLICAN
ZIP CODES & PRECINCTS

"METRO MAIL"
PHONE LIST

YIELDS:

UNREGISTERED LICENSE
HOLDERS IN REPUBLICAN
ZIP CODES & PRECINCTS
AND ALL PEOPLE ON THE
"METRO MAIL" PHONE LIST

PURGED:

ALL THOSE
NOT ON THE
"METRO MAIL"
PHONE LIST

60,000
UNREGISTERED LICENSE HOLDERS
IN REPUBLICAN ZIP CODES & PRECINCTS
WHO ARE ON THE "METRO MAIL" PHONE LIST

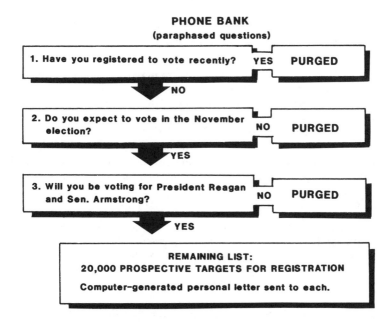

PHONE BANK
(paraphased questions)

1. Have you registered to vote recently?   YES   PURGED
↓NO

2. Do you expect to vote in the November election?   NO   PURGED
↓YES

3. Will you be voting for President Reagan and Sen. Armstrong?   NO   PURGED
↓YES

REMAINING LIST:
20,000 PROSPECTIVE TARGETS FOR REGISTRATION
Computer–generated personal letter sent to each.

Figure 6.9 Targeting Voters through "Merging and Purging"

lists at a time when postage rates were lower and the novelty of the approach increased its success (Sabato, 1985, p. 153).

Lists designed solely to influence voters have no mechanism for evaluating the effectiveness, and targeting is based on more creative hunches. Profiling voters by place of residence from census data on their zip code area gives clues to income, education, and ethnicity. An entire consulting profession of demographic targeting has developed around the ability to categorize census tracts politically. Car-registration data provide additional information on income and perhaps ideology and interests (Volvo owners tend to be yuppies—Young Urban Professionals). As one mailing-list master described it: "Hispanic surnamed individuals would get a different message than younger women who have been identified by their choice of the title 'Ms.'" (author's interview).

The Republican National Committee uses an "ethnic-surname file" computer program in its direct-mail program. The computer combs its huge voter-registration lists in search of potential voters with particular interests. The program is at least 90 percent accurate and can pick out Italian, Jewish, Irish, and even Serbo-Croation voters and automatically code them for special mailings (Salholz, 1984, p. 13).

The value of mailing lists emerges when the parties attempt to take over list management or attempt to coordinate list creation and use. General voter lists present little problem, but volunteer and contributor lists become a touchy subject. In one party executive's words,

> Defeated candidates and those who don't plan to run again are about the only politicians who will give up their lists without some quid pro quo....The legacy of the Reagan campaigns is a set of extensive computerized voter lists left with the state party organizations. They were much more willing to share them after 1984 than before. (Author's interview)

For the parties as continuing organizations, becoming the repository of voter, volunteer, and contributor lists gives them something of value to give candidates. One state chairman explained:

> Candidates find it difficult to keep their mailing lists up to date and we are the natural vehicle. Now with the computer, voter lists are not thrown away like they used to be. Having good lists allows us to recruit more viable candidates and gives us a good answer to elected officials who ask "Who have you done for me lately?" (Author's interview)

One of the most important legacies of the two Reagan campaigns is the extensive computerized lists of voters categorized by demographic groups. Republicans made sure that their lists would become the property of the state party organizations. Democratic efforts in this realm have more often been used to help specific campaigns, and the information gained was often lost after the election. Republicans learned earlier the contribution of such resources to the continuity and strength of the party organization (Edsall, 1985b).

Designing the message properly is another important factor in successful mailings. Not only must the message appeal to the targeted group, but it must be designed in such a way that people will open it. More than 75 percent of all direct-mail appeals get thrown away unopened (see Schram, 1982, p. A2). Personalization of the address (rather than "Dear Occupant") and of the content increases the impact, as does mentioning the person in the body of the letter ("I am sure the Jones family shares my concern over..."). With more organizations both in and out of the political realm using direct mail, the tactics have become more extreme. Official looking letters declaring "Enclosed: Urgent Information about Your Social Security" sent to senior citizens or "Official Tax Questionnaire Enclosed" sent to businesspersons increase the likelihood they will be opened. Contrary to common sense, the more ideological and conflictual messages seem much more effective than reasoned discussions of the issue (see Cotter et al., 1984, p. 167). The consultants argue as follows:

> Targeted mail is much better for attack advertising. It is safe since you can specify your audience much more clearly....Potential subjects of attack often use "inoculation letters." A preemptive letter outlining your position

on a sensitive issue protects you from future negative information the voter might receive. (Author's interview)

What is the future of targeted mailing? Although targeted mailing still works, the proliferation of groups and individuals using it and the wide availability of relatively standardized lists reduces its effectiveness. As one party leader put it:

> We are beyond the awe of seeing thousands of letters per day directed to individuals with narrow interests. The challenge for the future is over who can reach the most voters cheapest. So far we have not been very economical. We know how to use the technology; now we have to bring the cost down. (Author's interview)

Although few observers question the effectiveness of targeting and the underlying assumption that voters respond more to messages of interest to them than to messages seen as extraneous to their needs, the technique does engender some fears. From the individual voter's perspective, questions of privacy arise as voter characteristics, preferences, and behavior become part of huge data banks with little control over their use (see Arterton, 1983, p. 78). From a broader perspective, targeting techniques encourage an atomization of the electorate with candidates appealing to and voters responding to narrow messages and motivations rather than general goals for the political system. To the degree this happens, the campaign and political party roles of aggregating and compromising political interests diminish. Mass-media approaches force the party to come to a set of positions that can be sold to a wide segment of the population, whereas targeting approaches enable the party to support sending different messages to subsets of the population.

Getting the Voters to the Polls

The campaign is not over when the last speech is given and the last piece of targeted mail is delivered. Convincing voters which candidate to support means little if those voters fail to appear at the polls. Political parties traditionally took on the task of get-out-the-vote (GOTV) drives on election day through facilitating transportation to the polls, using poll watchers to identify nonvoters, and making personal contact through telephone banks. One consultant argued that "there is no magic to getting out the vote. It just takes work. We take the Dr. Pepper 10-2-4 approach. We call our supporters at ten to see if they have voted, and check up on the non-voters at two and four" (author's interview).

In many areas, candidates distrustful of party effectiveness duplicate the party efforts, and the task for the party lies in coordinating and increasing the efficiency of the various drives. The success of the Republican party in California in 1982 in stimulating absentee balloting added a sophisticated new technique to the party arsenal. Using computer lists to identify others likely to vote by absentee ballot (traveling salespersons, nursing home residents, military personnel, and so on), the party contacted likely Republican voters and offered them help in casting their ballots. The number of absentee ballots increased by more than 50 percent with 61 percent supporting the Republican candidate for governor. The large plurality of Republican absentee ballots offset the narrow Democratic victory in regular votes delivering the governor's mansion to the Republicans (see Arterton, 1983, pp. 28–29).

Assessing the Impact of Campaigns in the Technological Age

Complex phenomena like political campaigns seldom have simple explanations. There is a tendency to explain election results as being based on clever decisions by candidates and their staffs. Winners' campaigns are looked on as textbook examples of infallible decisions, whereas losers represent examples of all of the pitfalls. In reality, election results are often out of anyone's control. In some districts at certain times the best campaign cannot win, whereas in other situations seemingly disastrous decisions still do not spell defeat. The explanatory variables do not exhibit a clear pattern.

Assessing the electoral implications of new ground rules and new campaign technology is difficult. Few campaigns are completely modern or traditional. Uncertainty about the impact of new approaches means that new technology tends to be added to traditional approaches rather than replacing them (see Agranoff, 1979, pp. 235–236). In many headquarters, the microcomputer for mailing lists serves as the stand for a bucket of traditional campaign buttons. Without irrefutable evidence as to what works, candidates are schizophrenic about new approaches.

> The technology creeps down slower than you'd think it would. In House campaigns you still have arguments between the media people and the door knockers. People win for sewer commissioner because they mailed out 25,000 potholders and think the way to win for Congress is to mail out 50,000 potholders. (Michael Murphey, quoted in Ehrenhalt, 1985b, p. 2564).

Although candidates with the most money or the most sophisticated uses of technology do not always win, one sees few candidates or campaign activists willingly running underfinanced campaigns and eschewing new technology.

THE ADOPTION OF CAMPAIGN TECHNOLOGY BY THE PARTIES

The story of the political parties fighting back into the political game by becoming the vendors of campaign technology begins largely with the Republican party on the national level. The Republicans pioneered most of the current applications, and the Democrats followed their lead (see Chapter 3 for full discussion). As two observers put it, "Typically, it is the Republicans who take the lead in organizational development, with a lag of eight to twelve years...before the Democrats catch up" (Kayden & Mahe, 1985, p. 92). Only relatively recently did national Democratic leaders begin to recognize the problem and do something about it. A former national Democratic party official mused, "We Democrats were blindsided by technology, and tried to live on our reputation and democratic procedures. After a few years it took no genius to see that we were losing out, so we patched up our pride and began to determine how we could rejoin the game" (author's interview). Even old-style politicans such as former House Speaker Tip O'Neill recognized the problem:

> Candidates need the financial and technological support of the party. The preoccupation of the Democratic National Committee with presidential politics must cease. The congressional campaign committee must serve as a genuine political and financial resource for Democratic incumbents and challengers. (Hershey, 1984, p. 127)

A similar pattern of Republican leadership in providing services applies on the state party level as measured by the Party Transformation Study (see Gibson, Cotter, Bibby, & Huckshorn, 1985). Much of the stimulus for state parties to enter the provision of services came from the provision of resources, expertise, and models by the national party, with the Republicans more active earlier in providing such stimuli. The Republicans placed a great deal of effort on areas of electoral weakness, but significant opportunity, such as the South. For example, the Florida State Republican party is the best-financed and one of the most technologically sophisticated providers of services and has been heavily helped by the national party.

The Democratic party is clearly playing a game of "catch up" when it comes to becoming a service-vendor party. Its slow start places it at a disadvantage, but certainly has not placed a damper on its ardor in expanding its capabilities. The Fairness Commission, the Democratic procedural response to the 1984 loss, was clearly deemphasized, and an attempt was made to "get it out of the way so we can get on with the important task of providing candidate services" (state party leader, author's interview).

THE CONSEQUENCES OF THE RISE OF THE SERVICE-VENDOR-BROKER PARTY

Although American political parties are still in transition (and probably always will be to some degree), we seem to be well into a new age for the parties in which party image, ideology, labor-intensive human resources, and party decision-making procedures (expressive goals) have largely given way to competitive goals primarily dominated by the ability of the parties to provide services to their candidates and subordinate organizational units. These service-vendor parties have taken the essentially technologically based services, which once dramatically weakened their role in contemporary politics, and have begun to use these services to rebuild the party organization.

There is little disagreement that neither political parties nor the process of politics is the same as it was a few decades ago. Some of those changes are directly related to the rise of the service-vendor party as either causes or consequences, and others are merely coincidental happenings. It is important to recognize the danger of assuming single causes.

> We must be careful to avoid becoming technological determinists. There is nothing inherent in the technologies of communication that will necessarily cause politicians to use them in a certain manner. To predict more accurately, we need to understand both the physical capacities (and limitations) of the hardware as well as...the institutional form in which the technology is available to politicians. An even more important factor in determining how the hardware will be used is the incentive structure of campaigns. (Arterton, 1983, p. 3)

Winning Elections

Politics is a game of both perception and reality. Although it is difficult to prove once and for all whether enhanced party-based campaign resources are key factors in winning more elections,

> the important point may be that the entire political establishment—both Democrats and Republicans, political analysts from both the media and academia—BELIEVES that what the Republicans do makes a difference. (Salmore & Salmore, 1985, p. 219)

As Charles Jones put it, "hard disk politics will not magically turn defeat into victory, but it allows a political party to make the most of its other strengths" (Jones, 1986, p. 4). The test of campaign technology lies in its ability to affect election outcomes. According to the pattern of previous postwar midterm elections, the Republicans should have lost between 40 and 60 seats in the House; yet they lost only 26 seats in 1982 and 5 seats in 1986. At least some of that relative success can be accounted for by their heavy use of technology (Edsall, 1984b, p. A1).

Technology seems to be more important in campaigns with low expenditure limits, since in a battle where everyone has the same resources, efficiency counts for more. Special elections have become "orgies of technological innovation," since with little else going on, the national parties use these campaigns to try out all of the new approaches.

Practitioners point out that new technologies are not well understood by politicians.

We are still fighting the battle of unrealistic expectations. Candidates and party activists view new technology and especially computer applications as magical instruments which will win elections with no work on their part. Too many campaigns and parties purchase expensive hardware and software only to have the machine sit there while the purchasers wait to see it do something. (Author's interview)

The impact of services may be more indirect than direct.

Whatever the actual effect of the GOP's national advertising, media and polling services as well as the guarantee of full party financing offered by the Republicans were of immense value in recruiting top-quality candidates. "We locked them in with our resources," admitted Richard Bond of the Republican National Committee. (Sabato, 1982, p. 79)

Some analysts argue that the new technologies give Republicans an inherent advantage that may never be matched by the Democrats. Part of this argument rests on timing. The Republicans pioneered new technologies such as targeted mailing at a time when initial investment costs (largely postage) were relatively low and the technique had not been overused.

For local campaigns, computer technology may well have a democratizing effect by lowering the cost of mounting an efficient campaign (see Smith 1984b, p. 26; Clendinin, 1984, p. 1). With relatively little training and off-the-shelf software most small campaigns can manage their schedules, budget, and mailing lists.

The perceived importance of new technology for winning has driven up the cost of campaigns. Combined with the growth of PACs, the increased expenditures make candidates more beholden to those providing the resources for modern campaigning.

Linking Voters to the Party

Translating organizational activities into causes of change in individual behavior is dangerous at best, but some effects seem to be emerging. The slight reversal of declining voter participation in recent elections can be at least partially attributed to massive registration and activation programs by the parties. F. Christopher Arterton argued persuasively that more effective communications strategies spearheaded by the parties provide more and better information that could help link voters to a party:

We should note the less direct implications of the direct mail success. For the first time in American political history, there exists a substantial number of citizens who consider themselves to be MEMBERS of a national party; they can carry cards in their wallets to prove it. . . . While we are still very far from a European conception of party membership. . .we should not ignore the fact that a concept of identity as "members" of a party, rather than as voters or identifiers, is developing. (1982, p. 105)

Controlling Elected Officials

The ultimate goal of reestablishing the party's campaign role and success with the electorate lies in having some influence over the policy process. The rise of the service-vendor party sets up conditions increasing such influence by helping the party affect the issue agenda and, as the next chapter demonstrates, facilitating compliance from newly dependent elected officials.

Xandra Kayden and Eddie Mahe argued that during the campaign

> weekly computer feeds to candidates...present a speech outline, [or] a possible press release and [are] designed to help Republican candidates handle critical questions about the day's events and the administration's role in them. Those candidates who are elected to office will come to Washington with a common history on positions on a wide range of issues—positions written by professional party staffers. (1985, p. 82)

To the degree that elected officials credit the party for their electoral success, and to the degree that the party links the provision of services to party support, the rise of the service-vendor party promises the party organization an enhanced role in the policy process.

> The new directions in which both major parties are moving appear to be changing the relationship between party and candidate in a fundamental way. The coordinated expenditures, institutional advertising, media services, tracking polls, candidate schools, and all the rest are having the effect of drawing candidates closer to the parties. Particularly on the Republican side, where party renewal is in full bloom, the candidates voice similar policy themes, take much the same approach on at least some basic issues, and have a stake in the party's present well-being and future development. They are beholden to the party....It may well be that congressional party cohesion on basic issues will increase, that voters will begin to perceive more strongly the connection between that party and its issues and candidates, and that a more party-responsible system will gradually emerge in the future. If so, the national party committees, thanks to their institutional adaptation of the new campaign technologies, will be able to take much of the credit. (Sabato, 1985, p. 104)

Revitalizing the Party Organization

The ability of the parties to discover a new role in providing campaign services promises both to revitalize party organizations and to change their very nature. Thirty years ago, two experts on American politics boldly asserted:

> There is perhaps no point on which writers on American politics are so...agreed as that our state and local party organizations, taken collectively, are far more powerful than our national organizations. (Ranney & Kendall, 1956, pp. 160–161)

Little could be further from the truth today.

Historically, national parties have not had much of an independent existence. . . . Where national committees were little more than confederations of state parties, they now have an independent existence. . . . Now the national parties are reaching out to help their state affiliates in a complete reversal of roles. (Arterton, 1982, p. 123)

Both reform initiatives—the Democratic commitment to expressive procedural reform and the Republican lead in building a service-vendor party—contributed to a nationalization and centralization of the parties. The Republican lead in developing service-vendor parties came as the second of a "one-two punch" to redefine the organizational influence within the parties. Since strong national parties require active state and local parties, the national parties worked hard to keep them in the game but constantly reminded state and local affiliates of their status. Although local party activity has increased dramatically in recent years (see Gibson, Cotter, Bibby & Huckshorn, 1985), national party activity increases make it pale in comparison and have often been the stimulus for state and local party change. As Leon Epstein concluded, "The Republicans have nationalized their party effort by a method analogous to the federal government's grant-in-aid system" (quoted in Conlan, 1985, p. 40). Even the Party Transformation study, which boldly challenged the conventional wisdom by asserting that state and local parties are alive and well, was forced to face the reality of national party power:

As party organizations have developed as more stable institutions it is probable that some sort of relationship between different levels of party have emerged. Relationships today are clearly not hierarchical, although both national committees have attempted, with varying success, to exert some degree of control over state party practices and activities. But perhaps the most significant change in intra-party relations is the emergence of a service role for party organizations. Through joint activity and the provision of services the national party organizations have developed a means for inducing state party cooperation and coordination. Similarly, the state parties have used a variety of "carrots" to integrate the local party organizations. (Gibson, Frendreis, & Vertz, 1985, p. 9)

CONCLUSION

Political campaigns are considerably different from what they were a generation or more ago. New approaches capitalizing on modern communications technologies affect the substance and resources of campaigning as well as redefining the meaningful players. In revising their campaign role to play a service-vendor-broker function political parties have not regained their traditional role or power, but they have guaranteed a continued position in the campaign process. This new position allows the parties some influence over the substance and consequences of campaigns and sets the stage for enhanced influence over the policy-making process.

7

The Party in Office

The morning after an election the media proclaim "A Democratic Landslide" or "Republicans Sweep the Senate." The implication of such headlines is that elections are more than a series of individual contests and that the party identification of elected officials has something to do with their behavior in office. In reality, postelection impact of the parties could be much more indirect, with the parties doing little more than facilitating the election of candidates who differ consistently on the issues and follow their personal and political instincts once in office. Each party appeals to candidates with different policy perspectives, potentially screening out candidates incompatible with party positions in the primary and more likely to elect candidates in certain types of constituencies. Personal political perspectives combine with differing constituency pressures to insure that Republican officeholders will behave differently from Democratic ones. The different constituency pressures are heightened by the fact that elected officials tend to define their constituency not in terms of legal boundaries or characteristics of all eligible voters but in terms of their personal electoral coalition—those voters who supported them in the last election—a definition that tends to heighten the importance of fellow partisans. Once in office, officials tend to hear more from voters who supported them in the last election and who support their current policy positions than from those who oppose them (Congressional Quarterly, 1976, p. 533), reinforcing the behavior pattern on which they have embarked.

THE RESPONSIBLE-PARTY MODEL

Although the indirect electoral impact of parties on the behavior of elected officials would be enough to warrant the study of partisanship in office, both political theory and reality imply that the parties as organizations can and

229

should do much more. Despite the fact that even during the period of party hegemony winning elections was more important to parties than was carrying out policy, a predominant undercurrent of political thought in the United States has always striven for a more responsible-party system. The model of responsible parties begins with an electoral process involving parties with clear and consistent differences on the issues. During the campaign, party candidates are expected to appeal to the voters on the basis of these party differences. Voters, according to the responsible-party model, express their policy preferences by voting more for the party than for the candidate. Once in office, the party organization is expected to use its power to carry out the party positions expressed during the campaign.

Responsible parties were promoted as providing voters with the necessary information to make their votes count in the way they intended and to make the party an entity that could be rewarded or punished based on its performance in office. This party accountability would make voting more meaningful. Furthermore, in a political system marked by a separation of powers, political parties were viewed as the glue that held the various branches and levels of government together, promoting the necessary cooperation for getting something done.

> Party government is good democratic doctrine because the parties are the special form of political organization adapted to the mobilization of majorities. How else can the majority get organized? If democracy means anything at all it means that the majority has the right to organize for the purpose of taking over government. (Schattschneider, 1942/1982, p. 208; see also Ranney, 1962; Committee on Political Parties of the American Political Science Association, 1950, p. 15)

Considerable debate continues over both the desirability and the possibility of the type of party government envisioned by the promoters of more responsible parties. Opponents of more centralized and powerful parties assert that such a system promotes more powerful and active government, limits creativity, discourages compromise, and limits the routes for citizen impact on government. The criticisms of the concept of responsible parties have been superseded in recent years by significant evidence concerning the possibility of making such a system work in contemporary America. The preconditions—differentiated parties, bound candidates, issue-oriented voters—all fall far below the level perceived as necessary for true party government to prevail. More party-oriented government seems to work better in parliamentary systems lacking the separation of powers characteristic of the American system, in societies with more homogeneity, and under electoral rules supporting centralized parties. In the British system, for example, the national parties have the right to screen local party nominees for support of the party position and control a staff of government-paid party organizers in each district. Once in office, the party winning a majority in Parliament chooses the executive branch leaders, and the party is held responsible for government action. Voters in such a system have a firmer grasp of the partisan implications of their vote, and candidates are motivated to campaign on the basis of party and support the party once in office.

American parties lack many of the resources for keeping candidates and elected officials in line. Candidates realize that they can get nominated through the primary system and often are elected without party help. Voters see party identification as only one of the characteristics they take into account when choosing between candidates. The parties have responded to candidate-centered campaigns and ticket splitting voters by moving away from enforcing issue and ideological constraints. Today the parties serve as service vendors and brokers for any candidate willing to wear the party label. Increased dependence on party services holds the potential for binding candidates closer to the party, but currently, many candidates have sufficient alternatives on which to rely. Unaccustomed to taking cues from the party organization to issues during the campaign, elected officials enter office with little intention of becoming more constrained in their behavior. As political journalist David Broder argues, "Party government is a tool that rusts when it is not used; we have gone a long time without using the political parties as they were meant to be used" (1972, p. 212).

THE PARTY IN THE LEGISLATURE

"Party is the most important reference group in structuring legislative behavior...and in the absence of party, no other kind of reference group serves a similar purpose" (Harris & Hain, 1983, p. 238). The legislative serves as the primary focus for understanding and explaining the potential and reality of party influence on elected officials. Since coalition building in legislatures is a necessity, lacking party involvement, other groups or individuals will take over the task. "Parties are most valuable to members of Congress when those members act as legislators, writing and passing laws....The party is the basic mechanism for arranging cooperative action in pursuit of legislative goals" (Crotty, 1984, p. 201).

Given the complexity of modern legislatures with numerous committees and simultaneous consideration of a variety of issues, the party has the potential of serving as the source of relevant information, the provider of voting cues, and the vehicle for forging compromises. The majority party is expected to control the administration of the chamber and take the lead in scheduling activity, whereas the minority party takes on the responsibility of monitoring majority party actions for fairness and wisdom.

232   The Party in Office

Partisanship and Responsible Parties

"Partisanship" is the degree to which individual legislators work together in pursuing party-defined goals through the consensual establishment of goals, the preferential treatment of fellow party members, and the use of party power resources to bring about cohesive behavior among the party members in office. Partisanship is not the same as responsible-party government unless the voters are given the opportunity to pass judgment on the content of the party goals, both prospectively and retrospectively through successive elections. Elected officials could demonstrate cohesive partisanship and be responsible to no one but themselves. Party responsibility implies that party members act in behalf and under the direction of the voters who put them in office, not that they simply work together in a disciplined manner as a group for their own benefits. Party responsibility is not possible without significant party discipline, but discipline is not enough.

The Changing Environment of Legislative Partisanship

The External Environment

"The important change that has taken place is not that strong parties have suddenly become weak, but that conditions favoring individualistic politicians have become even more prevalent now than in the past" (Mann, 1981, p. 39). Newly elected legislators arrive in Congress, and especially in most state legislatures, owing their party little and less prepared to follow the dictates of a political party organization. A century ago, a legislator's electoral fate lay with the party organization that controlled nominations, printed the ballots, and dominated the resources necessary for election (see Brady & Hurley, 1985, pp. 66–67).

> The new-style members of Congress...reflect the individualism of the organizations from which they come.... Today's members are likely to have never followed any leaders at all from the beginnings of their political careers. The new-style members won their seats, in all probability by their own efforts....Not having needed the party at home, and not beholden to it, they keep the party in Congress somewhat at a distance too. (Sundquist, 1982, pp. 49–50)

Familiar and comfortable with candidate-centered campaigns, the members of Congress followed by political scientist Richard Fenno as they visited their constitutents emphasized trust, constitutency service, and being "one of them" more than issues or party. The campaigns were not so much antiparty as placing party in the category of irrelevance (see Fenno, 1978, p. 55 and passim). Morris Fiorina argued that

> as the federal role has expanded, and federal programs have come to touch the lives of countless citizens, the relationship of a congressman to his

constituents has changed. Increasingly, congressmen are elected as individuals, not as members of a party, and increasingly they are reelected as nonpartisan, nonideological providers of constituency services. (1978, p. 41)

The nature of legislative districts also mitigates against party control. Congressmen and congresswomen are "fifth wheels" on the party wagon. With the national party focusing on the presidential races and the local party on state and local races, the congressional candidate can be caught in limbo with no party organization primarily interested in his race (Mikva & Saris, 1983, p. 68). The link between legislators and their parties was further weakened by the reapportionment rulings that required districts of equal population. Strict mathematical equality makes it almost impossible to respect the local jurisdictional boundaries around which party organizations are built. Legislative district boundaries overlap a number of jurisdictions while dividing others. Rather than creating legislative-district party organizations with the sole purpose of electing a legislator—who has little patronage and is not perceived as affecting local concern very much—most parties have abdicated much of their role in legislative elections to the personal organization of the candidates.

Voting studies indicate that legislative candidates may place too much trust in their personal efforts and standing with their constituents when "paradoxically, most voters base their voting decision on the candidate's party" (Crotty, 1984, p. 211). Most voters have very little information in legislative contests and revert to partisan cues, but in politics perceptions are as important as reality. As long as elected officials believe that they have secured their position on their own, their behavior will be guided by that perception. Furthermore, it is one thing to realize that party labels guide less-informed voters and to believe that the party organization should hold some sway in the candidate's postelection behavior.

The Internal Environment

The meeting of legislative party members is called a *caucus*. The caucus selects party officials (such as the majority and minority leader, whips, and a campaign committee chair) and nominates chamber leaders (the Speaker, committee chairs, and so on). The candidates nominated by the majority party almost always win, since no matter how splintered the party is, its members almost always vote cohesively at least on procedural and leadership votes. In some settings it is difficult to separate party and leadership positions. For example, although the Speaker of the U.S. House of Representatives serves as the presiding officer and is expected to show some degree of fairness, at the same time he plays a partisan role leading fellow party leaders. On the other hand, the presiding officer in the U.S. Senate (the president pro tempore in the absence of the vice-president) leaves partisan leadership to the majority leader and is expected to preside in an even-handed manner.

The majority and minority leaders guide the party fortunes on the floor. The Constitution, chamber, and party rules are silent about the duties of these leaders, but tradition has them serving as party spokespersons on the floor, helping to plan the legislative agenda, gauging party opinion on key issues, and encouraging support for party positions. In the final two tasks, the majority and minority leaders are assisted by a team of whips, who attempt to assess the level of party support for specific legislation, influence their colleagues, and get supporters to the floor for key votes. The term *whip* comes from fox hunting, in which the "whipper-in" is assigned to keep the hounds from leaving the pack (Granat, 1985, p. 2502). "Whips frequently stand by the doors to the floor, and signal their arriving colleagues to vote yea (thumbs up) or nay (thumbs down) on legislation. They also prepare weekly 'whip notices' advising members of the upcoming floor agenda" (Davidson and Oleszek, 1981, p. 173). Although the whips lack a continuous supply of rewards and sanctions to keep members in line, loyalty to the party is taken into account when making committee assignments, distributing favors, and scheduling legislation. Loyal partisans are allowed the public exposure of presiding over the chamber and can have some impact on the consideration of legislation in which they are interested.

Each party maintains a number of committees under the caucus. The congressional (or senatorial) campaign committees for each party provide contributions and services to incumbents and increasingly extend their largesse to challengers. Each party maintains a policy and steering or research committee designed to outline the long-term policy goals of the party, but they have not had significant influence in recent years.

Although not formal party leaders, committee chairs in the U.S. Congress come exclusively from the majority party in the chamber. The partisan division on most committees mirrors the division in the chamber, with a few key committees (such as the Rules Committee, which does scheduling in the House) having extraordinary majority-party control.

Particularly in the House with its unwieldy size, members have organized themselves into a variety of caucuses, many of which have a partisan basis. Organizations such as the Democratic Study Group (liberal Democrats), the Wednesday Group (moderate Republicans), and the Conservative Opportunity Society (conservative Republicans) meet regularly to exchange information. They also have their own intelligence gathering and influential whip system. Responding to the increased independence of members, legislatures revised their internal structures and procedures to accommodate these interests. Party organizational strength has ebbed and flowed in Congress based on the wishes of the membership and the skills of particular party leaders, with a general decline in organizational power during this century. The watershed in the House occurred in 1910 when Speaker Joseph Cannon (R.-Ill.)—who had dominated the House through his power to assign members to committees, appoint committee chairs, and regulate the flow of bills—became the focus of

REINING IN THE CHAIRS: THE PARTY FIGHTS BACK

In 1974, after having their ranks swelled by more than 70 new Democratic members, the Democratic party in the House used its newly adopted rule change providing for the election of chairpersons to remove three of the least representative committee chairs from office. The freshmen members forced the issue by asking all chairpersons to justify keeping their positions and respond to questions at a freshman caucus meeting. Some of the most senior chairs, offended by the presumptuousness of the freshmen, were vague and patronizing. When the full caucus met, three chairpersons with the lowest level of party support in the last session were defeated. Although the average Democrat supported the party 69 percent of the time on floor votes dividing the parties, F. Edward Herbert (D-La.), chair of the Armed Services Committee, had supported the party position only 15 percent of the time. W.R. Poage (D-Tex.), chair of the Agriculture Committee, with a 24 percent support rating and Wright Patman (D-Tex.) chair of the Banking and Currency Committee, with a 51 percent support rating proved to be tempting targets also. Although the deposed chairpersons maintained similar voting records in the next Congress, other chairs receiving a significant number of negative votes in the caucus became more receptive to fellow partisans in committee affairs and more supportive of the party on the floor. George Mahon (D-Tex.), chair of the Appropriations Commitee, for example, increased his party support from 34 to 45 percent from one session to the next.

Although voting on chairpersons has not led to wholesale changes, chairs now feel a greater responsibility to the party. During the 100th Congress, Les Aspin (D-Wis.), chair of the Armed Services Committee, almost lost his position—one he had won in the last Congress by defeating a number of senior members not seen as responsive to the Democratic majority—over charges that he was arrogant and not a team player. After numerous promises of a change in behavior, the initial negative vote was reversed.

revolt against power centralized in the hands of a party leader. Successive Congresses further limited the power of the party leadership, and the development of the seniority system, which automatically awarded the chair to the majority party member with the longest tenure on the committee, gave independent power to chairpersons (see box). Because of their electoral security, these chairpersons could block the will of party leaders and the majority of their party with impunity (see Broder, 1972, p. 217; Schlesinger, 1985, p. 1164). In an attempt to make more sense out of committee jurisdictions and cut down on the number of committees, a series of reforms beginning in the 1940s had the unanticipated effect of vastly increasing the number of subcommittees in Congress. This process served to decentralize power even more and to reduce the leverage of party leaders (see Brady & Hurley, 1985, p. 67). "One of the most remarkable trends of the twentieth-century House has been the isolation of the party leadership from the committee structure" (Cavanaugh, 1982, p. 633).

Specific rules, such as that allowing filibusters (unlimited debate) in the Senate, contribute to party decline by allowing the minority party to put roadblocks in the way of a party majority (See Broder, 1972, p. 217). Party caucuses, which in times past met virtually to bind members to a party position on the floor by rewards or sanctions, had begun to meet only once at the beginning of each session to choose their leaders and thereafter play virtually no role within the party (see Ornstein & Rohde, 1979, pp. 291).

By the 1970s frustration with weakened party organizations led to a series of reforms designed to reduce the autonomy of committee and subcommittee chairs and to draw some power resources back to the party. Chairpersons no longer claimed their positions on the basis of seniority but faced a vote within the party caucus. The removal of some chairpersons and the placing of selected ones under the fear of party disapproval resulted in a dramatic improvement in cooperation and increased voting support by chairpersons for party positions (see Schlesinger, 1985, p. 1164). In the House, the Speaker was again allowed to nominate the membership of the Rules Committee and to play a greater role in the committee assignments of all members. After one of their members (Phil Gramm, D-Tex.) sponsored Ronald Reagan's budget plan, the Democratic caucus proceeded to strip him of his Budget Committee position as a warning to others that party loyalty on key issues was expected.

The example made of Gramm lost some credibility when he resigned a few weeks later and won in a special election as a Republican and later went on to the Senate. In both houses and for both parties, the caucus was revitalized as a forum for the discussion of party policy (see Ornstein & Rohde, 1979, p. 292). "Without question the most important party-related change to hit Congress in the 1970's was the emergence of the Democratic caucus as a powerful party agency. An increasingly assertive caucus has effected major changes in the way House business is conducted" (Crotty, 1984, p. 237). Although such rules changes do not guarantee increased party power, they control some of the competing power centers and make resources available to party leaders with the skill and will to use them.

With the increased costs of campaigns and the increased capabilities of the congressional campaign committees controlled by the members, the party has another resource to influence partisan colleagues. Generally, though, the campaign committees have been hesitant to reward or punish colleagues on the basis of their partisan support.

A variety of technological changes could affect the party role in the legislature. The computerization of substantive information and the monitoring of information in the Congress reduces the party leadership resource of trading information for compliance (see Frantzich, 1982, p. 238). Electronic voting, adopted by the House in 1979, reduced the time available for partisan maneuvering on the floor and increased the number of recorded votes on which party leaders traditionally had less influence. At the same time it gave the leadership the ability to monitor ongoing votes via computer and to use the information to target particular members for influence attempts. During the vote members have become accustomed to party leaders confronting them with the fact that "you are the only Democrat from Florida voting against us on this vote. Is that what you really mean to do?" (see Frantzich, 1982, p. 239). The presence of gavel-to-gavel television coverage of the House and Senate holds the potential for party leaders to play a more visible role in national politics as the spokespersons for their parties. A corollary danger exists that more-telegenic and less-party-oriented members will capture some of the attention away from the party leaders.

Generalizing about party power in state legislatures is more difficult given the wide variety of conditions. In general, state legislative leaders gave up less power than their national counterparts; yet the increase of candidate-centered campaigning affected state legislative parties also. Analyzing differences in the state legislative party power verifies the assertion that stronger state party organizations tend to result in stronger legislative parties (Harris & Hain, 1983, p. 238). Effective partisan competition in state legislatures requires a large enough minority that perceives that its interests are being disadvantaged (Harmel, 1985, pp. 11–12). Virtual one-party state legislatures develop factions based on strong personalities, regional divisions, or interest-group associations (Harris & Hain, 1983, p. 238). The party leadership in some state legislatures matches the party services provided on the national level. As a California party leader explained it:

> The Democratic Speaker controls as a state funded research arm, Majority Consultants, which does legislative research for party members during the session, but really comes to the fore during the election. For those members of the majority in the speaker's favor, the staff of Majority Consultants become campaign staff members—after going off the state payroll temporarily. They are highly qualified and motivated to keep their state jobs by keeping the Democrats in power. The Speaker independently raises a considerable amount of campaign funds and donates them to his supporters. (Author's interview)

Partisanship within Legislatures

The ultimate test of a party's organizational strength in legislative bodies lies in its ability to control the legislative agenda and the policy outcome. In respect to the individual legislator, the power of the party organization is in its ability to facilitate, encourage, or coerce cohesive support for the party position within committees and on floor votes. Measuring party power becomes difficult when one realizes that cohesive party voting patterns may develop alternatively from personal convictions, constituency pressures, or organizational efforts. Party leaders taking positions in tune with the personal convictions and constitutency preferences of the majority of party members can register high levels of partisan cohesiveness without any organizational effort. Lacking strong preferences or pressures, legislators often go along with the party position out of habit. As one legislator expressed it:

> After thirty years of yelling "Republican" at campaign rallies and having the label attached to my name, it becomes like the bell for Pavlov's dogs. I hear "Republican" attached to a course of action and lacking conflicting information begin to see that position as inherently better and wiser. (Author's interview)

Unlike representatives in parliamentary systems whose vote against the party position could be seen as a "vote of no confidence," bringing the government down and ending each legislator's current term in office, American legislators do not have their personal political fortunes so closely intertwined with that of the party.

The very fact that the election process brings into political office a group of officials with common outlooks and a sense of common destiny sets the stage for "natural" party coalitions that would occur whether or not the party leaders actively encouraged them. Parties relying exclusively on such coalitions, though, place themselves at a political disadvantage since the factors naturally encouraging partisanship are declining and the party that successfully harnesses more direct means of influence will gain over the party that sits back.

The Mechanisms of Partisanship

Traditionally, political parties could control elected officials to a large degree through indirect methods such as the recruitment of candidates, control over the nomination process, and their critical role in the campaign communications process. With the rise of candidate-centered campaigns, the parties flailed around for a number of years bemoaning their loss of influence. More recently, the parties have begun to find ways to affect postelection behavior indirectly by recruiting and training candidates in both the techniques and substance of modern campaigns and by setting the policy themes of campaigns through advertising and the sharing of issue research. By providing candidates with issue memos, poll results, draft speeches, and coordinated advertising copy, the party can redirect the issue thrust of particular campaigns and set the stage for more cooperative behavior by officials once they get into office (see Hershey, 1984, p. 143; Kayden & Mahe, 1985, p. 189; Arterton, 1982, p. 128). Just as they lead with most new technology, the Republicans lead in this realm too. The national party claims credit for redirecting the 1982 congressional campaigns toward the Reagan economic policy through such methods. Republicans have added the mystique of technology to their delivery of substantive information to candidates by equipping field workers with portable computers and communicating with candidates through electronic mail. As a field staff member put it: "The information coming through the computer terminal may not be much different than that we can mail out, but it arrives much faster and has the enhanced credibility technology adds. Candidates who simply would not read a ten-page document will sit transfixed in front of the CRT screen" (author's interview).

For the party, it is obviously better to have members arrive on the legislative scene amenable to the party message and ready to be team players. The parties are just beginning to find new ways to make this happen partially through the harnessing of new campaign technology. The degree and spread of the impact of such indirect techniques for enhancing the conditions for natural coalitions are still somewhat limited. Therefore the parties must expend considerable direct effort to bring fellow party members into line.

Often, more direct methods of influence are necessary. *Influence* is one of those terms like love and democracy for which we all have a definition but may find little overlap with others on how we view the term. For the purpose of this discussion, influence is the ability to get someone to do something he or she would not otherwise do. A variety of distinct processes fall under the general term *influence*. *Persuasion* is the ability to change the behavior of an influence target on the basis of the issue at hand by convincing someone that what you want is what that person would really want if he or she had the information. The potential for persuasion increases for individuals or organizations knowing the interests of their targets, having access to relevant information, and possessing superior communications skills. *Leadership* involves a personal sense of respect and trust that encourages an influence target to accept the direction of the leader with few questions. Personal attributes such as charisma and reputation bolster the potential for leadership. *Rewards* and *sanctions* involve the promise of specific benefits or detriments for compliance. Access to the benefits or detriments relevant to an influence target and the reputation for delivering them enhance the utility of rewards and sanctions.

High-quality, timely, and relevant *information* is always in short supply in legislatures. Although legislators are often overloaded with information from constituents, the press, and interest groups, such information often lacks the credibility and political sensitivity of information provided by fellow politicians. Legislators regularly seek out fellow partisans in the halls or on the floor, while party leaders seek out partisan colleagues to encourage their support. The whip's office

> offers an information service for members. Beside publicizing the daily floor schedule, the whip distributes memos summarizing a bill's provisions and possible amendments. The whip also gives members "recess packets" and "speech cards" to help discuss legislation with constituents. (Granat, 1985, p. 2502)

Republicans in the U.S. House currently use computerized electronic mail to send out whip notices and legislative strategy information. The uniqueness of the delivery form tends to heighten its influence.

A reciprocity arrangement often develops between party leaders and their followers. The whip network "conveys members' wishes to the leadership as often as vice versa" (Granat, 1985, p. 2502). The party leadership in Congress serves as a conduit for members to express their opinions to the president and key administration officials, and in exchange the members are more willing to accept some direction from the party leadership.

All individuals develop information strategies in which they trust. Tried and true sources hold more sway than new approaches that must slowly prove their utility.

> Congressmen, because of the greater likelihood of their sustained exposure to partisan agents including party elite, as compared to less involved citizens at large, are people for whom the potential for partisan policy influence is maximum. (Clausen, 1979, pp. 278–279)

Leaders often acquire their positions through personal skills that inspire trust and confidence. These personal characteristics help party leaders to get their way on legislation. Recent periods recalled for strong party leadership have been marked by powerful personalities such as Lyndon Johnson. When a party controls the presidency, presidential skills and efforts become inextricably intertwined with internal chamber leadership, providing an additional impetus for party cohesion.

A major weakness of contemporary legislative party leaders is their lack of access to sufficient resources with which to force compliance through relevant *rewards* or meaningful *sanctions*. Although the legislative party generally cannot strike very deeply to control the electoral fortunes of members, it can indirectly provide them with public exposure, support for desired legislation, and desirable committee positions. Although the link between party campaign services and party cohesion is tenuous, it has the potential for encouraging members to take the party into account more seriously. As a national party official put it: "We don't threaten our candidates and expect absolute loyalty. That would be unrealistic given the heterogeneous nature of their constituencies. We just hope to affect who is elected and build a sense of good will toward the party" (author's interview).

Few legislators report the parties using future access to campaign services as a threat to bring about compliance, but the implicit attempt to make them beholden is clearly there.

> The principal purpose of providing party services to candidates is to elect party members to office. Once elected, however, a secondary aim is often to encourage such officials to take cognizance of party views and to be active in party affairs. (Conlan, Martino, & Dilger, 1984, p. 7)

In providing services, the party is in a bind. The incumbents who have access to more nonparty support and are more likely to win need the party less than the long-shot challengers whose prospects for victory are dim at best.

> While the influence of national party may be crucial in a candidate's first election to the Senate or House, it is uncertain whether this will will hold for incumbents. (Orren, 1982, p. 26)

It is the incumbents, though, who control the congressional campaign committees. Only recently did the Democratic committees break the trend of financing incumbents and leaving the scraps for the challengers, a lesson the Republicans learned much earlier. To the degree that candidates view the national party as an important partner in their election or reelection quest, it "should heighten the party's influence over campaigners who win office with party help" (Hershey, 1984, p. 133).

Legislative parties tend to be inclusive rather than exclusive, avoiding serious criticism of less loyal members and very rarely punishing recalcitrants. The Democratic party censured some southern congressmen in 1964 when they publicly supported the Republican presidential candidate. More recently,

> House Democrats booted [Texas Representative Phil] Gramm off the Budget Committee in 1983 after he had sponsored the administration's tax bill and acted as a Republican in the subsequent election.... "I had to choose between Tip O'Neill and y'all," Gramm drawled in his TV ads. "And I chose y'all." His East Texas constituents ate it up, so much so [that] Gramm used the line as a battle cry in his [successful] Senate race the following year [as a Republican]. (Beiler, 1985, p. 43)

The lesson for legislative parties seems to be: legislators willing to challenge party interests enough to raise the ire of the entire party are unlikely to be politically damaged by any punishment the party imposes.

Full-blown party attempts to control a legislative vote arise relatively rarely. There are fewer than 20 votes a year (Granat, 1985, p. 2502) when the party organization works through the full set of resources from the "cheap" attempts to persuade through information and leadership to the more "expensive" bargaining use of rewards and sanctions. The battle over the budget and tax cuts early in the Reagan administration (1981) and the unsuccessful attempt to sustain his veto of the highway bill in the Senate (1987) stand out as full-blown attempts to keep the party in line (see box, "A Highway Accident").

The Level of Party Cohesion

"Careful analysis of hundreds of the most important congressional roll-call votes... supports the "tiresome old truism" that party is the best predictor of congressional votes" (Fishel, 1979, p. xxvi). The valid conclusion that a

A HIGHWAY ACCIDENT

The freedom to travel America's highways efficiently is not only an economic necessity for a large country dependent on interstate travel for delivering goods but almost ranks as high as basic freedoms such as speech and religion in the American social philosophy. When during the 1974 oil shortage Congress passed legislation mandating a 55-mile-per-hour speed limit to curtail gasoline use, the public begrudgingly acquiesced, given the crisis situation. As the energy crisis dissipated, opposition grew. Research challenged the absolute claim that lower speed limits save fuel, especially for trucks. Despite the threat of cutting off federal funds, there was a wide variation between states in the diligence of enforcement. Westerners, with long distances between destinations, felt particularly hampered. From a philosophical perspective, conservatives chafed at the heavy hand of the federal government and asserted that such decisions are better left to states and localities. The argument for retaining the lower speed limit rested primarily on data that seemed to show that highway fatalities had declined after the speed limit was lowered, but the cause and effect relationship was challenged.

President Reagan's western political base and his philosophical commitment to returning power to the states made him a natural ally to those hoping to change the law. In 1987, as momentum grew for changing the speed limit, Congress realized their advantage over Presidental Reagan and proceeded to attach a large number of highway projects to their highway bill. These public works projects broadened the appeal of the bill among congressional representatives and reduced the potential of a presidential veto, which would threaten such projects in isolation. After lopsided victories in both chambers (79 to 17 in the Senate and 407 to 17 in the House), President Reagan vetoed the bill citing the "budget-busting pork-barrel projects."

Citing the waste in the bill and the need to maintain the president's leadership position, the White House began the process of blocking a veto override. In the House, Democratic Speaker Jim Wright (D-Tex.) saw an opportunity to further cripple a presidency damaged by the Iran-Contra affair and to uphold the prerogatives of the Congress. He informed fellow party members that he "had a long memory" and would not forget their vote on this issue. All but one House Democrat heeded his warning. Recognizing the Democratic majority in the House and the appeal of the public works projects, little effort was given to that chamber. The House proceeded to override the veto (350–73) with more than 100 Republicans and almost the entire House Republican leadership rejecting the president's pleas. Even Republican minority leader Robert Michel (R-Ill.), lured by the completion of a highway in his district, failed to take up the president's cause.

The Senate, with its more even partisan alignment, served as the stage for the real battle. Minority Leader Robert Dole (R-Kans.) activated his party apparatus, arguing that the future of the Reagan presidency and therefore the fortunes of the Republican party were on the line, to garner what seemed like enough Republican votes to block the override. After an initial vote in which the

Senate sustained the veto by one vote (65 to 35), Freshman Senator Terry Sanford (D-N.C.) was pressured by the Democratic leadership to change his vote. With the Democrats unified in blocking President Reagan, emphasis focused on the 13 Republican senators who had voted to override the veto. Making a rare personal vote-hunting trip to Capitol Hill, Ronald Reagan met with the largely western state senators arguing the merits of his veto and the need for Republicans to stand together in leading the country. The president's extraordinary effort in bringing about party loyalty was to no avail, and all 13 senators voted to override, and the highway bill became law.

Postmortems on the president's failure vary. From a narrow perspective, this may have been evidence of a specific party leader weakened by the Iran-Contra scandal. From a broader perspective, it shows the limits of presidential and party leadership, especially when local needs and benefits hang in the balance.

---

betting man would be best off predicting congressional votes using a member's party rather than the common alternatives (region, personal characteristics of members, ideology, and so on) reflects as much on the weakness of other variables as on the strength of partisanship. Too ready acceptance of the conclusion also masks the complexities of the pattern and of contemporary trends.

Two common measures of partisan cohesion need to be looked at in tandem to get a fuller picture of the role of party in legislative voting. *Partisan division* in voting measures the degree to which votes split along partisan lines, and *party cohesion* indicates the degree to which party members vote with their party on votes resulting in different partisan divisions.

Partisan Division

Fewer than one-half of the congressional votes find the majority of the Democratic members opposing the majority of Republican members, and the percentage of such party-line votes has generally declined in recent years (see Figure 7.1). The limited frequency of partisan divisions within the U.S. Congress comes into focus when you realize that in the British House of Commons close to 100 percent of the votes find more than 90 percent of one party opposing 90 percent of the other (see Turner, 1970, pp. 16–17).

Different issues divide the parties in different ways. Issues such as social welfare, argicultural assistance, and government management divide both the House and Senate on clear partisan lines. Party is a much weaker predictor of votes concerning international involvement and civil liberties (see Clausen, 1979, p. 276).

For those who argue that it makes little difference whether Republicans

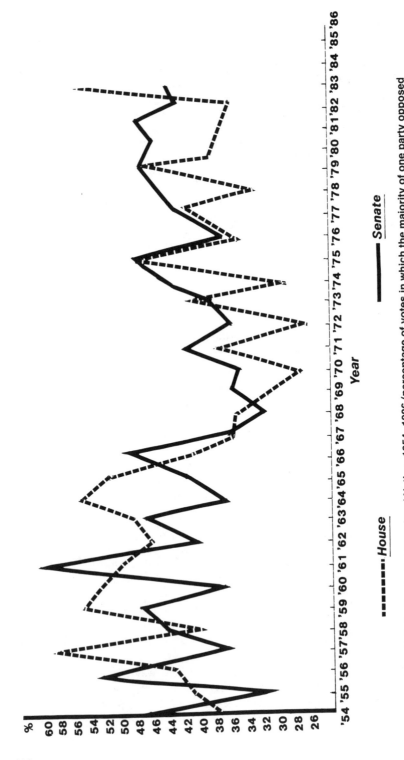

Figure 7.1 Party Polarization in Congressional Voting, 1954–1986 (percentage of votes in which the majority of one party opposed the majority of the other) (*Source: Ornstein, Mann, Malbin, Schill, & Bibby, 1984, p. 182*)

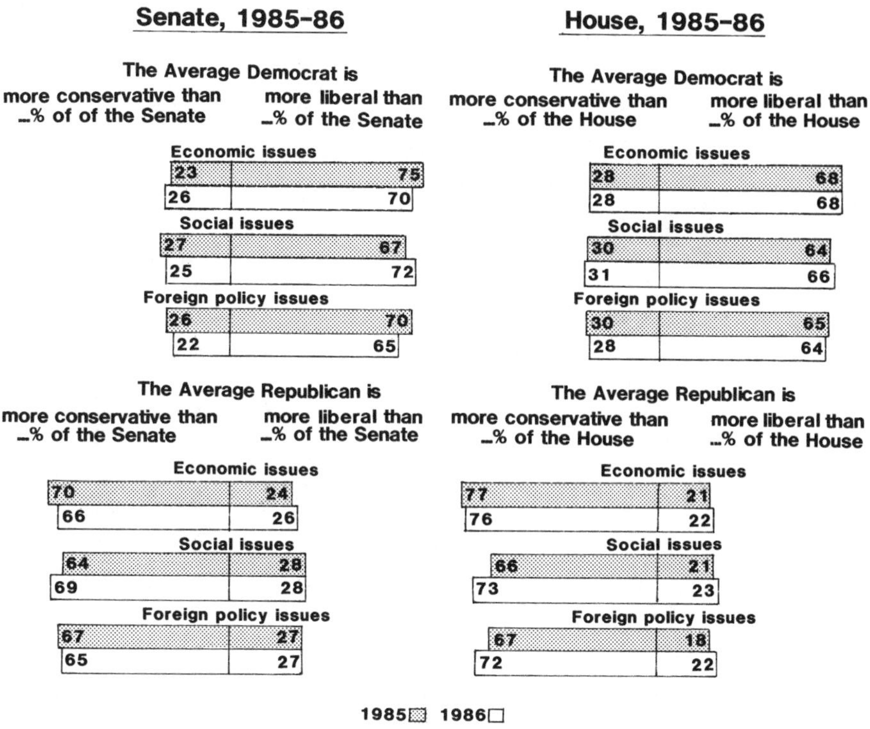

Senate, 1985–86

The Average Democrat is

| more conservative than | more liberal than |
| –% of of the Senate | –% of the Senate |

Economic issues

| 23 | 75 |
| 26 | 70 |

Social issues

| 27 | 67 |
| 25 | 72 |

Foreign policy issues

| 26 | 70 |
| 22 | 65 |

The Average Republican is

| more conservative than | more liberal than |
| –% of the Senate | –% of the Senate |

Economic issues

| 70 | 24 |
| 66 | 26 |

Social issues

| 64 | 28 |
| 69 | 28 |

Foreign policy issues

| 67 | 27 |
| 65 | 27 |

House, 1985–86

The Average Democrat is

| more conservative than | more liberal than |
| –% of the House | –% of the House |

Economic issues

| 28 | 68 |
| 28 | 68 |

Social issues

| 30 | 64 |
| 31 | 66 |

Foreign policy issues

| 30 | 65 |
| 28 | 64 |

The Average Republican is

| more conservative than | more liberal than |
| –% of the House | –% of the House |

Economic issues

| 77 | 21 |
| 76 | 22 |

Social issues

| 66 | 21 |
| 73 | 23 |

Foreign policy issues

| 67 | 18 |
| 72 | 22 |

1985▨ 1986☐

Figure 7.2 Ideological Voting by Democrats and Republicans in Congress
(Source: National Journal, March 21, 1987, p. 675)

or Democrats are elected, Figure 7.2 reveals the ideological variance in congressional voting. Using votes that clearly divide issues along liberal and conservative lines, it can be seen that the average Democrat is significantly more liberal than the chamber as a whole, whereas the average Republican is more conservative.

In general, the Senate reflects greater partisan division than the House. The various state legislatures reflect a wide variation in cohesion, with the average legislature more cohesive than Congress and the legislatures of the northeastern, urban, two-party states showing extensive party division (see Jewell & Patterson, 1977, pp. 384–385). In one-party states, the party is not the reference group for legislative voting. Legislative party divisions are strongest in states with a long tradition of two-party competition backed by relatively strong party organizations outside the legislature (p. 383).

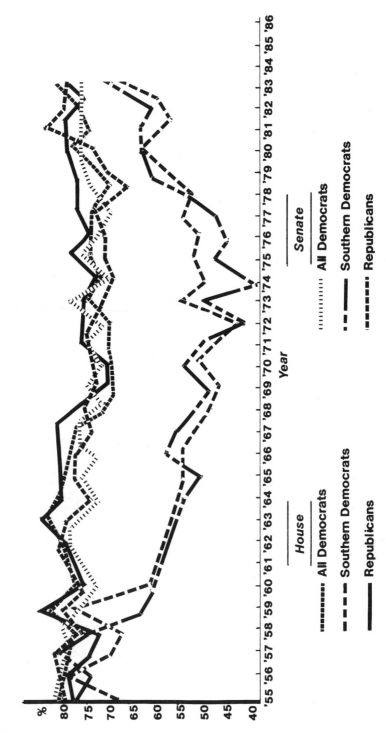

Figure 7.3 Party Support and Unity in Congressional Voting, 1955–1986 *(Source: Ornstein, Mann, Malbin, Schick, & Bibby, 1984, p. 183)*

Party Cohesion

The degree to which individual party members vote with their legislative parties varies independently from changes in the level of partisan division. As Figure 7.3 reveals, after considerable decline during the 1960s and 1970s, party cohesion regained importance during the 1980s for both parties. A number of factors could account for this, including the partisan challenge of the Reagan program and slight increases in party identification among the voters. But increased dependence on the parties during elections precipitated by the rise of the service-vendor party cannot be ruled out. Historical analysis shows that increased party cohesion tends to precede partisan realignments within the electorate (Brady & Hurley, 1985, pp. 65–66; Clubb, Flanigan, & Zingale, 1980, p. 234).

Legislative parties that control the presidency tend to reveal more cohesion than parties without the stimulus of the president's legislative agenda. An even more interesting pattern involves the tendency for Republican legislators to show more cohesion than their Democratic counterparts. A number of factors seem to contribute to this situation. The more common "bloated" majorities held by the Democrats make it easier for legislators to abandon the party without being noticed and without punishment. The greater heterogeneity of the Democratic party and, consequently, its elected officials—who encompass the whole range of southern conservatives to northeastern liberals—is harder to maintain by natural means. Contributing to this are the vast differences produced by pressures generated by campaign contributions. Most Republican political action committee (PAC) contributions come from conservative economic and issues groups. Democrats, on the other hand, have their liberal and labor-group contributions commingled with those from business groups hedging their bets by contributing to incumbents (Edsall, 1984a, p. 88). Added to these factors recently has been the bond of indebtedness built between the Republican party on the national level and the congressional candidates they support with contributions and services.

> The GOP has been collecting millions of dollars on a national scale and using those funds to recruit congressional candidates and provide them with a substantial proportion of their campaign resource. . . . The Republican candidates who win with this assistance arrive in Congress with what appears to be a deeper identification with the national party and a sense of obligation to it than do Democratic members helped less generously. (Sundquist, 1982, p. 52)

Figure 7.4 shows the party cohesion scores of recently elected members of Congress and indicates a cadre of legislators increasingly more supportive of party positions. The increase in party cohesion is most evident among freshmen Republicans elected since 1977, with newly elected Democrats following course a few years later. It does not seem to be a coincidence that the dramatic increases occurred about the same time as increased electoral efforts by the parties. As Gary Jacobson summarized it:

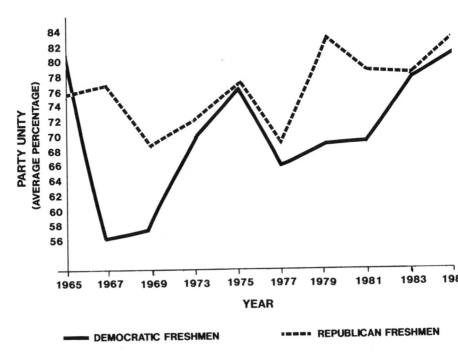

Figure 7.4 Party Support by Partisan Groupings of Freshmen in the House
(*Source: Data from* Congressional Quarterly Weekly Reports, *1965–1986*)

Some credit for Republican unity clearly belongs to the national party's electoral work. Party committees had, of course, assisted many of the new Republican members with campaign money and services and so established some degree of obligation. But the party's provision of training, information, campaign materials, and expertise also subtly injected common themes and issue positions into dispersed campaigns. (1985, p. 166)

It is still too early to determine whether a new age of partisan influence has dawned within legislatures or whether we are observing a temporary condition. The party organizations, both within the legislatures and in the national committees, are acting as if this is the opening that will regain some of their control over the legislative process.

PARTY INFLUENCE IN THE EXECUTIVE BRANCH

[The President] cannot escape being the leader of his party except by incapacity and lack of personal force, because he is at once the choice of the party and of the nation.... He can dominate his party by being spokesman for the real sentiment and purpose of the country, by giving direction to opinion, by giving the country at once information and the statements of policy which will enable it to form its judgments alike of parties and of men. (Wilson, 1908, pp. 67–68)

Former President Woodrow Wilson's forceful image of the president as party leader sounds correct from the contemporary perspective but fails to reflect the intentions of the Founding Fathers. The presidency was "envisioned and created as a nonpartisan office" (Bass, 1984, p. 59) consistent with the Founding Fathers' deep distrust of "divisive factions." As the first president, George Washington set the tone by asserting that the spirit of partisanship always seems to

> distract the public councils and enfeeble the public administration. It agitates the community with ill-founded jealousies and false alarms, kindles the animosities of one party against another, foments occasionally riots and insurrection. It opens the door to foreign influence and corruption, which find facilitated access to government through the channels of party passions.

As the political parties developed, the president became the inescapable leader since he emerged from a partisan selection process, headed the party ticket, and garnered the public attention, making him the most visible party functionary. Presidents became the personalized image of the party with which individuals could identify. Party electoral fortunes and image rose and fell with the public evaluation of the president. Despite his clear partisan role, the fact that the American system does not separate the ceremonial from the functional head of government (as Britain, for example, does with the queen and the prime minister) causes the public some discomfort. On the one hand, the president is expected to be an efficient and neutral public servant looking out for the interests of the entire nation; on the other hand, he needs to lead his party and cooperate with party goals in order to get the job done (see Cronin, 1980, p. 180).

On the state and local levels, governors and mayors also tend to be heads of their parties and many play an even more active role than the president in pursuing partisan goals.

The Partisan Nature of Executive Appointments

A number of factors came together to encourage partisanship in the selection of government officials. Political parties, requiring a vast stable of committed workers, used patronage as a reward for faithful party service. With the growth of government activities, executives sought to expand their control by appointing "their" people to key positions to carry out the executive's priorities. On the national level, a pattern developed whereby the chair of the national party committee became the postmaster general, allocating the vast patronage of that department and affecting appointments in other agencies. The development of an independent postal service in the 1960s continued the pattern of decreasing the range of nonpolicy-making presidential appointments that had begun with the Pendleton Civil Service Act in 1883. With modern-day presidents focusing their appointments on a few hundred key policy-making positions, the need for a party functionary in the White House declined. The public standing of the national party chair "has decreased as nonorganizational recruits have replaced him in such pivotal linkage roles as campaign manager, patronage dispenser, cabinet politician and political advisor" (Bass, 1984, p. 81).

Contemporary presidents tend to transfer their key personal campaign aides into top White House positions. In filling cabinet positions and those in the lower ranks, presidents seek out individuals who agree with them on policy, but "the party organization has not been a source of talent to fill them" (Seligman, 1979, p. 300). Although considerable variation exists, state executives have followed a similar pattern of appointing officials with personal loyalty to them over party functionaries.

Recognizing the danger of overloading high-visibility positions with recognized partisans, contemporary executives make a big show of appointing some key aides from the opposition party. John Kennedy's appointment of Republican Robert MacNamara as secretary of defense, Richard Nixon's appointment of Democrat Patrick Moynihan as a White House aide, and Ronald Reagan's appointment of Democrat Jeane Kirkpatrick as ambassador to the United Nations were all attempts to reveal bipartisanship. The legislation creating a number of the independent regulatory agencies reflects the fear of partisanship. The agency charters require the appointment of a minimum number of affiliates of each party, but like the bipartisan appointments above, presidents are often able to find appointees sharing their perspectives, if not their party label.

The President and the National Party Organization

The current recipe for presidential relations with their parties seems to call for one pound of dominance and another of neglect for every ounce of genuine leadership.... Recent presidents have largely ignored their party organizations when choosing administration personnel, when formulating policy (especially in the later years of an administration), even when planning for the reelection campaign. (Harmel, 1984, pp. 249–250)

By tradition, presidential candidates name the national party chair, who serves at the president's will if the candidate is elected.

Presidents expect national chairpersons and the national committee to do their bidding. The party chairpersons or the national committee appear to have no viable alternatives. Should a party chairperson resist, or simply be perceived to be not cooperating as fully as expected, he is quickly replaced. (Crotty, 1979, p. 41)

In recent years, the national organization of the party holding the presidency has been eclipsed by the White House organization and often has gone into periods of relative dormancy. Major advances in organizational activity and approach have "come to pass mainly during periods when the party has been out of power...[and] have tended to stall when the party nominee enters the White House" (Bass, 1984, p. 82). The party organization just cannot compete with a personalized presidency having its own resources, access to the media, and the mantle of party leadership.

The President as Party Leader in Congress

To fairly assess the power of the party organization or the party label, it is necessary to distinguish the support a president receives for his programs due to his role as president and the inherent qualities of the programs, from the support generated by partisan attachments and presidential activation of the party organization. Presidential scholar George Edwards concludes that "most of the votes a president's program receives from his party members are not because of party leadership...much of the support a president receives from his party in Congress is a result of the shared views of party members" (Edwards, 1984, p. 179).

The decreased willingness of congressional representatives to follow presidential initiatives blindly is recognized by most participants. As one State Department legislative liaison official puts it: "It used to be that a central piece of information on a vote was the president's position. Now the central information is the issue. With the breakdown of party discipline, it is clear that voters expect members to exercise independent judgment" (Crotty, 1984, pp. 266–267). Former President Gerald Ford lamented that "party leaders have lost the power to tell their troops that something is really significant [to the president] and to get them to respond accordingly" (Edwards, 1984, p. 189).

Despite the conventional wisdom that presidents have generally lost some of their potential as party leaders, they are not without resources. Within each of the categories of power resources (leadership, persuasion, and rewards and sanctions), presidents can find a foothold for exerting influence.

Presidential Leadership

The natural aura surrounding a national leader, made larger than life by media exposure and the mystique surrounding the office, enhances the president's ability to lead through the force of personality and respect.

Members of the president's party typically have personal loyalties or emotional commitments to their party and their party leader, which the president can often translate into votes when necessary. Thus, members of the president's party vote with him when they can, giving him the benefit of the doubt, especially if their own position on an issue is weak. (Milkis, 1984, p. 185)

Presidential Persuasion

Persuading legislators that what the president wants is really what they want, if they only knew the facts, is enriched by presidential superiority in the possession of factual information. With the growth of presidential legislative liaison staffs beginning in the Kennedy administration, the White House emphasized understanding the needs and goals of the individual members with whom they wanted to work. In recent years White House computer files containing political, district, and voting information on senators and representatives replaced sketchy notes and files. In the words of one legislative liaison official, "It is just a matter of effective targeting. We're trying to pick out the members who are 'gettable'" (author's interview).

The president's instantaneous access to reams of information on almost any topic, worldwide, increases the potential for persuasion. Presidents brief party leaders in Congress who then pass the "inside" information—often framed to support the presidential position—along to party followers. In recent years presidents used their access to sensitive national security information to add veracity to their position but often failed to share the information on which the judgments were based. Members of the president's party are often persuaded to support policies without having access to the full rationale.

The ability of presidents to "wow legislators with the facts" has declined in recent years as Congress harnessed expanded staffs and new technology enhanced its research and analysis capabilities. Although Congress used to go "hat in hand" to the executive branch for virtually all of its information, it has now become an independent information source, in some cases sought out by the executive branch. This is especially true in terms of budget analysis, in which the Congressional Budget Committee projections rival those of the president's Office of Managment and Budget (Frantzich, 1982, p. 242). "Congressmen no longer need to take the word of the executive branch....The congressional legislative party can now, if it chooses to do so, chart its own course with respect to policy fully in possession of adequate intellectual fortification" (Polsby, 1983a, p. 110).

Persuasion may involve encouraging specific legislators to support specific policy initiatives or convincing them that benefits would accrue to them by supporting the president in general.

Members of the president's party have an incentive to make him look good because his standing in the public may influence their own chances for reelection....All of the motivations to support the president are buttressed by basic distrust of the opposition party. There is a natural tendency for members of the president's party of view the opposition as eager to undercut the president. (Milkis, 1984, pp. 185–186)

Framed in such a way to get the competitive juices flowing among presidential partisans, presidents often present their case as a "we" versus "they" situation. Members of the president's party are admonished to come to the aid of a fellow party member, both for his own good and theirs also.

Presidential Party Leadership through Rewards and Sanctions

Presidents as party leaders share many of the limitations of intrachamber leaders—the lack of meaningful resources for directly affecting members:

> If members of his party wish to oppose the White House, there is little the president can do to stop them. The primary reason is that the parties are highly decentralized: national leaders do not control those aspects of politics that are of vital concern to members of Congress: nominations and elections. (Edwards, 1984, p. 194)

Despite the limitations, presidential favors in the form of promoting desired legislation, campaign help, and support of local public works projects hold considerable meaning. To the degree that presidents activate the "carrot and stick" of these favors, members of the president's party most often feel the impact since most of the bargaining is limited to them:

> When a president seeks to build his winning coalition, he typically "writes off" a large part of the opposition party and he can generally depend on a core of supporters from his own party. To obtain the additional votes he needs, a president usually begins with the members of his party who fall into the "undecided" or the "moveable" categories. . . . The threats of such actions are effective primarily with members of the president's party, of course, because members of the opposition party do not expect to receive many favors from the president. (Edwards, 1984, pp. 192–193)

In the electoral arena, presidents emphasize rewarding supporters as opposed to punishing party opponents. Presidential success in actively purging the party ranks of unsupportive legislators by involving themselves in nomination battles has shown very limited effectiveness (Milkis, 1984, p. 172). The accepted strategy involves helping supportive members through campaign visits, encouraging party and PAC contributions, and ignoring the less-supportive incumbents. The strongest party candidates in open seats and viable challengers of incumbents from the opposition party receive similar treatment. As one of Ronald Reagan's aides puts it, "The best way for us to encourage [party] discipline is for us to make it clear that the president is more

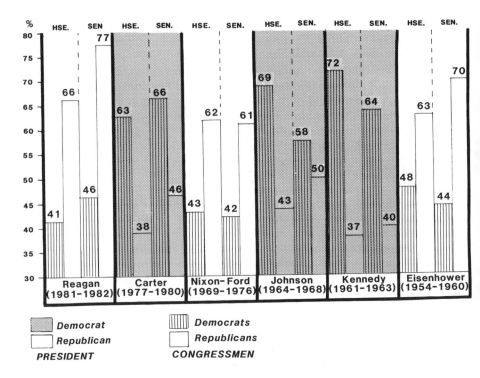

Figure 7.5 Presidential Mean Support Scores for the House and Senate
(Source: Data from Congressional Quarterly Weekly Reports, 1960–1983)

likely to raise funds for you if you support him than if you do not" (Hershey, 1984, p. 129).

The Reagan administration used the campaign-finance system in a direct way to gain both Republican and Democratic votes in Congress. Using data from the Federal Elections Commission, the White House computer identified PACs that had contributed to both Reagan and specific members of Congress. On key votes, the PACs were asked to lobby members to support administration bills (Jacobson, 1985, p. 166).

The president's access to the media allows him to go to the people directly and appeal for support. By generating public opinion favorable to his position or even stimulating direct contact with legislators, the president can increase his chances for success. As a key congressional staff member put it: "Every time the president goes on the air, we brace for an avalanche of mail and telephone calls. Nothing can stimulate mail like a direct request from the President to 'write your congressman'" (author's interview).

In close votes, presidents often bargain with would-be party supporters using other favors. Since the most desirable rewards are finite and expendable, wise presidents reserve them to acquire the last few votes needed for victory, relying on the "cheaper" techniques for building the base of the coalition.

Presidential Voting Support in Congress

Empirical analysis reveals (see Figure 7.5) that a president's fellow partisans serve as the backbone of his voting support in Congress. Members of the president's party support him more than two-thirds of the time, whereas the opposition party seldom supports him more than one-half of the time. There is little difference in the support that legislative parties give their respective presidents. Both voting analysis and interviews with members of Congress indicate that party and presidential efforts show most success on foreign policy issues where constituency cues are limited (see Kingdon, 1981, pp. 183–185).

Presidential Evaluations and Party Fortunes

Despite the fact that the president cannot control the party organization or vice versa, their fortunes are inextricably intertwined. Off-year elections are commonly viewed as a barometer of presidential success. High-visibility presidential contests often result in an abnormal division of party support favoring the congressional candidates of the winning president. Off-year elections generally result in a return to the more normal partisan division resulting in an average of more than 20 House seats being lost by the president's party. Variations from that average are seen as reflecting on the effectiveness of the president. Presidents entering an off-year election with a high degree of support in the public opinion polls generally do better than average. Part of this stems from the public transferring its support of the president to his party's candidates, but the full explanation is more complicated. Party officials report that when the president's support falls in the polls it is much harder to recruit good candidates for the upcoming election. As two party officials commented:

> 1974 was really a bummer for our recruitment effort. Just as state legislators and other viable candidates were deciding to give up their safe seats to run for Congress, the Republican administration was sinking under the weight of Watergate. Lets face it, we fielded a second string team and lost forty-nine seats. (Republican party official, author's interview)

> Jimmy Carter was our millstone in 1980. We had trouble getting good candidates to run knowing they would be tainted by Carter's low ratings in the polls. We lost thirty-four seats in the House, ten of them in open seats

where we just could not get the best candidates to run. In the Senate, every seat switching parties [12] went to the Republicans, giving them control. (Democratic party official, author's interview)

Similar patterns happen at the state and local levels, with presidential and national party fortunes affecting the outcome of state and local races. When the national party is having difficulty recruiting congressional candidates, state and local parties face similar problems. The failure to recruit effectively for lower-level offices denies a party a continuous stream of candidates for upper-level offices. The linkage between governors and the fortunes of their state and local parties is even more direct. Governors in many states serve as the de facto if not actual party chairpersons.

THE PARTIES AND THE BUREAUCRACY

Early in the development of the American political system, observers recognized that as in sports, in politics, too, the impact of the policy process "isn't over until it is over." General laws passed by legislatures must be administered by the bureaucracy. The discretion allowed in the administration of these laws grants bureaucrats significant power to make—rather than simply carry out—public policy. For example, in recent years, without specific changes in legislation, justice departments under Republican administrations have reduced the vigor of enforcement of voting rights and school-integration laws, and the Environmental Protection Agency has softened the impact of the more extreme environmental policies. On the other hand, under Democratic administrations, bureaucrats in the Department of Health and Human Services placed less emphasis on welfare "cheating" and those in the State Department enforced new standards of human rights while placing less emphasis on protecting longtime U.S. allies. Realizing the effect of the actual application of the laws, and seeing government bureaucracies as a reservoir of resources with which they could reward the party faithful, political parties took an early and deep interest in the composition of the bureaucracy.

For the first century of the American Republic, the limited role of government and the relatively nontechnical character of bureaucratic positions allowed a principle of "to the victor belongs the spoils." Government positions were highly sought-after rewards for loyal party work and provided the personnel to maintain the party organization. Each new administration arrived with its partisan backers, often cleaning house of the previous partisans. "Good Republicans" or "good Democrats," as the case may be, were assumed to be available for any open job. In some cases, incompetents were given appointments, and extreme partisanship was allowed to affect the decision-making process. The excesses of partisanship were combined with the increased complexity of governmental tasks and the need for continuity to usher in civil service reform, first nationally and then spreading to state and local governments. An increasing percentage of positions was protected from the partisan whims of mayors, governors, and presidents. In most cases, civil servants were protected from partisanship at the selection, promotion, and retention stage by specifically denying the use of partisanship as a criterion. For other positions, such as on boards and in regulatory commissions, the laws provide for a specific balanced partisan composition. Although traditional partisan machines continued at the local level—with some relatively pale copies existing even today—the trend toward a nonpartisan bureaucracy shows little evidence of reversal.

To provide some level of loyalty and teamwork, presidents and other chief executives retain the right to appoint their key advisors and administrative personnel (although many must be approved by the legislature). Except when attempting to portray a bipartisan flavor for a particular office, chief executives highly favor members of their own party who are personally loyal to them. Members of the president's cabinet virtually all arrive with considerable political experience, often in partisan politics. Lower-level personnel are often recruited from the campaign effort and/or from partisan activists.

The power to appoint often does not mean the chief executive has the power to control. Although the same political outlook that leads a particular appointee to become associated with one political party colors the way he or she perceives policy decisions in an agency, competing pressures often arise. To lead an agency made up primarily of career civil servants, an effective administrator must often speak for the interests of the department and its client groups and not be seen as a partisan messenger from the chief executive. The breadth of concern of most chief executives means that most appointees receive little day-to-day guidance from their partisan patron, making it even more likely they will take on the perspectives of those they wish to lead. The substantive constituencies of agencies become more potent and visible forces than the partisan constituencies (see Aberbach, Putnam, & Rockman, 1981, pp. 246–248). By the time a chief executive realizes that an appointee has begun to "go native" it may be too late. It may be more of a political detriment to fire an appointee popular with his department and constituency than to put up with deviation from the party line on all but the most significant issues.

THE PARTIES AND THE COURTS

American tradition and procedure make it almost unseemly to discuss the political parties and the courts in one breath. The ideal of equal justice for all runs counter to the implications of partisanship. We tend to forget that most judges are elected to office, often under a partisan label, or appointed by elected officials who gained office as nominees of a party. Once in office, these justices carry with them the political outlooks that associated them with one partisan outlook over another, that facilitated their selection, and that continues to affect their preferences in decisions.

The Selection Process

Election
Thirteen states hold partisan elections for most judges, and eight states use partisan elections for some judges. Twenty states use nonpartisan elections for some portion of their judges (Berkson, 1980, p. 178). No matter which method of election is used, viable candidates tend to have had significant experience in public service, often as party activists. Partisan judicial elections are yet to feel the dramatic impact of modern campaign technology, although some state and local parties do serve as providers of campaign services.

> The basic requirement is to obtain one's political party's nomination and then hope for the best in the general election. However, *real* contests are more often the exception than the rule and active "politicking" by judicial candidates, especially incumbents, is usually, albeit certainly not always, regarded as improper...in several states the "sitting judge" principle is in vogue, whereby both political parties at least theoretically are pledged to support the incumbent. (Abraham, 1987, p. 52)

Appointment
All federal judges are appointed by the president with the advice and consent of the Senate. Judges of the major state courts are appointed by governors in 21 states and by state legislatures in 4 others. In the above-mentioned states, only four governors have direct appointment power (with approval of the legislature), and the remaining 17 states use public commissions to recommend lists of potential appointees on the basis of their qualifications from whom the governors must choose. Overall, 31 states use some form of commission recommendation for at least some of their judges (Berkson, 1980, pp. 179–180).

For both presidential and gubernatorial appointments, prior political experience plays a role. Presidents clearly wish to affect the direction the courts are going and assume that a potential nominee's party label serves as an indicator of future decisions. In recent years, every president except Gerald Ford filled more than 90 percent of his judicial appointments with members of his own party (Gitelson, Conway, & Feigert, 1984, p. 297). Efforts to downplay partisanship through the 1978 Omnibus Judgeship Act and the Carter administration's suggestion that senators create "merit-selection" committees to recommend new appointees may have increased the quality of judges but did little or nothing to adjust the partisan composition of the courts.

Recognizing the unspoken importance of judicial appointments for policy outcomes, the parties have begun to encourage appointments promoting their ideology. The 1980 Republican platform explicitly called for the appointment of judges believing in decentralized government and opposing abortion (Gitelson et al., 1984, p. 297).

The approval of the Senate for federal appointments can become a partisan battle. Members of the president's party take up the battle to get his appointees through the process, whereas members of the opposing party see denial of an appointee as both a way to force the appointment of a more-acceptable nominee and as a method of wounding the president and decreasing his power.

The Party Stake in Judgeships

Patronage and Motivation

Political parties need a vast reservoir of volunteers to carry on their functions. Lawyers possess the skills and resources highly desired by party organizations. The possibility of obtaining a judgeship (through partisan activity), with its relatively high pay, prestige, and security enhances the motivation of lawyers to contribute their time and effort to the party. Even for those lawyers not aspiring to elective or appointive office, the day-to-day administration of justice allows sitting judges to dispense concrete benefits to legal colleagues known through partisan activity. It is generally easy for a judge to find deserving and competent members of his or her party to serve as receivers in bankruptcy cases or guardians for minors, each of which carries with it significant legal fees. In some localities, county or district judges draw on these vestiges of patronage to serve as the behind-the-scenes party leaders.

Partisanship and Judicial Decision Making

Evidence of judges deciding cases on purely partisan grounds is very hard to come by and, when apparent, almost impossible to verify. Judicial decisions are justified publicly in nonpartisan terms. The charges of direct partisanship most often come into play when the courts are called upon to mediate disputes between the parties such as legislative redistricting, voter-registration requirements, and ballot challenges, but it is precisely in these cases that judges most often take the "high ground" and justify their decisions on the basis of abstract, nonpartisan principles.

The fact that it is difficult to prove partisan motivations does not indicate that the partisan composition of the judicial bench is not important. Although failing to match the levels of party cohesion in legislatures, considerable research indicates that Republican and Democratic judges decide differently on certain types of cases. Studies of Democratic and Republican judges serving on the same court show that the Democrats are generally more likely to support the defense in criminal cases, the claimant in unemployment cases, the tenant in landlord-tenant cases, the labor union in labor-management cases, and the private citizen when confronting the corporation and a more expansive view of basic freedoms such as speech and assembly (see Nagel, 1961; Goldman, 1975). The tendency for Democratic judges to be more liberal and Republicans to be more conservative stands out most dramatically in states in which judges are elected rather than appointed (Goldman, 1975, p. 496).

The explanation for differing behavior patterns among judges from different parties is relatively simple, if one accepts the argument that judges become involved in conflicts involving significant ambiguity and a confrontation of values over which reasonable people can differ. Judges first entering their chambers after a significant period of partisan activity do not check their values and perceptions at the door. The same ideological outlooks and guidelines for interpreting the world that led them to an association with one of the political parties guide them in specific judicial decisions. The role of state superior courts and the Supreme Court in interpreting constitutions provides significant opportunities for ideological predispositions to hold sway. To the degree that American political parties bring together individuals with similar values, judges selected from that membership will tend to act in accordance with these commonly held perspectives.

CONCLUSION

The concept of the "party in office" as a cohesive team agreeing on the ultimate purpose of government and guided by a fixed set of party leaders misses the reality of contemporary American politics. It is not so much that the parties are irresponsible but rather that the individuals elected or appointed to run government under the party label find themselves responsible to a number of masters, of which the political party organization is only one. To the degree that elected officials credit their election to a personal, rather than a party, organization and to the use of communication technology not linked to the party, the party has few resources to force compliance. Sorting out the direct impact of the party organizational activities and the indirect impact of the internal agreement on policy preferences among elected and appointed officials from a particular party is difficult. Despite the limitations of party organizational power, knowing the political party of a government officials remains a useful, albeit imperfect, indicator of behavior in office.

8

The Future of Parties in the Technological Age

Less than two decades ago political journalist David Broder reflected the academic and journalistic consensus of the time, asserting in his book title that *The Party's Over*. Most observers sadly agreed with the commentary on the passing of a great political tradition. A spate of books used titles to assert the impending change: *The Decline of American Political Parties* (Wattenberg, 1984,), *The Current Crisis in American Politics* (Burnham, 1982); *Dismantling the Parties* (Kirkpatrick, 1979); *Parties and Elections in an Anti-Party Age* (Fishel, 1979). Even when the conclusion was not stated in the title, the vast majority of writings on political parties began with the assertion of a significantly diminished role and revealed very little hope for a reversal of fortunes.

By the early 1980s, some titles were making more hopeful statements: *Party Renewal in America* (Pomper, 1980b) and *Bringing Back the Parties* (Price, 1984). In 1985, Xandra Kayden and Eddie Mahe used a play on words from the title of Broder's stimulating book; *The Party Goes On* (1985). Larry Sabato went a step further, asserting *The Party's Just Begun* (1987). I was tempted to tip my hand by entitling this book *Come to the Party: New Place, New Time, New Music*. As should be clear from Chapters 1–7, the main argument of this book is that political parties continue to play an important, albeit changed, role in American politics. A primary source of that change is the ability of the party organizations to adapt the new technologies of political communications to their purposes.

There is a temptation to flush our memories of conclusions superseded by events and simply agree with Joseph Schlesinger that "the grab bag of assumptions, inferences, and half-truths that have fed the decline-of-party thesis is simply wrong" (1985, p. 1152). Such an approach too easily turns us away from the continuing challenges facing the parties and fails to captures the full

261

range of arguments underlying the conclusions of previous scholars. In particular, the continued existence and renewed vitality of the parties should not be seen as a refutation of Broder's thesis of party failures. He saw his book as more than a dire prediction of inevitable party decline. In fact, he points out that his central argument is the challenge that "if we engage ourselves in politics, and particularly concern ourselves with the workings of those strangely neglected institutions, the political parties, that we may find the instrument of national self-renewal is in our own hands" (Broder, 1972, p. xi). Party activists took the warnings of Broder and others to heart in their attempt to rebuild the potential for party influence in light of social and technological changes.

THE ROLE OF TECHNOLOGY IN PARTY RENEWAL

A major source of party decline stemmed from the reduced ability of political parties to control, or even influence, political communications and the election results they spawn. New technologies of communication and persuasion developed in such a way that the parties were largely bypassed as critical links between candidates and voters. Perceived as increasingly irrelevant to the electoral process, the parties found it difficult to motivate volunteers and candidates alike. Candidate-centered campaigns required increased amounts of nonparty funding that focused voters away from partisan considerations, adding to the perceived irrelevance of the parties. One solution to breaking the reinforcing vicious circle of party decline lies in reinserting the party as a significant player through which candidates could effectively communicate with voters. In effect, the parties had to "beat the providers of communications technology at their own game." A wide range of observers came to the conclusion that technology could be as much as a part of the solution as it had been the source of the problem:

> The parties have been weakened by their failure to adapt to some of the social and technological changes taking place in America. (Broder, 1972, p. xxiii)

> Today the prospects for stronger party committees lie not in recapturing that pivotal role in deciding nominations, but in enhancing the influence in exchanges with candidates on the one hand, and voters, on the other. The provision of money and services to officeholders will increase the influence of party committees. (Arterton, 1982, p. 135)

> The same telecommunications technologies which have eroded the dominance of political parties offer the means whereby parties can effectively recapture a share of political influence. (American Assembly, 1982, p. 7)

> A revitalized national and state Republican party organization, fueled by the marvels consultants had previously themselves monopolized, has provided

the model that can tame consultant abuses and develop a healthier, party-based electoral system. (Sabato, 1981, p. 8)

THE CONSEQUENCES OF THE TECHNOLOGY-BASED SERVICE-VENDOR-BROKER PARTY

Although the emerging role of stronger and more viable technology-based service-vendor-broker parties is clearly the model for the near future, we must be wary of becoming technological determinists. Technology is only one factor affecting political parties, and it can be used for the benefit or detriment of the party. As with all tools, technology can be used or misused. "There is nothing inherent in the technologies of communication that will necessarily cause politicians to use them in a certain manner" (Arterton, 1983, p. 3). Targeted mailing, for example, can be used equally to build party consensus or exacerbate intraparty conflicts, no matter who provides the service. Furthermore, not all technologies are likely to have a similar impact. Some technologies support organizational centralization and others, decentralization. Some technologies impact on the party in the electorate, whereas others focus on the party organization. The way in which technologies are provided and the setting in which they are adopted may well determine the impact as much as the technology per se. Finally, the infusion of party-provided services interacts with a number of other societal and organizational changes that are either well in progress or currently on the horizon. For example, in assessing the contemporary Republican resurgence and its ability to dominate the policy agenda during the mid-1980s, it is difficult to prove the relative contributions of the party's advantage in providing services, the ability of the party to reach a policy consensus on ideas with wide public acceptance, and the force of Ronald Reagan as party leader (see Everson, 1982, p. 49). All of the factors undoubtedly contributed, but it would be hard to prove that any one was a necessary condition or a sufficient cause of what looked like a period of emerging responsible party government. Despite the difficulties in analysis, the emergence of the service-vendor-broker party has some relatively clear consequences.

The Consequences for the Party Organization

Emerging from a period of long predicted demise, party organizations, especially at the national level have "attained a degree of institutional permanence that they have never known before and have carved out a secure niche for themselves by virtue of their fund-raising and campaign-services capabilities" (Price, 1984, p. 297).

Revealing the common resiliency of organizations to maintain themselves through adaptation, political parties have entered the age of technology with a belated, but committed, vengeance. In the fight for survival, the party organizations realized that "organizations must cultivate a constituency—they must generate support by making themselves useful" (Gibson, Bibby, & Cotter, 1983, p. 201). Service-vendor-broker parties have attempted to make themselves indispensable to candidates as they compete for office (see Hershey, 1984, p. 148). Defining the critical linkage as one between the party organization and the candidates it chooses to support reflects a very different philosophy from the emphasis the national Democratic party put on building the link between the party and voters through the "expressive" reforms of the 1970s. Although "expressive" and "competitive" reforms are not inherently in conflict, limited resources and competing views of the most effective course of action tend to mean that one approach clearly dominates. Both parties today have cast their lot with a primary emphasis on the technology-based competitive reforms. In the process, the role of the party in expanding political involvement and serving as the source of policy initiative has declined. In the short run, emphasis on services has strengthened the party organizations in terms of participation, resources, and activities. As one state party chair put it:

> During the 1960's and 70's we spent a long time as a debating society casually fighting over the wording of resolutions and platform planks, but losing vitality as an organization. Now with the party more important in elections we find increased interest in our activities. The internal battles are real since we are no longer playing "sandbox" politics. We can help candidates win and they know it. We fight among ourselves, but it is a good sign that the party is worth fighting for. (Author's interview)

The potential negative sides of the competitive emphasis of service-vendor-broker parties emerge in at least three realms.

Technology as a Jealous Lover

Attempting to maintain parity and hopeful of a strategic lead over the opposing party in the provision of resources and services requires constant vigilance. The speed of technological innovation does not allow political parties to rest on their laurels. Although technology "has provided an entirely different basis of power for the parties," they have "no natural monopoly over these sources of power" (Arterton, 1983, p. 57). A new generation of technologies could again make the parties obsolete to candidates.

The "new" technologies of today are likely to follow the path of previous new technologies. New generations of technological adaptations for political use traditionally do not completely replace earlier applications but rather are add-ons to the reservoir of approaches. Radio did not replace personal contact nor was it replaced by television as the only means of political communication. Targeted mail coexists with the more mass-communications strategies of newspaper advertising and door-to-door literature drops. Candidates in the future will simply have more options for communicating their messages, and success will depend on the appropriate choices and effective use of the chosen means. The cost and technical requirements of these new technologies promise to the parties a new realm in which they can become vendors, distributors, and brokers of the new technology (see political consultant Robert Squire, quoted in Havlicek, 1982, p. 84). The challenge to the parties lies in riding the wave of new technology rather than having to play "catch up."

The Next Generation of Technologies

The next generation of communication techniques available to party organizations and candidates alike promises to expand the two-way aspects of political communication and refine the ability to communicate effectively with desired audiences.

What direct mail was to politics in the 1970s, *telemarketing* promises to be in the 1980s. It has already proved effective by adding the personal touch of a telephone call with the targeting of messages based on voter's interests. As a current user puts it:

> We give our professional callers cards which summarize the political biases and interests of each potential contributor or voter. We can then work those interests into the script and personalize the approach. Whereas the mass media message just floats around out there trying to find a receptive target, effective telemarketing seeks out people and talks to them about issues in which they are interested. Aside from the contact with a real person, it has the added capability of allowing the target to talk back—thus giving us even more information on their interests to follow up on. (Author's interview)

Videodiscs offer the promise of "video campaign literature in both visual and textual form that can be distributed to targeted audiences" (Brotman, 1981, p. 33). Distributed to civic and political groups for meetings, or to interested individuals, such a format increases the impact of the message.

The time constraints and cost of sending candidates or party officials around the country make *videoconferencing* an appealing technology. Through a satellite hookup party representatives can talk to campaign rallies or meetings of campaign workers and engage in a dialog, not unlike facing each other in the same room (see Neustadt, 1982a, p. 222).

The distinction between television as a "mass" media and targeted mail or telemarketing as more personalized begins to break down with the application of *cable television* to politics. Cable television allows "narrowcasting," rather than "broadcasting," by allowing selective groups of voters to tune in. The low cost of cable transmission makes such an application possible. The cable television audience in general is a very useful target group. Cable subscribers tend to be younger, better educated, employed, and much more politically active than the average television viewer. In 1984 cable subscribers were 19 percent more likely to have voted and 32 percent more likely to have worked for a political party or candidate than the population as a whole (Paley & Moffett, 1984, p. 6).

The emergence to two-way cable appliations promises to increase public interest and provide parties and candidates with information on the most interested voters. Political programs could end with a straw poll on the issue at hand. Although some fear that such instantaneous feedback would make candidates less likely to take controversial stands and diminish the necessary tempering of purely representative government (Brotman, 1981, p. 33), the potential for representing the most interested citizens is very tempting. A related approach, *videotext*, allows viewers to select political messages from a menu and respond to simple questions (Paley & Moffett, 1984, pp. 10–11). Whatever the format, viewer responses could be used to discover potential volunteers or contributors and to enhance mailing lists for more effective targeting.

It is likely that by the end of the 1980s both parties will develop their own cable networks "reaching out to the party faithful, educating them to the party's principles and the skills required for running campaigns" (Kayden & Mahe, 1985, p. 199).

The Triumph of Form over Substance

The genius of political parties has traditionally been in their capacity to involve large numbers of citizens, aggregate their political interests, and change the personnel *and* policies of government. Service-vendor-broker parties may potentially lose their policy content through lack of attention to responsive activities (caucuses, issue forums, platform, conventions, and so on) or their inability to favor candidates selectively with organizationally defined policy positions. In 1986 the Democratic party made a conscious choice to drop its midterm convention designed to get more party members involved in the policy process and reserve its resources for the development of campaign services. In the 1986 election, the Republican National Committee failed to come up with a substantive party theme and focused its efforts on resources and services. The image of the national parties (and to some extent those on the state and local levels) serving as giant vending machines distributing highly effective services to all comers without regard to their policy perspective smacks of a party system that has lost its soul.

The Distribution of Party Organizational Power

Economies of scale making large multistate applications of technology more cost effective, available resources, and technological expertise have combined during the current wave of technology provision to shift power from state and local party organizations to the national party committees. Combined with the court decisions relating to the Democratic party delegate-selection reforms (see Conlan, 1985, p. 40), the development of the service-vendor-broker party has revised the traditional images of the national party organizations as relatively powerless shells (see Bibby, 1981, p. 102). The nationalization of the parties could pave the way for more responsible parties and diminish the organizational vitality of state and local units, but neither result is clear at this point. The national parties are clearly having more voice in the affairs of local units, but both parties have established extensive programs to build the party from the bottom up while upgrading the role of the national party as a provider of services.

Some of the new technologies on the horizon could have just the opposite effect of current technology. Therefore a centralizing trend within the parties may not be inevitable.

> ...changes in communications technology may reverse the nationalizing thrust that characterized the early years of television. New technology— including cable television, video recorders, satellite-to-home broadcasting, and personal computers—may create a fragmented and decentralized style of communications (from broadcasting to "narrowcasting") and with it a more segmented style of campaigning. (Orren, 1982, pp. 25–26)

Microcomputers on the campaign trail provide the surest bet for decentralization. Their low cost makes a powerful technology available to more candidates and party activists than ever before. Microcomputers also enhance the role of volunteers by giving them the capacity to organize fellow citizens and contact more voters than ever before. Far from becoming Big Brothers, they are enhancing the democratic nature of the country's political process (Smith, 1984c, p. 25).

Whether ultimately centralizing or decentralizing, the emphasis of new technologies on information requires a permanent depository for records of volunteers, contributors, census data, voting data, and sophisticated analysis routines. As Colorado Republican chairman Howard Calloway sees it, "The data must be updated on a regular basis, which cannot be done by candidates in campaigns that are specific, intensive efforts that end on a given day. Only the parties are in a position to provide that necessary continuity" (Advisory Commission on Intergovernmental Relations, 1982).

Retaining the Human Element in Parties

One of the challenges for the parties remains either in finding ways to use volunteers in an effective way or turning the parties into little more than paid consulting firms hiring themselves out to the highest bidder. In the era in which door-to-door canvassing and stuffing envelopes for mass mailings dominated, technologically unsophisticated volunteers played a necessary role. High technology has initially diminished the party need for volunteers. This reduces the party role of getting more citizens involved in politics. More importantly, not needing to cater to volunteers, the parties are tempted to cut off the traditional impact of volunteers on policy decisions. Volunteers often serve on formal party committees, attend conventions, and participate in party-issue forums, giving the party leaders and staff a "real-world" test of their policy proposals. A well-oiled high-tech machine, run by professionals and capable of assessing policy perspectives through polling and demographic analysis, is tempted to bypass the "bother" of having to deal with the human resources of a party.

Parties that forget they developed as means for individuals to affect the personnel and policy of government and become little more than supervendors may win elections—for a while—but cannot long maintain themselves.

The "Myth" of Organizational Vitality

Political parties forgetting that organizational activity and presence represent only one component of party vitality pursue organization building in isolation at peril. Viable political parties are more than permanent headquarters, professional staffs, and high-tech workshops. Without a meaningful presence among voters and elected officials, the organization means little. To some degree, attempts to build the organization component of parties represent a response to their weakness in these other realms and a short-term hope that such efforts will have a payoff among voters and elected officials.

Consequences for the Party in the Electorate

Only a small portion of the revival of party identification within the electorate can be attributed to the effective use of new technology. Indirectly, the reemergence of the party as significant for candidates upgrades the general image of the party and encourages candidates to campaign as partisans. The increased tendency of the press to focus on the internal workings of campaigns has led to a proliferation of stock stories from party headquarters, beginning with shots of computer tapes whirring and targeted mail envelopes being spit out. The image of party capacity creates a sense of pride among potential partisans.

Polling and demographic analysis by the parties give them the potential for reflecting more accurately the interests of voters and thereby making party stands more appealing. It may well be that "political parties that can adapt, can equip themselves for a new and exciting electronic age, one in which advances in information storage, retrieval, analysis and communication will bring expanded meaning to democracy, if we let them" (Jones, 1986, p. 4).

Technology may also begin to refine the linkage between citizens and their party. With the advances in direct-mail technology, "there exists a substantial number of citizens who consider themselves to be MEMBERS of a national party; they can carry cards in their wallets to prove it...rather than as voters or identifiers" (Arterton, 1982, p. 105).

On the negative side, some of the new technologies raise important questions about citizen involvement and privacy. Political parties have traditionally been instruments for involving citizens directly in politics through face-to-face contact; yet many of the new technologies make the involvement more remote. There is a considerable difference between discussing politics among partisan activists and listening to paid advertisements, responding to targeted mail, or answering an opinion poll (see Arterton, 1982, p. 136). Political party development of vast data banks on the opinions and political habits of citizens involves serious questions of privacy and increases the potential for misuse. This is particularly true when data not collected for political purposes (credit information, magazine subscriptions, and so on) are brought into the political realm (see Arterton, 1983, p. 78).

Technology presents a competing challenge to parties as they attempt to be representative. The growth of the mass media and the centralizing tendencies of new technologies have nationalized politics. In attempting to present a more unified party position, national preferences have offended local interests. The Democratic party has found it hard to shield its traditional white southern base from the "Tip O'Neill-Ted Kennedy liberals" they abhor, whereas moderate suburban Republicans find the Jesse Helms contingent of their party just as offensive. Bowing to local interests, the party can use technology to target messages more narrowly and eschew a national party line, but in the process it faces a new era of technology-supported fragmentation, and any vestige of party responsibility enhanced by technology will be lost.

Technology may have had a more direct role in the increased importance of partisanship and the shifting partisan alliances. Automated registration drives, targeted mailing, and get-out-the-vote drives place more partisans on the voting rolls and increase the percentage of partisans among voters. Republican party activists credit technology with much of their success. As one party leader put it: "We may have been more in tune with what the public wanted, and we did have Reagan as a leader, but without our organizational abilities we could not have capitalized on these factors. We found a void and used our computers and telephone banks to make a difference" (author's interview). Despite the impact of new technology, many of the partisan trends in party identification and voting are largely beyond the impact of communications technology alone.

Demographic shifts have dramatically changed the political landscape. Changing economic well-being of the Democratic New Deal Coalition during the past 50 years has split blue-collar workers into those with increased economic security who find conservative Republican principles more appealing and those less favored by economic shifts still tied to the appeals of the Democratic party. Resting largely on differential economic progress, race has increasingly served as a predictor of partisan preference, with blacks playing an increasing role in the Democratic party. Population shifts to the Sun Belt states of the South and West and increased Republican gains in those areas stem as much from a match between basic Republican policies and voter preferences as from organizational capabilities. Republican gains among younger voters give the party renewed hope of an eventual realignment but must be tempered by the general trend away from party-line voting even among partisans. The "realignment watch" of the past decade resulted time and time again in identifying a seeming critical shift, only to see it diminish a short time later. Gains in party identification increasingly hinge on short-term forces such as the personality or performance of key political leaders. Just as most observers began talking about Republican parity in party identification, Ronald Reagan's Iran-Contra aid policy embarrassment resulted in a dramatic drop in Republican party preference. All of the high-tech communications available cannot completely stem public perceptions about the inadequacy of party leaders or policy. Even if technology could have significantly tempered public perceptions, the Democratic party has moved to a position where it could use many of the same technologies for its own purposes.

The lesson of high-tech communications capabilities to the parties is only one aspect of the political battle. It

> should not obscure the fact that revitalization [of the parties] depends on more than organization, hardware, and short-term strategy. It also depends on restoring citizen loyalties to the parties. Such a restoration in turn depends on a widespread perception that parties are relevant to the policy concern of citizens. (Everson, 1982, p. 58)

The Impact on the Party in Office

Both parties would probably like to build their influence in a neat and organized way from the bottom up, starting with a strengthened popular base. The seeming political ineffectiveness of Democratic "expressive" reforms confirmed both their conclusions and earlier ones by their Republican colleagues who recognized that a direct attack on the public base of parties is difficult to accomplish. Both parties have settled on a campaign and candidate focus for affecting the policy and personnel of government. The goal is not transparent. By offering candidates the services they need in a superior form and at a reduced rate, the parties are attempting to build a sense of indebtedness lost during the era of candidate-centered campaigns. Although the parties are unlikely to recover their control over candidate recruitment and elections, they have found a method of making themselves indispensable to more and more candidates. Once in office, these elected officials who were drawn closer to the party during the campaign have begun to act in a more cohesive manner (see Sabato, 1982, p. 104; Price, 1984, pp. 298–299; Sorauf, 1984, p. 84).

THE AGENDA FOR PARTY REFORM

"It is a basic article of faith in the American creed that for every ill there is a remedy; by now experience with party reform should have taught that, at least where political institutions are concerned, for every remedy there is probably an ill" (Kirkpatrick, 1978, p. 31). In many ways, political parties in America have always rested on a shaky foundation. Lacking a constitutional mandate, the parties have been easy and prime targets for reform directed at them and unwitting victims of other reforms in society and government. As Gerald Pomper summarized it:

> Americans have denounced parties in theory, restricted them in legislation, almost eliminated them in reform, and scorned them in public opinion polls. Nevertheless, we have continued to employ them, and even cherish them, in practice. Americans—like other people—are often ambivalent. (Pomper, 1980b, p. 4)

Over the years, public ambivalence, differing perceptions of what the parties should be doing, and conflicting perceptions of self-interest have combined to promote reform efforts pulling the parties in different directions.

THE FOUR WAVES OF PARTY REFORM

Opening the Parties and Strengthening Their Resources

From the 1820s to the 1840s exclusive legislative caucuses began to be replaced by mass-membership parties. National and subnational nominating conventions and the election of local party leaders opened up the parties to a larger segment of the population. The infusion of democracy into the parties gave them new vitality but in the process reduced cohension and increased localism (see Pomper, 1980b, p. 2). Legislative caucuses could concern themselves with more national issues and keep their members in line. Expanding the role of local activists meant less centralized control and increased attempts to use the party for solving local problems.

Taming Party Excesses and Reducing Their Role

New rules and procedures allowed the parties to prosper, controlling the electoral process, rewarding the faithful with elective and appointive positions, and setting the policy agenda. The strength of the parties and the image of undemocratic and smoke-filled-room decisions led to a new wave of antiparty reforms beginning in the 1880s. Civil service reform denying parties government jobs with which to reward their faithful workers stripped the parties of a major motivating tool. The shift to the secret ballot reduced party control over voters. Most importantly, the adoption of the direct primary removed party control over access to the ballot. With primaries, partisan loyalty was no longer a condition the party could impose on potential candidates, and more candidates began to use the primary to circumvent the party.

Setting the Stage for the Contemporary Reform Eras

The early portion of this century was marked not so much by reform as by societal changes that indirectly affected the parties. Population mobility and national mass communications combined to break some of the localism that traditionally marked American politics. New communications technologies, beginning with the mass media and eventually leading to methods of personalizing massive numbers of communications, emerged outside the political realm but found political applications.

During the 1950s idealists and practitioners alike came to the conclusion that the parties were not living up to their potential. The publication of the American Political Science Association's set of prescriptions for the future of the parties, *Toward a More Responsible Two-Party System* (1950), was hailed as the blueprint for more distinct and viable parties but led nowhere. The attempt of political scientists to redirect the parties away from winning elections as a primary goal toward setting the direction of public policy ran counter to American tradition and the desires of party activists. On the 20th anniversary of the report, Evron Kirkpatrick, former executive director of the American Political Science Association and a member of the committee, lamented that the committee report stands "therefore as a monument to the inadequacies of the discipline and the failure of the members of the Committee as political scientists" (1979, p. 54).

Two competing reform movements began in the 1970s. Both prove the dictum that "nothing greases the gears for reform like failure." Massive electoral failures by each of the parties set into motion the pressures to change internal party procedures and to pursue legislative changes that would support the internal initiatives.

"Expressive" Reforms: Making the Democratic Party More Democratic

The loss of the presidency to Richard Nixon after a bitter Democratic Convention in 1968 encouraged the Democratic party to pursue reforms that would ameliorate the demands of its various component groups and to reduce the Republican advantage in financial resources. Attempting to revitalize the parties through an additional dose of democracy, the Democrats led the movement with a series of reforms increasing the "expressive" capabilities of the parties. Revising the convention delegate-selection process by making it more representative, increasing the importance of primaries versus the more exclusive conventions, and providing government financing for campaigns in order to increase the number of viable candidates were all, at least partially, designed to give more people a voice in the outcome of elections. Although some pressure to make parties more internally democratic continues to exist, the seeming lack of electoral payoff dimmed the motivation.

"Competitive" Reforms: The Rise of the Service-Vendor-Broker Party

Massive defeat in 1964 shocked the Republican party and opened the door for enhancing its capabilities. The party slowly moved from being "a second-rate answering service" (Broder, 1981, p. A25) to a provider of services, trainer of political activists, and collector of resources. The damaging effects of Watergate, which led to massive congressional and local level defeats in 1974 and loss of the presidency in 1976, gave the party a renewed impetus to focus on providing the resources to make the party more competitive electorally. Electoral success of the Republicans led Democrats to abandon slowly the emphasis on expressive reforms and join the Republicans as providers and brokers of services. Unlike previous reforms, the primary emphasis has been on redirecting the internal resources and energies of the party organizations, rather than pursuing legislative adjustments.

The Contemporary Reform Agenda

The public reform agenda of the service-vendor-broker parties is short. Although some might hope for dramatic changes such as dropping the primary system for nominations or making the parties the only players in the election process, most practitioners are more realistic and modest (see box, page 274). They desire laws that unfetter the ability of the parties to contribute to campaigns both directly and indirectly while keeping the limits on PACs and individuals (see Malbin, 1983, p. 17). For states with public financing, they proposed procedures making the party the conduit by which candidates receive the funds. More generally, they push for laws that distinguish the party as the preferred participant in elections and the removal of laws that disadvantage the parties. For example, both parties in California are fighting for the right to provide preprimary endorsements.

The Complexity of Reform

It is good advice to be wary of reformers bearing gifts. The proponents of reforms always oversell their advantages and underestimate their disadvantages, whereas the opponents do just the opposite. Reformers promote their reforms on the basis of "transcendent rhetoric"—linking their reforms to goals such as "efficiency," "democracy," or "justice," with which few people can disagree—but reformers tend to be motivated by more pragmatic concerns such as how the change will affect their political well-being. One must ask: "Efficiency in reaching which goal?" "Democracy for whom?" "Justice by which criteria?"

The consequences of reform, particularly in the political realm, are not always clear. The history of party reform reveals a plethora of unanticipated consequences. The new ills created may well be worse than those the reforms

A CONTEMPORARY REFORM AGENDA

Assessing the workings of the Constitution in its bicentennial year, the Committee on the Constitutional System made a number of suggestions bearing directly on the political parties. This blue ribbon, bipartisan commission asserted that "at the root of many of our current national problems—from huge budget deficits and trade deficits to the contradictions in our foreign policy—there is a common theme; deadlocks caused by the decline in cohesion of our political parties" (Cutler & Robinson, 1987, p. D2). The emphasis of the commission's suggestions concerned strengthening the parties so that they could reclaim their traditional role. Among the suggestions were:

- Financing congressional races with federal funds, with at least part of the money to be distributed to candidates by the parties.
- Amending the Constitution to allow reasonable limits on campaign expenditures, thereby limitng the influence of PACs and individuals making unlimited indirect expenditures
- Increasing House terms to four years and Senate terms to eight years, making all federal elections ones in which congressional representatives and presidents run at the same time, thereby encouraging mandates for a partisan team
- Making all party nominees for House and Senate races delegates to the national convention, thereby making them feel more a part of the party organization and enhancing their commitment to the party once in office

(See Cutler & Robinson, 1987, p. D2 and Macrcus, 1987, p. A19; Taylor, 1985a, p. A1.)

were designed to eradicate. Jeane Kirkpatrick asserts that the trend toward party decomposition stemmed from a number of sources—"cultural, social, technological, demographic, political, and legal—but the decisions [were] taken by persons attempting to reform the parties" (1978, p. 2).

Finally, the limitation of our capacity to anticipate the impact of broad-based reform leads us to focus our efforts on segments of the problem, whereas political parties are complex and interrelated phenomena. Although the three components of political parties—the party organization, the party in the electorate, and the party in office—are conceptually distinct, they do interact. Without organizational capabilities, elected officials are unlikely to perceive the party as important. Simultaneously, having elected officials ignore the party organization over the long term diminishes the ability of the party organization to capture human and material resources for providing services continually. The party organization needs some continuing presence in the electorate to whom appeals may be directed, and a viable party organization makes that presence in the electorate more likely. This does not necessarily mean that party activists should unduly bewail the decline of party identification and party-line voting.

> Persuasion of uncommitted voters, even temporarily, may be just as important to achieving a party's organizational objectives as mobilizing comitted adherents through conversion. . . . The ultimate electoral objective of a party is not the number of people who express an attitudinal preference for it, but rather, the number of votes a party's members receive at the polls. (Frendreis, Gibson, & Vertz, 1985, p. 2)

The goal for the parties is to be perceived as an important political actor by their candidates first, and the shift to the service-vendor-broker party is the best way to accomplish that. As candidates increasingly frame issues and carry out conflicts from a partisan perspective, their legitimization of the party will force voters to view the political world in similar partisan ways. The key for the party reformer is to determine which component of the parties to attack first. Since the party organization is most immediately malleable and organization members have the greatest stake in bringing about change, it is no surprise that its resources and activities have seen the most change in recent years. Reformers, though, must anticipate the impact that changes in party organization have on the party in the electorate and the party in office to understand the full implications of their efforts.

CONCLUSION

It is an unfair charge that service-vendor-broker parties are simply supercampaign facilities. The appropriate application of new communications technologies holds the potential for allowing the parties to adapt to the modern electoral environment in an effective way. It is more important that the parties continue to exist as meaningful organizations to voters and elected officials alike than it is that they recapture some image of past glory. Rebuilding the popular base for the parties and ensuring the responsiveness of the party organization to that popular base is more likely to occur as the parties more securely assert their position as prime players in the election process. The challenge for the future lies in maintaining the technological superiority of the parties while searching for ways to ensure that their policy initiatives are based on popular support.

References

ABC-CLIO. 1983. *The Democratic and Republican Parties in America: A Historical Bibliography*. Santa Barbara, Calif.: ABC-CLIO Information Services.

Abraham, Henry J. 1987. *The Judiciary*. Boston: Allyn & Bacon.

Abramowitz, Alan. 1978. "The Impact of Presidential Debate on Voter Rationality." *American Journal of Political Science* 22 (August): 680–690.

Advisory Commission on Intergovernmental Relations. 1984. Testimony for "Transformations in American Politics and the Implications for Federalism" project. Washington, D.C.

———. 1986. *The Transformation in American Politics: Implications for Federalism*. Washington, D.C.

Agranoff, Robert. 1979. "The New Style of Campaigning: The Decline of Party and the Rise of Candidate Centered Technology." In Jeff Fishel (Ed.), *Parties and Elections in an Anti-Party Age* (pp. 230–240). Bloomington: Indiana University Press.

Aldrich, John, Gary J. Miller, Charles W. Ostrom, Jr., & David Rohde. 1986. *American Government: People, Institutions, and Policies*. Boston: Houghton Mifflin.

Alexander, Herbert. 1983. *The Case for PACs*. Washington, D.C.: Public Affairs Council.

American Assembly. 1982. *The Future of American Political Parties*. Ed. Joel Fleishman. Englewood Cliffs, N.J.: Prentice-Hall.

American Political Science Association, Committee on Political Parties. 1950. *Toward a More Responsible Two-Party System*. New York: Holt, Rinehart and Winston.

Anderson, Jack, & Joseph Spear. 1985, December 16., "PACs: Political Muscle with Bucks." *Washington Post*, p. B15.

Andersen, Kristi. 1979. *The Creation of a Democratic Majority, 1928–1936*. Chicago: University of Chicago Press.

Arterton, F. Christopher. 1982. "Political Money and Party Strength." In Joel Fleishman (Ed.), *The Future of American Political Parties* (pp. 101–139). Englewood Cliffs, N.J.: Prentice-Hall.

————. 1983. *Communications Technology and Political Campaigns in 1982: Assessing the Implications.* Washington, D.C.: Roosevelt Center.

Baker, Gorden E. 1985. "Excerpts from Declaration of Gorden E. Baker in Badham vs. Eu." *PS* 18 (Summer): 551–557.

Baker v. Carr, 369 U.S. 186 (1962).

Banfield, Edward C., & James Q. Wilson. 1963. *City Politics.* Cambridge Mass.: Harvard University Press.

Bass, Harold. 1984. "The President and the National Party Organization." In Robert Harmel (Ed.), *Presidents and Their Parties* (pp. 59–89). New York: Praeger.

Beiler, David. 1985. "Short Takes." *Campaigns and Elections* 6 (Summer): 39–43.

Bell, Julie Davis. 1985. "The Decline of Party Revisited: Motivational Change among Party Activists." Paper presented at the September 1985 annual meeting of the American Political Science Association. New Orleans.

Berelson, Bernard, Paul Lazarsfeld, & William McPhee. 1954. *Voting.* Chicago: University of Chicago Press.

Berkson, Larry C. 1980. "Judicial Selection in the U.S.: A Special Report." *Judicature* 64 (entire issue).

Bibby, John, & Robert J. Huckshorn. 1983. "Parties in State Politics." In Virginia Gray, Herbert Jacob, & Kenneth Vines (Eds.), *Politics in the American States* (pp. 59–96). Boston: Little, Brown.

Boren, David. 1985. *Congressional Record.* 99th Cong., 1st sess., December 2, pp. S16604–16607.

Born, Richard. 1985. "Partisan Intentions and Election Day Realities in the Congressional Redistricting Process." *American Political Science Review* 79 (June): 305–319.

Brady, David, and Patricia A. Hurley. 1985. "The Prospects of Contemporary Partisan Realignment." *PS* 18 (Winter): 63–68.

Broder, David. 1972. *The Party's Over.* New York: Harper and Row.

————. 1981, August 12: "Bliss Remembered." *Washington Post,* p. A25.

————. 1985a, February 3: "Democrats Remain in Doldrums." *Washington Post,* p. A15.

————. 1985b, June 27: "Democrats New Motto Bland Is Beautiful." *Washington Post,* p. A1.

————. 1985C, October 13: "Battle Lines Drawn for 1991." *Washington Post,* p. A4.

————. 1986a, January 2: "Stakes Are Unusually High as Midterm Elections Near." *Washington Post,* p. A1.

————. 1986b, April 2: "The Force." *Washington Post,* p. A23.

————. 1986c, May 18: "GOP Gains Strength in Political Cauldron." *Washington Post,* p. A1.

Brotman, S. N. 1981. "New Campaigning for the New Media." *Campaigns and Elections* 2 no. 3: 32–34.

Buckley v. Valeo, 424 U.S. 1 (1976).

Burnham, Walter Dean. 1970. *Critical Elections and the Mainspring of American Politics.* New York: W. W. Norton.

————. 1982. *The Current Crisis in American Politics.* New York: Oxford University Press.

Cain, Bruce. 1985. "Excerpts from Declaration in Badham vs. Eu." *PS* 18, no. 3: 561–574.

Cain, Bruce, & Ken McCue. 1985. "Do Registration Drives Matter: The Realities of

Partisan Dreams." Paper presented at the September 1985 meeting of the American Political Science Association. New Orleans.

California Commission on Campaign Finance. 1985, October 16. Press release.

Campbell, Angus, Philip E. Converse, Warren E. Miller, & Donald E. Stokes. 1960. *The American Voter*. New York: Wiley.

Campbell, James. 1985. "A Comparison of Presidential and Midterm Elections." Paper presented at the September 1985 annual meeting of the American Political Science Association. New Orleans.

Cantor, Joseph E. 1984. "Political Action Committees: Their Evolution, Growth, and Implications of the Political System." Congressional Reference Service Report no. 84–78 GOV.

Castle, David, & Patrick Fett. 1985. "When Politicians Switch Parties—Conscience or Calculation." Paper presented at the September 1985 annual meeting of the American Political Science Association. New Orleans.

Cavanaugh, Thomas. 1982. "The Dispersion of Authority in the House of Representatives." *Political Science Quarterly* 97 (Winter): 623–637.

Cavanaugh, Thomas, & James L. Sunquist. 1985. "The New Two-Party System." In John E. Chubb and Paul E. Peterson (Eds.), *The New Directions in American Politics* (pp. 33–68). Washington, D.C.: The Brookings Institution.

City of Mobile v. Bolden, 446 U.S. 55 (1980).

Civil Service, Inc. 1985. "Attitudes toward Campaign Financing." Washington, D.C.: Author.

Claggett, William. 1985. "Conversion, Recruitment, Mobilization, and Realignment." Paper presented at the September 1985 annual meeting of the American Political Science Association. New Orleans.

Clausen, Aage. 1979. "Party Voting in Congress." In Jeff Fishel (Ed.), *Parties in an Anti-Party Age* (pp. 274–279). Bloomington: Indiana University Press.

Clendinin, Dudley. 1984, February 15. "Small Computers Aid People of Small Means in Elections." *New York Times*, p. 1.

Clubb, Jerome, William Flanigan, & Nancy Zingale. 1980. *Partisan Realignment: Voters, Parties, and Government in American History*. Beverly Hills, Calif.: Sage Publications.

Colella, Cynthia. 1984. "Intergovernmental Aspects of FECA: State Parties and Campaign Finance." *Intergovernmental Perspective* 10 (Fall): 14.

Coleman, Milton. 1985, July 5. "Making Black Votes Count." *Washington Post*, p. B5.

Committee on Political Parties of the American Political Science Association. 1950. *Toward a More Responsible Two Party System*. New York: Rinehart.

Congressional Quarterly. 1976. *Guide to the U.S. Congress*. Washington, D.C.: Congressional Quarterly Press.

Conlan, Timothy J. 1985. "Federalism and American Politics: New Relationships, A Changing System." *Intergovernmental Perspective* 11 (Winter): 32–45.

———. 1986. Unpublished draft of Advisory Commission on Intergovernmental Relations. "The Transformation in American Politics: Implications for Federalism." Washington, D.C.

Conlan, Timothy J., Ann Martino, & Robert Dilger. 1984. "State Parties in the 1980's." *Intergovermental Perspective* 10 (Fall): 6–13.

Converse, Philip. 1975. "Public Opinion and Voting Behavior," In Fred I. Greenstein & Nelson Polsby (Eds.), *Handbook of Political Science*. Vol. 4 (pp. 75–169). Reading, Mass.: Addison-Wesley.

Conway, Margaret. 1985. *Political Participation in the United States*. Washington, D.C.: CQ Press.

Cook, Rhodes. 1984, November 3. "Third-Party Standard Bearers Struggle for Attention and Votes." *Congressional Quarterly Weekly Report*, pp. 2849–2851.

————. 1985. "Many Democrats Cool to Redoing Party Rules." *Congressional Quarterly Weekly Report* 43 (August 24): 1687–1689.

————. 1986, April 5. "LaRouch and His Followers: Angry, Noisy, and Persistent." *Congressional Quarterly Weekly Report*, pp. 742–746.

Cook, Rhodes, & Tom Watson. 1985. "New Generation Poised to Tip Voting Scales." *Congressional Quarterly Weekly Report* 43 (November 23): 2421–2427.

Cotter, Cornelius, & John F. Bibby. 1980. "Institutional Development of Parties and the Thesis of Party Decline." *Political Science Quarterly* 95 (Spring): 1–27.

Cotter, Cornelius, & Bernard Hennessy. 1964. *Politics without Power: The National Party Committees*. New York: Atherton Press.

Cotter, Cornelius P., James Gibson, John F. Bibby, & Robert Huckshorn. 1984. *Party Organization in American Politics*. New York: Praeger.

Craig, Stephen. 1985. "Partisanship, Independence, and No Preference: Another Look at the Measurement of Party Identification." *American Journal of Political Science* 29 (May): 274–290.

Crittenden, John A. 1982. *Parties and Elections in the U.S.* Englewood Cliffs, N.J.: Prentice-Hall.

Cronin, Thomas. 1980. "The Presidency and the Parties." In Gerald Pomper (Ed.), *Party Renewal in America* (pp. 176–193). New York: Praeger.

Crotty, William (Ed.). 1979. *The Party Symbol*. San Francisco: W. H. Freeman.

————. 1983. *Party Reform*. White Plains, N.Y.: Longman.

————. 1984. *American Parties in Decline*. Boston: Little, Brown.

Cutler, Lloyd, & Donald Robinson. 1987, February 1. "Breaking Our Political Gridlock." *Washington Post*, p. D2.

Dalton, Russell J. 1984. "Cognitive Mobilization and Partisan Dealignment in Advanced Industrial Democracies." *Journal of Politics* 46 (Fall): 264–284.

Daniels, LeGree S. 1985, April 11. "Still in Bondage—To a Political Party." *Washington Post*, p. A21.

David, Paul T., Ralph M. Goldman, & Richard C. Bain. 1960. *The Politics of National Party Conventions*. Washington, D.C.: The Brookings Institution.

Davidson, Roger H., & Walter J. Oleszek. 1981. *Congress and Its Members*. Washington, D.C.: Congressional Quarterly Press.

Davis v. Bandemer, 106 S. Ct. 2810 (1986).

Delli Carpini, Michael X. 1985. "Party Support and the Sixties Generation." Paper presented at the September 1985 annual meeting of the American Political Science Association. New Orleans.

DeNardo, James. 1980. "Turnout and the Vote: The Joke's on the Democrats." *American Political Science Review* 74 (June): 406–420.

Dennis, Jack. 1986. "Public Support for the Party System, 1964–1984." Paper presented before the September 1986 meeting of the American Political Science Association. Washington, D.C.

Downs, Anthony. 1957. *An Economic Theory of Democracy*. New York: Harper and Row.

Drew, Elizabeth. 1983. *Politics and Money: The New Road to Corruption*. New York: Macmillan.

Duverger, Maurice. 1954. *Political Parties*. New York: Wiley.

Edsall, Thomas. 1984a. *The New Politics of Inequality*. New York: Norton.

————. 1984b, June 17. "Money, Technology, Revive GOP Force." *Washington Post*, p. A1.

————. 1984c, June 18. "GOP Purchasing Technological Edge." *Washington Post*, p. A1.

————. 1985a, February 18: "Democrats' Fund-Raising Skids." *Washington Post*, p. A5.

————. 1985b, July 8: "Flush with Cash, GOP Looks to High-Tech Races in 1986." *Washington Post*, p. A3.

————. 1985c, July 8: "Pulpit Power: Converting the GOP." *Washington Post Weekley Edition*, p. 8.

————. 1986a, January 25: "Republicans See Signs of '86 Majority." *Washington Post*, p. A4.

————. 1986b, September 14. "Why the GOP Is Still Waiting on Realignment." *Washington Post*, p. A1.

————. 1986c, November 3: "Is the FEC Undermining Federal Election Law?" *Washington Post Weekly Edition*, p. 14.

————. 1986d, November 3: "Yeah, We Know What the Law Says, but This Is Different." *Washington Post Weekly Edition*, p. 13.

————. 1986e, November 6: "GOP's Cash Advantage Failed to Assure Victory in Close Senate Races," *Washington Post*, p. A46.

Edwards, George. 1984. "Presidential Party Leadership in Congress." In Robert Harmel (Ed.),. *Presidents and Their Parties* (pp. 179–214). New York: Praeger.

Ehrenhalt, Alan. 1985, August 31. "Seattle Area Politics: A Media Takeover." *Congressional Quarterly Weekly Report*, p. 1739.

Eldersveld, Samuel. 1964. *Political Parties: A Behavioral Analysis*. Chicago: Rand McNally.

————. 1982. *Political Parties in American Society*. New York: Basic Books.

————. 1984. "The Condition of Party Organization at the Local Level." Paper presented at the 1984 annual meeting of the Southern Political Science Association. Atlanta, Ga.

Epstein, Leon. 1980. *Political Parties in Western Democracies*. New Brunswick, N.J.: Transaction Books.

————. 1986. *Political Parties in the American Mold*. Madison: University of Wisconsin Press.

Erickson, Jack. 1982. "The Democrats: Rebuilding Support Groups." *Campaigns and Elections* 3 (Spring): 4–14.

Erickson, Robert S., & Kent L. Tedin. 1986. "Voter Conversion and the New Deal Realignment," *Western Political Quarterly* 39 (December):729–732.

Everson, David. 1982. "The Decline of Political Parties." In Gerald Benjamin (Ed.), *The Communications Revolution in Politics* (pp. 49–60). New York: Academy of Political Science.

Fenno, Richard. 1978. *Home Style*. Boston: Little, Brown.

Fiorina, Morris. 1978, September/October. "The Incumbency Factor." *Public Opinion*, p. 41.

————. 1981. *Retrospective Voting in American National Elections*. New Haven: Yale University Press.

Fishel, Jeff, Ed. 1979. *Parties and Elections in an Anti-Party Age*: American Politics and the Crisis of Confidence. Bloomington: Indiana University Press.

Flanigan, William, & Nancy Zingale. 1987. *Political Behavior of the American Electorate* (6th ed.). Boston: Allyn & Bacon.

Frantzich, Stephen E. 1982. *Computers in Congress: The Politics of Information.* Beverly Hills, Calif.: Sage Publications.

————. 1986. *Write Your Congressman.* New York: Praeger.

Frendreis, John P., James L. Gibson, & Laura L. Vertz. 1985. "Local Party Organizations in the 1984 Elections." Paper presented before the September 1985 annual meeting of the American Political Science Association. New Orleans.

Gibson, James L., John F. Bibby, & Cornelius P. Cotter. 1983. "Assessing Party Organizational Strength." *American Journal of Political Science* 27 (May): 193–222.

Gibson, James L., Cornelius P. Cotter, John F. Bibby, & Robert T. Huckshorn. 1985. "Wither the Local Parties?" *American Journal of Political Science* 29 (May): 139–160.

Gibson, James L., John Frendreis, & Laura Vertz. 1985. "Party Dynamics in the 1980's." Paper presented at the April 1985 annual meeting of the Midwest Political Science Association. Chicago.

Gitelson, Alan R., M. Margaret Conway, & Frank B. Feigert. 1984. *American Political Parties: Stability and Change.* Boston: Houghton Mifflin.

Goldman, Sheldon. 1975. "Voting Behavior of the U.S. Courts of Appeals Revisited." *American Political Science Review* 69 (June): 496.

Granat, Diane. 1984, May 5. "Parties' Schools for Politicians Grooming Troops for Election." *Congressional Quarterly Weekly Report*, pp. 1036–1037.

————. 1985, November 30. "Six Seeking Democratic Whip Position." *Congressional Quarterly Weekly Report*, pp. 2498–2503.

Grofman, Bernard (Ed.). 1985. "Political Gerrymandering: Badham v. Eu, Political Science Goes to Court." *PS* (Summer): 538–576.

Hadley, Arthur. 1978. *The Empty Voting Booth.* Englewood Cliffs, N.J.: Prentice-Hall.

Hadley, Charles. 1985. "Dual Partisan Identification in the South." *Journal of Politics* 47 (February): 254–268.

Harmel, Robert (Ed.). 1984. *Presidents and Their Parties.* New York: Praeger.

Harmel, Robert. 1985. "Minority Party Leadership in One Party Dominant Legislatures." Paper presented at the September 1985 annual meeting of the American Political Science Association. New Orleans.

Harris, Fred R., & Paul L. Hain. 1983. *American Legislative Process.* Glenview, Ill.: Scott, Foresman.

Havlicek, Franklin J. (Eds.). 1982. *Election Communications and the Campaign of 1982.* Chicago: American Bar Association.

Hayden, Tom. 1985, January/February. "Going West: California and the Future of the Democratic Party." *The Economic Democrat*, pp. 3–10.

————. 1986, June 1: "Democrats: Go West or Face Political Extinction." *Washington Post*, p. C1.

Hennessey, Bernard. 1981. *Public Opinion.* Monterey, Calif.: Brooks-Cole.

Herrnson, Paul S. 1985. "Parties, PACs, and Congressional Elections." Paper presented at the 1985 annual meeting of the Midwest Political Science Association. Chicago.

————. 1986. "National Party Organizations and Congressional Campaigning: National Parties as Brokers." Paper presented at the annual meeting of the Midwest Political Science Association. Chicago.

Hershey, Marjorie. 1984. *Running for Office: The Political Education of Campaigners*. Chatham, N.J.: Chatham House.

Hotelling, Harold. 1929. "Stability in Competition." *Economic Journal* 39 (March): 41–57.

Huckshorn, Robert. 1984. *Political Parties in America*. Monterey, Calif.: Brooks/ Cole.

Huckshorn, Robert, & John Bibby. 1982. "State Parties in an Era of Political Change." In Joel Fleishman (Ed.), *The Future of American Political Parties* (pp. 70–100). Englewood Cliffs, N.J.: Prentice-Hall.

———. 1983. "National Party Rules and Delegate Selection in the Republican Party." *PS* 16 (Fall): 656–666.

Jackson, John S., III, Jesse C. Brown, & Barbara L. Brown. 1980. "Recruitment, Representation, and Political Values: The 1976 Democratic National Convention Delegates." In William Crotty (Ed.), *The Party Symbol* (pp. 202–218). San Francisco: W. H. Freeman.

Jackson, John S., III, Barbara Leavitt Brown, & David Bositis. 1982. "Herbert McCloskey and Friends Revisited: 1980 Democratic and Republican Elites Compared to the Mass Public." *American Politics Quarterly* 10 (April): 158–180.

Jacobson, Gary C. 1985. "The Republican Advantage in Campaign Finance." In John E. Chubb & Paul E. Peterson (Eds.). *The New Directions in American Politics* (pp. 143–174). Washington, D.C.: The Brookings Institution.

Jennings, M. Kent, & Kenneth P. Langton. 1969. "Mothers vs. Fathers: The Formation of Political Orientations among Young Americans." *Journal of Politics* 31 (May): 329–358.

Jennings, M. Kent, & Gregory P. Markus. 1984. "Party Orientation over the Long Haul." *American Political Science Review* 78 (December): 1000–1018.

Jennings, M. Kent, & Richard G. Niemi. 1981. *Generations & Politics*. Princeton, N.J.: Princeton University Press.

Jewell, Malcolm E., & Samuel Patterson. 1977. *The Legislative Process*. New York: Random House.

Jones, Charles O. 1981. "House Leadership in an Age of Reform," In Frank H. Mackaman (Ed.), *Understanding Congressional Leadership* (pp. 117–134). Washington, D.C.: Congressional Quarterly Press.

———. 1986, August. "Hard Disk Politics." *Dirksen Congressional Center Report*. Pekin, Ill.: The Dirksen Center.

Jones, Ruth. 1981. "State Public Campaign Finance: Implications for Partisan Politics." *American Journal of Political Science* 25 (May): 342–361.

Joslyn, Richard. 1984. *Mass Media Elections*. Reading, Mass.: Addison-Wesley.

Kayden, Xandra. 1980. "The Nationalizing of the Party System." In Michael Malbin (Ed.), *Parties, Interest Groups, and Campaign Finance Laws*. (pp. 257–282). Washington, D.C.: American Enterprise Institute.

Kayden, Xandra, & Eddie Mahe, Jr. 1985. *The Party Goes On: The Persistence of the Two-Party System in the United States*. New York: Basic Books.

Keech, William R., & Donald Matthews. 1979. "Patterns in the Presidential Nominating Process, 1936–1976." In Jeff Fishel (Ed.), *Parties in an Anti-Party Age*. (pp. 203–218). Bloomington: Indiana University Press.

Keefe, William. 1987. *Parties, Politics and Public Policy in America*. Washington, D.C.: Congressional Quarterly Press.

Key, V. O., Jr. 1949. *Southern Politics in State and Nation*. New York: Alfred A. Knopf.

King, Gary, & Gerald Benjamin. 1985. "The Stability of Party Identification among U.S. Senators and Representatives, 1789-1984." Paper presented at the September 1985 annual meeting of the American Political Science Association. New Orleans.

Kingdon, John. 1981. *Congressmen's Voting Decisions*. New York: Harper & Row.

Kirkpatrick, Evron. 1979. "Toward a more Responsive Party System: Political Science, Policy Science or Pseudo-Science." In Jeff Fishel (Ed.), *Parties and Elections in an Anti-Party Age* (pp. 33–54). Bloomington: Indiana University Press.

Kirkpatrick, Jeane. 1978. *Dismantling the Parties: Reflections on Party Reform and Party Decomposition*. Washington, D.C.: American Enterprise Institute.

Ladd, Everett Carl. 1985a. *The Ladd Report #1*. New York: W. W. Norton.

_____. 1985b. "Party Time: Realignment." *Campaigns and Elections* 6 (Summer): 58–60.

_____. 1986a. *The Ladd Report #3*. New York: W. W. Norton.

_____. 1986b. *The Ladd Report #4*. New York: W. W. Norton.

Ladd, Everett Carl, & Charles Hadley. 1975. *Transformations of the American Party System*. New York: Norton.

LaFollette, R. M. 1913. *Autobiography*. Madison: Author.

Lamis, Alexander. 1984. "The Rise of the Two-Party South: Partisan Dynamics and Trends Since the Early 1960's." *Campaigns and Elections* 5 (Fall): 6–17.

Lane, Dale. 1983, November 8. "Suit Seeks to Widen Powers for State Political Parties." *San Jose Mercury News*.

Lang, Gladys, & Kurt Lang. 1984. *Politics and Television Reviewed*. Beverly Hills, Calif.: Sage Publications.

Lazarsfeld, Paul F., Bernard Berelson, & Hazel Gaudet. 1944. *The People's Choice*. New York: Duell, Sloan and Pearce.

Light, Paul C., & Celinda Lake. 1985. "The Election: Candidates, Strategies, and Decisions." In Michael Nelson (Ed.)., *The Elections of 1984* (pp. 83–110). Washington D.C.: Congressional Quarterly Press.

Lipset, Seymour Martin, & William Schneider. 1983. "The Decline of Confidence in American Institutions." *Political Science Quarterly* 98 (Fall): 379–402.

Longley, Charles. 1980. "National Party Renewal." In Gerald Pomper (Ed.). *Party Renewal in America* (pp. 69–86). New York: Praeger.

Lowi, Theodore J. 1983. "Toward a More Responsible Three-Party System." *PS* 16 (Fall): 699–706.

Madison, James. 1961. *The Federalist No. 10*. New York: New American Library.

Maggiotto, Michael A. 1986. "Party Identification in the Federal System." Paper presented at the September 1986 annual meeting of the American Political Science Association. Washington, D.C.

Malbin, Michael. 1983, January. "The Problem of PAC Journalism." *Public Opinion*, pp. 15–17.

Mann, Thomas. 1981. "Elections and Change in Congress." In Thomas Mann & Norman Ornstein (Eds.), *The New Congress* (pp. 32–54). Washington, D.C.: American Enterprise Institute.

Mauser, Gary. 1983. *Political Marketing: An Approach to Campaign Strategy*. New York: Praeger.

Mayhew, David. 1974. *Congress: The Electoral Connection*. New Haven: Yale University Press.

Mazmanian, Daniel. 1979. "Third Parties in Presidential Elections." In Jeff Fishel (Ed.), *Parties in an Anti-Party Age* (pp. 305–317). Bloomington: Indiana University Press.

McCloskey, Herbert, Paul J. Hoffman, & Rosemary O'Hara. 1960, June. "Issue Conflict and Consensus among Party Leaders and Followers." *American Political Science Review*, pp. 406–427.

McCorkle, Pope, & Joel Fleishman. 1982. "Political Parties and Presidential Nominations." In Joel Fleishman (Ed.), *The Future of American Political Parties* (pp. 140–168). Englewood Cliffs, N.J.: Prentice-Hall.

McWilliams, Wilson Carey. 1980. "Parties as Civic Associations." In Gerald Pomper (Ed.), *Party Renewal in America* (pp. 51–68). New York: Praeger.

Michels, Robert. 1949/1915. *Political Parties*. Glencoe, Ill.: Free Press.

Mikva, Abner, & Pati Saris. 1983. *The American Congress: The First Branch*. New York: Franklin Watts.

Mileur, Jerome M. 1986. "Federal Constitutional Challenges to State Party Regulation." Paper presented at the September 1986 annual meeting of the American Political Science Association. Washington, D.C.

Milkis, Sidney. 1984. "Presidents and Party Purges." In Robert Harmel (Ed.), *Presidents and Their Parties*, (pp. 175–195). New York: Praeger.

Miller, Arthur, & Martin Wattenberg. 1983. "Measuring Party Identification: Independent or No Preference." *American Journal of Political Science* 27 (February): 106–121.

Mitofsky, Warren, & Martin Plissner. 1980, October–November. "The Making of the Delegates, 1968–1980." *Public Opinion*, p. 43.

Nagel, Stuart S. 1961. "Political Party Affiliation and Judges' Decisions." *American Political Science Review* 55 (December): 845.

Neustadt, Richard. 1982, March 14. "Watch Out Politics—Technology Is Coming." *Washington Post*, p. D1.

Norpoth, Helmut. 1985. "Changes in Party Identification: Evidence of Republican Majority." Paper presented at the September 1985 annual meeting of the American Political Science Association, New Orleans.

Ornstein, Norman, & David Rohde. 1979. "Political Parties and Congressional Reform." In Jeff Fishel (Ed.), *Parties in an Anti-Party Age* (pp. 280–294). Bloomington: Indiana University Press.

Ornstein, Norman J., Thomas E. Mann, Michael J. Malbin, Allen Schick, & John F. Bibby. 1984. *Vital Statistics on Congress, 1984–1985 Edition*. Washington, D.C.: American Enterprise Institute.

Orren, Gary. 1982. "The Changing Styles of American Party Politics." In Joel Fleishman (Ed.), *The Future of American Political Parties* (pp. 4–41). Englewood Cliffs, N.J.: Prentice-Hall.

Orren, Gary, & Sidney Verba. 1983. "American Voter Participation: The Shape of the Problem." Paper presented at a symposium on American voting participation, Washington, D.C., ABC Inc.

Paley, William C., & Shelly Moffett. 1984. "The New Electronic Media: Instant Action and Reaction." *Campaigns and Elections* 4 (Winter): 4–12.

Patterson, Thomas. 1980. *The Mass Media Election*. New York: Praeger.

Patterson, Thomas, & Robert McClure. 1976. *The Unseeing Eye.* New York: G. P. Putnam's Sons.

Perl, Peter. 1985, March 21. "Kirkland Says Party Misdiagnoses Its Ills." *Washington Post,* p. A9.

Peterson, Bill. 1984, November 18. "Jesse Helm's Lesson from Washington." *Washington Post,* p. C1.

———. 1985, August 23. "GOP 'Open Door' Deemed Success Despite Shortfall." *Washington Post,* p. A3.

———. 1986a, July 22. "Megapolitics: The Florida Senate Race." *Washington Post,* p. A6.

———. 1986b, August 16. "Lt. Governor Baxter Becomes Gubernatorial Nominee." *Washington Post,* p. A4.

———. 1986c, October 8. "Computing an Audience for a Tailored Message." *Washington Post,* p. A1.

———. 1986d, November 3. "If Reagan Talks to You on the Phone Today, Don't Feel Special." *Washington Post Weekly Edition,* p. 11.

Phillips, Kevin P. 1986, July 6. "Once Reagan Goes, the Party May Be Over for the GOP." *Washington Post,* p. B1.

Piereson, James E. 1978. "Issue Alignment and the American Party System, 1956–1976." *American Politics Quarterly* 6 (July): 275–307.

Polsby, Nelson. 1983a. *Consequences of Party Reform.* New York: Oxford University Press.

———. 1983b. "The Reform of Presidential Selection and Democratic Theory." *PS* 16 (Fall): 695–698.

Pomper, Gerald M. 1975. *Voters' Choice.* New York: Harper & Row.

Pomper, Gerald M. (Ed.). 1980. *Party Renewal in America: Theory and Practice.* New York: Praeger.

Powell, G. Bingham, Jr. 1982. *Contemporary Democracies: Participation, Stability, and Violence.* Cambridge, Mass.: Harvard University Press.

Price, David. 1984. *Bringing Back the Parties.* Washington, D.C.: Congressional Quarterly Press.

Price, H. Douglas. 1971. "The Congressional Career—Then and Now." In Nelson Polsby (Ed.), *Congressional Behavior* (pp. 14–27). New York: Random House.

Ranney, Austin. 1962. *The Decline of Responsible Party Government.* Urbana: University of Illinois Press.

———. 1975. *Curing the Mischiefs of Faction: Party Reform in America.* Berkeley: University of California Press.

———. 1979. "Changing Rules of the Presidential Nominating Game: Party Reform in America." In Jeff Fishel (Ed.), *Parties in an Anti-Party Age* (pp. 219–229). Bloomington: Indiana University Press.

Ranney, Austin, & Wilmoore Kendall. 1956. *Democracy and the American Party System.* New York: Harcourt, Brace and World.

Reichley, A. James. 1985. "The Rise of National Parties." In John E. Chubb & Paul E. Peterson (Eds.), *The New Directions in American Politics* (pp. 175–202). Washington, D.C.: The Brookings Institution.

Reiter, Howard. 1984. "The Gavels of August: Presidents and National Party Conventions." In Robert Harmel (Ed.), *Presidents and Their Parties* (pp. 96–121). New York: Praeger.

Rossiter, Clinton. 1960. *Parties and Politics in America*. Ithaca, N.Y.: Cornell University Press.

Rusk, Jerrold. 1970. "The Effect of the Australian Ballot Reform on Ticket-Splitting." *American Political Science Review* 64 (December): 1220–1238.

Sabato, Larry. 1981. *The Rise of the Political Consultants*. New York: Basic Books.

———. 1985. *PAC Power*. New York: W.W. Norton.

———. 1988. *The Party's Just Begun*. Boston: Little, Brown, Scott Foresman.

Salholz, Eloise. 1984, September 10. "Periscope." *Newsweek*, p. 13.

Salmore, Stephen, & Barbara Salmore. 1985. *Candidates, Parties, and Campaigns*. Washington, D.C.: Congressional Quarterly Press.

Sandman, Joshua. 1984. "The Reemergence of the Political Party: Campaign '84 and Beyond." *Presidential Studies Quarterly* 14 (Fall): 512–518.

Schattschneider, E. E. 1982/1942. *Party Government*. New York: Holt Rinehart.

Schlesinger, Joseph A. 1985. "The New American Political Party." *American Political Science Review* 79, no. 4: 1152–1169.

Schram, Martin. 1982, March 23. "Why Can't the Democrats Be More Like the Republicans? They're Trying." *Washington Post*, p. A2.

Seligman, Lester. 1979. "The Presidential Office and the President as Party Leader." In Jeff Fishel (Ed.), *Parties in an Anti-Party Age* (pp. 295–302). Bloomington: Indiana University Press.

Smith, Rodney. 1984a. "National Committees: Party Renewal through Campaign Assistance." *Campaigns and Elections* 5 (Spring): 12–19.

———. 1984b. "The New Political Machine: Small Computers Are Having a Big Impact in Local Elections." *Datamation* 30 (June 1): 22–26.

———. 1984c, July 16. "The New Political Machine." *Computer World*, p. 19.

Sorauf, Frank. 1980. *Party Politics in America*. Boston: Little, Brown.

———. 1982. "Accountability in Political Action Committees: Who's in Charge?" Paper presented at the September 1982 annual meeting of the American Political Science Association. Chicago.

———. 1984. *What Price PACs?* New York: Twentieth Century Fund.

Stanley, Harold W., & Richard G. Niemi. 1988. *Vital Statistics on American Politics*. Washington, D.C.: CQ Press.

Steed, Robert. 1985. "Party Reform and the Nationalization of American Politics." Paper presented at the September 1985 annual meeting of the American Political Science Association. New Orleans.

Stokes, Donald E., & Warren Miller. 1962. "Party Government and the Salience of Congress." *Public Opinion Quarterly* 26 (Winter): 531–546.

Sundquist, James. 1982. "Party Decay and the Capacity to Govern." In Joel Fleishman (Ed.), *The Future of American Political Parties* (pp. 42–69). Englewood Cliffs, N.J.: Prentice-Hall.

———. 1983. "Whither the American Party System Revisited." *Political Science Quarterly* 98 (Winter): 573–594.

Sussman, Barry, & Kenneth E. John. 1984, July 15. "Delegates Enthusiastic about Mondale, but Fear He'll Lose." *Washington Post*, p. A6.

Taebel, Delbert A. 1975. "The Effect of Ballot Position on Electoral Success." *American Journal of Political Science* 19 (June): 519–526.

Tarrance, V. Lance. 1979. "Suffrage and Voter Turnout in the U.S.: The Vanishing Voter." In Jeff Fishel (Ed.), *Parties in an Anti-Party Age* (pp. 77–85). Bloomington:

Indiana University Press.

Taylor, Paul. 1985a, August 10. "State Seeks to Revive Open Primary." *Washington Post*, p. A1.

———. 1985b, October 5. "2 Parties Crossing Lines in Gerrymandering Suits." *Washington Post*, p. A4.

———. 1986a, May 20. "GOP Offensives Produce Dramatic but Fragile Gains." *Washington Post*, p. A1.

———. 1986b, November 3. "GOP Drops Ballot Security Program." *Washington Post Weekly Edition*, p. 11.

Tucker, H. J., A. Vedlitz, & J. DeNardo. 1986. "Does Heavy Turnout Help Democrats in Presidential Elections?" *American Political Science Review* 80, no. 4: 1291–1304.

Turner, Julius. 1970. *Party and Constituency: Pressures on Congress* (rev. ed. by Edward Schneier). Baltimore: Johns Hopkins Press.

U.S. Department of Commerce. 1985, January. "Current Population Reports." Series p-20, no. 397.

Verba, Sidney, & Norman Nie. 1972. *Participation in America*. New York: Harper & Row.

Walker, Jack L. 1966. "Ballot Forms and Voter Fatigue: An Analysis of the Office Block and Party Column Ballots." *Midwest Journal of Political Science* 10 (August): 448–463.

Wasby, Stephen. 1970. *Political Science: The Discipline and Its Dimensions*. New York: Charles Scribner's Sons.

Watson, Tom. 1985. "All Powerful Machine of Yore Endures in New York's Nassau." *CQ Weekly Report* 43 (August 17): 1623–1625.

Wattenberg, Martin. 1982. "From Parties to Candidates." *Public Opinion Quarterly* 46 (Summer): 216–227.

———. 1984. *The Decline of American Political Parties*. Cambridge, Mass.: Harvard University Press.

———. 1985. "The Hollow Realignment: Partisan Changes in a Candidate Centered Era." Paper presented at the September 1985 annual meeting of the American Political Science Association. New Orleans.

Will, George. 1986, November 6. "In 1986, There Is Not a Party Majority." *Washington Post*, p. A19.

Wilson, Woodrow. 1908. *Constitutional Government in the United States*. New York: Columbia University Press.

Index